D1712578

REX CUM MAGISTRO

MAGISTER REGIS

Studies in Honor of

ROBERT EARL KASKE

Edited by

ARTHUR GROOS

with

EMERSON BROWN, Jr.   THOMAS D. HILL
GIUSEPPE MAZZOTTA   JOSEPH S. WITTIG

FORDHAM UNIVERSITY PRESS
NEW YORK
1986

© Copyright 1986 by FORDHAM UNIVERSITY PRESS

All rights reserved

LC 86–80020

ISBN 0–8232–1161–4

Printed at
CULTURA PRESS
Wetteren, Belgium

CONTENTS

ACKNOWLEDGMENTS

It is a pleasure to thank some of the people who have helped us produce this volume. The contributors were generally most prompt and courteous, and Winthrop Wetherbee deserves special mention for his advice and help at a crucial stage of the manuscript. The secretaries of several Cornell departments, Carol Cook, Vicky Leccese, and Phillis Molock were unfailingly helpful in typing, photocopying, and assembling material, often at short notice. Gina Psaki provided invaluable assistance in checking references for the list of R. E. Kaske's publications. George Simian generously provided us with a copy of his photograph of 'Rex cum Magistro,' which first appeared in the *Cornell Alumni News* in April 1976. Finally, we would especially like to thank Cultura Press and the Fordham University Press for unfailing and generous *auxilium et consilium*.

R. E. KASKE: *MAGISTER REGIS*

By EMERSON BROWN, JR.

Robert Earl Kaske was born in Cincinnati, Ohio on June 1, 1921.[1] As is often the case with great and saintly men, accounts of his early years are colored by the well-intentioned hyperbole that responsible hagiographers must greet with pious admiration but treat with scientific detachment. Can it really be true, as one *vita* would have it, that little Robert memorized Migne's *Patrologiae cursus completus series latina* before he learned to walk? We must balance such reports against the statements of reliable witnesses that even ten years later he had not thoroughly committed to memory certain passages in the pseudo-scientific writings of the pseudo-Venerable Bede and a few of the more arcane and error-ridden indices.

The achievements of young Robert during his high school and university years are better documented. He attended Elder High School, an all-male institution established in 1923 as the first of Cincinnati's interparochial high schools.[2] In a curriculum not overburdened with frills, he completed four years of English, Latin, and religion without a grade below A, worked on the school newspaper and the yearbook, won the Latin contest, and played baseball. Something of a Lou Gehrig in attendance, he didn't miss a day his senior year and was tardy only once in his entire high school career.[3] The compilers of the Class of 1938 Prophecy were not above indulging in the subtle

---

[1] A century earlier, the Queen City of the West was already making scholarly news. In 1802, for example, discerning the sort of atmosphere in which academic committees do their best work, a group of citizens met at Griffin Yeatman's Tavern and decided to establish a library. The library opened just three weeks later. Having set a record for academic committee efficiency that still stands, Cincinnati turned its attention to educational fund raising. In 1807, the City Council authorized a lottery to raise $6,000 for the benefit of the University of Cincinnati. Apparently the Council neglected to meet in Mr. Yeatman's Tavern, for the city never got around to holding the event. Undaunted, in 1822 Cincinnatians founded a Society for Investigation, whose ambition was 'to solve profound problems of life' (Robert I. Vexler, *Cincinnati: A Chronological and Documentary History, 1676–1970* [Dobbs Ferry, NY 1975] 5–11). Happily, the Society for Investigation left some problems unsolved, among them — to the good fortune of the child born a hundred years later — the meaning of Dante's DXV and Langland's *Ex vi transicionis*.

[2] Toby Heile of the Elder High School Development Office kindly provided information about Elder and about Robert Kaske's years there.

[3] Gehrig himself was much in the news in 1938, his last full season. But the biggest baseball story in Cincinnati that spring was that the Reds' own Johnny Vander Meer pitched two no-hit games in a row and had won nine straight by the end of June.

humor characteristic of the genre: 'Edward Schneider, French Foreign Legion
. . . James Held, Dog-Catcher . . . Adam Nicolai, Pretzel-twister.' However, to
scholars who have benefited from his careful vetting of their work and to
readers of *Traditio*, one prediction speaks with the clarity of revealed truth:
'Robert Kaske, Editor.'

Entering Cincinnati's Jesuit university, Xavier, in the fall of 1938, Robert
Kaske continued to prepare himself for the scholarly career he had not yet
even begun to imagine. He studied German and belonged to the Heidelberg
Club, whose goal was to 'further interest in the language, culture, history,
and traditions of the Germanic peoples.'[4] His column 'Quid Ergo?' appeared
in the Xavier University *News*, and he was secretary of the recently organized
Philosophical Society. He was a member of the Traditionists, a new student
organization that combined Christian devotion with serious literary study.
The Traditionists 'study the masterpieces, not of the modern era, but of the
pre-Reformation centuries. They hope to recapture something of the spirit
and atmosphere of those wholly Catholic times, as well as to obtain an appreciation of our literary traditions.' During Robert's senior year, the Traditionists devoted their weekly meetings to 'an appreciative reading of Dante's
Inferno.'

An organization at Xavier of which Bob Kaske still speaks with affection
was the Mermaid Tavern. Founded and sponsored by the Rev. Paul J. Sweeney,
s.j., the Mermaid Tavern met weekly in its 'tradition-steeped quarters,' where
members presented their own literary creations and discussed the writings of
the masters. Prefiguring a role brought to perfection in his later years, Robert
Kaske was the Mermaid Tavern's official host. Quickly fulfilling the Elder
High School prophecy, he was also editor of the Xavier literary magazine, the
Athenaeum. Revealing a fondness for drama familiar to those fortunate enough
to have heard his renditions of medieval poetry, he was a member of the Masque
Society. In his senior year, his performance of 'the heavy-set Italian, Joe
Salvatore' contributed to the 'smashing success' of the Society's production
of the mystery comedy 'Whistling in the Dark.' He also found time to play
baseball for Sonderman's Delicatessen. Yet with all this extra-curricular activity, his academic record was nearly flawless. He was graduated *magna cum
laude* and was elected, his junior year, to the Jesuit academic honorary frater-
nity Alpha Sigma Nu.

---

[4] Quotations in this and the following paragraph are from the 1942 Xavier Yearbook. For
that and other information concerning Robert Kaske's undergraduate years, I am grateful
to Wendy Fahrnbach of the Xavier Registrar's Office and Mary Alice LaPille of Development
Services.

In the spring of 1942, while Robert Kaske was putting the finishing touches on his splendid undergraduate career, the allies suffered one defeat after another in Europe and the Pacific. Cincinnati *Enquirer* headlines tell the story:

Passenger Liner Is Sunk;
Women and Children Die
JAP PLANES BOMB AUSTRALIA
MANY KILLED IN RAIDS ON BRITISH TOWNS
Japs Achieve Victory on Bataan

To greet Robert Kaske on the morning of his graduation from Xavier on June 3, 1942, twin headlines displayed some good news:

British Take Big Toll Of Tanks
Using U.S. 'Grants' In Libya
Reich Munitions City Is Shattered
By Thousands of Tons of Bombs

But such news was rare, and the war was getting closer to home, as the next morning's *Enquirer* revealed:

U.S. BASE IN ALASKA RAIDED TWICE
WITHIN SIX HOURS BY JAP BOMBERS

Commissioned as a second lieutenant in the field artillery at his graduation from Xavier, Robert Kaske entered the Army almost immediately. Although he was married while home on a short leave, the war left him little time for domesticity. It was nearly four years before he could return to civilian life. David, his son from that marriage, now lives near Cincinnati with his wife and two children. Lieutenant Robert Kaske, a platoon leader and company commander with the 819th Tank Destroyer Battalion, served in various posts in the United States, Hawaii, Peleliu and Angaur in the Palau Islands, and Guam and Saipan in the Marianas. Of his various assignments, those in the Palau Islands are best documented. Overshadowed by campaigns that were of more obvious strategic importance, the invasion of Peleliu was among the most horrible in the Pacific war. After a sea voyage of some 5000 miles from Hawaii, the 819th arrived at Peleliu on February 1, 1945, where it was assigned island defense duties. By then Peleliu and neighboring Angaur were in American hands, but the war was not over. The islands themselves were unsafe, for not all of the Japanese soldiers had surrendered, and there was good reason to fear a counterattack. Some Japanese troops had landed on Peleliu just the month before, and the enemy still held some nearby islands. The 819th searched for Japanese stragglers, shelled enemy islands, and prepared to defend the Peleliu airstrip against airborne attacks. For its participation in the Western Pacific Campaign, the 819th was awarded the bronze battle star.[5]

While an undergraduate at Xavier, Robert Kaske had looked forward to a business career, perhaps in advertising. At the end of the war, filling empty time on a bomb-shattered coral island in the Pacific, Lt. Kaske read a story about two professors who talked the night away. At dawn, one said that he hated to break up the conversation but had to get ready for class. His guest apologized in turn, remarking with some confusion that he had been so interested in what they were talking about that he had forgotten that he wasn't in his own house. This picture of absorbing intellectual conversation so fascinated Lt. Kaske that he soon decided that the academic life was for him. The G. I. Bill of Rights made that possible. After discussing the matter with Father Sweeney, he chose the University of North Carolina and entered its graduate program in English literature in the fall of 1946.

Chapel Hill has always been strong in literary studies and never stronger than in the 1940s and 1950s, when several of the most distinguished medieval scholars of our time received their graduate training there. At Chapel Hill, Robert Kaske nearly betrayed his Traditionist legacy by becoming a Renaissance scholar. Under Hardin Craig's direction, he wrote his master's thesis on Chapman's tragedies; and had Craig remained at Chapel Hill, Kaske might well have continued to work with him. As it was, with his philological skills further increased by North Carolina's strong requirements (and by Norman Eliason's rigorous enforcement of them), he turned to medieval literature for his dissertation. He wrote it, under George Coffman's direction, on *Piers Plowman*.

Completing the doctorate in 1950, he began his teaching career at Washington University in St. Louis. The good company and learning of such colleagues as Vladimir Jelinek and Ernst Abrahamson enabled him to emulate those models of convivial intellectual concentration he had read about in the South Pacific. He taught a wide range of courses in medieval language and literature and began to publish the imaginative and meticulously researched historical criticism that has earned him an international reputation.

---

[5] The Modern Military Field Branch of the Military Archives Division of the National Archives and Records Administration provided a brief 'History of the 819th Tank Destroyer Battalion' and some other material concerning the 819th. Two fine accounts of the Peleliu invasion are the official Marine Corps history by Major Frank O. Hough, USMCR, *The Assault on Peleliu* (Marine Corps Monograph Series, 1950) and the more personal story of E. B. Sledge, *With the Old Breed: At Peleliu and Okinawa* (Novato, Calif. 1981). If one's tendencies to romanticize the war in the Pacific survive the experience of reading Hough and Sledge, one can turn to William Manchester's *Goodbye Darkness: A Memoir of the Pacific War* (Boston 1979).

A proper study of Robert Kaske's scholarly achievements would require a volume in itself. Without pretending to describe work of such range and depth in a few words, I shall make one observation. From the earliest of his essays to the most recent he has deftly joined imagination in literary interpretation with the painstaking historical research required to gather supporting evidence. There is nothing new about the desirability of this combination of attributes. Until traditional philological training began to disappear, literary scholars — except the most extreme New Critics — would routinely seek to support their insights with philological rigor. But philological rigor is never easy to achieve and is intermittently out of style. Too often, literary critics are oblivious to the essential first step of literary analysis: determining what the words meant, and all they might possibly have meant, at the time the work was created. On the other hand, no amount of philological rigor, no amassing of evidence, can rescue an inherently absurd interpretation. What we yearn for, and so rarely get, is the literary scholar who can see something in a text that we have overlooked and can produce the evidence needed to persuade us that the text could have contained what he sees in it. In that combination of insight and scholarly rigor Robert Kaske is a master. And he presents the results of that insight and rigor in a style as free of frills as the Elder High School curriculum but enriched with enough charm to mask the immensity of the scholarly enterprise that supports every sentence.

Leaving Washington University in 1957, Kaske taught briefly at the Pennsylvania State University (1957–58). In 1958, his first marriage over, he married Carol Vonckx of Elgin, Illinois. He taught at the University of North Carolina (1958–61) and the University of Illinois (1961–64) before arriving at Cornell to begin an association that has lasted more than twenty years. He has received most of the awards and honors possible for a medieval scholar, among them grants-in-aid and a fellowship from the American Council of Learned Societies, a grant from the American Philosophical Society, two Guggenheim Fellowships, a fellowship at Cornell's Society for the Humanities, a Senior Fellowship at the Southeastern Institute of Medieval and Renaissance Studies, and a grant and a fellowship from the National Endowment for the Humanities. He has served on the editorial and advisory boards of *The Chaucer Review*, *A Manual of the Writings in Middle English*, *Traditio*, and *Speculum*. In 1975, he was appointed chief editor of *Traditio*, was elected Councillor in the Medieval Academy of America, and was named Avalon Professor in the Humanities at Cornell. In 1982, he was elected a Fellow of the Medieval Academy.

At Cornell, he established a doctoral program that one of the survivors characterized as the 'Parris Island of medieval studies.' There, all students in medieval literature take course work and lengthy written comprehensive examinations in at least four medieval languages and literatures. All students have, or acquire, modern French and German and classical and medieval Latin. All take a demanding seminar in the methods and materials of literary study.[6] All have two semesters of Latin palaeography. All have the opportunity to work in one of the great research libraries in the country. And all have the opportunity to be part of a thriving scholarly community that balances the demands of its requirements with a way of life that celebrates the joy of learning. At Cornell, Robert Kaske and his colleagues and students have created a community of scholars who can share the thrill of intellectual discourse that so moved him when he read of it on a coral island in the Pacific.

To the casual observer, gatherings of medievalists at Cornell might seem little different from any crowd of people animated by drink and talk. But it is the quality of the talk, not the volume of the voices or the liquid refreshments, that we remember. Our heads were dizzy with learning and with ideas. We kept up with one another's projects and helped one another in our sometimes bizarre researches: studies of hypocritical bees, secondary meanings of the word *quoniam*, and curious *tableaux* staged in trees. Behind it all was hard work, work of a sustained intensity that some of us had never thought possible. Although students enter the Cornell Medieval Studies Program already better prepared in foreign languages than most doctors of philosophy in English literature, we were almost always learning and improving our languages at the same time we were taking graduate course work. Robert Kaske and other members of the Medieval Studies faculty realized that excellent scholarly work is only rarely possible in the few weeks a crowded semester permits for the usual seminar paper. They encouraged us to take incompletes and do the job right. For the more responsible among us, such a practice turned what are often mere exercises into apprentice scholarly work of great value. At Cornell, we were students all the time, not just for thirty weeks a year. At Christmas break or spring break or during summer vacation we learned what it was like to work steadily, full-time, day after day, on a single research project until we were satisfied that it was done right.

If we were students all of the time, Robert Kaske was a teacher all of the time. We called or dropped in unannounced to seek his help with passages of impossible Latin, to refine our growing knowledge of scholarly bibliography, or to consult one of his old books or borrow one of his newer ones. His extraordinary library, richer in essential Renaissance editions of medieval works than most university libraries, was not his private preserve but a continual source of help for his students and colleagues. His wife, Carol, herself a dedicated

---

[6] From the awesome bibliographical and methodological lectures he used as the basic material in that seminar, Robert Kaske built his *Medieval Christian Literary Imagery*, to be published shortly by the University of Toronto Press.

and productive scholar and teacher, had ample reason to grow weary of our presence, and yet she gave every sign of enjoying it. And their son, Richard, survived the influence of so much medievalism to become a giant in the world of computer whizzes — a successful businessman before finishing high school.

Wonderful things happen at the Kaske household. As a beginning graduate student, you might be sitting nervously in Professor Kaske's study, uneasy about opening your mouth and displaying your ignorance. You force yourself to ask the questions that are vexing you, and you are scribbling wildly, trying to take down the pages of bibliography that stream uninterruptedly from the Kaskean spring. Suddenly your revered professor shouts: 'I have an offprint of that right here!' And from his armchair he plunges headfirst toward the floor, a floor obscured by a sea of books, term papers, letters, offprints, microfilms, beer cans, score cards from Yankee ballgames, empty pizza boxes, used typewriter ribbons, announcements of department meetings, scurrilous postcards from traveling students, and plastic tepees from the St. Labre Indian School. You hold your breath and hope he is holding his. Trembling, you reflect with mounting concern that a less robust scholar, like Chaucer's Clerk, would be crushed under such a mass. Then, with a whoosh, the Kaskean form surfaces, offprint held triumphantly aloft: 'Knew I had it!'

Bob's prodigious learning and literary sensitivity are evident to anyone who reads his work. But of equal importance to his students is his unlimited generosity. That generosity does not end when his students complete their degrees. Too much of his time goes to continuing efforts on our behalf. He reads our work in draft and returns it, promptly, heavily marked with detailed suggestions that straighten out our clumsy thinking and writing and push us in productive new directions for further research. If we were working in the sciences, where team research is routine, Bob Kaske's bibliography would be many times its present length. It would be increased, as it should be, by the many books and articles he has, in effect, co-authored. He reads everything submitted to *Traditio*, and his hand has helped improve almost everything published in that most scholarly of scholarly journals. He has even turned the letter of recommendation into an art form.

Given the occasion to do so, Bob would have written the warmest of letters for one long-time companion who slept through some of his most animated lectures, who appears *coram pedibus magistri* in the frontispiece of this volume, and who inspired its title — Rex, his border collie. Well cared for, Rex lacked only the one thing his ancient bloodline most urged him to crave: a flock of sheep in serious and continual need of tending. In compensation, he tended the Kaske domicile. From his early years, he persuaded himself that all unfamiliar callers were wolves creeping maliciously toward the Kaske flock. This loyalty brought several visitors close to cardiac arrest. But only those few careless souls who placed parts of their bodies in the wrong place when Rex's jaws were playfully snapping shut would deny that he was among the mildest of dogs.

One afternoon, looking down from the seventh floor of Olin Library to the Arts Quadrangle, I saw Rex joyfully running circles around a dozen or so of his canine companions. Then, a mere speck from that vantage point, Bob emerged from Goldwin Smith Hall. He stood on the steps, looked around and quickly spotted Rex, who, when not *coram magistro,* was rarely far away. Shouting 'Here, Rex,' Bob started to move off, confident that Rex would follow. Rex stopped, looked toward his master, then looked back over his shoulder at his companions. Again he looked at Bob, again at his companions. Anyone who believes that animals don't think should have seen Rex weighing the pros and cons of obeying the Kaskean command. After a few seconds of intense canine psychomachia, he turned his back definitively on his fellows and, tail wagging, trotted after his master.

Rex is gone now. Nightmares of vast herds of sheep, dogless in the wilderness, will never more vex his sleep. But we hold his memory dear, for he was one of us during golden years, and never more so than on that day when he chose, so deliberately, to leave his play and to follow Bob Kaske. *Magister Regis* Bob was and *Rex Magistrorum* he remains. With this book we offer him a shadow of our gratitude.

Vanderbilt University

'INSULAE GENTIUM': BIBLICAL INFLUENCE ON OLD ENGLISH POETIC VOCABULARY

By CHARLES D. WRIGHT

In the past two decades, Old English scholars have been increasingly sensitive to Biblical themes, images, and motifs in Old English poetry, especially as interpreted in patristic tradition.[1] There has been less attention, however, to the influence of Biblical *words* and their traditional associations on Old English poetic vocabulary.[2] In the present paper I will try to show how Biblical usage and patristic tradition have affected the meaning of the Old English words for 'island' in specific contexts. Recognition of Biblical influence can thus contribute, I will suggest, not only to our lexicographical knowledge, but also to our literary understanding.

The Old English words *ealand* and *igland*, which both mean primarily 'island,' 'land surrounded entirely by water,'[3] occur several times in poetry in

---

[1] We owe to R. E. Kaske the formulation of a rigorous methodology, exemplified in his many articles, for the use of patristic exegesis in interpreting medieval literature. See esp. his 'Patristic Exegesis in the Criticism of Medieval Literature: The Defense,' in *Critical Approaches to Medieval Literature*, ed. Dorothy Bethurum (New York 1960) 27–60, 158–60; 'Chaucer and Medieval Allegory,' *ELH* 30 (1963) 173–92. His forthcoming *Medieval Christian Literary Imagery* will be a fundamental reference tool for future investigations.

[2] Still useful are the early studies by H. S. MacGillvray, *The Influence of Christianity on the Vocabulary of Old English* (Halle 1902); Albert Keiser, *The Influence of Christianity on the Vocabulary of Old English Poetry*, Illinois Studies in Language and Literature 5 (Urbana 1919); and James W. Rankin, 'A Study of the Kennings in Anglo-Saxon Poetry,' *Journal of English and Germanic Philology* 8 (1909) 357–422 and 9 (1910) 49–84. But these general works are only partly concerned with Biblical words, and do not attempt to trace the influence of their traditional interpretations. In a series of articles on name-meanings in Old English literature, Fred C. Robinson has demonstrated the influence of patristic onomastics: 'The Significance of Names in Old English Literature,' *Anglia* 86 (1968) 14–58; 'Some Uses of Name Meanings in Old English Poetry,' *Neuphilologische Mitteilungen* 69 (1968) 161–71; 'Anglo-Saxon Onomastics in the Old English *Andreas*,' *Names* 21 (1973) 133–36. See also H. D. Meritt, *Fact and Lore about Old English Words*, Stanford University Publications, Language and Literature 13 (Stanford 1954) 87–94 and 201–9.

[3] The two words are etymologically distinct, but fell together in meaning; both are used for the same place in *Andreas* and *Phoenix*. According to K. R. Brooks, 'Old English ĒA and Related Words,' *English and Germanic Studies* 5 (1952–53) 28, the simplexes *ēa* (<Proto-Germanic *áχwō-), 'water, water-course, stream, river,' and *īg, īeg, ēg* (<*αγωjṓ-), 'watery ground, island,' 'do not interchange except in the compounds *ēaland* and *igland* . . . which express the same idea in two different ways: the former is simply "water-land," while in the latter the second element defines the first.'

contexts that have led scholars to assume that they could also mean, more loosely, 'coastland,' 'land bordering on water.' This suggestion was made by George Philip Krapp for *Andreas*, where Mermedonia is called an *igland* and *ealand* (lines 15 and 28), a description without precedent in any other source or version of the legend. Krapp compares the 'island' paradise of *Phoenix* (lines 9 and 287), and concludes:

> The word in the above passages is evidently not to be understood in the specific sense of 'island,' but rather in the literal sense of 'water-land,' 'land that is reached by water.' To the insular Anglo-Saxons all foreign lands must have been 'water-lands'; perhaps in this poetical sense the word also carried with it the connotation of remoteness; in both the *Phoenix* and the *Andreas* it is used for the Orient.

Krapp further compares the 'islands' of *Solomon and Saturn* (line 1), where 'the elaboration of this passage makes *iglanda* refer to Lybia, Greece, and India, none of them islands.'[4] Krapp's suggestion has since been adopted or at least repeated by later editors of these poems: by K. R. Brooks for *Andreas*,[5] by A. S. Cook for *Phoenix*,[6] and by R. J. Menner for *Solomon and Saturn*.[7] Krapp does not refer to *Beowulf* 2334, where the *fæsten* of the Geats is called an *ealond*, but Bugge had already made a similar suggestion for that passage. R. W. Chambers adds his authority in support of the view that in *Beowulf* the word 'probably does not mean "island."'[8] Klaeber cites both Bugge and Krapp in favor of the sense 'land bordering on water,'[9] and this definition was in turn incorporated in C. L. Wrenn's edition and in W. F. Bolton's revision.[10] On the basis of *Beowulf* 2334, A. Campbell gives the sense 'land bordering the sea' in his *Addenda* to Bosworth–Toller,[11] and Clark Hall gives the sense 'maritime land, seaboard' in his *Concise Anglo-Saxon Dictionary*.[12]

Of the supposed poetic attestations of *ealand* and *igland* in the sense 'land bordering on water,' however, those in *Phoenix* and *Beowulf* are too doubtful to be counted. For *Phoenix*, J. E. Cross has pointed out that there is precedent

---

[4] George Philip Krapp, ANDREAS *and the* FATES OF THE APOSTLES (Boston 1906) line 15*n*.

[5] ANDREAS *and the* FATES OF THE APOSTLES (Oxford 1961) line 15*n*.

[6] *The Old English* ELENE, PHOENIX, *and* PHYSIOLOGUS (New Haven 1919) line 9*n*. Frederic G. Cassidy and Richard N. Ringler give the meaning 'land beyond the water, remote land' (*Bright's Old English Grammar and Reader*, 3rd ed. [New York 1971] 319).

[7] *The Poetical Dialogues of Solomon and Saturn* (New York 1941), glossary s.v. *igland*.

[8] BEOWULF: *An Introduction*, 3rd ed. (Cambridge 1967) 550. Cf. Chambers' revision of A. J. Wyatt's edition (Cambridge 1920) line 2334*n*.

[9] BEOWULF *and the* FIGHT AT FINNSBURG, 3rd ed. (Boston 1950) line 2334*n*.

[10] BEOWULF *with the* FINNESBURG FRAGMENT, 2nd ed. (London 1958), glossary s.v. *ēalond*: 'land by the water; sea-shore.' The 3rd ed., revised by W. F. Bolton (New York 1973) repeats this definition.

[11] (Oxford 1972) s.v. *ēaland* (Campbell introduces the definition with an 'apparently').

[12] (Cambridge 1960) s.v. *ēaland*.

for an insular Earthly Paradise in Christian tradition, concluding that 'we may disregard A. S. Cook's editorial explanation of *igland* (although etymologically possible and still permissible in context) and accept the common meaning of the word as "island." '[13] As for *Beowulf* 2334, there is simply no way to be sure that the unidentified place referred to is not really an island, as W. J. Sedgefield argues:

> By some commentators *ealond* is translated 'land bordering on water,' 'coast,' but the use of *fæsten* and *utan* seems to indicate the Geatish citadel is meant, and it is possible that it was on an island separated by a narrow channel from the mainland.[14]

The only clear attestations, then, are *Andreas* 15 and 18, and *Solomon and Saturn* 1. Presently I will suggest that *Maxims I* 15 provides another. But there are also two cases outside the poetic corpus in which a distant coastal region or city is identified as an 'island.' Meritt draws attention to a gloss, *ciliciae: ealonde* (i.e., Cilicia in Asia Minor).[15] To this citation may be added a gloss in the Rushworth Gospels in which Tiberias, a city on the shore of the Sea of Galilee, is supposed to be an *ealond*.[16]

Another kind of evidence, the evidence of native English place-names, must also be reviewed. There is no doubt that the simplex *ieg, eg* (like its Germanic cognates), besides meaning 'island,' also has meanings such as 'land partly surrounded by water, a piece of dry ground in a fen, well-watered land.'[17]

---

[13] 'The Poem in Transmitted Text — Editor and Critic,' *Essays and Studies* 27 (1974) 88–89. N. F. Blake also draws attention to the island paradise tradition in his edition, *The Phoenix* (Manchester 1964) 13–16.

[14] 'Further Emendations to the *Beowulf* Text,' *Modern Language Review* 28 (1933) 229. Cf. P. J. Cosijn, *Aantekeningen op den* BEOWULF (Leiden 1892) 34. Some commentators have identified the place with the island mentioned by Saxo (See Klaeber, BEOWULF xxii). Norman Eliason, *Anglia* 71 (1952–53) 454, would emend *ealond utan* to *eal ond utan*.

[15] Herbert Dean Meritt, *Old English Glosses* (New York 1945) 10 (4.199; the text is Bede's *Ecclesiastical History* 4.1). Meritt suggests a confusion with Sicilia, but he adds the citation to Clark Hall in his *Supplement*, s.v. *ēaland*, for the sense 'maritime land.'

[16] W. W. Skeat, ed., *The Gospel according to Saint John in Anglo-Saxon and Northumbrian Versions* (Cambridge 1878) 57, on John 6.23. In his glossary to the Rushworth Gospels, U. Lindelöf simply lists *ealond* as the equivalent of Latin *insula* (*Glossar zur altnordhumbrischen Evangelienübersetzung in der Rushworth-Handschrift* [Helsingfors 1897] s.v.). The Old English *Boethius* (ed. W. J. Sedgefield, *King Alfred's Old English Version of Boethius* DE CONSOLATIONE PHILOSOPHIAE [Oxford 1899] 34) renders the phrase 'nova litora' (II Met. 5.15) by 'ealand ne weroð,' but a comparison with the reading of the *Meters of Boethius* 8.30, 'ellend*ne wearod*,' suggests that the reading of the prose translation should be emended (George Philip Krapp, ed., *The Paris Psalter and the Meters of Boethius*, The Anglo-Saxon Poetic Records 5 [New York 1932]). Unless otherwise noted, subsequent references to Old English poetry will be to the ASPR by line numbers.

[17] A. H. Smith, *English Place-Name Elements*, English Place-Name Society [EPNS] 25.1 (Cambridge 1956) s.v. *ēg*.

As for the compounds, Ekwall's *Concise Oxford Dictionary of Place-Names* claims that 'OE *ēaland* and *ēgland* have the same senses as *ēg*,'[18] and various place-name monographs give similar meanings.[19]

Although I am not sufficiently versed in the mysteries of place-name scholarship to render a confident judgment, it seems to me that the place-name evidence for these senses, at least for the Old English period, is not conclusive. Of the names Ekwall cites, only two seem to be attested as early as (and no earlier than) the Domesday Book: *Elant* on the River Calder (modern Elland, West Riding of Yorkshire), and *Eilanda* on the Stour (modern Nayland, Suffolk).[20] As for the peninsulas called 'islands' cited by Chambers, Portland Island is joined to the mainland by only a narrow strip of land, and Hayling Island, at least at present, is surrounded by marshes.[21] Of course, topographical conditions slowly but constantly change, so that — lacking contemporary description or archaeological confirmation — it is difficult to be sure that a place on a river or coast, or in the fens, was not once a real island.[22]

---

[18] 4th ed. (Oxford 1960) s.v. *ēg*.

[19] See J. McN. Dodgson, *The Place-Names of Cheshire*, EPNS 48.5 (I.ii) (Cambridge 1981) s.v. *ēg-land*: '"an island; water-meadow land," also "a surrounded plot"'; A. H. Smith, *The Place-Names of the West Riding of Yorkshire*, EPNS 36.7 (Cambridge 1961) s.v. *ēa-land*: 'island, land by the water.'

[20] For Elland, see A. H. Smith (*n*19) Part III 43; for Nayland, see W. W. Skeat, *The Place-Names of Suffolk*, Cambridge Antiquarian Society 46 (Cambridge 1913) 76. Skeat quotes a statement that Nayland (which he would derive from Old Norse *eyland*) is 'subject to occasional inundations.'

[21] Chambers, *Beowulf* 550. Chambers (*n*8) also refers to a citation in the *Oxford English Dictionary* in which Norway is called 'a great Ilond compassed abowt almost wyth the See.'

[22] I am able to find only a single example in the new *Microfiche Concordance to Old English*, edd. Robert Venezky and Antoinette di Paolo Healy (Newark, Del. 1980), where an English place that is not now an island is called an *igland* or *ealand*. This is *Heabureagh*, which in a grant to Medeshamstede (Peterborough) is called an 'island': '686. Her Ceadwala 7 Mul his broðor forhergodon Cent 7 Wiht. Þæs Cædwala gef into sce Petres minstre Medeshamstede Hoge. Ʒ is an igland Heabureagh hatte.' Charles Plummer, ed., *Two of the Saxon Chronicles Parallel* (Oxford 1892) I 39 (the Laud text, *E*). *Heabureagh* must be placed at the modern Hoo peninsula (it has been identified with Avery Farm; see J. K. Wallenberg, *Kentish Place Names* [Uppsala 1931] 19–21). But J. H. Evans' comment illustrates well the difficulty of determining ancient topography: 'The description of Hebureaghe as an island is confirmed by an element in the name, but it has been a stumbling block to commentators, for Hoo is not now and never has been an island, and it is not very obviously a peninsula to those unfamiliar with maps. It does not seem to have occurred to anyone that there may have been islands very close to the shores of the Hoo, which, under land level changes, may now be merely marshes; yet there are two remaining today . . . and there was certainly one other in the Saxon Age.' Evans goes on to suggest that Heabureagh be identified with a particular meadow island that is known to have existed in the Roman Age ('Archaeological Horizons in the North-Kent Marshes,' *Archaeologia Cantiana* 66 [1953] 136–37). The 'Isle' of Ely is so called by a folk etymology as venerable as Bede, who refers to it in the *Ecclesiastical History*

But even if we admit, on the evidence of place-names, that Old English *ealand* and *igland* had these senses, this still would not account for the poetic examples collected here, since all refer to *distant, foreign lands across the sea*, an application that English place-names obviously do not explain. The key to this use of Old English *igland/ealand* is found in glosses and translations of the Bible. For the Hebrew word transliterated *'i* (plural *'iyyim*), usually translated 'island' in English Bibles, and always *insula* in the Vulgate and Old Latin versions, has a range of meaning that overlaps Old English *ealand* and *igland*. I quote a convenient listing of the various senses:

> The Hebrew term may refer to an island in our sense of the word . . . to habitable land in opposition to water (Isa. 42,15); to the coastland, as of Palestine (Isa. 20,6), Phoenicia (Isa. 23,2.6), the Mediterranean (Jer. 22,22); to islands and coastlands (Gen. 10,5; Isa. 11,11; Jer. 2,10; Ez. 26,15.18; 27,6.15) and to distant lands and their inhabitants (Is. 41,1.5; 42,4.10.12; 49,1; Ps. 76,10; 97,1; etc.).[23]

In Biblical geography, then, the word means not only 'island' in the strict sense, but also, like Old English *ealand* and *igland*, any land bordering the sea, or simply any and all distant lands. In medieval and ecclesiastical Latin these senses seem to be restricted to Biblical contexts. The *Thesaurus linguae latinae* gives the definition, '*laxius* in script. sacris per hebraismum sec. "*'i*" de qualibet ora maritima (fere plur. . . .).'[24] For English, the *Oxford English Dictionary* duly lists the 'Biblical sense' of the word 'island,' giving the Coverdale Bible (1535) as the earliest citation.[25] But of course in Old and Middle English, Biblical *insula* is always rendered by some form of *ealand, igland* and *ile, ilond*.[26] For example, Ælfric renders the phrase *insulae gentium* of Genesis

---

4.19: 'Est autem Elge . . . regio . . . in similitudinem insulae uel paludibus, ut diximus, circumdata uel aquis' (edd. R. A. B. Mynors and B. Colgrave [Oxford 1969] 396); the correct etymology is *ēl-gē*, 'eel-district'; see Ekwall, *Concise Oxford Dictionary* s.v. 'Ely.'

[23] *Catholic Biblical Encyclopedia*, edd. J. E. Steinmuller and K. Sullivan (New York 1956) s.v. 'isle, island.' See also Armin Schwarzenbach, *Die geographische Terminologie im Hebräischen des Alten Testaments* (Leiden 1954) 78–79.

[24] S.v. *insula* I.B. Commenting on *Beowulf* 2334, Klaeber, following Siebs, remarks that '*insula* is found in medieval Latin in this wider sense,' but Siebs gives no references and does not mention Biblical usage.

[25] See s.v. 'Island' 1.b.: 'In Biblical lang., after the corresponding Heb. word, applied to lands across the sea, the coasts of the Mediterranean'; similarly s.v. 'Isle' 1.b.

[26] For Middle English, see the *Middle English Dictionary*, edd. Hans Kurath and Sherman Kuhn (Ann Arbor 1956ff.) s.v. 'ile' 2.b.: '? in O.T. usage: a land on the seacoast, a coastland; also, the people of such lands,' and s.v. 'ilond' 1.b.: '? in *Bible* trans.: coastland.' Charles Osgood draws attention to the Biblical sense of the word in *Pearl* 693n, with citations from other Middle English texts (*The Pearl* [Boston 1906] 80–81). Cook quotes Osgood's note in connection with *Phoenix* 9 without comment. Theodore Silverstein, in his ed. of *Sir Gawain and the Green Knight* (Chicago 1984) 113, draws attention to the Biblical use of *insula* in connection with the phrase *western iles* ('western realms').

10.5 — where the sense embraces at least 'coastlands' as well as 'islands' — by *þeoda hilænd*,[27] while the Psalter glosses all render the *insula* of Psalms 76.10 and 96.1, which appears to mean 'distant lands and their inhabitants,' by some form of *ealand* or *igland*.[28]

Now, if we consider the Biblical word *insula* in its various contexts, we find that it also has an ethnological connotation in addition to its various geographical denotations. 'Islands' can be Biblical shorthand for the vast multitude of (non-Israelite) nations and peoples spread throughout the world, 'the lands of the *gentes*.'[29] For example, in Isaiah 40.15, 'ecce gentes quasi stilla situlae et quasi momentum staterae reputatae sunt / ecce insulae quasi pulvis exiguus,' the parallelism makes *gentes* and *insulae* equivalent, and the force of the simile depends precisely on the fact that the 'islands' *are* numberless, except to God, who can measure the waters and the heavens in His hand (40.12). In the Major Prophets, especially Deutero-Isaiah, this connection between *insulae* and *gentes* is frequent.[30] The phrase 'islands of the gentiles' (*insulae gentium*) occurs three times in the Old Testament: Soph. 2.11, 1 Macc. 11.38, and — most prominently — Gen. 10.5, in the description of the division of the world among the descendants of Noah: 'ab his [i.e. the descendants of Japheth] divisae sunt insulae gentium in regionibus suis / unusquisque secundum linguam et familias in nationibus suis.'

This recurrent Biblical association, in which the word *insulae* is identified with the heathen nations, explains a curious gloss in the Lambeth Psalter (Ps. 105.27), where *regionibus*, parallel with *nationibus* and clearly meaning distant, heathen lands generally, is rendered *on yglondum*.[31] The glossator,

---

[27] S. J. Crawford, ed., *The Old English Heptateuch*, EETS os 160 (London 1922) 109.

[28] Cf. the poetic renderings in the Paris Psalter (ed. Krapp, ASPR 5 [New York 1932]). For the Psalter glosses, see Minnie Cate Morell, *A Manual of Old English Biblical Materials* (Knoxville 1965). For other examples of translations of Biblical *insula* in its broader sense, see the translation of Is. 42.1–2 printed in Michael Korhammer, *Die monastischen Cantica im Mittelalter* (Munich 1976) 340–41 ('Canticum 24'). and the gloss to Is. 49.1 in the Durham Ritual, ed. U. Lindelöf, *Rituale ecclesiae Dunelmensis*, Surtees Society 140 (London 1927) 55.

[29] *The International Standard Biblical Encyclopedia*, edd. Geoffrey W. Bromley *et al.* (Grand Rapids 1979) I s.v. 'Coast; Coastland; Coastline' is more explicit on this point than the list quoted above: 'In Isa. 40–66; Jer. 31.10; and Ezk. 26.15, *'i* refers to distant heathen nations.'

[30] Other Biblical passages in which *insulae* and *gentes* (or *populi*, specifically non-Israelite) are parallel or closely associated are Ecclus. 47.17; Is. 11.10–11; 24.14–15; 41.1, 5; 42.1–4; 49.1; 51.4–5; 59.18 (referring to God's enemies); 60.3, 9; 66.18–19; Jer. 31.10; Ez. 39.6–7; Soph. 2.11. Some of these examples will be discussed more fully below.

[31] U. Lindelöf, ed., *Der Lambeth Psalter*, Acta Societatis Scientiarum Fennicae 43.3 (Helsinki 1914) II 171. Another hand has added, *l on eardum*. Lindelöf cites this gloss with an exclamation mark in a list of 'Inkorrektheiten und Eigentümlichkeiten' (29). I have not been able to consult J. R. Stracke, 'Studies in the Vocabulary of the Lambeth Psalter Glosses' (unpubl. Pennsylvania diss. 1970) 102, cited in Angus Cameron *et al.*, *Old English Word Studies: A Preliminary Author and Word Index* (Toronto 1983) s.v. *yglond*.

familiar with the 'insular' habitat of the heathen nations in the Bible, including the Psalms, has simply assigned them their proper place. But the context of the Psalm verse, a threat that God will disperse the Jews among the heathen nations as punishment for their lapses of faith,[32] suggests that the Biblical association of 'islands' and the *gentes* is not theologically neutral, for from the Old Testament point of view the *gentes* are those who do not know or refuse to acknowledge Yahweh. The 'island' passages in the Prophets stress this repeatedly; thus in Isaiah 66.19, God announces a mission 'ad insulas longe ad eos qui non audierunt de me et non viderunt gloriam meam.'

An interpretive gloss such as this from the Lambeth Psalter reflects what Jean Leclercq calls the 'Biblical imagination' of monastic authors, whose 'memory, fashioned wholly by the Bible and nurtured entirely by Biblical words and the images they evoke, causes them to express themselves spontaneously in a Biblical vocabulary.'[33] Leclercq of course is speaking of literary expression in Latin, but the Biblical imagination can express itself equally well in the vernacular, especially in literary cultures like the Anglo-Saxon, with ist strong tradition of Biblical translation and glossing.[34] Evidence for the influence of Latin on Old English vocabulary is especially plentiful in Biblical glosses, and most studies of semantic borrowing from Latin to Old English have relied heavily on them.[35] But we should also not forget that for monastic readers and authors, trained to read and understand the Bible by the associative method of *ruminatio*,[36] Biblical words could be charged with moral and theological connotations handed down by homilies, commentaries, and Biblical lexica or *distinctiones*, which record their 'total meaning, not merely the philological meaning.'[37]

---

[32] 'et pro nihilo habuerunt terram desiderabilem. Non crediderunt uerbo eius. et murmurauerunt in tabernaculis suis non exaudierunt uocem Domini. Et eleuauit manum suam super eos ut prosterneret eos in deserto. Et ut deiceret semen eorum in nationibus et dispergeret eos in regionibus' (Ps. 105.24–27).

[33] Jean Leclercq, *The Love of Learning and the Desire for God*, trans. Catharine Misrahi, 3rd ed. (New York 1982) 75. J. L. Rosier has pointed out that 'among the OE psalter glosses, those in Lambeth are the most learned and often give witness to the glossator's knowledge of patristic commentary' ('Ten Old English Psalter Glosses,' *Journal of English and Germanic Philology* 63 [1964] 1). Cf. Meritt, *Fact and Lore* (n2).

[34] For bibliography see Morrell (n28).

[35] See esp. Helmut Gneuss, *Lehnbildungen und Lehnbedeutungen im Altenglischen* (Berlin 1955).

[36] On *ruminatio* see Leclercq, *Love of Learning* 72–75; for its application to OE literary structure, Thomas D. Hill, 'Notes on the Imagery and Structure of the Old English *Christ I*,' *Notes and Queries* 217 (1972) 87–89.

[37] Leclercq, *Love of Learning* 77. On Biblical lexica and *distinctiones*, see Harald Dickerhof, 'Canum nomine gentiles designantur,' in *Secundum regulam vivere: Festschrift für P. Norbert Backmund* (Windberg 1978) 43–54.

In this way, an Old English word might reflect not only the denotative
'Biblical sense,' but also, in certain contexts, the traditional associations and
connotations of a Biblical-Latin word. Thus, while lexicographers should be
aware of the possible influence of Biblical usage on Old English vocabulary,
literary critics should be sensitive to the play of Biblical associations and
traditional interpretation in poetic contexts. To turn to *Maxims I*, we can
recognize the influence of Biblical *insula* in the poet's allusion to the 'island'
homes established by God for the races of men:

> He us geþonc syleð,
> missenlicu mod,   monge reorde.
> Feorhcynna fela   fæþmeþ wide
> eglond monig.   Eardas rume
> meotud arærde   for moncynne,
> almihtig god,   efenela bega
> þeoda and þeawa.   (12b–18a)

As in Biblical usage, the poet seems to have meant distant lands generally
(especially in view of the parallel statement with *eardas*), and here too the
'islands' are thought to be the homelands of the multitude of the nations
(*þeoda*).[38] The statement is reminiscent of Genesis 10.5 specifically: the poet
emphasizes the great number of the islands *and* their inhabitants, mentioning
(as does Gen. 10.5) their diverse languages. But we may also recognize, I
would suggest, the trace of the Biblical judgment upon the island nations. The
context of the so-called 'Table of Nations,' in which the reference to the *insulae
gentium* of Genesis 10.5 is embedded, is particularly relevant for *Maxims I*,
whether or not the poet had this verse in mind, since it merely reflects associations that are generally Biblical. Von Rad says of this passage:

> As it now stands, the sentiment underlying the Table of Nations is an amaze-
> ment at the richness of Jahweh as creator, who by his command to be
> fruitful brought the vast multitude of the nations into being out of one
> stock. This positive statement about the nations is followed by a purely
> negative one, however, in the story of the Tower of Babel. . . . Thus, ac-
> cording to the primeval history, the phenomenon of the nations is not clear.
> They derive from God's wealth in creation; but at the same time in their
> disorder they bear the deep scars of God's judging intervention. . . . For
> after the division of mankind and the confusion of their language, the gulf
> between the various nations and God opened still more widely than it had
> before.[39]

---

[38] That *feorhcynna* (14a) means races of men specifically is clear from the surrounding
references to languages, mankind, and nations. For the plural *þeoda* as 'heathen nations'
(= *gentes*), see MacGillvray, *Influence of Christianity* 15–16.

[39] Gerhard von Rad, *Old Testament Theology*, trans. D. M. G. Stalker (New York 1962) I
162–63.

Or we may cite an early medieval reading of the primeval history that manifests the same ambiguity. Freculph, a ninth-century chronicler, after ascribing the building of the tower of Babel to human pride and loss of the fear of God, shifts his focus from the sinfulness of man to the goodness of God when he describes the ensuing migrations of mankind to their various homelands, including the 'islands':

> Inde autem migrationes ubique agentes, et terram apprehendentes unusquisque felicem quam Deus unicuique distribuit: et ita omnis terra per eos completa est, mediterranea simul atque maritima. Quidam etiam navibus transeuntes, insulas habitaverunt.[40]

The passage from *Maxims I* evokes a similar tension. The references to the diversity of men, their homelands, languages, and customs bespeak 'an amazement at the richness' of the creator. But the poet has just invoked God's creation of men as proof of their obligation to praise Him (4b–7a),[41] and a reader sensitive to the Biblical associations of an allusion to the 'island' nations in such a context would discern, not an implicit reference to Babel (though the poet surely believed that the multiplication of languages and dispersal of nations was a result of its building), but at least a 'negative note' such as von Rad sees in the Table of Nations: these island races would be, by Biblical definition, largely heathen. Such is the explicit meaning, for example, of an allusion to the 'island' races in an Irish poem from around 1000, which also presents the multitude of nations and races as witness to the richness of the creator:

> The number of races that remain in the islands of the Great Sea no-one under heaven can relate or count them.
> Few of these believe in Christ. Doom and a dark heavy curse have overtaken them, their souls are not pure, their deeds have corrupted them.[42]

The poet's ethnological perspective is thus also a moral one. 'God sceal mon ærest hergan' (4b) ought to be more than an admonition; it ought to be an ontological truth, 'forþon þe he us æt frymþe geteode / lif ond lænna willan'

---

[40] *Chronicon* 1.28 (PL 106.936). Freculph knows that the 'islands' of Gen. 10.5 include coastlands and peninsulas: 'Japheth itaque filii seu nepotes has habuere gentes, et quae forsan nunc ignorantur. Omnes tamen pene insulas et totius orbis littora terrasque mari vicinas legimus Graecis accolis occupatas' (1.27 [PL 106.934]).

[41] In some versions (including the Sixto-Clementine Vulgate) Ecclus. 43.25ff. refers to God's creation of the 'islands' and the variety of living things as proof of both the richness of creation and of man's obligation to praise God: 'In sermone ejus siluit ventus, et cogitatione sua placavit abyssum, et plantavit Dominus in illa insulas. . . . Illic praeclara opera, et mirabilia: varia bestiarum genera, et omnium pecorum, et creatura belluarum. . . . Benedicentes Dominum, exaltate illum quantum potestis: major enim est omni laude' (verses 25, 27, 33; the modern critical edition of the Vulgate reads 'plantavit illum Dominus Iesus' for 'plantavit Dominus in illa insulas').

[42] Maura Carney, ed. and trans., 'The Works of the Sixth Day,' *Ériu* 21 (1969) 163.

(5b–6a).[43] Man's very nature is, or should be, to praise God; that he does not, that there are many races of men in the 'islands' who do not know Him, insinuates — like the Table of Nations — 'the gulf between the various nations and God.'

This same Biblical association of 'islands' with the unredeemed multitude of nations helps make sense of the geography of Saturn's opening speech in *Solomon and Saturn*:

> Hwæt, ic iglanda   eallra hæbbe
> boca onbyrged   þurh gebregdstafas,
> larcræftas onlocen   Libia and Greca,
> swylce eac istoriam   Indea rices.   (1–4)[44]

Here too the poet thinks of the diversity and multitude of the nations, and here too the word *iglanda* appears to mean distant, foreign lands generally, or at least 'coastlands,' since, as Krapp points out, it is parallel with Lybia, Greece, and India (cf. Is. 66.19, in which the 'islands' are part of a series including Africa, Lydia, Italy, and Greece). The Biblical associations discussed above would be appropriate in a general way, since Saturn is, in the poem's terms, the representative of the collective wisdom of the pagan world, as Solomon is of the Hebraic and, proleptically, of the Christian.[45] But the poet is here making a more exact Biblical allusion. According to Ecclesiasticus 47.17–18, Solomon was famed in the 'islands' for his riddles and parables:

> et replesti in conparationibus enigmata / ad insulas longe distulisti nomen tuum / et dilectus es in pace tua / in cantilenis et proverbiis et conparationibus / et interpretationibus miratae sunt terrae. . . .

So too Psalm 71, entitled 'In Salomonem,'[46] declares that the nations and 'islands' will pay homage to him:

> reges Tharsis et insulae munera offerent / reges Arabum et Saba dona adducent / et adorabunt eum omnes reges / omnes gentes servient ei . . . .
>   (10–11)

Thus Saturn, who has traversed the 'islands' in a bookish voyage, has heard of Solomon's amazing wisdom of riddles and parables, and wishes to match his own against it. But Saturn's wisdom is by implication limited, because the islands to not know the true God; and indeed, it is precisely in religious wisdom (or arcana) that Solomon surpasses Saturn in their debate.

---

[43] For gnomic *sceal* implying inherent state or quality as well as being hortatory, see P. L. Henry, *The Early English and Celtic Lyric* (London 1966) 94–104.

[44] Quoted from Menner's ed. (n7).

[45] See Menner 22 and 47–48.

[46] On the Psalm's connection with Solomon, see Menner 47. Of course, Saturn's home was supposed to be the island of Crete.

Up to this point, I have been concerned with the contextual associations of Biblical *insula* which, while they have theological implications, are contained within the literal sense, and I have tried to show that the poets of *Maxims I* and *Solomon and Saturn* have drawn on these associations in their allusions to 'islands.' Now from the *Andreas*–poet's perspective, the salient fact about Mermedonia (aside from its being inhabited by cannibals) is that it is a distant heathen land, and that would be reason enough for calling it an 'island,' simply as a reflex of Biblical usage. But by doing so, the poet exploits, I believe, a specific typological tradition of the 'island' passages in the Prophets, especially Isaiah. We have already seen that in many of these passages the inhabitants of the 'islands' represent those who do not know or acknowledge God. More often than not, these passages prophesy that the unbelieving nations will eventually be subjugated and converted.[47] These prophecies, like Sophonias 2.11, proclaim how the nations will turn to the Lord when faced with His judgment and law:

> horribilis Dominus super eos / et adtenuabit omnes deos terrae / et adorabunt eum vir de loco suo omnes insulae gentium . . . .

The conversion of the island nations is a virtual refrain in Deutero-Isaiah. Good examples are the following from chapter 42:

> ecce servus meus suscipiam eum . . . dedi spiritum meum super eum iudicium gentibus proferet / . . . non erit tristis neque turbulentus / donec ponat in terra iudicium et legem eius insulae exspectabunt . . . . (1, 4)
> cantate Domino canticum novum laus eius ab extremis terrae / qui descenditis in mare et plenitudo eius / insulae et habitatores earum . . . . (10)
> ponent Domino gloriam et laudem eius in insulis nuntiabunt . . . . (12)

It is not surprising to find that Christian interpretation of such passages makes them prophecies of the conversion of the *gentes* to Christianity; indeed, according to the influential commentary of Jerome, the prophecy of Isaiah 42.10 refers to the conversion of the *gentes* by the apostles:

> In omnem terram exiit apostolorum sonus, et in terminos orbis uerba eorum. . . . *Qui descenditis*, inquit, *in mare*, et nauigatis illud, siue *plenitudo maris*. Apostolos enim uidens Iesus in litore iuxta mare Genesareth reficientes retia, vocauit et misit in magnum mare; ut de piscatoribus piscium faceret hominum piscatores. . . . Uel certe descenderunt in mare et nauigauerunt illud; tempestates et persecutiones istius saeculi sustinentes. Insulas quoque et habitatores earum, uel diuersitatem gentium intellege, uel ecclesiarum multitudinem.[48]

---

[47] Of the verses quoted in *n*30, all except Ecclus. 47.17 and Ps. 71.10 allude to the conversion of the *gentes*.

[48] CCL 73A.483–84; cf. also CCL 73A.534 and Augustine, *De civ. Dei* 20.21 (CCL 48.739); *Enarr. in Ps. 96*.4 (CCL 39.1357).

The interpretation referring Old Testament 'island' prophecies to the apostolic mission became commonplace.[49] Remigius of Auxerre repeats Jerome's comment almost verbatim.[50] On Isaiah 66.19 ('et ponam in eis signum et mittam ex eis qui salvati fuerint ad gentes / in mare . . . ad insulas longe'), Isidore of Seville comments, 'in quo sententia specialiter missi apostoli prophetatur.'[51] A Psalter gloss, possibly of Irish origin, comments on Psalm 88.14 in a similar way:

> nunc mare gentes intelleguntur, quae subditae sunt dauid . . . similiter et omnes gentes, quae subditae sunt apostolis intelleguntur mare, et ubique insulas, hoc est ecclesias fundaverunt.[52]

This typological tradition, according to which the apostles are said to navigate the sea, traveling to the island nations and founding churches there, fits seamlessly into the literal narrative of *Andreas*. The apostles Andrew and Matthew travel on a ship piloted by Christ to a distant, heathen *island*,[53] and bring about the conversion of its inhabitants; Mermedonia is henceforth an *ecclesia gentium*. By making Mermedonia an island, the poet has taken advantage of the sea journey he inherited from his source, thereby drawing out and heightening its

---

[49] The *Thesaurus linguae latinae*, after giving the Biblical usage of *insula*, adds, 'script. ecclesiastici passim allegorice interpretantur,' with a number of references.

[50] PL 116.925–26 (attributed to Haymo of Halberstadt). Remigius makes the islands 'diversitates gentium ecclesiarum.' On Is. 41.1 ('taceant ad me insulae et gentes mutent fortitudinem') he comments, 'taceant, inquit, insulae ad hoc ut audiant me primum, hoc est gentes per apostolos' (915). These Biblical verses could easily be applied to the conversion of England. Bede quotes a letter of Pope Vitalian to Oswiu (*EH* 3.29) which cites a series of verses from Isaiah as testimony to the conversion of the English, including Is. 49.1, 'Audite insulae, et adtendite populi de longe,' and Bede concludes his work with a quotation of Ps. 96.1, 'laetentur insulae multae'; the latter verse is glossed 'restitutio gentium' in the Canterbury Psalter (facsimile ed. M. R. James [London 1935]) fol. 172ᵃ. For the post-medieval survival of this tradition, see Josephine Waters Bennett, 'Britain among the Fortunate Isles,' *Studies in Philology* 53 (1956) 129ff. The tradition outlined here explains a stanza in a Peter and Paul sequence of Nicholas of Clairvaux, which contrasts the spiritual victories of the apostles with the martial conquests of the Romans: 'Sanguis horum subiugavit / que Romanus ignoravit / insularum spatia' (ed. John F. Benton, 'Nicholas of Clairvaux and the Twelfth-Century Sequence,' *Traditio* 18 [1962] 168). The phrase 'insularum spatia' is clearly a general reference to the heathen lands converted by the apostles, and not, as Joseph Szövérffy assumes, a specific reference to Ireland ('Nicholas of Clairvaux and Ireland's Conversion,' *Medium Ævum* 34 [1965] 122–25).

[51] *De fide catholica contra Iudaeos* 2.1.10 (PL 83.493–94).

[52] Franz Unterkircher, ed., *Die Glossen des Psalters von Mondsee*, Spicilegium Friburgense 20 (Freiburg 1974) 364. On the origin and date (fifth–seventh centuries) of these glosses, see 25–26.

[53] Mermedonia is also an island metaphorically, because it is 'morðre bewunden' (19a); cf. Jerome's comment, 'gentes, id est insulae, quae falsis amarisque huius saeculi tunduntur fluctibus' (CCL 73ᴀ.468).

function as a paradigm of the apostolic mission,[54] and placing the entire narrative in a specific context of Biblical prophecy: the conversion of the *insulae gentium* by the apostles.

To summarize the lexicographical findings presented here: the evidence of English place-names (most attested after the Old English period), two Old English glosses on the Latin place-names *Cilicia* and *Tiberias*, and — very doubtfully — *Beowulf* 2334, suggests that Old English *ealand* and *igland* could mean not only 'island' in the strict sense, but also 'land by the water,' 'land partly surrounded by water.' But the parallel range of Biblical-Latin *insula* raises the possibility that these extended senses are not native, but semantic loans.[55] The use of the plural to refer to 'distant (heathen) lands across the sea,' attested in glosses on Biblical *insula* but also in a Lambeth Psalter gloss, *Andreas* 15 and 18, *Solomon and Saturn* 1, and *Maxims I* 15, is clearly indebted to Biblical usage, which has not only influenced the words' geographical denotation but has also contributed the contextual association of 'islands' with the heathen nations (*gentes*), a connotation developed in patristic tradition and exploited by the authors of the three Old English poems.[56]

Texas Tech University

---

[54] Owing to Paul's sea journeys in Acts; but the sea journey is also a stock motif of the apocryphal stories of the apostles. See Rosa Söder, *Die apokryphen Apostelgeschichten und die romanhafte Literatur der Antike* (Stuttgart 1932) 42ff.

[55] A semantic loan, whereby a native word adopts another sense from a Latin word with which it already shares a basic sense (a *Lehnbedeutung* in Gneuss' terminology), is often difficult to distinguish from independent parallel development, especially when the discrepancy between the two senses is not wide. But semanticists, as well as students of borrowing in OE, have warned against too hastily assuming parallel development before the possibility of borrowing has been fully explored. See Walter Ullmann, *The Principles of Semantics* (Oxford 1957) 231; Gneuss, *Lehnbildung* 25–27; Samuel Kroesch, 'Change of Meaning by Analogy,' in *Studies in Honor of Hermann Collitz* (Baltimore 1930) 188. An influential treatment of the subject is Einar Haugen's 'The Analysis of Linguistic Borrowing,' *Language* 26 (1950) 216–31.

[56] After the present paper had been completed, I found that Marie Walsh makes a similar suggestion for *Andreas* in an unpublished dissertation, 'Ecclesiastical Backgrounds of Imagery in the Old English *Andreas*' (unpubl. Catholic Univ. diss. 1975) 128–31. Walsh refers to the 'island' prophecies of Isaiah in connection with her thesis that the poet has portrayed Andreas as the 'Suffering Servant.' However, Walsh says nothing of the lexicographical problem, and seems not to have been aware of the special Biblical usage. The allegorical interpretation she quotes from Jerome makes the prophecies refer to Christ rather than to the apostles, although she does suggest that Andreas' mission is 'a perpetuation of the mission of the Servant to the nations' (129). It seems to me that the christological and the 'apostolic' interpretations are entirely compatible; but I would prefer to stress the latter, since the apostolic mission is the poem's literal subject. A rather different explanation has been proposed by Oliver J. H. Grosz, who suggests that 'an island symbolizes the religious exile's complete isolation from an outer world' ('The Island of Exiles: A Note on *Andreas* 15,' *English Language Notes* 7 [1970] 241–42).

AN UNPUBLISHED STORY OF MICHAEL THE ARCHANGEL AND ITS CONNECTIONS

By J. E. CROSS*

The unpublished story of Michael is found earliest (at present) in the MS Cambridge, Pembroke College 25 (saec. xi, Bury),[1] which is a representative of what Henri Barré[2] regarded as a reading-collection of pieces for preachers to use on appropriate days of the liturgical year, and some also *quando volueris*. The composer rarely accepted the sermons, homilies, or tracts of his predecessors without some selection and adaptation, and thus he normally created the individual sections from a variety of sources. His latest known and dateable sources are Amalarius, *De ecclesiasticis officiis*[3] and Rhabanus Maurus, *De clericorum institutione*;[4] thus the collection was produced some time after the 820s.[5] The fullest representative of the collection is the Pembroke manuscript, but almost as large is a collateral descendant from the exemplar in Oxford, Balliol College MS 240 (saec. xiv),[6] which offers additional information about the extent of the 'original' collection. Other manuscripts which contain, or indicate that they contained, runs of items are: Chartres, Bibliothèque Muni-

---

* In my experience of conversation in his company, Professor R. E. Kaske has always been alert to new information about mediaeval matters, however tangential it may appear to his major interests on first presentation. No excuse need be offered for my straying into areas away from my own and his dominant interests.

[1] For a description of the MS, including date and place of origin, see M. R. James, *A Descriptive Catalogue of the Manuscripts in the Library of Pembroke College, Cambridge* (Cambridge 1905) 25–29.

[2] Henri Barré, *Les Homéliaires carolingiens de l'école d'Auxerre* (Vatican City 1962) 24. Rosamond McKitterick, *The Frankish Church and the Carolingian Reforms 789–895* (London 1977) 107–9, has some comments on the collection.

[3] Barré 17 identifies the use of Amalarius.

[4] The tractate by Rhabanus Maurus was used for Pembroke 25 fol. 73ʳ, *Item alia* (*in Parasceuen*), although much of the section in Rhabanus was abstracted from Isidore, *De ecclesiasticis officiis*; fol. 75ʳ *In Sabbato Sancto*; fol. 111ᵛ *De sapientia*; and also fol. 159ʳ *De officio missae*. Barré 18 thought that the last of these items was not in the original collection, but I hope to argue otherwise.

[5] Rhabanus' *De clericorum institutione* was composed during the abbacy at Fulda of Eigil, who died in 822; see *Rabani Mauri* MARTYROLOGIUM, ed. John McCulloh, CCcM 44 (Turnhout 1979) xv. On Amalarius see Barré 17.

[6] R. A. B. Mynors, *Catalogue of the Manuscripts of Balliol College, Oxford* (Oxford 1963) 260–63. Abbé R. Étaix directed me to this manuscript, in which the collection occupies fols. 56ʳ–136ʳ, and is preceded by a list of contents (fol. 55ʳ⁻ᵛ). This list indicates that the original collection contained one more item which is not extant in any of the manuscripts noted in this paper.

cipale MS 25 fols. 119–162 (saec. x/xi, Saint-Père, Chartres);[7] Cambridge, St. John's College MS 42 fols. 13–62^v (saec. xii, Worcester [?]);[8] London, British Library MS Royal 5 E XIX fols. 21–37 (probably 1089–1125, Salisbury);[9] and Canterbury, Cathedral MS Addit. 127/12 (saec xi$^{1in.}$), a fragment of two folios.[10] I shall argue elsewhere that all of these manuscripts are representatives of the original homiliary to a larger or smaller degree, but all at removes from the exemplar. Two more collections select and include items from the Pembroke-type collection: Paris, Bibliothèque Nationale MS Lat. 3794 fols. 18–31 (saec xii, Germany ?);[11] and Grenoble, Bibliothèque Municipale 278 (470) (saec. xii, Chartreux).[12] At present, it appears that the collection was comparatively popular in England and had influence on the Continent.

This popularity in England is also indicated in vernacular sermons of the Anglo-Saxon period. Six anonymous Old English sermons use material from the Pembroke-type collection: Vercelli Homilies iii, xix, and xx;[13] two sermons

---

[7] *Catalogue général des manuscrits des bibliothèques publiques de France: Départements* XI: *Chartres* (Paris 1890) 12. At the time of the catalogue, the collection occupied fols. 119–62 and included an item numbered xxxii, beginning: 'Spiritus sanctus per prophetam,' as Pembroke 25 fol. 77^r, xxxii *In die sancto Paschae.* The manuscript was burned in 1944 and is extant only as a box of fragments, now interleaved and numbered. Abbé Étaix considered the fragments and left a letter of 21 January 1957 at Chartres identifying many fragments from the non-homiletic items in the manuscript and also six fragments from the sermon-collection (those with fragments of title remaining). Through generous aid from the British Academy, I have seen Abbé Étaix's letter at Chartres and considered the fragments, sometimes of two or three part-words, against the text of Pembroke 25. I have been able to confirm five of Étaix's identifications, sometimes with the addition of a verso reading, and rejected a sixth (now generously agreed by Abbé Étaix). I have also identified ten more. At present the fifteen identified fragments indicate that Chartres 25 (44) included folios within the range of Pembroke 25 fols. 81^v–108^v, thus for the items Pembroke xxxiiii *Omelia octauas Paschae* up to xlvii *Omelia in natale martyres in kalendas Agusti* (Maccabees). Clearly Chartres 25 (44) was another text at least of a considerable section of the collection.

[8] M. R. James, *A Descriptive Catalogue of the Manuscripts in the Library of St. John's College, Cambridge* (Cambridge 1913) 57–64.

[9] N. R. Ker, 'Salisbury Cathedral Manuscripts and Patrick Young's Catalogue,' *The Wiltshire (Archaeological) Magazine* 53 (1949) 154, 158, 168, 174; and N. R. Ker, 'The Beginnings of Salisbury Cathedral Library,' in *Medieval Learning and Literature: Essays Presented to Richard William Hunt*, edd. J. J. G. Alexander and M. T. Gibson (Oxford 1976) 23–49.

[10] N. R. Ker, *Medieval Manuscripts in British Libraries* II, *Abbotsford–Keele* (Oxford 1977) 316–17.

[11] R. Étaix, 'Le sermonnaire carolingien de Beaune,' *Revue des Études Augustiniennes* 25 (1979) 106–21.

[12] *Catalogue général des manuscrits des bibliothèques publiques de France: Départements* VII: *Grenoble* (Paris 1889) 112–13. Abbé Étaix directed me to this MS, which includes some items as in Pembroke 25.

[13] For an edition of Vercelli Homily iii see *Die Vercelli-Homilien: I.–VIII. Homilie*, ed. Max Förster (Hamburg 1932; rpt. Darmstadt 1964) 53–71. For editions of Vercelli Homilies xix and xx see Paul E. Szarmach, *Vercelli Homilies IX–XXIII*, Toronto Old

edited by Bruno Assmann[14] as his numbers xi and xii; and one sermon edited by Hildegard Tristram[15] as her number iii (for the Ascension). The evidence for these statements will be presented elsewhere, but two interesting results of the linking of items in the Vercelli Codex with the Pembroke-type collection may be stated. The first is that the Vercelli Codex was clearly not composed until after the 820s, when the 'original' Latin homiliary was written. The second is that the Vercelli items were copied from items already in the vernacular, since variant readings for Vercelli Homilies iii, xix, and xx in other vernacular manuscripts where the items occur[16] are occasionally closer to the direct Latin source. Such variants obviously indicate that, on occasion, Vercelli is an inaccurate copy of earlier translations or adaptations into Old English, for which more accurate copies are extant elsewhere. It is, of course, unfortunate that there is no dedicatory prologue to the Pembroke-type collection as with Rhabanus Maurus' similar 'reading-collection,' which allows a more precise date of writing for the latter work.[17] But mediaevalists, like Gregory the Great, proceed in steps, and we can continue to hope, think, and work.

The Pembroke-type collection contains two sections on the archangel (in three of the manuscripts only — Pembroke 25, St. John's 42, and Balliol 240): the first item, Pembroke 25 fols. 125ʳ–127ʳ as LIIII *Omelia in Festiuitate sancti Michaelis archangeli*, beginning: 'Angeli Grece uocantur, Aebraice Malaoth'; the second, Pembroke 25 fols. 127ʳ–129ʳ as LV *Item alia*, which is printed below.

The first *omelia* is one only in title since its whole narrative is an abstract corresponding to Isidore, *Etymologiae* 7.5.[18] A comparison of the Pembroke text with its variants against the texts, with variants, of Isidore's chapter, both in Arévalo's edition, reprinted by Migne in the *Patrologia*, and in W. M. Lindsay's edition,[19] indicates that our author copied the chapter in Isidore entire, in the same order of paragraphs, and — most probably — almost ver-

---

English Series 5 (Toronto 1981) 69–72, 77–80. Helen L. Spencer, 'Vernacular and Latin Versions of a Sermon for Lent: "A Lost Penitential Homily" Found,' *Mediaeval Studies* 44 (1982) 271–305, has already identified the source of Vercelli Homily iii and has printed the relevant item from the Pembroke-type collection.

[14] *Angelsächsische Homilien und Heiligenleben*, ed. B. Assmann, Bibliothek der angelsächsischen Prosa 3 (Kassel 1889; rpt. Darmstadt 1964) 138–50.

[15] Hildegard L. C. Tristram, *Vier altenglische Predigten aus der heterodoxen Tradition* (Diss., Freiburg i. Br. 1970) 162–72.

[16] For an edition of the variant texts for Vercelli Homilies xix and xx, see *Eleven Old English Rogationtide Homilies*, edd. Joyce Bazire and J. E. Cross, Toronto Old English Series 7 (Toronto 1982) 16–23, 31–38.

[17] Rhabanus Maurus' first collection of items as a reading-collection (PL 110.13–134) was dedicated to Haistulf, Archbishop of Mainz, who died in 826.

[18] PL 82.272–74. I owe this identification to J. D. Pheifer of Trinity College, Dublin.

[19] *Isidori Hispalensis episcopi Etymologiarum siue Originum libri XX* (Oxford 1911).

batim from one Isidorean manuscript. The only concession to the title *omelia* is a final addition of part of a benediction: 'per infinita secula seculorum. AMEN' (Pembroke 25 fol. 127^r).

The second, the object of discussion here, is more typical of our writer's normal methods of composition. For his first two paragraphs of eulogy for Michael, the composer abstracted and interwove phrases which are found as antiphons and responses of the liturgical feast for the archangel. Such phrases appear in the earliest antiphonary, the pseudo-Gregorian *Liber responsalis sive Antiphonarius* (LR),[20] and elsewhere:[21]

(i)   'qui constitutus est a deo . . . princeps super omnes animas hominum susci-
      piendas' [lines 2–3];
      Cf. 'Archangele Michael, constitui te principem super omnes animas susci-
      piendas' LR [PL 78.806].

(ii) 'Ipse est enim prepositus paradysi' [lines 6–7]; and 'quem honorificant an-
      gelorum ciues' [lines 3–4];
      Cf. 'Michael praepositus paradisi, quem honorificant angelorum civis' LR
      [PL 78.805].

(iii) 'Hic est princeps militię angelorum cuius honor prestat beneficia populis
      et oratio eius perducit ad regna caelorum' [lines 5–6];
      Cf. 'Hic est Michael archangelus princeps militiae angelorum, cujus honor
      praestat beneficia populorum, et oratio perducit ad regna coelorum' LR
      [PL 78.805].

(iv) 'Uenit Michael cum multitudine angelorum cui tradidit deus animas sanc-
      torum ut perducat eas in paradysum exultationis' [lines 7–8], as LR [PL
      78.805] *verbatim*.

Echoes of two more antiphons or responses occur within the narrative of Michael's fight with the dragon (lines 13–41):

(v)   'Factum est autem silentium in caelo dum pręliaretur Michael archangelus
      cum dracone. Cumque fecisset uictoriam . . . exaudita est uox milia milium
      dicentium: Salus, honor, uirtus et imperium semper omnipotenti deo' [lines
      25–28];
      Cf. 'Factum est silentium in coelo, cum committeret bellum draco cum
      Michael archangelo; et audita est uox millia millium dicentium: Salus, honor
      et uirtus omnipotenti Deo' LR [PL 78.805], and 'Factum . . . bellum, et
      Michael pugnauit cum eo, et fecit uictoriam, alleluia' LR [PL 78.806].

---

[20] This text is placed in Compiègne, dated 860–80, and described in *Corpus antiphonalium officii* I, ed. R.-J. Hesbert, *Rerum ecclesiasticarum documenta*, Series Maior, Fontes VII (Rome 1963) xvii–xx. CAO III (RED IX; Rome 1968), illustrates *Invitatoria et antiphonae*; CAO IV (RED X; Rome 1970) illustrates *Responsoria*. Although the earliest collection (*Liber responsalis*) is late ninth century, individual antiphons and responses were obviously of earlier date. For some such examples see H. Barré, 'Antiens et répons de la Vierge,' *Marianum* 29 (1967) 153–254.

[21] As illustrated in Hesbert's volumes.

The manuscript of the LR as printed in PL has lines and a page missing at the end of the section on Michael, but R. J. Hesbert's record of antiphons and responses indicates that later collections have words somewhat closer to those in Pembroke: 'Dum proeliaretur Michael archangelus cum dracone audita est uox.'[22]

Echoes of other antiphons and responses of the church are found in other items of the Latin collection to be a distinctive habit of composition, often in eulogy of notable figures, particularly Christ and the Virgin. See, for example, Pembroke v *In Natale Domini* fols. 10ᵛ–11ᵛ, which briefly describes portents and events at the Nativity, but includes the speaking ox in Rome and the lamb in Egypt, both of which are found in *The Old English Martyrology*;[23] vii *Item alia (in natale Domini)* fols. 13ᵛ–15ʳ; xv *In Purificatione S. Mariae* fols. 27ʳ–28ᵛ; and xlviiii *In Assumptione S. Mariae* fols. 113ᵛ–117ᵛ. A brief but clear illustration of the habit occurs in Pembroke xl *In Ascensione Domini*, which concludes (fol. 95ᵛ): 'O rex glorię, domine uirtutum, qui triumphat[o]r hodie super omnes cęlos ascendisti, ne derelinquas nos orphanos, sed mitte promissum patris in nos spiritum ueritatis,' to echo the *Liber responsalis* (PL 78.781) *verbatim*, and to be turned into vernacular prose in an Old English anonymous sermon on the Ascension: 'Eala wuldres cyning, drihten mægna, þu ðe nu to dæg sigorgend astige ofer ealle heofonas, ne forlæt þu us na fæderlease, ac asende to us þines fæder behat, þæt is soðfæstnysse gast.'[24]

Apart from the echoes of antiphons, two other discernible sources are used after the story of Michael's fight with the dragon (lines 13–41). Both of these sources illustrate another habit of the composer, his willingness to use the same material in different sections.[25] The phrases of lines 43–64, 'nouem esse or-

---

[22] Hesbert IV 288 no. 7151: 'Dum proeliaretur Michael archangelus cum dracone, audita est vox milia milium dicentium: Salus Deo nostro.' The *Breviarium ad usum insignis ecclesiae Sarum*, edd. F. Procter and C. Wordsworth, Fasc. III (Cambridge 1886) 867 col. 1 (for the feast of Michael) reads: *et audita*, which is a little nearer the *exaudita* of Pembroke 25.

[23] Pembroke 25 fol. 11ʳ reads: 'In eius tempore animalia fari humana locutione non dubitatur; bos enim in Roma sub misterio natiuitatis eius locutus est; nihilominus et agnus in Egypto humana usus est loquęla.' For a discussion of these portents in relation to the *Martyrology* see J. E. Cross, 'Portents and Events at Christ's Birth: Comments on Vercelli v and vi and the *Old English Martyrology*,' *Anglo-Saxon England* 2 (1973) 219.

[24] Tristram 171, Homily iii lines 235–39.

[25] One clear example is the addition to an item in Pembroke 25 no. xxxvi entitled *Alia in III feria* [Rogationtide] *sermo beati Maximi episcopi*. The item is based mainly on Maximus of Turin, *Homilia* 90 (PL 57.459ff.), but a section is added at fol. 87ʳ⁻ᵛ which speaks of fasting and almsgiving, beginning: 'Quantum autem ualeat ieiunium uirtus Isidorus explanat dicens: Ieiunum est res sancta, opus caelestę, ianua regni.' The passage, mainly on fol. 87ᵛ, corresponds with two passages (fols. 44ᵛ and 45ʳ) on fasting and alms, printed by Helen Spencer, *Medieval Studies* 44 (1982) 287, 291. These derive from *Collectio canonum Hibernensium* 12.3 (fasting), 13.2 (almsgiving), as noted by Joan Turville-Petre in *Traditio* 19 (1963) 59, 60, in terms of a derivative of Vercelli Homily iii.

dines . . . non praesint,' are selections from Isidore's *Etymologiae* 7.5, the
whole of which was abstracted for Pembroke LIIII as noted above. The phrases
of lines 64–80, 'Alii quidem . . . peruenire mereamur,' are selections (with
adaptation in lines 76–80) from a section of the influential sermon *Legimus in
ecclesiasticis historiis*, which is included within augmented versions of Paul
the Deacon's homiliary, a variant text of which is copied as items LVI–LXIII
(fols. 129ʳ–133ʳ) of the Pembroke collection.[26] The section used in the present
sermon is Pembroke LVIII entitled *De angelis* (fols. 130ʳ⁻ᵛ). All that remains
is the benediction: 'prestante . . . saeculorum, AMEN' (lines 80–82) and the
story of St. Michael.

For the story of Michael in Pembroke, the brief hints in BHL (Supp.)[27] allowed
some suspicions which are now confirmed. The incipit and desinit in a Vatican
Library manuscript, recorded as BHL 5951b, refer to a *draco*, eventually cut
into twelve parts, as in the Pembroke text. The incipit and desinit for another
Vatican manuscript, recorded as BHL 5956b, exactly equates the incipit of
our sermon and echoes the final words of paragraph 3 (lines 40–41), being the
end of the story of the contest, and is entitled *Apparitio et victoria in Asia*, in
which area the Pembroke confrontation is also placed.

The manuscript reference for BHL 5956b is the Vatican Library MS Reginensis Lat. 703ʙ (saec. XII ᵐᵉᵈ·), a well-studied manuscript, since it is the only one
containing most of Books VII and VIII of the ecclesiastical history written
by Ordericus Vitalis.[28] The end of Book VIII, in Marjorie Chibnall's most recent
edition of Ordericus, is transcribed from Reg. Lat. 703ʙ fol. 100ᵛ. Then, without
break, in the same hand, a few chronicle-type statements are entered which
Dr. Chibnall rejected, obviously as being of a different manner of writing from
the fuller narrative of the historian. These record events from 'Anno ab
incarnatione Domini milesimo .c. xxx.iii,' in both France and England, and
conclude: 'Anno ab incarnatione Domini .m.c.x.l.iii fuit fames ualida et mor-
talitas hominum. Deinde altero anno fuit uentus magnus. Eodem anno sub-
jugata est Normannia Gaufrido, Andegauensi comiti, reddita ei ciuitate Roto-
magensi.' With no break in the sequence of words the scribe continues:
'Memorare et recitare decet memoriam Sancti Michaelis archangeli, fratres
karissimi, cunctis gentibus,' as a variant text of Pembroke 25 lines 1–41, and
ending on fol. 101ʳ as Pembroke: 'multas uirtutes et signa et mirabilia ibi perfi-

---

[26] On the sermon *Legimus* see J. E. Cross, '*Legimus in ecclesiasticis historiis*: A sermon for
All Saints and its Use in Old English Prose,' *Traditio* 33 (1977) 101–35. Pembroke 25 is one
of the texts used for the edition of the sermon in that paper.

[27] Bibliotheca Hagiographica Latina (BHL), edd. The Bollandists, *Supplementi* (Brussels
1911) 231.

[28] See *The* ECCLESIASTICAL HISTORY *of Orderic Vitalis*, ed. Marjorie Chibnall, I (Oxford
1980) 121 on the manuscript; IV (1973) 340 on the last lines of Book VIII in this manuscript.

cere cotidie prestat dominus,' but with addition of a benediction: 'ad laudem et gloriam nominis sui quod est benedictum in secula seculorum. Amen.'

Experience in source-study teaches that a later manuscript may well contain a more original form of a story than an earlier manuscript. Had Vat. Reg. Lat. 703B merely contained a simple narrative of the dragon-fight (as Pembroke lines 13–41), I would have said that the Vatican manuscript contained a record of the original story, since the narrative is the only major section within the Pembroke sermon without source, and evidence already known to me indicates that the composer of the Pembroke-type collection was not normally an originator of ideas, certainly not for the vast majority of the items whose sources are identified. We should clearly assume that sources existed, even if they are not already identified. But the text of Vat. Reg. Lat. 703B is not solely the story of Michael's fight, since it includes sections corresponding to the edited text of Pembroke 25 lines 1–12, 25–28, including the phrases based on antiphons and responses, a distinctive habit of composition by the writer of the Pembroke-type collection, as illustrated above. Clearly a text of the Pembroke sermon has been abstracted for the Vat. Reg. Lat. 703B section on Michael.

BHL 5951b is already in print, within the analysis of Vatican Reginensis Lat. 542 (saec. xii) in the catalogue of the Vatican Library hagiographical manuscripts.[29] Albert Poncelet, the cataloguer, regarded it as an *epilogus* to the well-known story of the *Apparitio S. Michaelis in Monte Tumba* (BHL 5951 fols. 33r–34r) which it follows (fol. 34r). The significant details (idea, word, number) in his printing, however, indicate that it is an abbreviation of the story at base for the one in Pembroke 25 and Vat. Reg. Lat. 703B, but with two interesting differences. Where the Pembroke text says that the fight took place 'in the southern part of Asia' (line 13), the abbreviation in Vat. Reg. Lat. 542 places it 'in illis regionibus,' that is, presumably near *Mons Tumba* (probably Mont-Saint-Michel in Normandy);[30] and the phrases of Pembroke 25 lines 25–28 which echo antiphons or responses are missing from Vat. Reg. Lat. 542, which reads for this section of the story:

> 'Et misit eis Christus Michahelem archangelum in forma avis cum gladio ignito, qui drachonem in duodecim partes scidit. Unaquaeque[31] pars eius drachonis paene a duodecim iugis[31] boum ad mare allata est, ne suo foetore[31] homines et iumenta mortificarentur' (cf. the text printed below, lines 26–31).

---

[29] Albertus Poncelet, *Catalogus codicum hagiographicorum latinorum Bibliothecae Vaticanae* (Brussels 1910) 369.

[30] D. H. Farmer, *The Oxford Dictionary of Saints* (Oxford 1978) 278 is a convenient reference.

[31] These are Poncelet's emendations. The manuscript readings are respectively: *una quoque, iuga, fetoris.*

It must be obvious that the composer of the legendary in Vat. Reg. Lat. 542 and of the sermon in Pembroke 25 have adapted the same original story. But Vat. Reg. Lat. 542 has changed the place of the fight to link this story with that of the events at *Mons Tumba*; the composer of the Pembroke sermon has followed his practice of using suitable antiphonal phrases, here to inflate the account. The record (in context) of the three Latin manuscripts indicates that there was a separate story, unconnected with the events at *Mons Tumba*, which was at base for the Pembroke account. In my view, the three accounts should now be grouped together in the revision of Bibliotheca Hagiographica Latina,[32] most suitably under the number 5956, which appears to deal with separate *Apparitiones*.

One more recorded story should be added to this group, that used in a sermon on Michael within the Irish vernacular collection of the fourteenth-century manuscript known as the *Leabhar Breac* ('The speckled book').[33] The Irish sermon, besides using Gregory on angels[34] and including other interesting material, narrates two anecdotes about St. Michael, the second being the popular *Apparitio in Monte Gargano* (BHL 5948), which is the very common choice for the festival of the archangel in both homiliaries and legendaries.[35] Both Ælfric and Blickling Homily xvii[36] on the feast use this *Apparitio*, but with less freedom than the Irish writer. But the first anecdote in *Leabhar Breac* includes details which correspond with those in the Pembroke narration. In the free translation and the nineteenth-century style of Robert Atkinson (but with one correction) the story goes:[37]

> Many signs preceded the consecration of the church in that spot [Mount Garganus]; for the beginning of the magnifying of St. Michael's name in the

---

[32] A revision is being undertaken by François Dolbeau of the Centre Nationale de la Recherche Scientifique, Institut de Recherche et d'Histoire des Textes, Paris.

[33] *The Passions and the Homilies from* LEABHAR BREAC: *Text, Translation, and Glossary,* ed. Robert Atkinson, Royal Irish Academy: Todd Lecture Series 2 (Dublin 1887). The text of our sermon is 213–19; the translation, 451–57.

[34] The preacher names Gregory twice (text 214; translation 451.2) and cites (text 214): 'supernorum ciuium numerus [infinitus] et finitus exprimitur, ut qui [est] numerabilis Deo esse [hominibus] innumerabilis demonstretur,' from the *Moralia in Job* 17.25.18 (PL 76.20); and continues to discuss angels *stantes et ministrantes* from the same paragraph. The nine orders of angels, which follow this brief discussion, come from Gregory's *Homilia in Evangelia* 34.8–10 (PL 76.1250–52).

[35] For some examples see J. E. Cross, 'An Unrecorded Tradition of St. Michael in Old English Texts,' *Notes and Queries* 28 (1981) 12n4.

[36] *The* SERMONES CATHOLICI *or* HOMILIES *of* Ælfric, ed. B. Thorpe, I (London 1844) 502–18. *The Blickling Homilies,* ed. R. Morris, EETS, os 58, 63, 73 (London 1874–80; rpt. 1967) 197–211.

[37] Atkinson 453–54; text 216.

present world was the mighty contest he had with the dragon in that place. The demon had assumed the form of a huge dragon, and entered into a cave on the top of Mount Garganus, from whence he assailed the seeds and fruits and cattle of the districts and countries with his plagues and pestilences. The rude pagans were afraid of that, and thought that the dragon, in whom was the demon, was a god, so that they offered sacrifices and almsgiving to him. But the educated Christians and believers besought aid from God with tears and fasting and prayers, praying the Lord that Michael might come to their assistance. Thereafter it was revealed to them one night, that they should go to the mountain on the morrow; and when they went thither, they beheld the archangel, who clave the dragon asunder into nine parts, each part as much as ten oxen could carry,[38] when it was taken off to be burned. So the name of God and the name of St. Michael were magnified through that miracle.

The skeleton of the Pembroke 25 story is here, although retold by a writer who did not use one word where more could be added. There are differences, the attachment to the famous Mount Garganus, which is in no other example of BHL 5948 and clearly the Irish writer's own; the difference of number, which misleads no one who realises how often scribes err on number, particularly Roman number. But the desolation caused by the dragon, and particularly Michael's dissection of the beast, together with the indication of its size in terms of the loads on oxen, all these point to an echo of the distinctive story, and there is a little more.

The Irish writer continues by reflecting and approximating to events already told in the *Apparitio in Monte Gargano* (BHL 5948),[39] the story of the straying bull, the war between the pagans and Christians, and then the uncertainty of the Sepontine bishop about the consecration of the church. At this point in both BHL 5948 and the Irish vernacular sermon, Michael himself makes an appearance to confirm the church's consecration and to command the Christians to use it. The Irish sermon then inserts a statement which is not found in BHL 5948: 'After this the Archangel went into it in the form of a splendid bird, and marked out the length, breadth, and height of the church, and left on the rock the marks of his fingers,[40] which remain there still.' BHL 5948 does have a record of Michael's physical presence earlier in the narrative, but the information is different:[41] 'uidentes mane iuxta ianuam septemtrionalem . . . instar posteruli pusilla quasi hominis vestigia marmori artius impressa, agnoscuntque, beatum Michaelem hoc presentiae suae signum voluisse monstrare.' The impression is as of a man's footsteps as in Ælfric and in Blickling Homily xvii,

---

[38] Atkinson 454: 'each part the weight of ten oxen.' R. L. Thomson generously checked the translation and made this correction.

[39] The best edition of this text is by G. Waitz, MGH SRL I (Hanover 1878) 541–43.

[40] One would expect 'claws.'

[41] Waitz 542.

although the latter adds that the footsteps 'swa hie on wexe wæron aðyde,'[42] possibly from a variant manuscript of the Latin text of BHL 5948. But in the Pembroke story Michael takes the form of a bird ('in speciem alitis' line 24) for his contest, and as a result his physical presence later is in the same form: 'Non omitendum quoque quod in illo loco ubi stetit sanctus Michael in forma auis quando draconem occidit signa ungularum eius in petra quasi in caera mollissima apparent omni tempore' (lines 37–40). Here the Irishman has fused information from the two separate *apparitiones* of St. Michael the Archangel.

Within the Old English vernacular we also have a fascinating eulogy[43] of St. Michael which enumerates the qualities of the archangel and examples of his aid to humans in what may be termed a series of prose stanzas, each beginning 'þis is se halga heahengel Sancte Michael.' In the introduction to the series, the homilist notes that 'he is strong on gefeohte wið ðane miclan drocan swa hit sagað her on pocalipsis þære bec.' The reference is to Apocalypse 12.7: 'Et factum est proelium magnum in coelo; Michael et Angeli eius proeliabantur cum dracone, et draco pugnabat, et angeli ejus,' which verse is recalled by the Pembroke homilist, via an antiphon or response in his extension of the basic dragon story. The apocalyptic dragon, as indicated in the succeeding scriptural verses, is that old serpent Satan who is thrown down to earth. I suspect, however, that sometime someone felt that Michael should be accorded a conquest of a real dragon, set in distant lands, and the story was created which is now found in Pembroke 25, Vat. Reg. Lat. 703ʙ, Vat. Reg. Lat. 540, and in the account in the *Leabhar Breac*.

University of Liverpool

THE LATIN TEXT

Except for Balliol 240 all the texts below have been read on clear microfilm and presented no problems. The spelling of the base text (Pembroke 25) is retained unless there could be misunderstanding and variant texts confirm a more acceptable spelling. Transpositions of words in variant manuscripts have not been recorded; abbreviations in the base text (Pembroke 25) have been expanded; punctuation, however, has been modernised for easier reading.

Manuscripts:

i.   Cambridge, Pembroke College MS 25 (P), saec. xi, Bury; fols. 127ᵛ–129ʳ.
ii. Cambridge, St. John's College MS 42 (B20) (J), saec. xii, Worcester (?); fol. 53ʳ⁻ᵛ.

---

[42] Thorpe I 506; Morris 203, 205.
[43] Ed. Tristram (n15) as no. ii, 152–61. The quotation is from 152.

iii. Oxford, Balliol College MS 240 (B), saec. xiv, fols. 111ʳ–112ʳ.
iv. Vatican Library MS Reginensis Lat. 703ʙ (olim 703ᴀ) (V), saec. xii ᵐᵉᵈ·,
      St. Stephen's, Caen; fols. 100ᵛ–101ʳ (lines 1–41 of our text).

P fol. 127ʳ ʟᴠ Item alia.

      Memorare et recitare decet memoriam sancti Michaelis, fratres karissimi,
      cunctis gentibus toto orbe terrarum dispersis, qui constitutus est a deo
      dux et princeps super omnes animas hominum suscipiendas, quem honorifi/
127ᵛ cant angelorum ciues.
   5 Hic est princeps militię angelorum cuius honor prestat beneficia populis
      et oratio eius perducit ad regna caelorum. Ipse est enim prepositus para-
      dysi sicut scriptum est: Uenit Michael cum multitudine angelorum cui
      tradidit deus animas sanctorum ut perducat eas in paradysum exultationis
      et habitare ibi faciat cum iocunditate et cum gaudio magno. Huius ergo
  10 rei gratia ab omnibus fidelibus ueneranda est sancti Michaelis solempnitas
      ac precipue quia in multis locis terrarum in auxilium frequenter ueniens
      populis dei.
      Hanc quoque inmensam et ammirabilem in dextrali parte Asiae fecisse
      legimus uirtutem. Draco enim ingens mirae magnitudinis, montem quen-
  15 dam altum occupans in illis regionibus uenit, cuius flatus flamiuomus
      quantoscumque in giro suo tangi potuisset omnes interficiebat. Incolae
      igitur regionis illius uacuas terras miserabiliter relinquentes ad alias
      exierunt gentes. Uidentes autem suam regionem esse desertam, diuina
      gratia edocti et inluminati, ad deum omnipotentem toto corde conuersi
  20 sunt, et ab Ihesu Christo auxilium petentes, multa deo promittebant uota
      dicentes quod in nomine eius templum aedificarent cum magna honori-
      ficentia si hunc draconem suam deuorantem patriam ab eis expelleret ne
      ultra eis nocere potuisset. Misit igitur deus archangelum suum Michaelem
      auxilium eis ferre, in speciem alitis praeclari cum gladio ignito, ut draco-
128ʳ nem inter/ficeret. Factum est autem silentium in caelo dum pręliaretur
  26 Michael archangelus cum dracone. Cumque fecisset uictoriam, draconem
      in xii partes interficiens, exaudita est uox milia milium dicentium: Salus,

---

   1. V *adds* archangeli *after* Michaelis.   2. V *adds* in *before* toto; 2. V: dispersi.
5. B, V *add* enim *after* est.   5. V: princes.   10. P. J: rei; B: regi; V *omits.*
11. P, J, V: quia; B: qui.   11. V *omits* frequenter.   15. P, J, B: occupans; V:
occupatus.   16. J *omits* suo.   17. P, J, B: miserabiliter; V: miseraliter.
21. P, J, B: dicentes; V: dicebant.   21. P, J, B: magna; V: magno.   22. V *omits*
eis.   27. P, J, V: exaudita; B: et audita.

1-9   Antiphons and/or Responses, see discussion above.

honor, uirtus, et imperium semper omnipotenti deo. Sed cum incolae
regionis illius post haec deum glorificantes reuertissent, uix unamquamque
30 partem huius draconis per xii iuga bouum ad mare usque trahere conantes
prẹualuerunt ne suo fetore homines et iumenta mortificarentur. Deinde
post haec in illo loco aecclesiam magne structurae, in dei nomine, sub
honore sancti Michaelis, gens illa iuxta promissionem construxit. In
qua dehinc centum quinquaginta uiri huius rei gratia cotidie pascuntur,
35 quinquaginta ad adorandum et supplicandum deum caeli, et quinquaginta
ad legendum et scribendum, et quinquaginta ad praeparandum ea quae
necessaria sunt eis in presenti uita. Non omitendum quoque quod in illo
loco ubi stetit sanctus Michael in forma auis quando draconem occidit
signa ungularum eius in petra quasi in caera mollissima apparent omni
40 tempore, cui gratia huius uictoriẹ, multas uirtutes et signa et mirabilia ibi
perficere cotidie prestat dominus.

   Sed hoc quoque commemorandum his dictis de sancto Michaele quod
nouem esse ordines angelorum sacrae scripturae testantur, id est, angeli,
archangeli, throni, dominationes, uirtutes, principatus, potestates, cheru-
128ᵛ bin et seraphin. Angeli grece uocantur,/ Ebraice malaoth, Latine uero
46 nuntii interpretantur, ab eo quod domini uoluntatem populis nuntiant.
Angeli autem sunt qui parua et minima annuntiant hominibus; archangeli
dicti eo quod primatum teneant inter angelos maxima quẹque annun-
tiantes. Quidam autem archangelorum priuatis nominibus appellantur
50 ut per uocabula ipsa in opere quid ualeant designetur. Gabriel enim Ebraice in lingua nostra uertitur 'fortitudo dei' quia ubi potentia diuina uel
fortitudo manifestabitur Gabriel mittitur. Unde et eo tempore quo erat
dominus nasciturus et triumphaturus de mundo Gabriel uenit ad Mariam
ut ad illam annuntiaret qui ad debellandum aerias potestates humilis
55 uenire dignaturus esset. Michael interpretatur 'qui[s] ut deus'; quando
enim aliquid in mundo mire uirtutis fit, hic archangelus mittitur et ex
ipso opere nomen eius est quia nemo potest facere quod facere praeualet
deus. Raphael interpretatur 'curatio uel medicina dei'; ubicumque enim

---

28. J *omits* cum.   30. P, J, B: huius; V: eius.   32. P, J, V: aecclesiam; B:
ecclesie.   35. B, V *omit* ad *before* adorandum.   35. P, J, V: deum; B: deo.
40. P, J: cui . . . huius; B, V: cuius.   41. V *adds after* dominus: ad laudem et gloriam
nominis sui quod est benedictum in secula seculorum, Amen.   44. J *adds* et *before*
potestates.   47. B *omits* archangeli . . . nominibus (49).   54. P, J: debellandum;
B: debellandam.   54. P: aerias; B, J: aereas.   55. P: qui; B, J: quis.
56. J *adds* a deo *after* archangelus.   57. B *omits* facere.

43–64 Isidore, *Etym.* 7.5 (PL 82.272–74) in the order §§ 4, 1, 6, 9, 10, 11, 12, 13, 28, 29, almost
as phrases from text in Pembroke 25 fols. 125ʳ–127ʳ.

curandi uel medendi opus necessarium est, hic archangelus a deo mittitur
60 et inde 'medicina dei' uocatur. Unicuique autem eorum propria officia
data sunt, nam quod angeli et locis et hominibus presunt per prophetam
testatur angelus dicens: Princeps regni Persarum resistit mihi [Daniel
10.13]. Unde apparet nullum esse locum nullumque hominem quibus
angeli non praesint. Alii quidem ex his ad nos in mundum mis[s]i futura
129ʳ predicando deueniunt. Alii ad haec sunt constituti ut per eos / signa et
66 mirabilia frequentius fiant. Alii subiectis angelorum spiritibus praesunt
eisque ad explenda diuina misteria principantur. Alii mira potentia ceteris
prae[e]minent pro eo quod eis ad oboediendum alia angelorum agmina
subiecta sunt. Alii tanta diuinitatis gratia replentur ut in eis dominus
70 sedeat et per eos sua iudicia discernat. Alii tanto perfectiori scientia
pleni sunt quanto claritatem dei uicinius contemplantur. Alia uero ita
deo coniuncta sunt angelorum agmina scientia ut inter haec et deum nulli
alii spiritus intersint, tanto autem magis amore ardent quanto subtilius
claritatem diuinitatis eius aspiciunt.
75 Talibus ergo, ut diximus, a primordio incipien[ti]s uitae beatorum spirituum distinctionibus superna cęlorum regna a deo conditore in perpetuum
mirabiliter collocata subsistunt. Sed quia de caelestium ciuium secretis
disputauimus, fratres karissimi, conemur ante oculos nostri conditoris
tergere peccatorum maculas ut ad consortia eorum, de quibus locuti
80 sumus, peruenire mereamur, prestante domino nostro Ihesu Christo qui
cum patre et spiritu sancto uiuit et regnat per infinita secula seculorum.
AMEN.

---

64. P, J: praesint; B: praesunt.   64. P: misi; B, J: missi.   65. P, B: deueniunt;
J: deuenerant.   67. B *omits* diuina.   68. P, B, J: praeminent.   71. P, J:
pleni; B: perfecti.   72. P: coniuncta; J: coniuncti.   72. B, J *omit* scientia.
75. B *omits* ergo.   75. P: incipiens; B, J: incipientis.   77. B *omits* subsistunt . . .
secretis; *reads* ut.   78. P, B: disputauimus; J: disputamus.   81. P, B: per infinita;
J: in.

64–76   The sermon, *Legimus in ecclesiasticis historiis*, ed. J. E. Cross, *Traditio* 33 (1977)
        108–9, almost as text in Pembroke 25 fol. 130ᵛ.
76–80   Based on statements in *Legimus*.

SCYLD SCEFING AND THE 'STIRPS REGIA':
PAGAN MYTH AND CHRISTIAN KINGSHIP IN 'BEOWULF'

By THOMAS D. HILL

Kings and kingship are central in the historical world which *Beowulf* depicts. There are of course the rich and elaborate depictions of court life in both Denmark and the realm of the Geats, and most of the major figures in the poem are either kings or *æpelingas*, princes on whom the succession might devolve.[1] Even in small details the poet reveals his concern for the dignity and authority of kings. As the Danes celebrate Beowulf's magnificent victory over Grendel, the poet is careful to specify that while they praised Beowulf, 'ne hie huru winedrihten wiht ne logon, / glædne Hroðgar, ac þæt wæs god cyning' (862–63).[2] And in the conclusion of the poem it is not only the death of King Beowulf, but also the end of the royal line he represented which presage the future troubles of the Geatish people. The *Beowulf*-poet, however, is not only scrupulously respectful of the kings and royal families with which he deals; he also begins his poem with a mythical digression which explicitly concerns the origin of one of the great royal families of the north and implicitly the institution of kingship itself. Curiously, this myth has not attracted much interest in modern *Beowulf* scholarship. *Beowulf* scholars of an earlier generation discussed this myth and identified a number of analogues, thus demonstrating that it was current in Anglo-Saxon England apart from *Beowulf*.[3] Modern scholarship has tended to emphasize the æsthetic aspect of the poem, and this digression — though justifiable — has seemed a bit irrelevant to the main concerns of the poem. My concern here is with the ideological implications of this episode which are both interesting in themselves and important for understanding the aesthetic rationale for the opening scene in *Beowulf*. In discussing this 'myth', I wish to break the discussion down into two parts — what the myth itself implies, and how the *Beowulf* poet presented and adapted it in the context of the poem as a whole.

Since the term 'myth' itself is often used in quite different senses, it might be useful to offer a brief definition here. Myth can simply be defined as an

---

[1] On the definition of the *æpeling*, see David N. Dumville, 'The Ætheling: A Study in Anglo-Saxon Constitutional History,' *Anglo-Saxon England* 8 (1979) 1–33.

[2] All citations and quotations of *Beowulf* are from the Anglo-Saxon Poetic Records by line numbers.

[3] The evidence and the texts themselves are conveniently assembled in R. W. Chambers, BEOWULF: *An Introduction*, 3rd ed., rev. C. L. Wrenn (Cambridge 1963) 68–88.

ordering story which explains some feature of the world of experience. It can
be historically true or wildly fabulous, but the explanation which the story
offers must at some point have been thought to have some cogency, or otherwise the myth would not have any currency. In this instance, the story of
Scyld Scefing 'explains' how the Scylding dynasty was first established and
also 'explains' why legitimate kings — in Denmark at least — must be
descendants of Scyld. Since the story also involves the implied guidance and
protection of some divine power, it could be argued that the story of Scyld
Scefing is also a myth in the more conventional sense of that term, a story
about 'sacred beings and semi-divine heroes and the origins of all things.'[4]
But the important feature of a myth is that it explains, and the importance
of the political explanation which this story offers is obvious.

                                        I

   The story of Scyld Scefing fulfills exactly Victor Turner's dictum that 'myths
treat of origins, but derive from transitions.'[5] The story concerns the founding
of the Danish royal family of the Scyldings, but the larger implications of the
story concern the institution of kingship itself and the crucial question of
succession, for kingship as a social institution is tested most severely at that
juncture when kingship is transferred from one king to another.[6] Given the
question — what defines a valid claim to the throne? — the pragmatic answer
would be power and the ability to use it; in the context of Anglo-Saxon society,
these terms might presumably be defined as the allegiance of a sufficient body
of warriors and the skill to command them effectively in war. In purely
pragmatic terms, this answer would seem to be self-evident; in fact, historians
know of a number of instances of self-made kings and presume that the paucity
of records as well as the tendency of chroniclers to conceal awkward truths
about powerful men obscure many more such situations. Given these truths
about the actual process of ascent to kingship, the story of Scyld Scefing
in *Beowulf* and the truncated versions available in the various Latin sources
are utterly removed from the exigencies of real historical process. In terms of
historical reality, one would expect the most powerful magnate to ascend to
the throne after a period of civil war. But according to this myth it is Scyld
Scefing, a young boy whose antecedents are unknown, who accedes to the

---

   [4] Stith Thompson, *The Folktale* (1946; rpt. Berkeley 1977) 9.
   [5] Victor W. Turner, 'Myth and Symbol,' in the *International Encyclopedia of the Social
Sciences*, edd. David L. Sills *et al.* ([New York] 1968) X 576.
   [6] On this issue, see Janet W. Nelson, 'Inauguration Rituals,' in *Early Medieval Kingship*,
edd. P. H. Sawyer and I. N. Wood (Leeds 1977) 50–71.

throne; and according to the *Beowulf*-poet and the other extant versions of the story, his accession occurs by acclamation.

The gap between reality and myth suggests a perspective from which we can understand the most significant features of the story of Scyld Scefing. The essential point of the myth is a simple one: *true* kingship is given, not won. If this assumption is granted, the potential conflict which might occur whenever the current king dies or is seriously weakened is avoided. It is also significant that Scyld is (on a *de facto* basis) fatherless and motherless, and therefore exists outside of the kinship structure of the people over whom he will rule. This is a very anomalous situation in certain ways. In a traditional society a foundling, who exists apart from the bonds of kinship, is at the nadir of the social structure; in this instance, Scyld Scefing ascends from this humble beginning to the most exalted position within the society which adopted him. But the myth does not concern simply the story of a poor boy making his way in the world, for Scyld Scefing was not merely found — he was sent. There are various stories about the way in which he was found,[7] but all of them reflect the assumption that Scyld Scefing was not just an orphan whom someone wished to dispose of. There is thus a curious ambiguity about Scyld Scefing's ascent to the throne: on the one hand, he emerged from nowhere; and yet, on the other, his emergence was predestined and was duly recognized by those who received him. Scyld Scefing's rise thus depends upon the fact both that he was divinely sent, and that he was willingly and joyously received.

Another immediate significance of the 'fatherlessness' of Scyld Scefing is that the first king, Scyld, emerges from the people as a whole without any specific commitment to one family, clan, or region. One is reminded of the etymology of the Old English word *cyning*, which means literally 'the son of the *cyn*, the race, or people.' As a matter of historical fact, the conception that the leader of the people should be set apart from any particular region or family is one which might have a certain pragmatic appeal. Old Testament scholars, for example, have speculated that part of the logic of the Davidic kingship was that David came from a small tribe situated between other, more

---

[7] Since the two Latin summaries of the story are quite brief, I will quote them in full. Æthelweard writes: 'Ipse Scef cum uno dromone aduectus est in insula oceani que dicitur Scani, armis circundatus, eratque valde recens puer, et ab incolis illius terrae ignotus. Attamen ab eis suscipitur, et ut familiarem diligenti animo eum custodierunt, et post in regem eligunt; de cuius prosapia ordinem trahunt Adulf rex.' *The Chronicle of Æthelweard*, ed. A. Campbell (London 1962) 33. According to William of Malmesbury, '[Sceaf], ut ferunt, in quandam insulam Germaniae Scandzam, de qua Jordanes historiographus Gothorum, loquitur, appulsus navi sine remige, puerulus, posito ad caput frumenti manipulo, dormiens, ideoque Sceaf nuncupatus, ab hominibus regionis illius pro miraculo exceptus et sedulo nutritus: adulta aetate regnavit in oppido quod tunc Slaswic, nunc vero Haithebi appellatur.' *De gestis regum Anglorum* 2.116, ed. William Stubbs, Rolls Series 90 (London 1887) I 121.

powerful tr bes of the Israelite confederation, and hence was generally acceptable to all parties. And in this myth, Scyld Scefing is completely set apart from
any personal or regional loyalties — a point which is particularly relevant if
we assume that the Danes were subjected to civil strife in the period preceding
his accession.

Scyld, however, is not necessarily the son of Sceaf in the same sense that
Beow (to use the correct form of the name) is the son of Scyld. If the boy who
was found on a vessel by the seashore with a sheaf of wheat by his head was
called Scefing, it does not necessarily follow that a man named Scef was his
father. To raise an immediate, if somewhat naïve, question: how could the
people who found Scyld know the name of the father of this fatherless boy?
Again, the family that Scyld Scefing founded were called Scyldings rather
than Scefings — a detail which implies that Scyld, the penultimate name on
the genealogical list, is defined as the true founder of the family. In any case,
in the context of royal succession, fatherhood is as much a public and cere-
monial function as a biological one. But the fact that Scyld, not Scef, is the
originator of the royal line focuses attention upon another feature of the
Beowulf-poet's version of the myth — that Beow is the true heir, whose succession to the throne is absolutely unquestioned. Scyld has only one son,
so there can be no question of any conflict between brothers for succession to
the throne. Again, his father lives sufficiently long to ensure that his son can
succeed in due order, but not so long that the young man or his followers are
tempted to revolt or seize power prematurely. Lines 20–25 are damaged and
difficult in any case, but the general drift of the *Beowulf*-poet's meaning is
quite clear. Beow succeeded to Scyld with the consent, approbation, and
affection of the royal court, and this was a profoundly good thing:

> Swa sceal geong guma   gode gewyrcean,
> fromum feohgiftum   on fæder bearme,
> þaet hine on ylde   eft gewunigen
> wilgesiþas,   þonne wig cume,
> leode gelæsten;   lofdædum sceal
> in mægþa gehwære   man geþeon.   (20–25)

Another important aspect of this myth is its onomastics. Scyld is borne on
the waters; in one version he is surrounded by weapons; in another a sheaf is
set over his head; in yet a third legend the human child is no longer mentioned,
and a sheaf is set upon a round shield which then floats over a specific course
in order to establish particular boundary lines.[8] But in all of these various
stories, an important meaning of the myth is suggested by the names themselves. In the Anglo-Saxon coronation rituals, the king was acclaimed with the

---

[8] For a convenient summary and discussion of the analogue in which a sheaf, floated upon
a shield, vindicates the property rights of the monks of Abingdon, see Chambers 83–84.

formula *pax et habundantia salutatis*,[9] and the first king from whom these kings traced their descent was 'shield, the son of sheaf,' that is, he who brought the protection of the shield (*pax*) and the prosperity of the sheaf (*abundantia*).

Germanic kings were traditionally thought to enhance the prosperity of their kingdoms in that they brought good seasons and fertile crops.[10] The *Beowulf*-poet is not specific about the sufferings which the people endured during the lordless time, but he characterizes it as a time of *fyrenþearf*, a *hapax legomenon* which nonetheless can be readily rendered in terms of its elements as 'terrible need' and thus the opposite of *abundantia*. As Germanic kings were expected to lead their people to success in war, so Scyld Scefing did. The attempt of an earlier generation of *Beowulf* scholars to separate Scyld from Scef and to speculate about the diverse origins and significance of these figures seems to me misguided. Even if we concede that Scyld was originally a Scandinavian eponymous hero, whereas Scef is to be associated with West Germanic fertility ritual,[11] the *Beowulf*-poet and the various chroniclers and genealogists who preserved this myth associated these figures together in a story about the origins of kingship. The significance of these names provides an immediate explanation for their association.

The story of Scyld Scefing in its original form was thus an archaic Germanic etiological myth which concerns the problem of the origin of kingship within this particular grouping of peoples. To the potentially subversive questions — where do kings come from? how is kingship passed from one generation to another? — the myth proposes a simple and striking, if radically conservative, answer. The first king was sent among the people by an unnamed and presumably divine power; he was welcomed and made king, and from him his son succeeded in due course. An implicit conclusion from the myth is that a true king — among these peoples at least — derives his authority from his descent from this line. The myth can thus be seen as an attempt to suppress the disturbing social truth that any magnate who possessed good luck and the prerequisite military skills could conceivably aspire to make himself king. Myths are often concerned with the legitimization of the social order (one thinks of *Rígsþula*), and this myth serves to set the *stirps regia* apart from the other great families who might aspire to kingship.

What, then, does this myth imply for the real or imagined origin of Scyld? Obviously he is sent — someone put the baby with the signs of his special

---

[9] *Three Early English Rituals*, ed. V. Wickham Legg, Henry Bradshaw Society 19 (London 1900) 56.

[10] See R. W. McTurk, 'Sacred Kingship in Ancient Scandinavia: A Review of Some Recent Writing,' *Saga Book* 19 (1974–77) 139–69. As McTurk observes, part of the difficulty of this question hinges on the fact that 'sacred' is a rather amorphous term.

[11] Chambers 79 *et passim*.

status in the vessel which bore him to his new homeland and future realm. But who might this be presumed to be? Our texts are all quite silent on this point. One immediate candidate would be Woden, whose cult was closely associated with kingship in both the North and West Germanic world[12] and who figures, together with Scyld, as the ancestor of the various Anglo-Saxon royal lines. One could even cite the prose preface to *Grímnismál*[13] as a story which is at least broadly similar to the myth of Scyld Scefing in that it concerns the young son of a king who is favored by Odinn and sent back over the sea to his people to assume the kingship which has lain dormant. But despite these similarities, no feature in the myth of Scyld Scefing remotely corresponds to the episode of fratricide with which the Old Norse–Icelandic myth is centrally concerned. One could, perhaps, see the story of Geirroðr's ascent to the throne, with its brutally nonchalant endorsement of fratricide, as a cynical Icelandic response to myths such as the story of Scyld Scefing. According to the story of Scyld, the god (or divinely inspired human) sends the chosen king over the sea to his people. According to the prose preface to *Grímnismál*, the young king is indeed fostered, chosen, and sent over the sea by Odinn, but he is taught by the god to help himself to the kingship by a judicious act of fratricide.

But if it is possible that a more detailed and archaic form of the myth of Scyld Scefing might have included reference to Woden as the figure who sent Scyld Scefing to his people, there are other possibilities as well. We know very little about the pagan myths of the various West Germanic peoples, and one of the lesser-known figures of the Germanic pantheon might have served as the giver of kingship in this myth. In *Rígsþula*, for example, which also treats of the origins of the social order, Rígr, who is otherwise unknown, is the divine figure who orders society.

Interpreting myths which are well documented and whose social context is well understood is still often a controversial matter; in this instance, the texts with which I am concerned differ from each other and are preserved in fragmentary and abbreviated form. The *Beowulf*-poet, for example, presumes that his audience has heard the story of Scyld Scefing and hence only alludes to the story rather than retelling it. And, of course, our knowledge of Anglo-Saxon social and political life is very limited in some respects. But I would argue that the social significance of this myth is that it provides a charter, to use Malinowski's term, for kingship as the inheritance of the *stirps regia* of the Scyldings.

---

[12] See G. Turville-Petre, *Myth and Religion of the North* (London 1964) 64–74.

[13] For a convenient edition of *Grímnismál*, see *Edda*, ed. Hans Kuhn, 4th ed. (Heidelberg 1962) I 56–68.

II

If this was the general purport of the Scyld Scefing story as the *Beowulf*-poet knew it, the next question is what the poet made of it and how he adapted it in the context of *Beowulf* as a whole. The poet seems to have taken the myth quite seriously, to judge from the prominence he accords it; yet the Scyld Scefing story is one of the few 'pagan' moments in the poem in which it is apparent that these ancient Germanic peoples were not Christian. The *Beowulf*-poet is very much aware of the paganism of his ancestors, but for the most part he suppresses even the fact that the ancient Germanic peoples worshiped pagan gods.[14] This story of the mysterious origin of the Scyldings is thus quite unlike the rest of the poem. We can only speculate why the *Beowulf*-poet was so tolerant in this instance, but I suspect that two reasons were prominent. The first is that the divine origin of kingship was one pagan myth which Anglo-Saxon kings were reluctant to suppress — for obvious reasons. Without quite claiming to be god-born, the kings and their genealogists continued to circulate the old stories linking their descent to the ancient gods of the north. Even such an apparently implacable enemy of the Germanic heritage of Anglo-Saxon England as Alcuin was still distressed by the decline of true — i.e. Woden-descended — kingship in his age.[15] So a story which emphasized the special character of the royal line may well have seemed congenial to the *Beowulf*-poet, who was much concerned about the legitimacy of royal succession.

A second rationale for the poet's interest in this story is more speculative, but given the poet's attempt to synthesize pagan antiquity and the Christian world-view of his own times, the parallel between the arrival of Scyld and the discovery of Moses in the bulrushes might have interested him. In both instances, the divinely chosen leader who frees his people from a time of *fyrenþearf* arrives, apparently abandoned to the waters. And both depart as mysteriously as they arrived: no man knows where either's body rests.[16]

---

[14] The exception of course is lines 175–88; whether these lines are an interpolation or not is an open question. See Dorothy Whitelock, *The Audience of* BEOWULF (Oxford 1951) 79–80.

[15] For Alcuin's comments on the decline of ancient royal lineage in his time, see his remark in his letter to the people and nobles of Canterbury (Ep. 129), 'Et vix modo quod sine lacrimis non dicam, ex antiqua regum prosapia invenitur, et tanto incertioris sunt originis, quanto minoris sunt fortitudinis.' MGH Epp. 4: *Epp. Kar. Aevi*, ed. E. Dümmler (Berlin 1895) II 192.

[16] Chambers mentions this possibility (80). See J. E. Cross and Thomas D. Hill, edd., *The Prose* SOLOMON AND SATURN *and* ADRIAN AND RITHEUS (Toronto 1982) 110–11, for commentary on the burial of Moses.

But whatever interested the *Beowulf*-poet about this narrative, he made it very much part of his own poetic world. Although he touches upon Scyld's mysterious arrival, the emphasis falls upon his heroic success. And if this is one of the most pagan episodes in the poem, the *Beowulf*-poet characteristically emphasizes that it is God, the God of the Christians, who rules over human history. The *Beowulf*-poet says little about the origin of Scyld Scefing (although he does suggest that it was more than one person who sent him forth in the beginning), but he does insist that it was God, 'the Lord of Life, the ruler of glory' (16–17), who took pity upon the sufferings of the Danes and brought it about that a son, Beow, was born to Scyld in due succession. If the God of the Christians orders such mundane matters as the succession of Beow to Scyld's kingship, His providential ordering surely did not begin there; He must also have guided Scyld's vessel in the beginning to the land where Scyld would be king. But the *Beowulf*-poet does not makes this claim explicit: he offers an implicitly Christian revision of the old story about the coming of the first king, but this Christian revision does not undermine the old legends.

Adrian Bonjour and other scholars have already noted how this episode accords with the aesthetic structure of the poem as a whole.[17] The story opens with a digression which leads to a magnificent burial scene; it closes with a similarly elaborate burial. The opening concerns the Danes' *fyrenþearf* in those terrible years when they had no true king; the conclusion anticipates a similar period of war and suffering for the Geats. But in addition to these formal correspondences, the prologue to the poem also articulates one of the main ideological concerns of the poem, the importance of true kingship and orderly succession. The first true king, Scyld, was divinely ordained to rule the Danes; the poet implies that this miracle was granted by the God of the Christians, although he does not radically alter the old story. But he insists that the steady succession of son to father in the true royal line was the result of the kindly dispensation of God, who grants *woruldar*, glory in the world, as well as spiritual gifts. The genealogy of Scyld culminates in the portrait of Hroðgar, a magnificent, wise, and benevolent king. But the reign of Hroðgar is disturbed by the incursion of Grendel and by troubles which the poet only hints at. The poet clearly implies that the orderly succession of son to father, younger brother to older, which has hitherto characterized the Scylding line, will be violated by Hroðulf, who will challenge either Hroðgar's sons or the authority of Hroðgar himself for the throne.

The gravity of Hroðulf's offense, in the poet's view at least, is underscored by the fact that Beowulf, whose relationship to the royal line of the Geats is exactly that of Hroðulf to the Scyldings, refuses the throne when he is urgently

---

[17] Adrian Bonjour, *The Digressions in* BEOWULF (1950; rpt. Oxford 1970) 1–11.

pressed to accept it by no less a personage than Hygd, the mother of Heardred, the son of the previous and recently deceased King Hygelac:

> þær him Hygd gebead   hord ond rice,
> beagas ond bregostol,   bearne ne truwode
> þaet he wid ælfylcum   eþelstolas
> healdan cuðe,   ða wæs Hygelac dead.
> No ðy ær feasceafte   findan meahton
> æt ðam ædelinge   ænige ðinga,
> þæt he Heardrede   hlaford wære.
> oððe þone cynedom   ciosan wolde;
> hwæðre he him on folce   freondlarum heold,
> estum mid are,   oððæt he yldra wearð,
> Weder-Geatum weold.   (2369–79)

This episode is only marginally relevant to the narrative of *Beowulf* as a whole, since Heardred, the young king whom Beowulf served as regent, was killed shortly after assuming the throne in the first episode of the Swedish wars. The fact that the *Beowulf*-poet is so careful to explain Beowulf's role in this momentary interregnum suggests that he thought it important to emphasize Beowulf's respect for the direct order of succession from father to son and to contrast Beowulf's scrupulous regard for the ordering of succession with Hroðulf's unscrupulous and violent ambition. In real Anglo-Saxon political life this particular case seems to have been regarded somewhat differently. King Alfred had no hesitation about inheriting his brother's throne and then excluding his nephew from the royal succession. But the *Beowulf*-poet is concerned with an ideal hero, not a man who has to contend with the awkward ambiguities of real politics, and in this respect, as in so much else, Beowulf's behavior is beyond reproach.

If D. A. Binchy is right in arguing that some of the Anglo-Saxon royal establishments practiced a system of succession comparable to that in practice in early Ireland, where the son of the ruling king was not necessarily the successor to his father's throne,[18] the *Beowulf*-poet emerges as an unhesitating and zealous exponent of the new Christian patrilineal rules of royal succession. But the Christianity of the *Beowulf*-poet is hardly in question. One would expect him to defend a specifically Christian mode of defining true kingship.

Part of the tragedy of Beowulf's final moments is that his death involves not only the death of a hero, but also the extinction of a great royal line. The Geats are left kingless, and will recapitulate the terrible time of kinglessness which the Danes experienced before the coming of Scyld. It is perhaps necessary to point out that the *Beowulf*-poet's concern with true kingship and

---

[18] D. A. Binchy, *Celtic and Anglo-Saxon Kingship: The O'Donnell Lectures for 1967–68* (London 1970).

orderly succession does not simply reflect antiquarian piety and conservatism. In the early medieval world, a strong and prestigious monarch strengthened the state enormously; the absence of such a monarch could lead to civil war or foreign invasion, precisely the fate which the poet envisions for the Geats.

In concluding this discussion, I would like to raise again a suggestion which has been made before — although not of course in precisely this context. One of the problems in *Beowulf* scholarship is that the poem reflects a richly detailed and, as far as we can judge, surprisingly accurate historical understanding of the ethnography and political conflicts of sixth-century Scandinavia. And yet, with the exception of the allusion to Offa in lines 1949ff., very little of the historical detail in the poem seems relevant to Anglo-Saxon England. One possible explanation of this anomaly is that the *Beowulf*-poet was looking to the distant past to find precedent and justification for a contemporary situation. Even if we accept the dating of *Beowulf* to the age of Bede, the historical distance between the poet's present and the time he writes of was substantial — particularly since the lore on which the poet drew would have had to have been preserved orally for over a century at the least. But if we assume that there existed some Anglo-Saxon social group that believed it had ties with the Geats, then much of the political and historical content of *Beowulf* comes into focus. The social group in question need not be large — though it would need to be wealthy enough to sponsor and help preserve a poem as long as *Beowulf*. Let us imagine for the moment that we are dealing with as small a group as a magnate's immediate family. Such a group would wish to emphasize its ancestral greatness and would at the same time have to explain its presence in England. It is the landless and the poor who normally have incentives to emigrate, but in an aristocratic age, one would hardly wish to acknowledge that one's family was established as recently as the invasion. The *Beowulf*-poet's account of the Geats would, however, provide an appropriate charter for the family of the magnate in question. In the ancient Scandinavian world, the story went, the Geats were a great people and Geatish aristocrats were accepted as welcome guests in the great royal courts of the north. But because their kings were excessively brave and venturesome, the Geats incurred the enmity of their neighbors to both the south and the north.

It is sometimes held that the messenger's speech presages the complete destruction of the Geatish people, but the difficulty with this view is two-fold. Firstly, the messenger's speech does not say as much — he simply speaks of future wars and troubles. Secondly, if the Geats were simply extirpated, who would bother to preserve the memory of their kings? A simple solution, however, which would accord both with the desolate tone of the messenger's speech and with the preservation of so much Geatish history in England, is that the Geats, or some remnant of the Geats, pressed on both sides, found their position insupportable and left their continental homeland to win a new home in England. This history — whether true or fictional — would provide an appropriately aristocratic heritage for the social group in question and an honorable explanation for their emigration from the lands which they once ruled. The story would thus correspond to the long genealogies which extend behind such figures as Cerdic and which imply, as this story states, that this particular family was an exalted one long before it came to England.

The exact relationship of Wiglaf to Beowulf is a notoriously difficult question, but the frequent assumption that Wiglaf will succeed Beowulf as king of the Geats seems to be belied by the fact that he is not apparently directly related to the Geatish royal line and by the fact that his father fought against the Geats in the Swedish wars. The digression on Wiglaf's sword could thus be explained as an indication that Wiglaf, the heroic combatant against the dragon, is not eligible for the role which one might assume he would play as the next king of the Geats. If the Danes could not resolve the terrible crisis of their kingless period by electing some appropriate war leader, it would seem likely that the Geats would face similar difficulties in their crisis of succession.

Obviously this reconstruction of a specific political context for Beowulf is speculative; it is equally obvious that *Beowulf* is a rich and complex poem whose political significance — if this argument seems cogent — is only one aspect of the whole. The fact that Shakespeare's history plays are Tudor propaganda is probably the least interesting aspect of them for most modern readers, and yet this fact is of some importance for our historical understanding of them. Similarly, the political and social implications of *Beowulf* are only dimly discernible now, but we should nonetheless be aware of them.

There has been a good deal of discussion of the historical context of *Beowulf* and similar discussion about history *in Beowulf*. What I am arguing here is that it should be possible to relate these two discussions — to view history within *Beowulf* as a reflection of the political and social concerns of the poet. It is the consensus of scholars of quite different viewpoints that the *Beowulf*-poet was a Christian who was deeply serious about his faith. But it is also true that the poem reflects the poet's political interests as well, and the fact that he was a royalist of a specific sort — one concerned with preserving and honoring the ancient roots of Scylding kingship — is profoundly important for our understanding of the poem.

Cornell University

'INTERLACE' AS A MEDIEVAL NARRATIVE TECHNIQUE WITH SPECIAL REFERENCE TO 'BEOWULF'

By MORTON W. BLOOMFIELD*

Although Ferdinand Lot was probably the first modern scholar to use the term 'interlace' ('entrelacement') as applied to narrative technique,[1] the present emphasis on the notion in English studies, especially those dealing with medieval works and subjects, is largely due to John Leyerle[2] and Eugene Vinaver.[3] The term is, however, so broadly interpreted that a special effort is needed to keep notions separate which need to be separate, and to bring notions together which need to be together, in short to clarify it. This article, honoring Robert Kaske, who himself has been a great clarifier, especially in the field of the medieval exegetical tradition, attempts to bring some basic distinctions to light in the hope that they may make the use of 'interlacement' more accurate than has hitherto been the case.

The primary task in attempting to analyze the notion is to understand one of the major characteristics of narrative. The basic element of narration is sequentiality. Some literary theorists prefer to consider the notion of time rather than sequentiality as basic, but I think the former is more appropriate. It is time, of course, that sequentiality implies. Events described in words which follow each other do so primarily in time, but time is such an elusive

---

* I have not discussed in this paper the use of the term 'aural interlace' to indicate the repetition of sounds throughout a poem or part of a poem. I see even less justification for the term 'interlace' in this connection than in the use of the metaphor for lines of narrative action. There is no 'interlacing' in the repetition of sounds. I certainly do not object to the study of repetitive sounds, but I do think that the use of the term 'interlace' to describe this procedure is completely meaningless and barren as a descriptive or metaphoric term. On the subject, see Richard A. Lewis, 'Old English Poetry: Alliteration and Structural Interlace,' *Language and Style* 5 (1973) 196–205 and 'Plurilinear Alliteration in Old English Poetry,' *Texas Studies in Literature and Language* 16 (1975) 589–602, and James C. Addison Jr., 'Aural Interlace in "The Battle of Brunanburh,"' *Language and Style* 15 (1982) 267–76.

[1] See his *Étude sur le* Lancelot *en prose* (Paris 1918) 17–28. I am indebted to Carol J. Clover's *The Medieval Saga* (Ithaca and London 1982) 91–92 for this observation as I am for various other observations and ideas throughout. Her book is the best study of medieval (and classical) interlace in English, not to speak of her perceptive treatment of the Icelandic saga.

[2] See 'The Interlace Structure of *Beowulf*,' *University of Toronto Quarterly* 37 (1967) 1–17.

[3] 'The Prose *Tristan*,' *Arthurian Literature in the Middle Ages*, ed. R. S. Loomis (Oxford 1959) 344–46; *The Rise of Romance* (New York 1971) 74, 81, 85, 92–93, etc.; *The Works of Sir Thomas Malory*, 2nd ed. (Oxford 1967) lxx; and *A la Recherche d'une poétique médiévale* (Paris 1970) 129–49.

concept that it cannot, when dealing with story, be inscribed in words or written marks (as in music), whereas sequence can be. A reader or listener may be *told* about time, but time cannot be *described* to her in its existential import; whereas sequentiality can be so described if it is, as in most narrative, divided into episodes or events. Sequentiality is the outstanding and most general characteristic of time in words.

Dreams or attempted reproductions of characters' thoughts told directly or by a narrator are, moreover, sequential even if they cannot be simply broken down into events or episodes. It is easier to think of them as sequential rather than time-bound. They seem to occur out of time.

Narrative is, of course, not merely sequentiality because it is frequently interrupted by pure (that is static) descriptions or by the narrator (as there usually is in story), who gives us information or makes comments on the action. Some narratives do not even claim one or several lines of narrative but consist of various lines juxtaposed or intermingled, sometimes extensively. Normally, however, we can expect one or more lines of action to be distinguishable in narration.

Unlike art in its various manifestations which are more spatial than temporal, it is impossible to grasp two, let alone more, different sequential verbal lines at the same time. In verbal art, neither the creator nor the audience can follow two different lines at the same time. In plastic art, however, though the creator must paint, draw, or shape one thing or part of one thing at a time, the audience can take in two or more objects, persons, or scenes at the same time.[4] In fact, this distinction is a basic distinction between the fine arts and the verbal arts. In painting we can see and understand (even if not fully) two or more events, happenings, or objects (or people) present at the same time; whereas in reading we cannot read of two events at the same time in order to get (when appropriate) the illusion of simultaneity.

Motion pictures can make use of montage to put two (or more) lines of action or characterizations together, enabling us to grasp the whole, even if not in every detail or particular. With the content of books, however, montage will not work at all. We must look first at one side of the page (divided presumably by a line) and then at the other. It would be hard to get directly the content

---

[4] There are, of course, Oriental scroll paintings and Western cartoons using sequential boxes which can give us the illusion of time passing, but if we wish we can look at, if not the whole scroll or a sequence of cartoons at one time, at least much of it or certainly two or three episodes.

The Neoplatonists and particularly Plotinus considered the fine arts to be superior to the verbal arts just because of this characteristic. The fine arts are normally out of time, leaving the world of becoming for the world of being. Of course a full appreciation of two episodes in the fine arts normally requires two careful studies of one after the other, but one is clearly aware of both in some detail at the same time.

of simultaneous happenings (which is a major reason why montage is used in films) from any printed or written page.

The nature of verbal art is such that two lines of sequential happenings (not to speak of more) cannot be followed by a reader at one time. Unlike art, the very nature of narration demands one line of action at a time. This fact of verbal art makes interlace based on simultaneous events impossible. It does not, of course, make complexity impossible (and much great verbal art is complex), but it makes true interlace as it is used in art borders or in weaving[5] impossible. This latter point in turn makes the value of the notion dubious in discussing some of the characteristics of literature.

Because of this limitation in the verbal arts, the difficulty of suggesting simultaneity is one of the many literary compositional problems. How can two or more simultaneous events or scenes be indicated in words which must follow only one line of narration at any one time?

Of course, narrative can and usually does have more than one story line, especially if any complexity of development or structure is aimed at. Complexity is only loosely related to 'interlace.' Even then it does not normally correspond to the interweaving which is characteristic of real 'interlace.' In verbal art, one suggests or indicates but does not present simultaneous events.

A major but not only cause of several story lines is the attempt to indicate what is very hard to present in verbal art: simultaneous simultaneity. A major method of indicating simultaneous actions is sequential story lines, either introduced or assumed as such. Other purposes for various story lines could be the desire to introduce us to a variety of themes, or to present significant contrasts and similarities, or to present a rich mosaic of opinions and points of view. With these other purposes we shall not be concerned in this paper.

The classic article on simultaneity in literature was published by Th. Zielinski in 1901.[6] Being, as most scholars of his period, heavily under the influence of the notion of evolutionary progress, he tries to divide the various methods of indicating simultaneity into three progressively complex varieties.

Carol Clover[7] has summarized his categories as follows:

1. *Retrospective report* in which action A is described by the narrator and action B by a character in the narrative. The most famous example of this

---

[5] Etymology sometimes bears out this notion. Verbal art is occasionally spoken of in various languages as if it has been woven, as in terms like 'text.' There is some evidence that to early man (because the heart, not the brain, was thought to be the seat of ideas), the larynx or Adam's apple 'weaves' together words as they pass from thought to auditory form. See Heinrich Wagner, 'Studies in the Origins of Early Celtic Civilization II,' *Zeitschrift für Celtische Philologie* 31 (1970) 46–57 for some interesting etymologies bearing on this matter.

[6] 'Die Behandlung gleichzeitiger Ereignisse im antiken Epos,' *Philologus*, Supplementband 8 (1901) 405–49.

[7] 110–11.

method is that of Virgil in Book 2 of the *Aeneid*. There Aeneas tells Dido the story of the fall of Troy. The story of the fall of Troy, however, is not simultaneous with the night of its telling at the court of Dido. The major difficulty with this method is that a character cannot report a simultaneous happening to another (or a group of characters) without being present later to do so. If the two simultaneous actions are recited by two different characters later, furthermore, the idea of simultaneity is lost because both actions are in the past as compared with the time of recitation.

2. *Discontinuous retrieval* indicates *without any overlap as to time* two (or more) separate lines of action, one after the other. (An introductory phrase like 'meanwhile' can be introduced, but the reader or listener must mentally put the two lines of action together.)

3. *Continuous retrieval* must of course have separate lines of action, but there is some overlap in time. Action B overlaps in happening time with A or vice versa, partially or completely. Clover suggests that 'this type alone can lay a fair claim to simultaneity' (111). This type is still, however, restricted to doubling its tracks in action time and is no more simultaneously presented than the other two. (3) is perhaps more sophisticated than (1) or (2), but none can overcome the iron rule of narrative that two lines of action cannot be *presented to the reader or listener at the same time*. Verbal art cannot indicate simultaneity simultaneously. There are of course ways of indicating simultaneity in literature, but they cannot be presented in such a way that they can be simultaneously experienced. Art may be an imitation of life, but verbal art can only indicate or imply in its mode of presentation simultaneous actions or thoughts.

This limitation is not, however, as Zielinski proposed in his above-mentioned article, due to 'primitive thought,' but to the limitation inherent in literary art. Zielinski writes that Homeric narrative 'never retraces its steps to describe a second main thread of the narrative, because the account of his actions which take place at the same time is not possible for a primitive period, before the awakened reason permits a more abstract and reflective conception of events.'[8] Bassett and others, furthermore, have shown that Zielinski missed several examples of presenting parallel actions in both the *Iliad* and *Odyssey* (where Zielinski did find only two 'embryonic traces' of such actions).[9] Early literature besides the Homeric poems provides other examples in narrative — in the Sumerian *Gilgamesh* and the narrative parts of the Bible. We still cannot get around the basic fact that by its very nature, verbal art cannot display simultaneity directly, but only at different times.

---

[8] Translated by Samuel Eliot Bassett in *The Poetry of Homer*, Sather Classical Lectures 15 (Berkeley 1938) 34. The original is in Zielinski 418.

[9] Basset 35ff. He also refers to Bougot, *Étude sur l'*ILIADE *d'Homère* (Paris 1888) 531 for another example. Bassett categorically states, 'Homer knows how to describe two actions as parallel.'

Before turning to *Beowulf*, I shall discuss in a little more depth the use of retrospective narrative to indicate an event simultaneous with one that has happened, and present some further reasons why 'interlace' is not a good metaphor either for literary simultaneity or for the movement back and forth between several episodes which are not simultaneous.

From classical times on, it has been recognized that narrative, particularly epic narrative, can follow the line of action from the beginning to the end in a straightforward manner, that is, in the natural order of happenings and events ('ab ovo'); or the narrative can begin in the middle of the action ('in medias res') told by the narrator or rarely by a character, and then later in the story line introduce a second line (or even more) by one of the characters or more rarely by the narrator, who tells what has happened in the part of the action before the narrative has begun.

These two methods of approach, the *ordo naturalis* and the *ordo artificialis*, as is true of all narrative, are unable to present simultaneous actions simultaneously in words, but do give us the necessary other action so that we may participate in the story in a satisfactory manner. In the one case, we follow the natural movement of time; in the other, we are kept in suspense or at least ignorance until the earlier necessary part or parts of the story are told within the story line. Usually the two events (or groups of events) are not simultaneous in any case.

Carol Clover[10] has pointed to medieval discussions of these two orders and indicated, by quotations and references to those comments about the adequacy of the natural order for oratory and sermon and of the artificial order for artistic works (probably read privately), how both were distinguished by medieval literary rhetoricians. As has been noted, the telling of past events is usually *not* simultaneous with the tale that is being told at the time of its interjection into the later time. In spite of this, Carol Clover, to whose excellent work I am much indebted, discusses these two *ordines* in a chapter called 'Simultaneity.' Professor Clover does point out, however, that 'if o*rdo artificialis* is not *per se* an adumbration of simultaneous narration, it certainly sets the scene.'[11]

What this demonstrates is the confusion between happenings at the same time and the order of the main story line, a confusion which is widespread in the discussion of 'interlace' and simultaneity. Another story may be brought into the main story line, but it either must be told within the main story line by a character or the narrator, or it may be presented alongside the main story line with some kind of explanatory remark (e.g., 'meanwhile' or 'while all this was happening, something else was happening,' etc.), or even boldly without

10 137–40.
11 140.

explanation. More frequently, however, the second story line refers to what has happened earlier, and is not simultaneous with the present scene. The term *ordo artificialis* normally refers to the latter. Complexity (more than one story line), however, is always possible, but complexity is not, at least in classical and medieval literature, *per se* an indication of simultaneity. *No narrative can present more than one story line at a time, but may present others at other places in the story in the same or another story line.*

Part of the confusion in this matter of narrative lines is due to the ambiguity of the Aristotelian phrase that plot must have 'a beginning and middle and end' (*Poetics* 1450B). It may mean 'the beginning and middle and end' of the central line of action (that is, if it has a main story line) or it may mean the beginning, middle, and end of the story as presented (even a complex tale with multiple story lines has a beginning, middle, and end). I have always interpreted Aristotle's comment to apply to the story as told and presented, and not exclusively to the main line of action.[12] What Aristotle meant, I believe, is that a story should be properly proportioned to its sequential role and must have a beginning which is a beginning, a middle which is a middle, and an end which is an end. It must have, in other words, a shape or structure. Occasionally, it must be admitted, a story has only one line of action and in that case the terms apply to that line.

'Interlace' is a phrase we have already briefly discussed. Its basic meaning is to indicate physical interweaving as in cloth and in art, especially borders where various strands cross over each other. Metaphorically it has been used since the time of Ferdinand Lot (and possibly earlier) for several narrative threads or lines when used in medieval literature. The use of several narrative strands is a commonplace in literature of all periods and all countries, but as far as I know, the term 'interlace' seems to be applied only to medieval and occasionally classical literature. It is clear that a strand of narrative action cannot cross over another as threads of cloth or visual lines can do. Furthermore, it does not seem to apply to simultaneous actions at all. They may overlap but they do not interweave.

Eugène Vinaver writes, 'for several themes to be pursued simultaneously, they have to alternate like threads in a woven fabric, one theme interrupting another and again another, and yet all remaining constantly present in the author's and the reader's mind.'[13] Leaving the psychological guesswork aside,

---

[12] The notion of beginning, middle, and end as applied to medieval romance is dealt with at some length by William W. Ryding, *Studies in Medieval Narrative* (The Hague and Paris 1971) 38–61. Ryding does not define how he is interpreting the phrase, and seems to think that the remark does not apply to cycle stories (53) where many lines of action are being presented. There is, however, always (as far as I am aware) an enveloping story in cycle romances to which the Aristotelian remark does apply.

[13] *The Rise of Romance* 76.

this is not what narrative strands do. They follow each other sequentially. They do interrupt each other by shifting completely to a new or different story line, sometimes overlapping in time of action and sometimes not. When not being narrated, they disappear completely until they reappear further on, if they are still to continue as a line of action. The thread or line in art, if it disappears, disappears only slightly to let another line pass over it. It is still clearly 'there.' And often it does not disappear at all.

A much better word for the process is the term Clover uses, 'stranding' or 'stranded composition,' because it does not imply the regular interweaving of narrative lines.[14] Multi-strand narratives are very common at all periods of literary history, but the last half of the Middle Ages is particularly prolific in such a type of composition. One can even include the *Decameron* and the *Canterbury Tales* in such a category. There are no doubt various modes of stranding. In the latter two cases, the strands have a regular mode of operation which most multi-stranded narratives do not possess.

'Interlace' is often used in such a loose manner that it loses its specificity and the term is not very helpful. A new name for an old process or technique is not a new notion at all. Foreshadowing, a process in literary art long recognized by scholars, has been brought into the definition of 'interlace' by some scholars.[15] Connections and parallels have since the beginning of literary art been used by authors or singers or readers of tales to enable their narrative to cohere more closely. The process has often been called 'foreshadowing.' This procedure has little or nothing to do with the purpose of stranding. It most frequently appears in the same line of action. Narration contains similarities which enable the reader to make discoveries of likenesses and realize some kind of order and unity in the work he is reading or listening to. Nor is it confined to narrative but is found in other genres. Foreshadowing is not interlace, but the manipulation of similarities increasing the pleasure and memorability of literature both oral and written.

Foreshadowing as a feature of narrative (not to speak of drama and lyric) has been recognized by literary critics and analysts for a long time. Using a different name for the same notion, as has been done,[16] does not make a new notion.

Almost twenty years ago, Rosemond Tuve warned her readers that 'one must distinguish entrelacement from the mere practice, ubiquitous in narrative,

---

[14] See 61–108. The English term 'strand' for story line may have been first used by Bertha Philpotts in 1931, if I may judge from Clover's annotation.

[15] See, e.g., John Leyerle (*n*2) esp. 10–13.

[16] For an example of a different name, see Anne Heinrichs, ' "Intertexture" and Its Functions in Early Written Sagas,' *Scandinavian Studies* 48 (1976) 127–28, where 'intertexture' is used for 'foreshadowing.'

of taking one character through a series of actions, then deserting him tem-
porarily . . . while another character is given primary attention, then returning
to the first and so on. '[17] Tuve, however, does use the term 'entrelacement' and
distinguishes it from simply shifting the story line by the fact that 'when we
get back to our first character he is not where we left him as we finished his
episode but in the place or psychological state . . . of meaningfulness to which
he has been pulled by the events occurring in the following episodes written
about someone else.'[18]

This point is an extremely subtle interpretation of foreshadowing. When
we return to character A, Tuve argues, what we have found out about character
B influences, in many cases, our view of character A. This perceptive observation comes as close as possible to the effect of simultaneity in verbal art. We
should, however, hesitate to use the term 'interlace' to explain this psychological effect, but it is close enough to the literal meaning of the word for us to
realize how unlike interlacement most if not all other metaphoric uses of the
term are. It is, however, still a metaphor, and what happens when one strand
is 'off stage' so to speak is not known or even guessable enough to demand a
distinction between stranding and interlace. Even without 'interlace' or even
stranding, important events 'off stage' occur in narrative by report by either a
character or the narrator, or are assumed by the reader when he runs across
something new. There is, as Tuve suggests, some trace of the second or third
strand rubbed onto the first when we return.

With all these general comments finished, let us turn to *Beowulf*,[19] and see
how its complexity is handled and how simultaneity (if used at all) is presented.
Although rather elementary evolutionary explanations are no longer as popular
as in Zielinski's time, there is still to be found a residue of evolutionary thinking
in most scholars. Thus it is still believed that the *Beowulf* author (and other
early medieval writers) had difficulty in expressing simultaneous action. After
all, all that is needed is a phrase like 'in the meanwhile' or 'at the same time
as this was happening, that was happening' to present simultaneous action.
It was not a deep mystery even to the 'primitive' Anglo-Saxons.

One notable example of simultaneity in *Beowulf* was pointed out by Kenneth
Sisam.[20] In lines 837–927, the poet presents the simultaneous actions of the
various chieftains who come from afar to Heorot to witness the arm of Grendel
and his tracks, and those of the young retainers of Hrothgar who followed the

---

[17] *Allegorical Imagery: Some Mediaeval Books and Their Posterity* (Princeton 1966) 362.
[18] 363. It should be pointed out that the effect of foreshadowing is not always psychological
(as Tuve sees it), but could actually be a contribution to character A's or the narrator's
knowledge of something of which he has hitherto been completely ignorant.
[19] All references to *Beowulf* are taken from the Klaeber edition, 3rd ed. (Boston 1980).
[20] *The Structure of* BEOWULF (Oxford 1965) 29–32.

bloody tracks of Grendel to his mere home and who on return heard the ac-
companying scop singing Beowulf's praise in various ways. Here we have
some overlapping and an example of the third Zielinski type ('continuous
retrieval') discussed above.[21] Lines 917–18 seem to repeat line 837. There
are possibly other examples, but none so clear-cut as the 'morning-after' episode.

Beowulf is a very complex poem, although its type of complexity is not the
same as that of the French Vulgate romances. The unifying story line is longer
and more time-bound than that of these romances, which often has a rather
short length and covers a less detailed and circumstantial story. The basic
story line in Beowulf begins with the establishment of the Spear-Dane dynasty
and ends with the death of Beowulf. The complexity arises from the length
of time of the action and from the various references, mostly to the past (although there are a few to the future). Some of these references are long inter-
jections, like the Sigemund story (874b–97) or Hygelac's historic raid on the
Frisians (1069–1160 and elsewhere more briefly); even more frequent are the
continuing historical, Biblical (rare), fabulous, and usually brief contemporary
references, which turn back from the main action as similar, parallel, or contrasting statements and which establish a density of texture.

We have in Beowulf a polyphonic cross-section of Danish, Swedish, and early
Germanic history, pseudo-history, mythology, and beliefs, but never at the
cost of losing the always forward-moving main story line. The reader or listener
of Beowulf never loses the main thread. He may be slowed down by the density
of allusions, but never has to grope for the main thread of action.

Complex as the first part of Beowulf (to Beowulf's report to his chieftain
Hygelac, lines 2000–151) is, even more complex is the effect of the shorter allusions to the past and contemporary history in the second and last part of the
poem. Between the two parts is a gap of 50 years wherein Beowulf becomes
king of the Geats, an interlude which has given rise to much discussion. To
some, the gap spoils the power of the story; to others, the unity is preserved by
the continuity of the hero, Beowulf. We need not concern ourselves with this
problem.[22] What I am primarily interested in is why the second part, or at
last the part beginning at line 1925 (when Beowulf and his men leave Denmark
to return to Geatland), seems to be more broken and interrupted in style than
the earlier part, although both parts share similar back-curlings of reference.

The return to Hygelac (the king of the Geats preceding Beowulf) is interrupted by a story digression about Hygd (Hygelac's wife) and a Thryth or
Modthrythe who is as wicked as Hygd is good (1925–76). This digression has

---

[21] See above, p. 52.

[22] See the well-known essay by J. R. R. Tolkien, 'Beowulf: The Monsters and the Critics,'
Proceedings of the British Academy 22 (1936) 245–95. He argues for the poem's unity.

given rise to much discussion which is not relevant to my argument here. I wish solely to emphasize the interrupting quality of this story. Other major digressions from the main story line occur in the second part: the lay of the last survivor (2247–66), a return to the disaster of the Frisian raid (2354–69), followed by another digression about the Scylfings (Swedes) (2370–2400) and the Heathobards (2024–69).

Shorter digressions are also found throughout the poem, sometimes a short reference to an analogous event, especially in the last part of the poem, or to a contrasting event. 'The past is continually overlapping into the present.'[23] Examples such as the slaying of Daeghrefn by Beowulf (2502–8). Beowulf's relations with the Swedes and support of Eadgils (2379bff.), the accidental slaying of the Geatish prince Herebeald by Haeðcyn (2425ff.) spring to mind. The famous Breca story told by Unferth to insult the stranger Beowulf at the Danish court (499ff.), creation (90b–98), and the Heremod story (901–15 and 1709–10) are similar interrupting examples from the earlier part of the poem.

Many of these interrupting allusions or references are quite brief. The references to Cain and Abel (106–8 and again 1260–61), Hrothgar's brief allusion to the death of his older brother Heregār (465–69), the brief pointings to Eomer (1960–62), to Ingeld (2025), to Hereric (probably brother of Hygd, 2206) provide a short selection.

It is significant that these references to the past (real and mythic) and a few to the future occur in greater number in the last part of the poem than in the first. The past is the main theme of the poem throughout, and we are continually reminded of it, but in the last part of the poem the forward movement is slowed by numerous back references, more than ever before. As a human ages, his mind is less direct and precise than when he was younger. Clouds of memory and of vagueness descend on him and to some extent block the future. The past becomes much more important. The past is to the old what the future is to the young.

The narrator in *Beowulf* develops the last part not only in terms of the main story — the fight with the dragon — but by numerous references to the past or assumed past. This procedure blurs the clean and sharp effect of the main story line and thus reduplicates as far as is possible by structural means the mode of aged thinking. The tone is, of course, not confined to Beowulf, but the atmosphere is made heavy with these references. It is an atmosphere suitable to the story of an old and worn-out hero.

---

[23] See Howell D. Chickering, Jr., ed. and trans., BEOWULF: *A Dual-Language Edition*, (Garden City, N.Y. 1977) 359. 'Montage fashion' is the phrase used by Chickering for the method. Chickering indicates his dissatisfaction with the term 'interlace' as applied to verbal art: 'I question whether a visual analogy can characterize the poem's structure. . . . If the visual interlace has any symbolism, it is obscure' (20).

Much more could be done with an analysis of these curlings, mostly into the past, which occur in the poem and especially in the last part, but this work deserves a much more detailed and lengthy analysis than I can deal with here. The main point I wish to make is that the 'interlace' image is not useful when applied to verbal art and that the notion of simultaneity in literature needs to be more carefully used. Its built-in limitations in literature must be acknowledged, while at the same time it must be recognized that there is fundamentally no difficulty in presenting simultaneous actions in literature, provided that we do not attempt to present them simultaneously.

Harvard University

'BRUNANBURH' 12b–13a AND SOME SKALDIC PASSAGES

By JOSEPH HARRIS

Old English scholars have apparently accepted the 'synesthetic' image in 'feld dennade / secga swate' of *Brunanburh* 12b–13a, and most would now translate: 'the field resounded with the blood of men.'[1] The problematic verb has the manuscript variants *dæn'n'ede*, *dennode*, and *dennade* (twice), but is thought to be the frequent OE *dynode/dynede* (inf. *dynian/dynnan*), with the gemination carried over from the class I infinitive.[2] The *-e-* for *-y-* is explained as Kentish influence, and Carl T. Berkhout adds that the spelling with *-æ-* could be a scribe's attempt to restore a West Saxon form in view of the fact that *-æ-* would also show up in Kentish as *-e-*.[3] Berkhout supports the synesthesia with Biblical parallels, especially 'vox sanguinis fratris tui clamat ad me de terra' (Gen. 4.10), and seems inclined to credit the *Brunanburh* poet with a conscious Biblical allusion at this point. This does not seem impossible, especially in view of other evidence of bookishness in the poem,[4] but the allusion would not be very appropriate — are the enemies of the West Saxons treated as their brothers, does the bloodshed seem a sin? Instead I would prefer

---

[1] Fred C. Robinson, 'Lexicography and Literary Criticism: A Caveat,' in *Philological Essays . . . in Honour of Herbert Dean Meritt*, ed. James I. Rosier (The Hague and Paris 1970) 107.

[2] Alistair Campbell, ed., *The Battle of Brunanburh* (London 1938) 98–102, is the basic discussion, subsuming earlier work; Campbell rejects *dynnan/dynian* or a reformed **dynnian* (100) despite the fact that the lost Otho MS certainly had *dynede* (98), but Björkman ('brauste'), Ashdown ('resounded'), Klaeber ('resounded'), and Körner ('klatschte') [references in Anglo-Saxon Poetic Records VI 147] have been followed by recent scholars in accepting the usual verb in the usual sense. Klaeber, 'A Note on the Battle of Brunanburh,' in *Anglica: Untersuchungen zur englischen Philologie, Alois Brandl zum siebzigsten Geburtstag überreicht* II (Leipzig 1925) 2n3 anticipates my general argument by proposing to emend the obscure *Exodus* 40b–41a from 'land dryrmyde / deadra hræwum' to *dyn(n)ede*.

[3] Carl T. Berkhout, '*Feld dennade* — Again,' *English Language Notes* 11 (1974) 161–62, here 162n4.

[4] Lines 68b–69a; and see, for example, the literature on Biblical sources for the sun image: A. Brandl, *Geschichte der englischen Literatur*, Grundriss der germanischen Philologie, ed. Hermann Paul, 2nd ed. (Strassburg 1900) II 1077; Klaeber, 'A Note' [roundly rejected by Campbell 40n2]; W. F. Bolton, '"Variation" in *The Battle of Brunanburh*,' *Review of English Studies*, NS 19 (1968) 371; Traugott Lawler, '*Brunanburh*: Craft and Art,' in *Literary Studies: Essays in Memory of Francis A. Drumm*, ed. John H. Dorenkamp (Wetteren 1973) 59–61n8; and the healthy corrective of Earl R. Anderson, 'The Sun in "The Battle of Brunanburh," 12b–17a,' *Notes and Queries* 218, NS 20 (1973) 362–63.

to support the consensus reading by parallels in another relevant literary tradition: the Norse praise poem.[5]

It should be well known that *Brunanburh* contains a number of undoubted
and some doubtful Nordicisms. Dietrich Hofmann's judicious study proposes
to stand by *cnearr* from ON *knǫrr* and *eorl* (*eorlas Anlafes*) in the ON sense,
and he elaborates convincingly on the Norse connections of *sceard* and *guðhafoc*.[6]
Hofmann also shows a special relationship (short of a direct relationship) to the
poetry of Egill Skallagrímsson, and this is a point I will return to. First,
however, let us examine the ON cognate of OE *dynnan/dynian*. The verb
dynja (*dunði, dunit*) means generally 'resound,' and this basic sense is supported by etymological relations.[7] *Lexicon poeticum* gives 20 occurrences in
verse; two describe the resounding of feathers, one of fire, one of a river (of
words). Four convey the sound of weapons, e.g., 'dunði broddr á brynju' =
'point resounded on byrnie'; three more, the sound of waves on a ship, e.g.,
'láta snekkjur dynja á brim' = 'let the ships resound in the sea.' Three have
an extended sense, 'to rush (noisily),' e.g., 'jarlar dunðu undan' = 'the jarls
rushed away, fled.'[8] From the etymological connections of *dynja* and the
conservative poetic instances in *Lexicon poeticum*, it appears certain that the
meaning 'to pour' (cf. *n*6) is derived from the primary idea of noise.

Two instances appear to parallel *Brunanburh* a bit more closely. First:

> Dunði djúpra benja
> dǫgg ór mækis hǫggvi
> (bark með dýrum drengjum

---

[5] *Brunanburh* has been briefly compared with Norse praise poetry by Campbell 37–38;
Nora Kershaw (Chadwick), ed., *Anglo-Saxon and Norse Poems* (Cambridge 1922) 64–65;
and Andreas Heusler, *Die altgermanische Dichtung*, 2nd rev. ed. (Potsdam 1941; rpt. Darmstadt 1957) 126; and more fully by Heinrich Naumann, *Das Ludwigslied und die verwandten
lateinischen Gedichte* (Halle 1932), and by Heinrich Beck, 'Zur literaturgeschichtlichen Stel-
lung des althochdeutschen Ludwigsliedes und einiger verwandten Zeitgedichte,' *Anzeiger
für Deutsches Altertum* 85 (1974) 37–51.

[6] *Nordisch-englische Lehnbeziehungen der Wikingerzeit*, Bibliotheca Arnamagnæana 14
(Copenhagen 1955) 165–67; cf. 22–42. Kershaw adds the intransitive use of *lecgan* (65) and
considers *dennode*, etc. to be borrowed from ON *dynja* in the sense 'to pour' (65 and 180,
line 12). The latter suggestion (originating with Price in 1824) was rejected by Campbell,
partly because in Norse usage 'blood' should be the subject, as in the prose quotation given
by Kershaw: 'dunði þá blóðit um hann allan.' But here the expression, occurring in a famous
passage in *Njáls saga* (ed. Einar Ólafur Sveinsson, Íslenzk fornrit 12 [Reykjavík 1964] 291),
refers to dried and clotted blood, which would not have 'poured' in any liquid sense over
Flosi but 'rattled' down around him.

[7] Jan de Vries, *Altnordisches etymologisches Wörterbuch*, 2nd rev. ed. (Leiden 1977), s.v.
dynr, dynja, duna, dúni, dunkr, dúnn 2, dunsuðr, dynkr, dýja.

[8] Finnur Jónsson, *Lexicon poeticum antiquae linguae septentrionalis: Ordbog over det norsk-
islandske skjaldesprog oprindelig forfattet af Sveinbjörn Egilsson . . .*, 2nd ed. (1931; rpt.
Copenhagen 1966).

> dreyrugt sverð) á eyri;
> bera knáttu þá breiðan
> blóðvǫnd hjarar Þundar,
> þó munk, greipa glóðar
> Gerðr, strádauða verða.

That is: 'Dǫgg djúpra benja dunði á eyri ór mækis hǫggvi; bark dreyrugt sverð með dýrum drengjum; bera knáttu þá hjarar Þundar breiðan blóðvǫnd, greipa glóða Gerðr; þó munk verða strádauða' = 'The dew-of-deep-wounds (= blood) resounded [rushed resounding] on the beach out of the blow-of-the-sword (= wound); I bore the bloody sword together with brave men; swords-of-Odin (= warriors) bore the broad blood-wand (= sword), Oh Gerd-of-the-fire-of-the-hands (= woman), though I must die the strawdeath (= in bed).' Second:

> Gestr hefr Geitis hristi
> galdrs, miðjungi skjaldar
> dunði djúpra benja
> dǫgg, rǫskligast hǫggvit.

That is: 'Gestr hefr hǫggvit rǫskligast Geitis galdrs hristi; dǫgg djúpra benja dunði skjaldar miðjungi' = 'Gestr has most quickly struck the shaker-of-the-song-of-Geitir (= the man); the dew-of-the-deep-wounds (= blood) rushed noisily [resounded] from the giant-of-the-shield (= the man).'[9]

The first of these passages, from Kormakr, who lived in the tenth century and composed this *lausavísa* in Scotland as little as twenty years after the battle of Brunanburh, is especially suggestive; and the verb *dunði* must carry at least some of its original aural charge even if the passage also implies that the blood 'rushed noisily' out of the wound. If Finnur Jónsson is correct in construing *a éyri* with the resounding blood (and A. E. Kock agrees) rather than with *bark sverð*, then we have the three elements of the Old English — the resounding, the blood, and the land — but not their arrangement. For here the blood resounds on the land, rather than the land resounding in blood.[10] The second passage, by Gestr Þórhallason, whose *lausavísur* Finnur Jónsson places about 1007, is not quite so useful. Finnur Jónsson translates: 'blodet strömmede ud af manens dybe saar,' and in *Lexicon poeticum* he places both

[9] Finnur Jónsson, ed., *Den norsk-islandske Skjaldedigtning* (Copenhagen and Kristiania 1912–15) IA 91; IB 84–85 (= Kormakr, *lausavísa* 64); IA 199; IB 190 (= Gestr Þórhallason, *lausavísa* 2).

[10] Roberta Frank, to whose keen skaldic eye I owe the correction of several slips and a blunder, points out that *á eyri* could belong to either sentence. Since *eyri* could be acc. or dat., even the question of motion with *á* sheds no light. A. E. Kock prints *á eyri* with the second sentence in *Notationes norroenae: Anteckningar till Edda och skaldediktning* §2229 (Lunds Universitets Årsskrift, NF, Första avdelningen 28 [1932] 25) but with the first in *Den norsk-isländska skaldediktningen*, I (Lund 1946) 50; as he comments in §2229: 'Logiskt hör rums-adverbialet jivetvis till båda satserna.'

these passages under his fifth sense: 'falde, strömme hørlig, bevæge sig stærkt.' However, Gestr's 'dunði djúpra benja dǫgg' is fairly obviously an imitation of Kormakr's phrase and must, like it, still carry some of the primary aural quality.

This understanding of the verb is supported by the three simplest entries in *Lexicon poeticum*, those of meaning 1: 'dönne, dundre, (især om lyde der er eller ligner genlyd)':

> foldvegr dunði (*Baldrs draumar* 3)
> mána vegr dunði (*Haustlǫng* 14)
> bœr dunði (*Brot* 10).

The first of these, 'the earth-way resounded,' is closest to the OE passage, but the second, 'the way-of-the-moon (= sky) resounded,' is an extension of the same idea; the third is a restriction of the idea: 'the farm resounded.'[11]

All in all, then, the poetic occurrences of ON *dynja* tend to support the interpretation of the OE as 'the earth resounded with blood,' since we find the same verb in ON collocated with words for earth and with the synesthetically resounding blood of battle. A kenning of Þórmóðr Trefilsson's provides, but rather obliquely, another instance of resounding blood: 'feeder-of-the-swan-of-the-resounding-wave-of-wounds' (= warrior) employs the root of *dynja* in its included blood kenning *sára dyn-bára*, 'resounding-wave-of-wounds.' The noise belongs not only to the metaphorical element 'wave' but also, as we can now appreciate, to the final referent blood.[12] I believe other synesthetic blood images could be documented from ON battle poetry; *Hákonarmál* (ca. 961) comes to mind: 'umðu oddláar í Óðins veðri' (st. 8) = 'the-liquid-of-the-point (= blood) resounded (*ymja*) in Odin's-storm (= battle),' although it is true there is a pervasive metaphorical quality here not present in the Old English. But instead of hunting further limited parallels, I would like to try to make a case for a parallel that, like the lines from *Brunanburh*, seems to offer both the resounding earth and the noisy blood in a close parallel to the OE arrangement.

---

[11] A third passage in *Lexicon poeticum* with resounding blood is still more problematical but should be mentioned; Finnur Jónsson gives 'eggja spor dunði,' which would be 'the path-of-the-edges (= wound) resounded.' However, the word *spor* also appears as *spiðr* and *spiorr* in the manuscripts, and in his edition of *Njáls saga*, Einar Ólafur Sveinsson gives *spjǫr* 'spears' (336–37). The second helming of the verse, which is spoken by Skarpheðinn after his death and is placed in the twelfth century by Finnur Jónsson, is very corrupt, and both editors capitulate on most of the lines. However, Finnur Jónsson's partial reading seems superior to me, although the audible wounds may not belong to the idea we are pursuing at all, but to the literal 'sucking wounds' we hear of elsewhere.

[12] *Skjaldedigtning* IA 206; IB 196 (= *Hrafnsmál* 3).

Stanza 5 of Egill's famous poem *Hǫfuðlausn*, supposedly composed in York
in 948, has already been juxtaposed to the *Brunanburh* passage by T. M. Andersson in the course of his discussion of the shining blood on the 'fields' of
Ludwigslied, line 49.[13] In Finnur Jónsson's text the passage reads:

> Vasat villr staðar
> vefr darraðar
> fyr grams glǫðum
> geirvangs rǫðum;
> þars í blóði
> í brimils móði
> vǫllr of þrumði,
> und véum glumði.

Finnur Jónsson (by implication) takes up the words of the second helming
thus: 'þars brimils vǫllr of þrumði í móði [og] í blóði, glumði und véum,' and
translates: 'hvor sælens mark (søen) bruste oprørt og blodig, hørtes kamplar-
men under fanerne.'[14] Sigurður Nordal agrees in general about the first helming,
but in the second follows different manuscripts and principles to give:

> þars í blóði
> enn brimlá-móði
> vǫllr of þrumði,
> und véum glumði.

He paraphrases: 'þar sem hin brimsorfna strönd lá lauguð blóði, dundi í henni
undir fánunum (þegar fánarnir voru bornir fram).'[15] *Anglicè*: 'There where the
sea-weary shore lay bathed in blood, it resounded in/on it (the shore) under
the banners (when the war-banners were borne forward).' The main disagreement is, of course, between 'enn brimlá-móði vǫllr' and 'í brimils móði vǫllr,'
but more important to us is that Finnur Jónsson's interpretation offers a
'field' (*vǫllr*) that 'resounds' (*þrymja*) 'in blood' (*í blóði*): 'feld dennade
secga swate.' Whether the 'field' is the field of the seal, i.e., the sea, or the
sea-worn shore is less pertinent.

However, a second difference between the two readings of Egill's helming is
that for Nordal the bloody shore does not 'resound' but just lies there. The
difficulty cannot be fully resolved, but here are some considerations. ON has
two sets of almost homophonous verbs:

> þruma 1: ruhig liegen (de Vries); forblive stille og tavs paa et og samme
> sted (LexP);
> þrymja 1: ruhen, liegen, sich ausbreiten (de Vries); forblive paa samme sted
> urokkelig (LexP);

---

13 'Blood on the Battlefield: A Note on *Ludwigslied* v. 49,' *Neophilologus* 56 (1972) 12–17.
14 *Skjaldedigtning* IB 31.
15 *Egils saga Skalla-Grímssonar*, Íslenzk fornrit 2 (Reykjavík 1933) 187. E. V. Gordon,
An Introduction to Old Norse, 2nd ed. rev. A. R. Taylor (Oxford 1957) 233, combines Finnur
Jónsson's understanding of the first two lines of the helming with Nordal's of the verb:
'the surging sea, the field of seals, broke in wrath under the banners, as it lay in blood.'

þruma 2: donnern, lärmen (de Vries); tordne, larme (LexP);
þrymja 2: tordne, larme (LexP).

The first group lacks further etymological connections in de Vries (unless perhaps with his *þruma* 2 f. ['land, boden'], but de Vries does not propose this). De Vries does not list our *þrymja* 2, but it shows up as a separate verb in *Lexicon poeticum*. The second pair has many further etymological connections in de Vries' *þrymr* 1 m. ('lärm, krachen'), *þruma* 1 f. ('lärm, donner'), *þrima* f. ('lärm, kampf'), and an IE etymology (Lat. *turma* 'menge,' IE *tuer- 'drehen, wirbeln,' etc.). Cleasby-Vigfússon lists our *þruma* 1 with the additional meaning 'to mope, tarry, stay behind.'[16] *þruma* 1 and *þrymja* 1 are very common in *Lexicon poeticum*, but they cover an extraordinarily wide range of meanings. The noisy second pair is the easier to interpret because the nouns are so common, the semantic range is much tighter, and the three poetic occurrences of the verbs are crystal clear. The question is: could the *Hǫfuðlausn* passage be added as a fourth occurrence of our *þrymja* 2?

Finnur Jónsson seems to have been divided on this point: in *Lexicon poeticum* he gives the Egill passage under our *þruma* 1, but in *Skjaldedigtning* he translates 'bruste,' i.e. 'gush, roar, rush,' presumably with *þrymja* 2 in mind. Nordal, of course, takes the verb as *þruma* 1, glossing it 'vera kyrr' = 'lie quietly.' The reading 'í brimils móði vǫllr of þrumði' definitely demands *þrymja* 2: 'the sea in rage resounded'; but Nordal's 'enn brimlá-móði vǫllr of þrumði' could take either verb: 'the sea-weary shore resounded/lay quietly.' Presumably the question cannot be resolved without a theory of the manuscript variants and without taking a position on the hard question of skaldic diction (the simple word order of Nordal, entailing a complex *hapax legomenon* in *brimlá-móði*, vs. the Jónssonian kenning drawn from here and there and interrupting the natural syntax of *í móði*).

However, even in the absence of firm convictions on these questions, I think there is much to speak in favor of the resounding shore or sea at this point. For Nordal's translation and gloss seem self-contradictory: if the sea-weary shore 'lay quietly' in blood, what was 'resounding' under the banners? How could it '[dynja] í henni [sc. strönd]' if the 'strönd lá [kyr] [í] blóði'? Thus Nordal's translation or paraphrase ('lá lauguð blóði') somewhat obscures the contradiction that emerges clearly if we substitute his gloss ('vera kyrr') on the verb *þrymja/þruma*. Even his 'brimlá-móði' ('sea-weary') would seem to call for the active verb sense, and it is certainly more in harmony with the idea of 'und véum glumði.' I would translate Nordal's text: 'It resounded (*glymja*) under the banners there where the sea-weary field (= shore) resounded (*þrymja*) in blood.'

---

[16] R. Cleasby and G. Vigfusson, *An Icelandic–English Dictionary*, 2nd ed., supp. William A. Craigie (Oxford 1957).

Egill is supposed to have fought at Brunanburh and to have learned his rhyming meter in England; he certainly composed verse for Athelstan. Whether he also exchanged opinions on the virtues of 'synesthesia' in poetry we can never know, but the recent trend toward dating OE poetry late and accounting for Scandinavian connections in terms of borrowing or shared tenth-century milieu (rather than *Urverwandtschaft*) agrees with the fact that the extant Old English praise poems appear suddenly and strongly attested in the reign of Athelstan, the first West Saxon king to claim 'all Britain.'[17] In this context of Scandinavian influence, we may advance two further speculations. [1] *feld dynede is metrically weak beside its closest parallels 'healwudu dynede' and 'hruse dynede' (*Beowulf* 1317 and 2558), 'hleoþor dynede' (*Rhyming Poem* 28), and 'dyndan scildas' (*Judith* 204), and this in a metrically careful poem.[18] Perhaps a line like 'bœr dunði' (*Brot* 10) lies behind it, and the doubled *n* of the manuscript forms *dennade*, etc. might be an early scribal response to the metrical irregularity.[19] [2] Perhaps OE *secga* in our passage originally meant 'of swords,' yielding the even more Nordic: 'the field resounded with the sweat-of-swords (= blood).' This would eliminate the redundancy of 'blood of men' (whose else?) and the questionable pathos that could call to mind the Biblical analogue.[20] Even if these Nordicizing suggestions should prove ac-

---

[17] Cf. Patricia Poussa, 'The Date of *Beowulf* Reconsidered: The Tenth Century,' *Neuphilologische Mitteilungen* 82 (1981) 276–88, esp. 278. *The Dating of* BEOWULF, ed. Colin Chase (Toronto 1981) provides a cross-section of the recent dating discussion; Frank, here and in her other recent essays, is an especially eloquent proponent of the shared Norse and English literary context in the tenth century. On the Latin eulogy in Athelstan's period, Michael Lapidge, 'Some Latin Poems as Evidence for the Reign of Athelstan,' *Anglo-Saxon England* 9 (1981) 61–98.

[18] Klaeber and others cite as further parallels Lagamon's 'gurren þa stanes mid þan blodstremes'; Ashdown cites also Lagamon's 'þe eorðe þer dunede' and the apparent paraphrase in Henry of Huntingdon ('colles resonuerunt, sudaverunt armati') in justifying *dynede*.

[19] Campbell rejects *dynede* partly on metrical grounds, and Klaeber's idea of a 'reformed' verb is partly intended to save the meter.

[20] Rudolf Meissner, *Die Kenningar der Skalden: Ein Beitrag zur skaldischen Poetik* (Bonn and Leipzig 1921) 205, lists two ON kennings for blood with sweat as the base word: 'sára þorns sveiti' (*Skjaldedigtning* IB 90.1) and 'sœfis sveiti' (*Skjaldedigtning* II B 76.54), both meaning 'sweat-of-the-sword.' For OE, H. van der Merwe Scholtz, *The Kenning in Anglo-Saxon and Old Norse Poetry* (Utrecht and Nijmegen 1927) 82–83, accepts *heaþoswat* (*Beowulf* 1460, 1606, and 1668), *hiorodrync* (*Beowulf* 2358), and a few others as kennings, but the *heoruswat required to support my argument is not attested. Hertha Marquardt, *Die altenglischen Kenningar: Ein Beitrag zur Stilkunde altgermanischer Dichtung*, Schriften der Königsberger Gelehrten-Gesellschaft, geisteswissenschaftliche Klasse 14.3 (Halle 1938) 114, 155, and 216, does not admit any of these expressions as regular blood kennings, although some must be based on such. In both OE and ON the metaphorical relationship of the base *swat/sveiti* to the ultimate referent is problematic, since both languages show a frequent secondary meaning 'blood' for the simplex that originally meant only 'sweat' and according to Meissner's rule (28–29) the base word cannot have the same meaning as the ultimate

ceptable, of course, *Brunanburh* remains the most thoroughly 'English' Anglo-Saxon poem, but its peculiar kind of battlefield synesthesia may have roots in the poetry best known from the Northern kinsman-enemy.

Harvard University

---

referent in a (well-formed [cf. 430]) kenning. Marquardt 120–21 makes more allowance for the base to be an *Oberbegriff* for the ultimate referent, at least in OE. However, blood kennings with *swat/sveiti* would belong to a special category in which there is no proper kenning if we select one meaning, but a good one if we select the other for the ambiguous base. Since, however, *'blood of the sword(s)' would be fairly meaningless, it is safe to say that the two skaldic expressions are to be understood as containing 'sweat.' The problem with the *Brunanburh* passage is that the definer is also ambiguous, and we have no certain way of choosing between 'blood of men' and 'sweat-of-swords' (though the bathetic 'sweat of men' can be rejected along with 'blood of swords'). (Note, for what it is worth, that Henry of Huntingdon [n18 *supra*] must have understood 'sweat of men.') 'Sword' is a very common qualifier in skaldic blood kennings, and the plural in *secga* seems to be no grounds for rejection (Meissner 39–40).

'RANA LOQUAX' AND THE FROGS OF PROVENÇAL POETRY

By DANIEL J. RANSOM

In a major study of troubadour rhetoric, Linda Paterson remarks that the image of the frog, though rare in Provençal poetry, appears in Marcabru's work four times. And after demonstrating the likelihood that Marcabru was influenced by exegetical traditions in his use of other images drawn from nature, she cites exegetical sources that allow her to interpret frogs as symbols of sterile verbosity in three of Marcabru's poems, 'Al departir,' 'Bel m'es quan la rana chanta,' and 'Lo vers comens.'[1] She also suggests that in 'Bel m'es,' an attack on the troubadour Alegret, 'the *rana* may be an image of Alegret himself: noisy with empty flattery, and perhaps raucous with poor singing' (40). Paterson's discussion of this image is no more than a brief excursus within a larger argument concerning Marcabru's rhetoric and his use of exegetical interpretation. In this paper I wish to provide fuller background to the sketch she provides and to suggest how the image of the frog in Provençal poetry is a potentially rich allusion.

Earlier commentators were inclined to praise Marcabru for his close observance of nature and for his avoidance of cliché. Thus Carl Appel accounts for the appearance of the frog in Marcabru's *Natureingänge*.[2] But there are two reasons why the frog cannot be so simply accounted for. First, of the various novelties with which Marcabru particularizes his portrayal of spring — the specificity of trees in poem III, the shadows on the mountain in II, the owl in XXI — only the frog recurs. Second, Marcabru's fondness for the image of the frog is somewhat disconcerting. Indeed, Martín de Riquer regards that image as a source of irony in Marcabru's poems.[3] For while the song of the frog truly is a sign of spring — the troubadour Guillem de Berguedà clearly uses it as such[4] — it is at best an awkward addition to, or substitution for, the usual conventions of springtime poetry. Frogs, unlike blossoms and nightingales, are an aesthetic failure — repulsive certainly to most people today — unattractive to the touch, to the eye, to the ear. In this paper I am concerned

---

[1] Linda M. Paterson, *Troubadours and Eloquence* (Oxford 1975) 39–40. Further references to Paterson will be made parenthetically in the text. Unless otherwise indicated, citations of Marcabru's poetry are from J.-M.-L. Dejeanne, ed., *Poésies complètes du troubadour Marcabru* (Toulouse 1909).

[2] Carl Appel, 'Zu Marcabru,' *Zeitschrift für romanische Philologie* 43 (1923) 455.

[3] Martín de Riquer, *Resumen de literatura provenzal trovadoresca* (Barcelona 1948) 32: 'no olvida el croar de la rana, detalle sorprendente y cargado de intención paródica que luego repetirá su discípulo Bernart Martí, pero que los demás trovadores velarán discretamente.'

[4] See discussion *infra*, p. 83.

chiefly with the sound made by the frog, its *chant*, perhaps its least objection-
able attribute. Did twelfth-century listeners share our distaste for marsh
song? Given the opinion of one scholar that the ancients did not denigrate
the sound of the frog,[5] it will be necessary to review the evidence for medieval
antipathy to *rana loquax*.

Roman authors, even those writing as naturalists, not as poets or storytellers,
speak of the frog's voice as less than pleasant. Cicero, detailing the frog's
ability to foretell the coming of storms, writes:

> vos quoque signa videtis, aquai dulcis alumnae,
> cum clamore paratis inanis fundere voces
> absurdoque sono fontis et stagna cietis.
> [Ye, too, distinguish the signs, ye dwellers in waters delightful, / When, with
> a clamour, you utter your cries that are empty of meaning, / Stirring the
> fountains and ponds with absurd and ridiculous croaking.][6]

Columella refers to the curses of the querulous frog ('querulae semper convicia
ranae'), a theme that reappears in Virgil's first *Georgic* (378): 'et veterem in
limo ranae cecinere querellam.'[7] Columella and Virgil allude to a tradition
treated later in Ovid's *Metamorphoses* (6.317–81) of the Lycian peasants who
refused Latona a drink from their pond and were forthwith turned into frogs.
Of course this metamorphosis does not alter their boorish behavior:

> . . . sed nunc quoque turpes
> litibus exercent linguas pulsoque pudore,
> quamvis sint sub aqua, sub aqua maledicere temptant.
> vox quoque iam rauca est, inflataque colla tumescunt,
> ipsaque dilatant patulos convicia rictus.
> [But even now, as of old, they exercise their foul tongues in quarrel, and
> all shameless, though they may be under water, even under the water they
> try to utter maledictions. Now also their voices are hoarse, their inflated
> throats swell up, and their constant quarrelling distends their wide jaws.][8]

The precedents in Roman literature clearly are not the basis for interpreting
the *vox ranae* as a welcome sign of spring. Medieval commentators are even less
enthusiastic about the creature's vocal capacities. Isidore reports that *rana*
gets its name 'a garrulitate . . . eo quod circa genitales strepunt paludes, et

---

[5] See A. S. F. Gow, ed., *Theocritus*, 2nd ed. (Cambridge 1952) II 142.

[6] *De divinatione* 1.9.15, quoted from Cicero, *De senectute, De amicitia, De divinatione*,
trans. William Armistead Falconer, Loeb Series (1923; rpt. Cambridge, Mass. 1964) 238–39.

[7] Lucius Junius Moderatus Columella, *On Agriculture and Trees*, trans. E. S. Foster and
Edward H. Heffner, Loeb Series (Cambridge, Mass. 1955) III 6–7 (*De re rustica* 10.12); *Virgil*,
trans. H. Rushton Fairclough, rev. ed., Loeb Series (Cambridge, Mass. 1967) I 106.

[8] Ovid, *Metamorphoses*, trans. Frank Justus Miller, 2nd ed., Loeb Series (1921; rpt. Cambridge, Mass. 1946) I 314–15. For further instances of deprecation of the frog's voice, see
Horace, *Satires* 1.5.14–15 and Martial, *Epigrams* 3.93.8.

sonos vocis inportunis clamoribus reddunt.'⁹ This information is repeated in later encyclopedias by Rhabanus Maurus, Bartolomeus Anglicus, and Vincent of Beauvais.¹⁰ Less complimentary still are descriptions prompted by the lines in Virgil and Ovid. Virgil's reference to the frogs' old complaint is examined in the ninth-century Scholia Bernensia, which continue to be promulgated into the fifteenth century. The expositors are uncertain about the allusion Virgil makes ('multi ambigunt, quae sit ranarum vetus querela'), and they mistakenly report that Ovid's story concerns Ceres rather than Latona. However, they embellish Ovid's account in an interesting way: 'tunc eam [Cerem] Lycii rustici a potatu prohibuerunt, et conturbantes pedibus fontem cum contra eam emitterent turpem narium sonum, illa irata eos convertit in ranas, quae nunc quoque ad illius soni imitationem clamant.' They gloss *querela* as 'vox mu[l]ta, ut ipse [Virgil, *Aen.* 8.215f.] ait: omne querellis Inpleri nemus.'¹¹ We may note finally that Rhabanus Maurus, also in the ninth century, characterizes the sound of the frog with the verb 'latrare' (see *n*10).

Isidore's Iberian frog clamors, Rhabanus' barks, and the voice of Italian and Bernese frogs is ugly and foul (*turpis*); we might expect that the frogs of Provence sing in much the same register. Paterson (40*n*4) points to evidence to confirm this suspicion: 'The last lines of Peire d'Alvernhe's satire on the troubadours . . . where Peire praises his own singing, were altered [in two manuscripts] to read: "Peire d'Alvernhe a tal voz / que canta cum granolh' em potz."'¹² The evidence, then, is strong that Marcabru cannot have used the song of the frog to enhance an attractive portrayal of springtime. In Marcabru's poetry the frog appears always in the first or second strophe. Its song therefore must be a proleptic hint that the poem it introduces will not pursue a pleasant theme, despite the springtime imagery. Because the direction of the hint will vary from poem to poem, it will be convenient to review now the traditions upon which the image may draw.

In Biblical exegesis there are four passages that receive commentary on the frog: Exodus 8.1–15, Psalms 77.45 and 104.30, and Revelations 16.13.¹³

---

⁹ Isidore of Seville, *Etymologiae* 12.6.20–27, ed. W. M. Lindsay (Oxford 1911).

¹⁰ Rhabanus Maurus, *De universo* 8.2 (PL 111.228); Bartolomeus Anglicus, *De proprietatibus rerum* 18.91: see *On the Properties of Things: John Trevisa's Translation of* BARTHOLOMAEUS ANGLICUS DE PROPRIETATIBUS RERUM, edd. M. C. Seymour *et al.* (Oxford 1975) II 1242–43; Vincent of Beauvais, *Speculum naturale* 20.59 (Douai 1624; rpt. Graz 1964) 1492.

¹¹ For the uncertainty regarding the allusion, see 'Brevis expositio in Vergilii Georgicum' (11th century), ed. Hermann Hagen, *Appendix Serviana: Ceteros praeter Servium et Scholia Bernensia Vergilii commentatores continens* (Leipzig 1902) 261. Another version identifies the allusion as to the Latona story (365). For the version that substitutes Ceres for Latona, see Hagen, ed., *Scholia Bernensia ad Vergilii* BUCOLICA *atque* GEORGICA (1867; rpt. Hildesheim 1967) 204.

¹² See below, p. 81.

¹³ There is also a reference at Wisdom 19.10, but it draws virtually no commentary.

Earliest attention is given to Exodus, to the plague of frogs that descends on Egypt. Origen writes: 'Per secundam vero plagam, in qua ranae producuntur, indicari figuraliter arbitror carmina poetarum, qui inani quadam et inflata modulatione, velut ranarum sonis et cantibus mundo huic deceptionis fabulas intulerunt. Ad nihil enim illud animal utile est, nisi quod sonum vocis improbis et importunis clamoribus reddit.' To these remarks Origen adds a 'moralis figura': Any soul living in ignorance of truth is in Egypt; if God's law approaches, 'tum deinde educit . . . vanam et inanem loquacitatem, et adversum Dei providentiam ranarum similem querelam.'[14] As with so many of Origen's interpretations, this one is idiosyncratic; and though it continued to be copied in its second-century Latin translation, it did not have an impact on Biblical exegesis until its view of the plague frogs began to circulate outside of the original text. We find it promulgated in the *Glossa ordinaria* and in the commentaries of Bruno of Würzburg, Bruno the Carthusian, Bruno of Asti, Hildebert of Tours, Rupert of Deutz, Honorius of Autun, and Jacques de Vitry.[15]

A somewhat more influential theme was begun by Augustine, who says simply, 'Habes expressam significatamque vanitatem, si attendas ranarum loquacitatem.'[16] This interpretation was subsumed under a much more widely spread figural reading which compares frogs to heretics and philosophers, a comparison indebted to the express association of frog-likeness and demons

---

[14] Origen, *In Exodum* (Hom. 4), 'De decem plagis, quibus percussa est Aegyptus' (PG 12.322–23). For a comparison of frog and poet in Greek literature, see Theocritus, Idyll VII, Gow's edition (n5). Simichidas shows a modest appreciation for his own skill as a poet: 'For in my own esteem I am as yet no match in song either for the great Sicelidas from Samos or for Philetas, but vie with them like a frog against grasshoppers.' A late medieval instance of such a comparison is 'The Flyting of Dunbar and Kennedie' (341–44):

> And thou [Dunbar] come, fule, in March
> or Februere
> Thare [Pernaso] till a pule, and drank
> the padok rod [spawn]
> That gerris the ryme in to thy termes glod
> And blaberis that noyis mennis eris to here.

(ed. James Kinsley, *The Poems of William Dunbar* [Oxford 1979] 88).

[15] *Glossa ordinaria* on Exodus 8 (Venice 1588) I 139ᵛ (for references to the *Glossa* and to Hugh of St. Cher, I owe much thanks to Emerson Brown, Jr., who kindly provided me with transcriptions); Bruno of Würzburg, *Expositio Psalmorum* (PL 142.380); Bruno the Carthusian, *Expositio in Psalmos* (PL 152.1048); Bruno of Asti, *Expositio in Psalmos* (PL 164.1102); Hildebert of Tours, sermon for the Feast of the Assumption (PL 171.633); Rupert of Deutz, *In Exodum commentariorum* (PL 167.599–600); Honorius of Autun, *De decem plagis Aegypti, spiritualiter* (PL 172.267); Jacques de Vitry, *Sermones de tempore*, cited from Philipp Funk, *Jakob von Vitry: Leben und Werke* (Leipzig and Berlin 1909) 72.

[16] Augustine, sermon on the Ten Plagues and the Ten Commandments (PL 46.948–49).

in Revelations 16.13.[17] Revelations also encouraged a further association with uncleanness, 'vidi de ore draconis spiritus tres immundos in modum ranarum,' to which Eucherius and then Rhabanus add: 'Ranae haeretici, qui in coeno vilissimorum sensuum commorantes, vana garrulitate latrare non desinunt, ut in Exodo legitur.'[18] Honorius of Autun and Richard of St. Victor make the short step from uncleanness and the vile senses to *luxuria*.[19]

It may be that the association between frogs and sordid sensuality was encouraged by more than the muddy marsh ('limosa palus') mentioned by some commentators as the frog's natural habitat. Ancient tradition also records that the song of the frog was a mating call. Among the naturalists who so report are Aristotle, Aelian, Plutarch, and Pliny. The exegete Eustathius also states this natural fact. In the later Middle Ages it reappears under the name of Aristotle.[20] It is likely to have been understood as scientific fact in popular lore, and Marcabru's use of frog song in 'Bel m'es quan la fuelh'ufana' (21.7–12) suggests as much.[21]

What must be addressed now is the question of whether the exegetical traditions concerning the frog were, if not quite popular, at least current in Marcabru's day. About the time that Marcabru was active, Berengar of Poitiers wrote a satirical letter to the Carthusians blaming them for pursuing wrongful litigations. He reminds them that '*cultus iusticiae* teste propheta *est silen-*

---

[17] This comparison is recapitulated and emphasized by several commentators: Eucherius of Lyon, *Formulae spiritalis intellegentiae*, ed. Carolus Wotke, CSEL 31.1 (Prague 1894) 29; *Glossa ordinaria*, interlinear gloss on Ps. 77.45 (III 200ʳ); Peter Damian, *De decem Aegypti plagis* (PL 145.689); Bruno of Asti, *Expositio in Exodum* (PL 164.246–47), *Expositio in Psalmos* (PL 164.1001, 1102); Odo of Asti, *Expositio in Psalmos* (PL 165.1283); Peter Lombard, *Commentarium in Psalmos* (PL 191.737); Alan of Lille, *Liber in distinctionibus dictionum theologicum* (PL 210.921–22); Hugh of St. Cher, *Opera omnia in universam Sanctam Scripturam* (Lyon 1669) on Ps. 77.45 (II 204ʳ).

[18] For Eucherius and Rhabanus, also *Glossa ordinaria*, Peter Damian, Bruno of Asti, and Peter Lombard, see n17. In the *Glossa*, see also Exodus 8, 'in aquis immundis . . . in deliciis carnis' (I 139ᵛ).

[19] For Honorius, see n15. Richard of St. Victor, *In Apocalypsim libri septem*, '[in modum ranarum] exeuntium de luto, sic isti lutosi sunt per luxuriam' (PL 196.828).

[20] See Aristotle, *Historia animalium* 4.9 (536ᴀ), trans. A. L. Peck, Loeb Series (Cambridge, Mass. 1970) II 78–79; Aelian, *On the Characteristics of Animals* 9.13, trans. A. F. Scholfield, Loeb Series (Cambridge, Mass. 1959) II 232–33; Plutarch, *Moralia*, 'De sollertia animalium,' trans. Harold Cherniss and William C. Helmbold, Loeb Series (Cambridge, Mass. 1957) XII 460–61; Pliny, *Natural History* 11.65.173, trans. H. Rackham, Loeb Series (Cambridge, Mass. 1940) III 540–41; Eustathius, *In Hexaemeron S. Basilii: Latina metaphrasis* (PL 58.935). For the medieval Aristotle, see Jacqueline Hamesse, *Auctoritates Aristotelis* ([et] *Senecae, Boethii, Platonis, Apulei et quorundam aliorum*): I. *Concordance* (Louvain 1972) 156; see also Bartolomeus Anglicus (n10).

[21] In this poem birds sing, so too the frog, and the owl with his mate makes noise. The implication is that each species sings to its mate. In lines 13–14 we are told that these creatures couple up in pairs ('s'aparilha').

tium,' whereas they prefer 'cultus iustitiae multiloquium.' And he asks:
'Quid prodest, fratres, exire in eremum et in eremo habere cor Aegyptium?
Quid prodest Aegypti ranas uitare et obscenis detractionibus concrepare
[croak]?'[22] The allusion implies that its readers will know the passage in
Exodus and be aware of its figural possibilities. A related allusion is to be
found in Walter the Englishman's fable of the frog and the mouse (ca. 1175).
The treacherous 'rana loquax' deceives the mouse and tries to drown it,
which leads Walter to the following comment: 'Omne genus pestis superat
mens dissona verbis, / Cum sentes animi florida lingua polit.'[23] Even more
oblique is the reference made some years earlier by Serlo of Wilton in a distich
signalling his conversion from worldly to spiritual pursuits: 'Linquo "coax"
ranis, "cra" corvis vanaque vanis — / Ad logicam pergo, que mortis non timet
ergo.' The master of logic (and erstwhile poet of racy lyrics) will now leave
vain things to the vain.[24] The distich and the man thus touch upon four facets
of the exegesis we have been examining: vanity, sophistry, poetry, and frogs.

The same themes were made known to a wider audience through sermon
literature. Evidence that they were, at least in the early thirteenth century,
is to be found in the exempla of Jacques de Vitry (1170–1240). Jacques tells
of the miracle that led to Serlo's conversion and quotes the famous distich
cited above. More direct is his reference to frogs in one of his *Sermones de
tempore,* a diatribe against 'temporalis abundantia,' where he condemns the
wastefulness and vanity of chivalric culture. To the chorus of angels he contrasts the licentious sing-song that foolish girls take pleasure in because they
find in it food for their concupiscence. Furthermore, Jacques interprets the
frogs that entered the homes of the Egyptians and befouled their food as idle
songs, the lies of poets, the sing-song devoted to women, the smut of buffoons.[25]
We may suppose that he is not the first to sermonize in this way. Indeed, we
shall see that Marcabru himself writes in much the same vein.

Like Jacques, Marcabru deplores the licentious behavior of the aristocracy
in his day, but he attributes it, not to excessive wealth, but to a realignment of
values directly attributable to the interruption of blood lines in the family,
which leads to the decline of noble stock. In poem III, 'Al departir,' Marcabru
presents us with an allegorical garden full of prospering plants that bear no

---

[22] See R. M. Thomson, 'The Satirical Works of Berengar of Poitiers: An Edition with
Introduction,' *Mediaeval Studies* 42 (1980) 132.

[23] Quoted in Robert Pope, 'A Sly Toad, Physiognomy and the Problem of Deceit: Hen-
ryson's *The Paddock and the Mous,*' *Neophilologus* 63 (1979) 462.

[24] Jan Öberg, ed., *Serlon de Wilton: Poèmes latins* (Stockholm 1965) 121.

[25] For the reference to Serlo, see Thomas Frederick Crane, ed., *The Exempla or Illustrative
Stories from the* SERMONES VULGARES *of Jacques de Vitry* (1890; rpt. Nendeln, Liechtenstein
1967) 12 and 145–46. For the *Sermones de tempore,* see n15.

fruit. The 'plants' are the grafts ('l'empeut' 11), that is, the illegitimate offspring, of great men. They prosper but do not support those who tend them. In their midst, in the sweet season, sings the frog. What sounds do the scions make? They promise but do not fulfill, dispute but to no good end, boast but do no deeds of real value (20–21, 29–32). Paterson (39) relates their noise ('nausas' 31) to that of the frog and interprets both as 'sterile verbosity.' This is not quite the language of the exegetes, though the idea may be derived from them. But the expressions *vana garrulitas*, *loquax vanitas*, and *loquacitas vana*[26] do make the frog a fitting emblem of the puffed-up volubility of degenerate noblemen.

Poem XI, 'Bel m'es quan la rana chanta,' pursues much the same theme, but with a different allegory and with an added dimension. Marcabru says that he loves the time when the frog sings, the sap rises, and the nightingale conquers his mate 'per joi.' As in poem III we have a positive scene with ambiguous elements. The frog we may leave aside for a moment. 'Joi' of course is one of the premiere qualities or virtues of the courtly ethic. It is also an agent of conquest here, a conquest achieved 'ples d'orgueilh' and made possible only by the fair season (cf. Paterson 40). In the realm of nature this joy, conquest, and pride are as they should be. As Marcabru says in poem XXI, such joy follows the straight path ('via plana' 15). In the human sphere, however, all is perverted. In poem XI we find degenerate nobility seeking to conquer Jois, Jovens, and Proeza, whom they have besieged. Dukes and kings shut the mouth of Prowess by making big noise ('gran nauza' 43) about little deeds ('pauc fag'). The frog sings but Marcabru does not dare to speak ('non aus . . . dir' 9–10) of those who abuse Prowess.

The frog has its proper role in nature, but it also has an emblematic function here, as in poem III. The boasting of potentates is done, in large part, by court poets who compose panegyrics to honor the deeds of their patrons. Poets are the mouthpieces of princes, that is to say, their frogs. Peter Cantor identifies the frogs of Egypt as 'adulatores garruli.'[27] They are the singers of false praise, the kind of praise that must have grated badly on Marcabru's ear. Marcabru says that praise ('lauzenja' 60) should not be given to unworthy patrons, and blames the poet Alegret for trying to pervert truth in this way (65–67): 'Alegretz, folls, en qual quiza / Cujas far d'avol valen / Ni de gonella camiza?' ('Alegret, fool, in what way do you think to make from a wretch a worthy

---

[26] For these phrases, see Rhabanus Maurus and Peter Lombard (n17) and Remigius of Auxerre, *Enarrationes in Psalmos* (PL 131.556).

[27] Peter Cantor, *Verbum abbreviatum*, ch. 45 'Contra adulatores' (PL 205.140). Cf. the *Glossa ordinaria* on Apoc. 16.13: 'per istos tres significatur mali relatores, aduocati dolosi & adulatores, qui sua verbositate mundi potentes excitant ad contentiones' (VI 625ᵛ); also Hugh of St. Cher on Ps. 104.30 (II 273ʳ).

man or from sackcloth a silken shirt?'). Untrue poetry is, of course, another form of 'vana garrulitas,' and its emblem, as we have seen, is the frog.

Marcabru attacks Alegret because he believes that the disguise of truth, particularly in the houses of rich and powerful men, leads to social degeneration. A similar theme is to be found in commentary on Exodus regarding the entrance of the frogs into the houses of kings and potentates. Bruno of Asti writes: 'Istae ranae, poetae et philosophi, et Judaei et haeretici intelliguntur, qui, de sola loquacitate gloriantes, contra veritatem loqui non cessant. Et tales quidem regibus et potentibus familiares sunt, qui in eorum vanitatibus et erroribus delectantur.' Odo of Asti speaks of frog-heretics who 'confabulate' for purpose of entertainment in the houses of kings, 'uti mos est.' Rupert of Deutz warns of the consequences: 'istae autem ranae, id est fabulosi poetae corporaliter aures lectitando, et oculos gesticulando delectaverunt, sed animis exitiales exstiterunt.'[28] Marcabru follows this tradition, but particularizes the poetry-heresy at work in his own milieu. We have seen already in poem III how Marcabru deplores the vitiation of the nobility by illegitimate offspring. In poem XI he addresses the cause of illegitimacy — the infidelity of husbands and wives (stanza 7). Furthermore, he relates this cause to the (adulterous) courtly love ethic that was being enthusiastically celebrated by the poets of twelfth-century Provence. Alegret's *gonella cum camiza* is Marcabru's metaphor for the courtly lover. In lines 62–63 Marcabru tells us that the man who wears 'la blancha camiza' cuckolds his lord ('seinhor sufren') and possesses his lady ('ten si dons a sa guiza'). What seems pure and fine, Marcabru says to Alegret, is actually foul and coarse, or a mere cover for what is foul and coarse, something to be lifted and lowered as need requires ('levan cazen / Qual gonella qual camiza').[29]

It might be suggested, therefore, even without recourse to an established symbol system, that Marcabru's frog represents a lower and less appealing aspect of the sexual vitality inherent in the new season. Like the birds, the frog sings to attract a mate. But whereas song birds, creatures of the sky, offer a relatively ethereal image of sexuality, the frog, creature of earth, dwelling as Virgil says *in limo*, presents sexuality more as a chthonic force, dark and vaguely repellent. To be sure, Marcabru never situates his frogs *in limo* or even in the *coenosae paludes* to which some exegetes refer; rather, they sing in the pond (*vivier* 3.5) or by the fountain (*fontanilh* 21.10). But the frog's reputation for uncleanness was both longstanding and still current in Marcabru's day. It is noted by medieval naturalists such as Bartolomeus Anglicus; in

---

[28] Bruno of Asti on Ps. 104.30 (n15); Odo of Asti (n17); Rupert of Deutz (n15).

[29] Compare the clothing metaphors in Jonathan Swift's *Tale of a Tub*, sec. II: 'Is not . . . Vanity a *Shirt*, and Conscience a *Pair of Breeches*, which, tho' a Cover for Lewdness as well as Nastiness, is easily slipt down for the Service of both.'

Trevisa's fourteenth-century translation of *De proprietatibus rerum* the frog is said to be 'slymy.'[30] And given the exegetical association of this uncleanness with *luxuria* and with the verbal power to lead 'per suggestionem' to fornication, we may suppose that Marcabru's frog does represent the libido as well as its advocates, both desire and the promotion of it by court poets.

Marcabru takes up the theme of poetry again in a similar context in poem XXXIII, 'Lo vers comens.' This time Marcabru will begin his song when the bird and frog no longer sing. In this silence, Marcabru declares that he follows 'trobar naturau' (7),[31] for which petty troubadours ridicule him:

> E segon trobar naturau
> port la peir' e l'esc' e.l fozill,
> mas menut trobador bergau
>   entrebesquill,
> mi tornon mon chant en badau
> e.n fant gratill.   (7–12)

[And according to the natural art of composing I bear the flint and tinder and steel, but buzzing, petty troubadours with confused thoughts turn my song into nothing and make a mockery of it for me.][32]

To reveal truth, Marcabru implies, the poet must strike a spark, kindle a flame. To do this he must scrape together the flint and steel of his verse. He creates then a harsh kind of poetry (no pretty lies to disguise the truth[33]), a kind of verse that makes Marcabru's poetic voice rather more like that of the frog in nature.[34] But the frog follows natural law, and this is what Marcabru would have the degenerate nobility do. Instead they (and their petty poets) reject sound values, walk a crooked path, and put off shame. In failing to follow right reason, they are unnatural, kin to the figural frog, not the literal one.

Among the faults of the aristocracy Marcabru numbers illiberality or the failure to exercise generosity, that is, to make awards to those who deserve them, to those who serve the true good. Here too the theme of *trobar naturau* is present. The lords do not prize blame or praise ('E non prezon blasme ni lau / Un gran de mil' 35–36), exactly those goods which the righteous poet has to offer. And thus they do not give freely (presumably to those who sing the truth); instead they grudgingly pay what they owe, full of grumbling ('plen de grondill' 34). In grumbling, these lords make the sound of the frog (cf. 4),[35]

---

[30] See *n*10.

[31] On this concept of style, see Paterson 28ff.

[32] Text and translation from Paterson 28–29.

[33] Cf. lines 51–52 of this poem: 'no.i pot hom trobar a frau / Mot de roïll' ('one cannot find [in this poem] any false, blighted word').

[34] Cf. Paterson 53 and 73.

[35] One hears from neither the nightingale nor the frog 'chan ni grazill / grondill.' This poem exists in six manuscripts. Three read *grondill*, adopted by Dejeanne; three read *grazill*, which K. Lewent, 'Beiträge zum Verständnis der Lieder Marcabrus,' *Zeitschrift für ro-*

the querulous complaining noted long before by Columella, Virgil, and Ovid. The Roman writers allude to the metamorphosis of niggard peasants (who would give no water to Latona) into frogs. Marcabru decries the present-day transformation of Angevin lords into mean-minded serfs ('seigner sers e sers seignorau' 39). Perhaps it is no wonder that the petty troubadours would seek to turn Marcabru's song into foolishness ('mi tornon mon chant en badau'). In doing so, they practice the unnatural *loquacitas vana*, their own style of frog-speak.

Man's failure to follow nature's law is the dominant theme of 'Bel m'es quan la fuelh'ufana' (poem XXI). It begins with an extended *Natureingang*, two stanzas rather than one, which depict the nightingale, frog, and owl singing (or making such noise as they can) to their mates. Again we have 'alarm' words to indicate a two-tier structure of meaning: the very foliage grows proud ('la fuelh'ufana'), the owl grumbles ('grondilha'), and Marcabru refers to the coupling of 'creatura *vana*' (13, my emphasis). Of course, the frog is charged with his usual *in bono/in malo* burden. The joy of these creatures, however, follows 'la via plana' (15); it is innocent and good. Creation carries the germ of symbolic meaning but is not infected by it. The infection is in the soul of man, whose joy stumbles ('bruzilha' 16). It is man who has a fox's tongue ('volpils lengua' 19); and while animals couple ('s'aparilha' 14), deceitful human beings desert their mates or send them into exile ('desert' ez essilha' 22). Exile, of course, is in Christian allegory the condition of the human soul separated from God's love, and it is the central metaphor in anagogical interpretations of Exodus. Marcabru certainly knew this. Does he invoke the idea here? The poem ends with an indictment of 'falsa gent crestiana,' whose pursuit of deceitful love makes the 'baptismes de Jordana' seem noxious to them. In their foolish sin ('crim pec' 38) they turn rather to 'Corrossana,' the desert land of Persia, for Marcabru a convenient (rhyming) name for the Near East apart from Israel, perhaps Egypt itself. It is in any case a land of the infidel or, one might say, of the heretic, and thus a land that overflows with frogs.

It is not surprising that the image of the frog reappears in the verse of Bernart Marti, a follower and imitator of Marcabru. Like Marcabru, Bernart is a moralist. He deplores the debasement of the world and the inversion of right

---

manische Philologie 37 (1913) 438, argues to be the correct reading, since *grondill* appears in rhyme later in the poem (34). Paterson 40 adopts *grazill*, as does Aurelio Roncaglia, ' "Lo vers comens quan vei del fau," ' *Cultura Neolatina* 11 (1951) 25–48. Even so, *grondill* is clearly a word appropriate to the frog, and the conjunction with the noblemen is therefore especially apt.

(poem II).[36] He attacks the lying forked-tongues ('lengua forquat') who prosper in this world. He chastises infidelity and observes that though it may flourish, it will bear no fruit ('si floris, non grana' 3.20; cf. Marcabru III). He warns that the lover who cheats on his partner should expect the same treatment. He condemns frivolous poetry that leads to folly and sin, and castigates boasting and vanity (poem V). He complains of the venality of the world (poem VI). And he relies on the authority of Marcabru to declare that money-grubbers, gossip-mongers, and calumniators will go to Hell ('Cels c'auzis a Marcabru dir / Q'en enfer sufriran gran fais' 9.27–28).

What is surprising is that Bernart seems not to invest the image of the frog with the traditional meanings that attach so readily to Marcabru's use of it. The two poems in which we find the frog, III and VII, do not involve social criticism. And they hardly champion Christian values. Rather, they serve to confirm Bernart's devotion to the gallant eroticism that Marcabru forthrightly condemns. In this regard, Bernart is fundamentally different from his mentor. Marcabru has what we might call a middle-aged view of sexuality, a responsible insistence that it follow right reason, that it serve the social good. Marriage is the lawful contract that keeps human sexuality in harmony with nature. Although Bernart parrots this doctrine in 'Belha m'es la flors d'a-guilen,'[37] his most servile imitation of Marcabru, he defines a clearly different moral norm in poem III, 'Bel m'es lai latz la fontana':

> Dona es vas drut trefana
> De s'amor, pos tres n'apana;
>   Estra lei
>   N'i son trei.
> Mas ab son marit l'autrei
> Un amic cortes prezant.
> E si plus n'i vai sercant,
>   Es desleialada
>   E puta provada.   (10–18)

[A lady is disloyal to her lover, with respect to his love, when she refreshes three. It is against the law to have three of them. But aside from her husband I allow her one courtly and worthy lover. And if she seeks more, she is disloyal (literally, outside the law) and a proven whore.]

Bernart takes a young man's view of sex, a view much like that of Ami in the *Roman de la Rose*,[38] which we may characterize as follows. The adolescent

---

[36] All quotations from Bernart's poetry are from Ernest Hoepffner, ed., *Les Poésies de Bernart Marti* (Paris 1929).

[37] The attribution of this poem is unsure; it may actually be Marcabru's, but Hoepffner iv thinks it more likely to be Bernart's. The poem appears in Appendix I of his ed. (33–36).

[38] It is noteworthy that *puta* ('whore') is the strongest sex word that Bernart uses; he never speaks of genitals. Marcabru, like Reason in the *Roman de la Rose*, uses much blunter language and does not recoil from plain words for sexual organs.

moral thinker demands honesty and equity in the affairs of men, but he must, in deference to his hormones, make an exception in the affairs of the heart. The sexual impulse, a natural force, has its own imperative.[39] The young idealist reconciles himself to it as best he can, but deny it he cannot (will not). He is compelled to construct an ancillary code of behavior, carefully circumscribed so as to interfere as little as possible with the ethical norms to which he otherwise subscribes. Thus Bernart characterizes his love as 'dous' amor *privada*' (9, my emphasis), intimate but also private or set apart;[40] and he longs to be isolated with his lover:

> Em bosc ermita·m vol faire,
> Per zo qe ma domn' ab me·s n'an.
> Lai de fueill' aurem cobertor.
> Aqi vol viurë e murir:
> Tot autre afar gerpis e lais.   (9.38–41)

[In the woods I wish to make myself a hermit, provided that my lady come with me. There we would make a cover of leafy branches. There I wish to live and die; all other affairs (of men) I abandon and leave behind.][41]

Bernart would like to return to nature, the source of his sexual longing. His 'dous' amor privada' pleases him under the flower ('sotz la flor' 8), and it is beautiful there by the fountain. But he sees a fly in the ointment, a frog in the sand ('pel sablei' 4). The frog may sing, but not when it storms outside ('fors a l'aurei' 5). It seems that nature is not entirely pleasant or receptive. Does Bernart follow Marcabru's practice of darkening the *Natureingang* to warn us that not all is sweetness and light? It seems that he does. The second stanza of 'Bel m'es lai latz la fontana' defines the rules of love, the criteria by which a lady is deemed disloyal and a whore. Stanza three calls for infidelity as the proper response to infidelity. In 'Quan l'erb' es reverdezida' (VII), one hears the frog bray ('braire' 6) when the weather clears ('temps s'esclaire' 5). And we learn that Bernart's lady has forgotten him (23), has

---

[39] The impetus of love is suggested in 3.51–59, where we are told that the hawk of fair semblance breaks its tether to fly to Bernart's lady, and that Bernart breaks his harness like so much wool thread. In the second metaphor, Bernart is the horse that in traditional symbolism represents the flesh and its appetites (see, for example, Beryl Rowland, 'The Horse and Rider Figure in Chaucer's Works,' *Univ. of Toronto Quarterly* 35 [1966] 246–59). However, the irrepressible urge does not reduce him to bestiality. In breaking the restraints put upon his desire, Bernart also laces his tongue in a kiss and laces words in poetry ('entrebescant / los motz').

[40] See Emil Levy, *Petit dictionnaire provençal-français*, 2nd ed. (Heidelberg 1923) s.v. *privat*: 'qui vit à part, isolé.'

[41] Gottfried von Strassburg, a more mature student of love, knows that such isolation cannot be maintained: Tristan and Isolde abandon their love grotto, unable to live apart from the court society that is so important in defining them as individuals and as lovers.

lied to him and played him false (43–46). In this poem the nightingale does not
sing, but shrieks and cries ('brayl'e crida' 3; cf. Marcabru 26.13, and see
Paterson 53).

Even so, Bernart remains loyal in love, and thus his responses to its exigencies
are fundamentally different from Marcabru's. Disappointment in love leads
Marcabru to abandon it altogether (VII) and to warn others against it: Let him
whom Love will deceive not make the sign of the cross ('Ja el nos senh ab sa
ma / Cui Amors enguanara!' 55–56). Certainly Bernart will not sign himself,
and he advises rather to let the deceived deceive! ('enguanat enguanaria'
4.32). The sexual instinct is given a freer rein, not a tighter one. Also, in
recognizing that love will never be free of deceit so long as the world will last
(40–42), Bernart simply accepts the fact; he does not rage against it as Marcabru does. 'C'est un peu Philinte s'opposant à Alceste,' as Ernest Hoepffner
aptly remarks.[42] Thus, despite Bernart's other resemblances and debts to
Marcabru, his borrowed frogs cannot sustain the allegories or suggest the
allusions that Marcabru's originals do.

This is not to say that Bernart was unaware of the possibilities, only that
he was in no position to exploit them. His frogs can do no more than indicate
that Love is not always a many-splendored thing. That frogs could do more is
suggested by a revision made in a poem mentioned earlier, Peire d'Alvernhe's
'Cantarai d'aqestz trobadors.' After satirizing twelve other troubadours, Peire
turns to himself (79–81): 'Peire d'Alvernge a tal votz / que canta de sus e de
sotz, / e lauza·s mout a tota gen' ('Peire d'Alvernhe has such a voice that he
sings both high and low, and he praises himself before all the people'). In
two manuscripts, line 80 reads: 'que canta cum granolh em potz' ('that he
sings like a frog in a well').[43] On the literal level, this variant derides the quality
of Peire's voice and thus contradicts the line that it replaces. On the figurative
level, it leads very neatly to line 81, for self-praise is a species of vanity and
vanitas loquax is precisely what the frog represents. Indeed, Bernart Marti
attacks Peire precisely because of his vanity. In response to Peire's 'Sobre.l
vieill trobar,'[44] Bernart remarks scornfully that good workmanship will not
salvage a song made out of vanity ('qu'om de vanetat fezes' 5.17); such poetry,
he says, is frivolous ('vers de leujairia' 8) and gives rise to sin and folly (9).
Indeed, such poetry is 'vers . . . de truandia' ('a song of lies'), mere fables
('faulas' 25) that are nothing but lies ('enteiramen lecharia' 26). Bernart's
language is reminiscent of the exegetical condemnations of poetry that we

---

[42] Ernest Hoepffner, 'Le Troubadour Bernart Marti,' *Romania* 53 (1927) 146.

[43] Paterson 40n4. For the textual tradition, see the edition of Alberto Del Monte, *Peire d'Alvernhe: Liriche* (Turin 1955) 127.

[44] No. XI in Del Monte's ed.

examined earlier. It suggests that the variant line in 'Cantarai d'aqestz trobadors' proposes a simile that is apt indeed.[45]

Our final examples of frogs in Provençal poetry are to be found in two *sirventes* by Guillem de Berguedà. Guillem belonged to the landed aristocracy that Marcabru had chastized so heatedly for its empty boasting and sexual profligacy. And he seems perfectly suited to the frog symbolism that Marcabru employed. Indeed, to a certain extent Guillem may engage that symbolism in his own poetry. If so, he wears the emblem like a badge of honor. He is, like Chaucer's Miller, a *janglere* and a *goliardeys*; and just as Robin might enjoy the sexual reference inherent in his bagpipe, so does Guillem enjoy the innuendo to which the frog lends itself. In an insult poem addressed to Ponç de Mataplana, whom Guillem nearly unhorsed in a joust, Guillem remarks that Ponç, had he any strength in his hand, might have killed a great lover:

> cel qe·ls maritz escogossa,
> lo cortes drut qe·ls corns sap far enpeigner,
> e non tem glat ni crit ni huc de gossa,
> gerra ni fais, ni barrieira ni pon,
> anz es plus gais que raineta en fon,
> que ses aiga non poiria estar sana
> plus q'ieu d'amor un jorn de la setmana.   (12.26–32)

[. . . that one who cuckolds husbands, the courtly lover who knows how to make horns grow and who fears no slander, no cry, no bitch's growl; no battle, no burden, no barrier, no bridge. Instead, he is more gay than a little frog in a fountain who could no more thrive without water than could I without love one day of the week.][46]

Marcabru, Bernart, and the exegetes undoubtedly would have regarded such poetry as sheer vanity — frivolous, boastful, and immoral. And though Guillem's frog is specifically a sexual reference,[47] it is not improbable that in using it, Guillem thumbs his nose at all the moral standards implied by the image.

---

[45] Peire was profoundly influenced by Marcabru, and if he wrote the variant line himself, he likely borrowed the image directly from Marcabru. If so, he enhances the self-deprecation already implied by the stanza.

[46] Quoted from Martín de Riquer, ed., *Guillem de Berguedà* (Abadía de Poblet 1971) II 116.

[47] It is worth noting that the frog is here probably a phallic symbol. The fountain in Guillem's 'Joglars, no·t desconortz' is clearly a figure for the vulva: Guillem has cuckolded three men,

> c'ab lor moilliers ai jon,
> et abeurat cen vetz
> mon caval a lor fon,
> e passatz a lor pon
> amdos mos palafres . . .   (4.22–27)

[for with their wives I have joined, and a hundred times has my horse drunk from their fountain and both my palfreys have passed over their bridge].

Perhaps for a similar reason he employs it again in 'Chansson ai comensada' (VI), an attack on the bishop of Orgel. Guillem writes the poem because he is, he says, at war with a cuckold and wishes to show that he fears no boast of his enemy (6–12). Guillem protests that the bishop, presumably an ally of the aforementioned cuckold, disturbs the law (of religion) with his wicked preaching, which is related to or takes the form of rampant sexual promiscuity. The righteous poet is scandalized by reports that the bishop nearly split a girl in two with his prodigious virility, and he proposes to castrate that false prelate and take from him his ring and crosier as well as his scrotum — all before the frog sings ('anz que chant la granoilla' 16). As Martín de Riquer points out, the song of the frog is a perfectly legitimate time signature for the arrival of spring,[48] but there are others, so we may assume that Guillem chooses this one deliberately and not necessarily because he might have composed the poem in February. The frog is a symbol of sexuality, of boasting, of false preaching.[49] Guillem wants the bishop cut short on all counts. As so often in medieval poetry, the symbolic function of imagery here takes precedence over realism.

It is precisely the tendency to symbolic expression that knits medieval poetry into a coherent tradition. In this essay I have tried to describe a skein of linked themes that binds together the 'frog' poems of four Provençal poets. If one allows for poetic originality and individuality of purpose — the necessary interstices between the intersections of tradition — then it is reasonably clear that the 'frog' poems do reflect a unified understanding of the image they share. One might complain that the poems show less interest in tradition than in innovation, more interest in the open space than in the reticulations defining that space. But it remains necessary at least to highlight the twine that surrounds the creative space. If I have, like Bernart Marti, snapped some threads in my eagerness to seize upon them, still I think the outlines of the tradition remain intact and remain relevant to the poems considered here. If in fact they are not, one may say that I have heard the frog sing and have responded in kind: 'et sonum vocis importunis clamoribus reddunt.' But that is for the reader to decide.

University of Oklahoma

Riquer, *Guillem de Berguedà* I 182, observes that the same meaning for fountain occurs in the Old French fabliau *De la demoiselle qui ne pouvait ouir parler de foutre*. Vincent of Beauvais (n10) remarks on the frog's potency: 'Ranarum coitus magis est de nocte, quam de die, & in eorum coitu magna est mora, multumque seminis effundunt.'

[48] Riquer, *Guillem de Berguedà* II 75, line 16n. Cf. Nicander, *The Poems and Poetical Fragments*, ed. and trans. A. S. F. Gow and A. F. Scholfield (Cambridge 1953) 133: 'the vocal Toad of the fen [is] the first harbinger of delightful spring.' Angelo De Gubernatis, *Zoological Mythology or The Legends of the Animals* (New York 1872) II 373, refers to the *canta-rana*, frog-noises made by children at Easter time in Turin.

[49] As a figure for the false preacher, see Jacques de Vitry, Exemplum III (Crane 1). Pope, 'A Sly Toad' 468n18, also cites John Bromyard, *Summa praedicantium*.

COMIC SCRIPTURAL ALLUSIONS IN BEROUL'S 'TRISTRAN'

BY ALFRED KELLOGG

Perhaps no lines in the whole tradition more poignantly characterize the tragic nature of the love of Tristan and Yseut than Beroul's:

> Nule gent tant ne s'entramerent
> Ne si griment nu conpererent.   (1791–92)[1]

Yet it is Beroul's sense of the comic that more than any other element pervades the fragment of his work we still possess. Beroul is justly noted for his realism, yet no matter how startling that realism, it is the flow of comic scene after scene which dominates the reader's recollection — the brilliant disingenuousness of the tryst by the fountain, the transformation of Tristran's leap into a kind of divine comedy, the famous ambiguous oath of Yseut and the extraordinary ingenuity of the plot which precedes it. These are the great examples of Beroul's distinctive genius. However, Beroul's attitudes are never simple. The scenes alluded to, with their strong element of broad comedy, do not adequately represent the full range of his talent. In the Brother Ogrin scenes at the end of the poem, Beroul can be so bitterly satiric as to assure himself a position in the great goliardic and jongleuresque tradition of ecclesiastical satire.[2] However, whether satiric or simply comic, what is notable about Beroul's scriptural allusions is their economy and their functionalism. Each has its own particular purpose, whether the illumination of a character, the deflation of a melodramatic scene, or the subtle denunciation of the practices of a great institution.

I

The first allusion to be discussed is contained in a few inconspicuous words more or less buried in the immensely entertaining scene of the tryst by the fountain. In accordance with a plot concocted by the wily dwarf Frocin, King

---

[1] 'No people ever so loved each other, nor so bitterly paid the price for their love' (*The Romance of Tristran*, ed. A. Ewert [Oxford 1958] 54). All references are to this edition. A second volume, 'Introduction, Commentary,' was published in 1970. They are henceforth referred to as Ewert I and Ewert II.

[2] For the 'classes' of 'goliard' and 'jongleur,' and the lack of distinction between the two terms, see the classic discussion of J. Bédier, *Les Fabliaux* (Paris 1925) 392–95. In his edition of *Le Jongleur Gautier le Leu* (Cambridge, Mass. 1951) 126, Charles H. Livingston shows himself in agreement.

Mark has perched himself in a pine tree overlooking the anticipated meeting-place of the lovers. However, the meeting-place contains a fountain as well as a tree, and Yseut is the first to make out in it Mark's reflection. In a speech of superb duplicity — replete with simulated sobs — Yseut bewails to Tristran the unjust rumors of a love affair between them which have been implanted in the heart of her 'courtois' lord Mark by the 'felon' Cornish barons. Most frightening, these rumors have now rendered the King so violent that did he but know of their present encounter, death — or more precisely dismember-ment — would be her reward (1–68). In the course of her attack upon the Cornish barons, Yseut points out their cowardice in groveling at the challenge of Morholt — the fearsome would-be ravisher of the children of Cornwall — and Tristran's bravery in meeting it. In the heat of her diatribe, Yseut prophe-sies the heavenly reward to be expected by these despicable creatures:

> So may they see God and his kingdom !
> They shall never look upon his face.   (58–59)[3]

Ernest Muret, the prolific editor of the *Tristran*, explains the fashion in which the evil barons will see God in a rather covert way[4] as an allusion to Jeremiah 18.17, which relates God's ultimate treatment of those who persist in evil con-trary to Jeremiah's preaching: 'I will show them the back and not the face in the day of their destruction.'[5] However, despite what might be termed the general acceptance of Muret's allusion,[6] does the Jeremiah text in itself — the simple turning of the back of God upon those who have refused to heed His teachings — possess the force to convey those aspects of Yseut's character which are here relevant — her absolute lack of sexual inhibitions and her relentless vindictiveness toward the barons?

As regards the first, unparalleled sexual frankness, Yseut uses language in what might be considered an over-explicit fashion. When the expiration of the 'lovendrins' brings the lovers back to Ogrin, Yseut does not simply confess to him that their passion has ceased, but instead gives an almost verbally ana-

---

[3] 'Si voient il Deu et son reigne !
   Ja nul verroient en la face.'

[4] For the editions of Muret, see T. B. W. Reid, *The* TRISTRAN *of Beroul: A Textual Com-mentary* (Oxford 1972) ix. Muret, for reasons of his own, instead of identifying the Jeremiah text in his notes, places the reference under 'face' in his vocabulary.

[5] Commentary on Jeremiah 18.17 seems to echo St. Jerome, *Commentarius in Jeremiam prophetam* (PL 24.798). His point seems to be the same as that made by St. Augustine in his commentary on Exodus 33.10–23. See below, p. 88. Translation here as elsewhere is from the Holy Bible (Douai 1609).

[6] Ewert recognizes the allusion, but his comment is concerned rather with possible gram-matical constructions than with the significance of the allusion itself (II 83–84). Reid comments upon Ewert's note, but makes no mention of the Jeremiah passage (*Textual Commentary* 10–11).

tomical description of the cessation: 'De la comune de mon cors / Et je du suen somes tuit fors' (2329–30). In her 'ambiguous oath' at the Blanche Lande trial, her language is rather more exact than her oath requires (4205, 4227). In her dress, she seems by preference unconventional. When Mark finds them in their lodge in Morrois, he is able to convince himself Yseut's conduct is guiltless because she is wearing her shift (1995). He is not aware that earlier she has put on her shift because of the weariness and disinclination of her lover, and her costume 'icel jor' was not customary for that part of her day (1995, 1804–10). In her actions she is even more unrestrained. She lies nude with Tristran in the King's own bed, as well as elsewhere (589–94), and at the Mal Pas her riding Tristran 'janbe deça, janbe dela' (3940) creates a sensation of her own planning.

Of her passion for vengeance, P. Jonin has given an excellent account.[7] From the time that the three barons incur her wrath, her hatred never ceases. Perhaps the most striking example is afforded by her emotions at the time of the proposed execution of the lovers by King Mark (866). When about to be burnt at the instigation of the three 'felon' barons, Yseut hears of Tristran's escape and rejoices at the thought that, even though she herself may be brought to the flames, Tristran will take vengeance. Thus will the barons receive their just deserts (1045–63). To Jonin's vengeance thesis might be added the fact that Yseut's passion for vengeance extends even to the forester who found them in their lodge in Morrois. When there is a kind of prefatory tournament on the occasion of her trial at the Blanche Lande, Governal recognizes the forester and runs him through, leaving no time for confession; Yseut, frank and simple, smiles beneath her wimple (4055–56). As Jonin remarks, 'There remains something of the primitive in Yseut.'[8] For the feelings of a woman so constituted, could the divine tergiversation of Ezechiel 18.17, performed for the benefit of the barons, be equated with divine justice?

There does exist, however, a well-known passage, which in language and in situation could have suggested itself to Beroul as appropriate fortification of and conflation with the Jeremiah text. This is Exodus 33.9–23. There God appears to Moses and speaks to him 'face to face, as a man is wont to speak to his friend' (11). However, this conversation takes place after the catastrophic return to idolatry of the Israelites and its terrible consequences (32.26–28). Moses is deeply concerned over the continuance of God's favor toward the people over whom Moses had been given command, and he begs for God's assistance in leading His people from this tragic place to the land God has promised. As proof of God's favor, Moses asks that God walk with them, that

[7] P. Jonin, 'La Vengeance chez l'Iseut de Beroul et chez l'Iseut de Thomas,' *Neophilologus* 33 (1949) 207–9.
[8] 208.

they may be glorified before all peoples (16). Finding God's reassuring reply inadequately exact, Moses asks that God show him His Glory (18). God replies that no man may see His face and live. However, He assures Moses that there is 'a place with Him,' and that he (Moses) shall stand upon the rock. He will place Moses in a hole of the rock and protect him with His right hand until His glory shall pass (22):

> And I will take away my hand, and thou shalt see my back parts: but my
> face thou canst not see.   (23)

Of this passage, St. Augustine creates an elaborate allegory, making Moses a type of the Hebrew people, and 'posteriora' those things which are to take place after the death and resurrection of Christ.[9] Commentary in general followed this interpretation. However, given the attitude of God toward the Israelites at this time (3, 5), and Moses' reluctance to assume the leadership as God has directed (15), might not the jongleuresque mind perceive in God's showing Moses His 'posteriora' an example of a highly derisive gesture of great antiquity and durability, existing even unto the present day in a recrudescent form?[10] That God should receive the three 'felon' barons in this fashion, rather than simply turning His back on them, seems more in accord with Yseut's 'Vision of Judgment.'

II

Beroul's second scriptural allusion is to Ezechiel 33.11, which seems to have assumed the popularized form: 'God does not wish the death of a sinner, but that he turn from his ways and live.' The allusion occurs in the most dramatic scene of the poem — the capture of Tristran and the attempted execution of

---

[9] Since Moses cannot very well be expected to see events which happened after the death and resurrection of Christ, St. Augustine makes him a figure or type of the Jewish people. By rearranging verses 21–24 of the Exodus text, he arrives at the following sequence. At the time of the Crucifixion, there was blindness in part in Israel (Romans 11.25). However, immediately ('statim') — and St. Augustine stresses this — after the glory of God (Christ) passed to the Father, the Israelites were relieved of their blindness, and with the descent of the Holy Spirit and the preaching of the Apostles, were able to see and be converted, and so to stand upon the rock of the Church ('petra'). These events following the passing of Christ are the 'posteriora' (*Quaestiones in Heptateuchum*, PL 34.647–50).

[10] The current term is, I believe, 'mooning.' A modern secular reading of Exodus 33 is to be found in John Gregory Bourke, *Scatalogical Rites of All Nations* (Washington 1891), where he refers to 'The interview between Moses and Jehovah, where the latter refused to allow the prophet to see the glory of his face, but made him content himself with a view of his posterior' (160). It is perhaps to be recalled that Chaucer includes a tale related by a miller who was 'a janglere and a goliardeys,' in which the heroine subjects her would-be lover to a more ignominious fate on rather less provocation (*Canterbury Tales* I (A) 560; 3730–39, in the *Works of Geoffrey Chaucer*, ed. F. N. Robinson, 2nd ed. [Boston 1957] 22, 53).

the lovers. After their exploitation of Mark's credulity in the fountain incident, the lovers act, as previously noted, with incredible indiscretion — they lie together outside and inside, most notably in Mark's own bed — where they are duly observed by the three 'felon' barons (594). The barons righteously demand that Mark restore morality to his court, and present him with a plan devised by the same dwarf Frocin, whose previous plot at the fountain had turned out to be something less than an outstanding success.

The essential element of this plan is to call upon Tristran, entirely without warning, to carry a letter, purported to be of the greatest consequence, from Cornwall to King Arthur in 'well fortified Carlisle' (650). The double traversing of the realm of Logres from one end to the other means to Tristran a prolonged absence from his beloved, and Frocin calculates quite correctly that Tristran will feel compelled to pay Yseut a visit before he departs. The plan is put into action. Flour is strewn on the floor, and Mark shortly after receives an urgent message which requires his withdrawal from the bedchamber. Tristran, lying on his pallet, observes the flour covering the floor, but also observes that the use of flour has certain limitations: the intervening air space is left entirely unprotected. He therefore projects himself with the greatest accuracy into what Beatrix de Dia properly terms the 'luoc del marit'[11] recently vacated by Mark. What he has unfortunately forgotten is the unhealed wound received in a recent boar hunt. So intent is he upon his pleasure that he is unaware of the blood he is plenteously dispersing, and its inescapable value as evidence. When he hears the King returning, Tristran makes a magnificent return leap, and upon the arrival of Mark and the barons is found vociferously snoring (643–761).

Regrettably, Tristran's suddenly conceived ruse is not successful against the plenitude of evidence — the lovers are apprehended and condemned without trial to execution by fire.[12] Hands bound behind his back, Tristran is being led along a path near the edge of the cliff to the hastily prepared place of execution. He is under the guard of two knights. At the end of the path, Mark is directing the gathering of inflammable materials for the use of his beloved wife and nephew. Circumstances would seem to warrant the conclusion that the tragic ending of the two lovers is at hand, were it not for an authoritative communication from the narrator to the audience: God is not unmindful of the lovers' peril. In His mercy, He does not wish the death of one of His creatures, even though he be a sinner. The allusion is to Ezechiel 33.11: 'God does not wish the death of a sinner:'[13]

---

[11] 'Estat ai en greu cossirier' (21), in *Anthology of the Provençal Troubadours*, edd. R. T. Hill and T. G. Bergin (New Haven 1941) 53.

[12] For the legality of Mark's act, see Ewert II 130–31.

[13] Ewert shows no recognition of the allusion (II 137). Reid recognizes the allusion, and provides the very useful reference to the Thuasne edition of Villon (*Textual Commentary* 37).

> Oez, seignors, de Damledé,
> Conment il est plains de pité;
> Ne vieat pas mort de pecheor.   (909–11)

As Tristran and his guards proceed along the path, they come upon a little chapel set upon the cliff and overlooking the sea. The chapel is elevated upon a mound composed of slaty stone. If a squirrel had attempted to leap from this slippery surface, the narrator assures us, he would have committed suicide (923–24). Tristran turns to his guards and beseeches them to permit him to enter the chapel. The end of his life is at hand, and much has he sinned. Surely they can allow him to pray for God's mercy. There is no way out except past them, since they stand with drawn swords at the only doorway (928–36). The guards cut his bonds, and permit him to enter. He rushes toward the window overlooking the sea, pulls open the window, and leaps out. He quickly makes his way to a stone, large and broad, set in the middle of the slaty surface of the cliff edge. From it, he leaps down. The wind rushes beneath his clothes, supports him, and drops him up to his knees in the soft, muddy sand. The narrator exclaims: 'What a beautiful act of mercy has God performed for him!' (941–60).[14]

What has Beroul accomplished by incorporating the allusion to Ezechiel 33.11 into the turbulent scene of Tristran's apprehension and escape? Perhaps nothing less than possessing himself of the hearts of his audience. The Ezechiel text is no ordinary text, stating as it does the infinite mercy of God toward sinful man. No sin is so terrible as to be unforgivable. The conception of the infinite mercy of God has shown itself to be highly acceptable to mankind throughout the centuries, both in Scripture and in secular literature. In Scripture, it is found in some five complementary texts, differing only slightly in language.[15] As regards secular literature, the popularity of the text has been

---

[14] This is an extremely difficult passage to make out. Ewert (II 138) points out that what is called 'Tristan's Leap' is actually the flat stone 'pierre lee' (948) from which Tristran makes his leap, but believes that 'u milieu' (949) means that the stone is located half-way down the cliff. However, Tristran leaping blindly through the chapel window and landing on a rock in the middle of the cliff-face does not accord with the realism of Beroul. It is more probable that he leaped through the window (945) and landed on the slaty surface alluded to earlier. Knowing that he could not leap to the sand below from this uncertain footing (note the earlier remark on the squirrel), he looked about and made his way, possibly on hands and knees, to the broad flat stone at the edge of the cliff. From this he made his leap. For discussion of Ewert's textual emendations and interpretation, see Reid, *Textual Commentary* 37–38.

[15] The five texts, extending from the Old Testament to the New Testament, are as follows:

Ezechiel 18.23: 'Numquid voluntatis meae est mors impii? dicit Dominus Deus: et non ut convertatur a viis suis, et vivat?'

Ezechiel 18.32: 'Quia nolo mortem morientis, dicit Dominus Deus; revertimini, et vivite.'

demonstrated in remarkable fullness by Louis Thuasne in his edition of François Villon. He indicates that Villon's lines in which he paraphrases Ezechiel 33.11:

> . . . Dieu ne veut pas ma mort
> Mais convertisse et vive en bien   (105–7)

are to be found in Rutebeuf, Jean de Meun, and Christine de Pisan. Thuasne further indicates the use of the text as an appeal for mercy in an actual trial. Thus Charles d'Orléans pleaded for the Duc d'Alençon that he not die but turn to penitence and live.[16]

As story-teller, Beroul ought to be well content. By the use of the Ezechiel text, he has produced a love story of immense human appeal, in which a hovering divine presence presides over the fate of two supremely devoted lovers and, despite their sinful state, protects them. What more? The fascinating quality about Beroul's artistry is that there is always something more. Sometimes it is an arresting realism, more often a kind of irrepressible comic spirit rare in medieval romance. Thus, when Agravain and Mordred gain Arthur's consent to trap Lancelot and Guinevere in the latter's bedchamber — the end being their destruction — neither the unknown author of the Vulgate[17] nor Sir Thomas Malory[18] is able to detect any element of humor in the situation.

Ezechiel 33.11: 'Dic ad eos: Vivo ego, dicit Dominus Deus, nolo mortem impii; sed ut convertatur impius a via sua, et vivat. Convertimini, convertimini a viis vestris pessimis; et quare moriemini, domus Israel?'

1 Timothy 2.4: 'Qui omnes homines vult salvos fieri, et ad agnitionem veritatis venire.'

2 Peter 3.9: 'Non tardat Dominus promissionem suam, sicut quidam existimant; sed patienter agit propter vos, nolens aliquos perire, sed omnes ad poenitentiam reverti.'

The most popular form the text takes is that of an extract from Ezechiel 33.11: 'nolo mortem impii; sed ut convertatur impius a via sua, et vivat.' However, the use of this version was by no means exclusive. Brother Ogrin seems to be alluding to Ezechiel 18.32 in his exhortations to Tristran on the lovers' first visit to him:

> Assez est mort qui longuement
> Gist en pechié, s'il ne repent.   (1389–90)

It is interesting that Chaucer's *Parson's Tale* begins with an allusion to 2 Peter 3.9 conflated with 1 Timothy 2.4: 'Oure sweete Lord God of hevene, that no man wol perisse, but that we comen alle to the knowleche of hym' (X [I] 75, in *Works*, ed. Robinson 229). The occurrence of the text in English literature is beyond the scope of the present essay. However, it has been pointed out to me by Professor Valerie M. Lagorio of Iowa State University that the Ezechiel text is prominent in the Coventry or Hegge play of the *Woman Taken in Adultery*, where the text is prefixed to the first lines of the play, and Christ opens the play with an address on the availability of the mercy of God to those who sin, and its unavailability to those who judge (see the N. Town text of the play, ed. David Bevington, *Medieval Drama* (Boston 1975) 460–69. Not all texts of this play contain the Ezechiel allusion.

[16] *François Villon: Œuvres*, ed. Louis Thuasne (Paris 1923) II 103–5.

[17] *The Vulgate Version of the Arthurian Romances*, ed. H. Oskar Sommer (Washington 1908–13) VI 269ff.

[18] *The Works of Sir Thomas Malory*, ed. Eugène Vinaver, 2nd ed. (Oxford 1967) III 1161ff.

However, in the comparable scene in which the plot of Frocin and the three 'felon' barons has exactly the same end — the destruction of the lovers— Beroul seems to lack appropriate seriousness. In the story itself, Tristran's acrobatics in attempting to evade the flour trap have little sense of the tragic, and his snoring to indicate the non-existence of his activities has something of the childishly ridiculous about it. In addition, there is present Beroul, the first-person commentator. Threading his remarks through what one might regard as some very turbulent action, he observes confidentially that things are going badly (748), that if the Queen had only had the presence of mind to take the sheets off the bed, nothing could have been proved against the lovers. This is absolute nonsense. How the Queen could have gotten the sheets off the bed, what she would have done with them, and what difference all this could have made — since Tristran's bleeding leg and the blood on the flour would still remain — does not appear. The audience is left with several muddled visual images which make comedy out of a potentially tragic situation: that of Tristran in mid-air and snoring, the Queen desperately pulling the sheets off the bed as the narrator says she ought to have done, and a benign God in the background miraculously preserving the lovers (750–56). One is assured in two lines of the presence of a protecting God — we are *told* He is there — but the presence which makes itself felt throughout the scene is that of Beroul the narrator.

The same comic spirit which enlivened what ought to have been the tragic capture of Tristran and Yseut becomes that of the Biblical commentator and logician. The same Biblical text, Ezechiel 33.11, which has previously conveyed an almost mystical sense of God's mercy, is also found capable of serving as the major premise of a comic syllogism. Beroul as scriptural commentator would seem to have much in common with Alice of Bath. Each of them uses the technique of quoting part of a text, and ignoring the rest. Thus Alice cites 1 Corinthians 7.3 as reading, 'Let the husband render the debt unto his wife,' thus showing the Apostle's deference to female domination. What she has omitted is the second half of the text: 'and likewise the wife unto the husband.'[19] Beroul follows almost exactly the same procedure with Ezechiel 33.11. Rutebeuf, Jean de Meun, Villon, and Christine de Pisan all follow the usual version in which the key word is 'mais,' or in the case of Rutebeuf, 'ains.'[20] God does not wish the death of a sinner, *but* that he turn from his ways (i.e., come to penitence), and live. Beroul quotes only the first part of the text: God does not wish the death of a sinner (911), which he precedes with an exclamatory passage on the mercy of God, and follows with a description of God's hearkening to 'le cri, le plor' of the poor folk for those dear to them being

---

[19] *Wife of Bath's Prologue* 130 (*Chaucer*, ed. Robinson 76).
[20] *Villon*, ed. Thuasne II 104–5.

taken to torment. This drift into eloquent sentimentality, immediately following Beroul's statement of the first part of the text, effectively obliterates the customary '*but*' which normally follows, and thus yields Beroul his major premise unqualified: 'God does not wish the death of a sinner.' When Tristran begs to enter the chapel, he makes clear his need for prayer: 'I shall pray God that He have mercy upon me, for too much have I transgressed against Him' (931–32). In other words, 'I am a sinner — and a great one.' What should now follow to make the syllogism complete is: 'therefore, God does not wish my death.' When the wind supports Tristran in his leap, it is clear to all that God does not wish his death.[21] The syllogism then reads:

> Major Premise: God does not wish the death of a sinner.
> Minor Premise: I am a sinner.
> Ergo: God does not wish my death.

Whether or not one accepts the existence of a comic syllogism, a very clear contrast is drawn between God's merciful attitude toward the unfortunate sinner inextricably entangled in the toils of love, and Mark's clerically sanctioned[22] view of what is to be done with his sinning nephew. The syllogism simply gives the contrast a comic, but sharply penetrating edge.

III

The three scriptural allusions discussed in the present essay would seem to constitute something of a tribute to the scope and depth of Beroul's artistic abilities. The first should probably be classed as comic scatology; however, although its purpose is laughter, a no less important function is that of displaying Yseut's mind at work, and giving some indication of what sort of mind it is. The second comes within the realm of satire, in that — as discussed above — it deals with the harshness of human ecclesiastical justice and the mercy of divine justice. However, it is so filled with scriptural parody and comic intrusion by the narrator that, although it certainly possesses a satiric edge, the satire becomes in reality secondary to the comic narrative. It is

---

[21] See Ogrin's confirmation of this (2380–84).

[22] Beroul is perhaps here making use of time in his own fashion. He must have been aware that burning as a punishment for adultery was out of fashion, but no one so informs Mark, as is likewise the case with Arthur in the fifteenth century, where Guinevere expects her punishment to be burning (Malory, *Works*, ed. Vinaver III 1165). Both authors appreciated a dramatic scene, but whereas Malory is constantly looking to a past age (see his remarks on love in the same scene III 1165), Beroul's immediacy gives the sense of a contemporary happening. To the present writer, it would appear that Beroul would like to see the harshness of an ancient custom color the ecclesiastical law of his own time. For a discussion of various aspects of the punishment, see Ewert II 143–44.

with what the present writer takes to be the third allusion: 'Blessed are they whose sins are covered' (Psalm 31.1) — the second Penitential Psalm — that Beroul the satirist fully emerges. His satire takes the direction of an irony suggested in the language of the text itself and readily perceived by a jongleur whose sympathies with Church practices seem to have been extremely limited.

After the lovers escape from Mark's bonfire into the forest of Morrois, they lead a hard life. Bread they lack, and venison is their food. For fear of detection, they sleep only one night in the same place, but their love makes them oblivious to their hardships.[23] One day they happen upon the hermitage of Brother Ogrin.[24] He recognizes Tristran at once, and without hesitation begins fervently to preach repentance. Despite their pitiful pleadings that it is the love potion which places them in their unwilled situation, Brother Ogrin remains adamant: without their repentance, he can do nothing. When, on the expiration of the power of the 'lovendrant' (2159), Tristran and Yseut leave the forest of Morrois and return to him for the counsel they have previously rejected, Brother Ogrin becomes a very different person. On the first visit of the suffering but impenitent lovers, Brother Ogrin has meticulously observed the letter of sacerdotal law — no one can be absolved who is not contrite (1391–92). On the second visit, the lovers return contrite, but in no religious sense — a fact which fails to disturb Brother Ogrin. They are sorry for their sins, but only insofar as these sins have cost them their worldly positions — Tristran as knight and nephew of the King, Yseut as Queen.

To resume their positions at court requires reconciliation with the King. Ogrin, who is only too delighted at the recalcitrant lovers' surrender to his jurisdiction, is not without a plan. In words which sound like a parodic rendi-

---

[23] The above is a composite of several passages in which Beroul describes the privations of the lovers in the forest. He starts gently. Immediately after their escape to the forest, he observes that Tristran is an excellent archer and hence provider of venison. However, their cuisine is lacking in salt and milk (1279–98). On their first visit to Ogrin, their life is described as 'aspre . . . et dure' (1364), but they so loved each other that neither felt the pain of that existence (1365–66). On their return to the forest, Beroul stresses the hardship of daily moving, together with their paradoxical diet of plenty of venison and absence of bread (1424–30). In their continued life in the forest, the hardships are the same — especially lack of bread — and their love is the same (1640–50). Under these circumstances the invention of the 'arc Qui ne faut' (1752) appears as a curious redundancy. It is bread they need desperately, and venison constitutes a kind of forced feeding. Their flesh becomes pale. The irony of

> Mervelles fu de buen porchaz:
> De venoison ont grant plenté   (1772–73)

is penetrating. Beroul's Morrois is not a fairy forest.

[24] For the character of Ogrin, see Ewert II 164–65, with references.

tion of Psalm 31.1, 'Blessed are they whose sins are covered,' he announces his plan to his broken-spirited clients. Through a very slight reliance on the 'beautiful lie,' their shame may be removed and their evil — i.e., their sins — may be covered:

> Por honte oster et mal covrir
> Doit on un poi par bel mentir.   (2353–54)[25]

These lines, written in a kind of childlike, rockinghorse rhythm, are, in the present writer's opinion, some of the most quietly — and savagely — satirical lines ever set down. Applied to any situation, they could not fail to be ironic. Placed in the mouth of pious Brother Ogrin, their effect is devastating. Who is the father of 'beautiful lies,' and what is their result? The answer is, of course, Satan, and the result is perdition. What is the prime symbol of man's fallen state? His inability to tell the truth, when the truth brings with it unpleasant consequences: 'Only God is true; every man is a liar' (Romans 3.4). As already noted, Brother Ogrin has, on the lovers' first visit, been the model of orthodoxy in his treatment of penitence. Now, with only a passing reference to penitence (2345–50), he turns with great earnestness to the carrying out of his 'bel mentir.' The first step is a letter to Mark. With astonishing facility he outlines an argument which Mark will not be able to contradict. It may be summarized as follows: Tristran has been denied a trial, as everyone knows. In this situation, fear for his life led him to escape. When, in the course of his escape, he came upon Yseut in her pitiable situation, he had no choice but to carry her off. It was he, Tristran, who had won her in Ireland and brought her to be married to Mark. She was his responsibility and he could not ignore it. Since then, they have been living in the forest. Should the King wish to forget his ill-will toward Tristran, his Queen will be returned to him, and Tristran will resume his position as loyal retainer or serve another king overseas (2357–2409). Very practical reasons guarantee the success of this argument. First and primary, no one will question the letter because he would then need to face Tristran in judicial combat. Second, Tristran's leap has become famous, 'Si com il est oï assez,' and is attributed to divine intervention (2382–84). Lastly, though not mentioned by Ogrin, ineradicably fixed in the hearts of the people of Cornwall is Tristran's battle with the gigantic Morholt at a time when no Cornish knight could be found to defend his own child (844–59). Then

---

[25] The allusion considered verbally would be limited to 'tecta peccata' = 'mal covrir.' Since this is the second Penitential Psalm, one would suppose that Beroul could rely on its familiarity for recognition by his audience. However, the 'honte oster,' the removal of shame, necessarily precedes, because in Brother Ogrin's mind the restoration of the appearance of marital propriety takes precedence over any other consideration. The 'mal covrir' he forgets about. See following discussion. Neither Ewert (II 203) nor Reid (*Textual Commentary* 86) notes an allusion.

Tristran's selfless acceptance of judicial combat with so dreaded an opponent could not have been more welcome; now, when it has become a question of his own Queen, Mark has seen fit to seize Tristran without trial and deny him the very right which was the salvation of the children of Cornwall. Viewed from any perspective, Mark's actions can only be seen as indefensible.

One point in particular is to be noticed about Ogrin's argument. He skillfully avoids the direct assertion that the relationship between the Queen and Tristran has been that of unwavering chastity. Ogrin's language nevertheless clearly implies it, even though Ogrin himself has every reason to know the falsity of what he is implying.[26] However, an implication does not make a reconciliation, and Ogrin understands this perfectly. The letter, a kind of 'bel mentir' in itself, is, however, only the first part of Ogrin's plan. The second part of the plan is physical. If a 'beautiful lie' is to be successful, it must be beautiful. With this goal firmly in mind, Ogrin proceeds to the fair at St. Michael's Mount, and busies himself — very knowledgeably — with the acquisition of a stunning wardrobe for Yseut. Precious furs he buys, silks and brocades, along with a gentle palfrey adorned in lustrous gold (2733–44). He spares no expense, nor is he disappointed in the dazzling appearance Yseut makes. Her scarlet cape being removed:

> Rich was her robe, and elegant her body;
> Bright were her eyes, and blond her hair.   (2887–88)[27]

The lie is indeed beautiful, nor does Mark hesitate to accept it.[28]

What conclusions concerning the character of Ogrin may Beroul's audience be expected to draw? A possible guide is scriptural commentary on Psalm 31.1 — the second Penitential Psalm — to which Beroul's 'honte oster et mal covrir,' as has been noted, seems to constitute a kind of parodic allusion. In the usual commentary, the first verse of the Psalm is considered to fall into two parts. The first part, 'beati quorum remissae sunt iniquitates,' is held to apply to

---

[26] Yseut is completely frank with Ogrin on this matter (2329–30). See above, pp. 86f.

[27] Riche ert la robe et gent le cors;
Les eulz out vers, les cheveus sors.   (2887–88)
For the color of her eyes, Ewert's 'Glossary' reads 'bright.' However, since Ewert equates 'vers' with 'vair,' and in the 'Glossaire' of the Langlois edition of the *Roman de la Rose* 'vairs' associated with eyes is rendered 'bleu,' this deserves consideration (Guilaume de Lorris and Jean de Meun, *Le Roman de la Rose*, ed. Ernest Langlois [Paris 1914–24] V 322).

[28] There is no question that Mark receives Yseut without hesitation, but Beroul has neglected to furnish us with a description of what ought to be a climactic scene. We are told that Mark has been yearning to see her (2642–43) and that he loves her 'forment' (2520), but at the moment Tristran gives his speech in delivering Yseut to the King, Mark suddenly turns to consult his nephew, Andret, as to what to do with Tristran (2869–75). Yseut's beauty is not noted until later (2887–88). On the above scene, see Ewert (II 216–18) and Reid (*Textual Commentary* 101).

original sin, which is removed in baptism; the second part, 'tecta sunt peccata' to 'actualia,' or sins committed after baptism. All commentaries concur in defining penitence as the necessary means of removing actual sin. Although the language of the commentaries is bare and dogmatic, one figure is to be found as a constant, and that is of sin as a wound. Behind it of course lies the parable of the Good Samaritan (Luke 10.30), and the image of Christ the Physician. In his *Enarratio in Psalmum 31*, following a reference to the parable of the Good Samaritan, St. Augustine addresses the sinner very directly concerning the folly of concealing sin from God:

> Leave the covering of wounds to God; do not yourself attempt it. If in shame you should desire to cover the wound, the Physician will not cure it. . . . Under the dressing of the Physician the wound heals; under the dressing of the wounded [sinner], the wound is hidden. From whom do you hide it? From Him who knows all.[29]

Gregory the Great makes the image sharper:

> If the patient covers the wound, how may medicine be made of use to him by the physician? If he begins concealing the wound, will not the wound, more broadly diffused within the body, fester? Just so, sin, unless it is laid open through confession, spreads fatally within [the soul].[30]

If one is to take this wound metaphor seriously, what Brother Ogrin has done is to turn his back upon the doctrine of penitence and use it simply as a tool to pry the lovers back into conformity with social propriety. Once penitence has become equated with submission to his authority, Brother Ogrin leaves the wounds of the confused lovers to fester. The contrast between Brother Ogrin, the meticulous observer of the doctrine of penitence, and Brother Ogrin, the proponent of the 'beautiful lie,' is simply too great to be ignored. In Brother Ogrin, Beroul's audience would almost certainly have seen a finished exemplum of ecclesiastical hypocrisy.

Yet it is difficult to believe that Beroul created a character of such complexity as that of Ogrin if he wished only to present a simple ecclesiastical hypocrite. It is interesting that Guillaume de Lorris created just such a character, 'Papelardie,' the personification of hypocrisy (407–40), in the *Roman de la Rose*. She is a simple hypocrite in that she does, with complete consistency, all that a religious hypocrite ought to do. Her dress is that of a

---

[29] 'Deus tegat vulnera; noli tu. Nam si tu tegere volueris erubescens, medicus non curabit. . . . Sub tegmine medici sanatur vulnus, sub tegmine vulnerati celatur vulnus. Cui celas? Qui novit omnia' (PL 36.266).

[30] 'Si tegit infirmus vulnera, quomodo illi a medico adhibetur medicina? Nonne si celare vulnus coeperit, latius extensum introrsum putrescit? Sic et peccatum, nisi per confessionem detegatur, lethaliter in intimis dilatur' (*In septem Psalmos Poenitentiales Expositio* [PL 89.558–59]).

religious, and to this she adds a hair shirt. With psalter in hand, she pretends to be lost in prayer. Despite all appearances — including that of fasting — her mind is preoccupied with malicious thoughts. All this she does out of vainglory — a consuming passion to possess the reputation of holiness.[31] Ogrin does not fit this pattern at all. One pictures him as leading a meditative life — a very comfortable meditative life — supported by wealth of some little consequence and undetermined origin. From his epistolary skills, we know him to be a man of some learning. When the lovers unexpectedly come upon him, he is reading a book, not thrashing about to look as if he were reading a book. Nor does he make any point as to the pious nature of the book. Ogrin, though living in less opulence and with clerical rather than chivalric background, seems to belong to the vanished class of hermit represented by Malory's Sir Bawdwyn of Bretayne, who takes in the wounded Lancelot:

> For in thos dayes hit was nat the gyse as ys nowadayes; for there were none ermytis in tho dayes but that they had bene men of worship and of prouesse, and tho ermytes hylde grete householdis and refreyssed people that were in distresse.[32]

However, there is a significant difference in attitude between Sir Bawdwyn and Brother Ogrin. Before recognizing Lancelot, 'leening upon his sadyll-bowe and ever bleeding spiteously,' Sir Bawdwyn knows nothing of the wounded knight except that he has received his wounds in fighting Arthur. Bawdwyn says:

> I have seyne the day . . . I wolde have loved hym the worse bycause he was ayenste my lorde kynge Arthure, for sometyme I was one of the felyship, but now I thanke God I am othirwyse disposed. But where ys he? Lat me se him.[33]

Bawdwyn has progressed into a spiritual state that does not distinguish one suffering human from another. He has no reason to care for an enemy of King Arthur, yet he does. When the lovers first come to Ogrin in their pitiable state — so wasted away that Mark is able to draw the ring from Yseut's finger without awakening her (2044–47) — he is without pity. As events later prove, to Ogrin there is a vast difference between the sinner who resists his counsel — penitence — and one who submits to it. Back into the forest go the lovers. Charity as Paul defines it (1 Cor. 13.1–7) is no part of Ogrin.[34]

---

[31] *Le Roman de la Rose*, ed. Langlois II verses 407–40.

[32] *Works*, ed. Vinaver III 1076.

[33] *Ibid.* III 1075.

[34] It is not that Ogrin can be expected to break his canonical vows by granting false absolution. It is simply that he has no love for the human being as human being, the creation of a loving God. There is no sense about him of the divine mercy which has watched over the lovers throughout. Making the law of the Church prevail is his sole consideration.

Yet, can Ogrin's apparently contradictory treatment of the lovers be termed hypocritical? On their submissive return, Ogrin's thanks to God for guiding the lovers to him — or into his jurisdiction, for he quickly assumes that they have come to consult him concerning their 'pechié' — do not sound feigned:

> Ha! God, noble king omnipotent,
> With good heart I render you thanks,
> That you have permitted me to live so long
> As to see these two people come to me
> For counsel concerning their sin.   (2333–37)[35]

God has granted him his chance to serve. There is no indication that the moneys he has expended on Yseut's wardrobe are to be repaid with interest out of the King's treasury. Here again was his chance to serve, and he has not spared his personal finances. Nor is there about him any sense of a search for personal gain. Brother Ogrin, very simply, sees his role in the world as the maintenance of order in accordance with the law of the Church. And in this he is completely ruthless. If maintaining that law requires the covering of sins, then blessed are they whose sins are covered, and more blessed is he who does the covering. To quote Jean-Charles Payen in his essay 'Lancelot contra Tristan':

> The passion of the lovers appears as the touchstone which reveals a disquieting divorce between divine clemency and the law of the Church. There, it seems to me, lies the true subversion of the *Tristan* of Beroul.[36]

Rutgers University

---

[35] Ha! Dex, beaus rois omnipotent,
   Graces, par mon buen cuer, vos rent,
   Qui vivre tant m'avez laisiez
   Que ces deus genz de lor pechiez
   A moi en vindrent consel prendre.   (2333–37)

[36] 'La passion des amants apparaît comme la pierre de touche qui révèle un inquiétant divorce entre la clémence divine et la loi de l'Église. Voilà, me semble-t-il, la veritable subversion du *Tristan* de Béroul' (*Mélanges de langue et de littérature médiévales offerts à Pierre Le Gentil* [Paris 1973] 621).

IMAGINATION, MEDICINE, AND RHETORIC IN ANDREAS CAPELLANUS' 'DE AMORE'

By MARY F. WACK

According to Rule XXX of the second book of Andreas Capellanus' *De amore*, 'The true lover is engaged without interruption by the continual imagination of his beloved' ('Verus amans assidua sine intermissione coamantis imaginatione detinetur').[1] This dictum poses as duty what the first chapter of the treatise offers as definition: 'Love is a certain passion born within, proceeding from the sight and immoderate cogitation on a form of the opposite sex, on account of which one desires above all things to enjoy the embraces of another and by mutual wish to fulfill all the precepts of love in the embrace of the other.'[2] As these and other sentences reveal, Andreas uses both 'cogitation' and 'imagination' to designate the lover's preoccupation with the image of the beloved, which, in turn, is inseparable from sexual desire.[3] As he explains at the end of the first chapter, once a lover has a mental image of the woman he desires, he begins to think about her figure ('incipit cogitare facturas'), to distinguish her parts, to imagine their acts ('suosque actus imaginari'), and to investigate her body's secrets; he desires to enjoy fully the working of each part.[4] The power of imaginative thought to prefigure love's pleasure is thus by definition essential to the generation and sustenance of the *amor* that is the subject of Andreas' treatise.

---

[1] P. G. Walsh, ed., *Andreas Capellanus on Love* (London 1982) 2.8.48 (= Trojel 312). Quotations of the Latin text will be taken from Walsh's edition.

[2] 'Amor est passio quaedam innata procedens ex visione et immoderata cogitatione formae alterius sexus, ob quam aliquis super omnia cupit alterius potiri amplexibus et omnia de utriusque voluntate in ipsius amplexu amoris praecepta compleri' (1.1.1 = Trojel 3).

[3] The equivalence of 'cogitation' and 'imagination' in reference to the lover's contemplation of the beloved is also attested by such statements as the following: 'Nam si ex assidua et immoderata de aliquo cogitatione cum delectationis actuum imaginatione suam in muliere amor non sumit originem, in aeternum novum alterius amorem non curabit appetere' (1.6. 559 = Trojel 217); and is also noted by Eugenio Massa, *Il libero amore nel medioevo* (Rome 1976) II 83n20 and Massimo Ciavolella, *La 'malattia d'amore' dall'antichità al medioevo* (Rome 1976) 102–3. Edgar de Bruyne, *Études d'esthétique médiévale* (Bruges 1946) II 230 points out the close relationship between *cogitatio* and *imaginatio* in Hugh of St. Victor's psychology of meditation. On the term 'imagination' itself, see M.-D. Chenu, '*Imaginatio*: Note de lexicographie philosophique médiévale,' *Studi e testi* 122 (1946) 593–602.

[4] 'Postmodum mulieris incipit cogitare facturas, et eius distinguere membra suosque actus imaginari eiusque corporis secreta rimari ac cuiusque membri officio desiderat perpotiri' (1.1.10 = Trojel 5).

Given the centrality of imagination to Andreas' analysis of love, it is worth tracing its roots in the twelfth-century clerical culture that provided so much of the intellectual artillery directed against literary love in *De amore*. The task is unusually rewarding for our understanding of the treatise, because imagination not only creates and stores images of hoped-for pleasures, but also provides the means of achieving them. According to the precepts in 1.6.16, 'eloquence often compels the hearts of those who do not love to love' ('Sermonis facundia multotiens ad amandum non amantium corda compellit'). The dialogues of the first book, intended to create the presumption of moral probity, develop through standard principles of topical invention familiar in medieval rhetoric.[5] Rhetorical invention in turn depends on imagination for the images and commonplaces used to frame the arguments of a speech.[6]

This essay suggests that Andreas Capellanus saw imagination as a way to integrate two striking phenomena of twelfth-century love literature, erotic desire and rhetorical inventiveness, and that his understanding of imagination was based on Salernitan psychology.[7] In addition to providing him with a psychophysiology of desire, Salernitan theories of imagination allowed Andreas to couple the sexual psychology of the new science with the principles of rhetorical invention to generate the lovers' dialogues.

I

Throughout *De amore*, Andreas demonstrates his familiarity with ideas on human sexuality found in Salernitan medical works. Although the corpus of medical and scientific writing associated with Salerno is vast, only a few works need be mentioned here. The translator most responsible for Salerno's rise to fame was Constantine the African († 1085), who translated Arabic medical

---

[5] Discussed by Wesley Trimpi, *Muses of One Mind: The Literary Analysis of Experience and Its Continuity* (Princeton 1983) 328–35.

[6] On the importance of imagination to rhetorical and poetic invention, see Douglas Kelly, *Medieval Imagination: Rhetoric and the Poetry of Courtly Love* (Madison, Wisc. 1978) and Trimpi, *Muses* 25–49, 87–163. For a brief summary of twelfth-century ideas on imagination, see Winthrop Wetherbee, 'The Theme of Imagination in Medieval Poetry and the Allegorical Figure of "Genius,"' *Medievalia et Humanistica*, NS 7 (1976) 45–64, and for a lengthier treatment, Murray Wright Bundy, *The Theory of Imagination in Classical and Mediaeval Thought*, University of Illinois Studies in Language and Literature 12 (Urbana 1927).

[7] I use the term 'Salernitan' in a broad sense to refer to translations (primarily medical) made in Italy in the eleventh century and to the writings those translations stimulated directly (e.g., commentaries). On the school of Salerno, see Paul Oskar Kristeller, 'The School of Salerno: Its Development and Contribution to the History of Learning,' in *Studies in Renaissance Thought and Letters* (Rome 1956) 495–551; Heinrich Schipperges, *Die Assimilation der arabischen Medizin durch das lateinische Mittelalter* (Wiesbaden 1964) 17–49; and Gerhard Baader, 'Die Schule von Salerno,' *Medizinhistorisches Journal* 13 (1978) 124–45.

works into Latin as well as compiled his own treatises based on Arabic sources.[8] One such text ascribed to the 'cursed monk, daun Constantine,' as Chaucer calls him in the *Merchant's Tale*, is *De coitu*, a brief, authoritative, and widely-quoted treatise on sexuality.[9] Of the many masters who taught medicine at Salerno in the twelfth century, two of the most important were Maurus and Urso of Calabria, who composed, among other works, influential commentaries on standard medical texts.[10] The *Prose Salernitan Questions*, circulating before 1200, were collections of questions and answers based on and epitomizing the teachings of Salernitan masters.[11] The problems on sexuality in the *Prose Questions* incorporate material from Constantine's *De coitu* and the works of Maurus and Urso of Calabria, and hence can be viewed as summaries of Salernitan ideas. This is by no means an exhaustive catalogue of Salernitan works dealing with sexuality or sexual psychology; nonetheless, I think they are representative of the sources of medical ideas underlying *De amore*.

Salernitan medicine was esteemed in Paris in the later twelfth and early thirteenth centuries, in part through the efforts of Gilles de Corbeil (Aegidius Corbolensis), physician to Philippe Auguste.[12] Gilles studied in Salerno and returned to Paris with a high admiration for his former masters, Urso and Maurus. Since Philippe Auguste may have been Andreas' patron, it is possible that he had access to Salernitan ideas through royal physicians. Other writers with Parisian connections, such as Alexander Neckham and Raoul de Long-champ, mined Urso's *Aphorisms* and *Glosses* for their own works, further indicating the importance of Salernitan ideas in Paris in the late twelfth and early thirteenth centuries.[13]

---

[8] See Michael McVaugh's article on Constantine in the *Dictionary of Scientific Biography* III 393–95 and M.-T. d'Alverny, 'Translations and Translators,' in *Renaissance and Renewal in the Twelfth Century*, edd. Robert L. Benson and Giles Constable (Cambridge, Mass. 1982) 421–62, esp. 422–26, as well as Schipperges, *Assimilation* 17–49.

[9] Ed. Enrique Montero Cartelle, Monografías de la Universidad de Santiago de Compostela, 77 (Santiago de Compostela 1983).

[10] For an overview of these Salernitan authors, see Karl Sudhoff, 'Constantin, der erste Vermittler muslimischer Wissenschaft ins Abendland, und die beiden Salernitaner Früh-scholastiker Maurus und Urso als Exponenten dieser Vermittlung,' *Archeion* 14 (1932) 359–69; Kristeller, 'The School of Salerno,' 514–19; and Morris Harold Saffron, 'Maurus of Salerno: Twelfth-century "Optimus Physicus," with his Commentary on the Prognostics of Hippocrates,' *Transactions of the American Philosophical Society* 62 (1972) 9–11.

[11] For the origins and history of the Salernitan problem literature, see Brian Lawn, *The Salernitan Questions* (Oxford 1963) and *The Prose Salernitan Questions* (London 1979).

[12] On Gilles de Corbeil, Maurus, and Urso, see John Baldwin, *Masters, Princes, and Merchants: The Social Views of Peter the Chanter and his Circle* (Princeton 1970) I 41 and 83.

[13] R. W. Hunt, *The Schools and the Cloister: The Life and Writings of Alexander Nequam (1157–1217)*, rev. ed. Margaret Gibson (Oxford 1984) 70–73. On Philippe as Andreas' patron see Alfred Karnein, 'Auf der Suche nach einem Autor: Andreas, Verfasser von *De amore*,' *Germanisch-Romanische Monatsschrift* NS 28 (1978) 1–20. Raoul de Longchamp, *In* ANTI-CLAUDIANUM *Alani commentum*, ed. Jan Sulowski (Wrocław 1972), quotes Urso on 48, 56.

Salernitan ideas on sexual physiology, thus easily accessible in the Paris of Andreas Capellanus, provide the physical basis for amorous practice in *De amore*. Early in the first book (1.5.1–5), Andreas discusses who is fit for love, and notes that Love's arms can be born only by women between twelve and fifty and by men between fourteen and sixty. After these ages, insufficient innate heat and excessive moisture hinder love. According to Salernitan medical works, properly balanced heat and moisture are essential for the sexual activity that, according to Andreas, is the goal of the lover's efforts (1.2.2).[14] In the *reprobatio amoris* of the third book, *physicalis auctoritas* teaches the dire physical consequences of indulgence in the acts of Venus — loss of appetite and sleep, with such resulting debility that the lover becomes *amens et furiosis* (3.57–61). In less sensationalized form, the Salernitan masters investigated the physiological consequences of sexual activity.[15] An even closer parallel occurs in the same passage. When Andreas claims to recall having seen in certain books of physic that intercourse causes premature aging, he may well be referring to Constantine's *De coitu*, where this information appears, based on the authority of Galen.[16]

The strongest evidence for Andreas' knowledge of Salernitan medical ideas lies in the quotation of Johannitius that has proved to be a long-standing crux. After noting that love deprives the lover of sleep, from which follow a host of ills, Andreas appends the following definition of sleep: 'Est enim somnus, ut ait Iohannicius, quies animalium virtutum cum intensione naturalium; ergo privatio somni nil aliud est nisi animalium virtutum fatigatio cum diminutione naturalium' (3.58). ('As Johannitius says, sleep is a resting of the animal powers [= the mind] accompanied by a strengthening of the natural powers [= the body]; therefore, deprivation of sleep is a fatiguing of the mind with a weakening of the body.') Since the sentence is not found in Johannitius'

---

[14] Constantine, *De coitu* 5, ed. Martelle, explains that heat and moisture provoke sexual desire; cf. also Constantine, *Viaticum* (in *Opera Rasis*, Lyons 1510) 6.1; Lawn, *Prose Salernitan Questions* B 6, B 16, B 245. On the suitable ages for sexual activity, see Lawn, *Prose Salernitan Questions* B 9: 'Queritur cum pueri calidi sint et humidi quare huic operi [coitus] non conveniant?' and B 174 (a discussion of sterility) 'pueri non emittunt sperma ante quintumdecimum annum. Ex vetustate quia iam deficit materia spermatis scilicet sanguinis. Deficiunt et virtutes post vero sexagesimum annum, dum etiam in mulieribus deficiunt menstrua.' Rüdiger Schnell, *Andreas Capellanus: Zur Rezeption des römischen und kanonischen Rechts in* DE AMORE (Munich 1982) 90–92, however, suggests that Andreas derived his statements on age and sexuality from legal sources.

[15] E.g., *Prose Questions* B 17, P 119, K 3, K 4; *De coitu* 11.

[16] 'Sed memini me quodam tempore in dictis quibusdam physicalibus invenisse quod propter Veneris opera homines tempore breviori senescunt, et ideo te ad non amandum precibus admonere contendo' (3.61 = Trojel 337); *De coitu* 11.

Isagoge, some have theorized that it may be drawn from Avicenna.[17] The line is, however, an exact quotation from an early twelfth-century Salernitan commentary on the *Isagoge,* repeated by Guillaume de Conches and later incorporated into the *Prose Salernitan Questions.*[18] Although there is no way of telling by which route Andreas learned of this definition of sleep, its presence in *De amore* shows familiarity with Salernitan medical ideas in one form or another.

Given Andreas' use of Salernitan ideas on sexuality, it is not surprising to find that the theory of imagination's role in erotic desire found in Salernitan literature closely parallels the love psychology in *De amore.* According to the Salernitan physician and teacher Urso, all the passions of the soul originate in the imagination and are completed in the heart.[19] He and other Salernitan writers moreover term imagination 'the appetite of the soul,' one of the four factors necessary for intercourse, the others being heat, moisture, and *spiritus.*[20] This appetitive imagination is also termed 'cogitation,' as when Constantine says that 'appetite from cogitation' is necessary for intercourse.[21] As I have pointed out, Andreas also equates cogitation and imagination, and his definition of love ('Amor est passio' etc.) leaves no doubt that intercourse is the goal of the lover's imaginative thoughts.

The imaginative origin of love and its definition as a *passio* are elaborated in 1.1.8–11, where Andreas' description of the progress of desire to action tallies well with one of Urso's discussions of imagination. In explaining how love is 'born within' ('innata'), Andreas sets forth his theory of erotic desire:

> Quod autem illa passio sit innata, manifesta tibi ratione ostendo, quia passio illa ex nulla oritur actione subtiliter veritate inspecta; sed ex sola cogitatione quam concipit animus ex eo quod vidit passio illa procedit. Nam quum aliquis videt aliquam aptam amori et suo formatam arbitrio, statim eam in-

[17] Robert Bossuat, *Drouart la Vache, Traducteur d'André le Chapelain* (Paris 1926) 82–83, followed by J. J. Parry, *The Art of Courtly Love* (New York 1969) 198; Walsh, *Andreas* 305.

[18] Lawn, *Prose Salernitan Questions:* 'Quare aliquis spermatizat in sompnis propter imaginationem et non in vigiliis? Responsio. Somnus est quies animalium virtutum cum intensione naturalium' (Ba 96, p. 186). Lawn notes the following parallels: Anon. *Comm. in Isagogen Ioannit.*; Guillaume de Conches, *Dragmaticon* vi (264); and Maurus, *Super Isagogen Ioannit.* The line is also quoted by Raoul de Longchamp, *Commentum* 52.

[19] Rudolf Creutz, 'Die medizinisch-naturphilosophischen Aphorismen und Kommentare des Magister Urso Salernitanus,' *Quellen und Studien zur Geschichte der Naturwissenschaften und der Medizin* 5 (1936) 73: 'In cerebro vero per ymaginationem seu cogitationem omnis animae passio sumit exordium, eademque ymaginatione peracta per reductionem spirituum ad cor in corde accipit complementum.'

[20] Constantine, *De coitu:* 'Tria vero sunt in coitu: appetitus ex cogitacione fantastica ortus, spiritus et humor' (1.1, p. 80); Urso, *Aph. Glos.:* 'vis imaginaria, quae virtus animae est appetitiva'; 'Ymaginatio enim appetitus animae, sicuti appetitus naturae et sicut illo natura appetit sibi convenibilia cibaria, sic per imaginationem appetit varia anima' (Creutz 119, 120); Lawn, *Prose Questions* N 1: 'imaginatio que appetitus anime dicitur'; cf. B 245.

[21] See previous note.

cipit concupiscere corde; postea vero quotiens de ipsa cogitat, totiens eius
magis ardescit amore, quousque ad cogitationem devenerit pleniorem. Postmodum mulieris incipit cogitare facturas, et eius distinguere membra suosque actus imaginari eiusque corporis secreta rimari ac cuiusque membri
officio desiderat perpotiri. Postquam vero ad hanc cogitationem plenariam
devenerit, sua frena nescit continere amor, sed statim procedit ad actum.

Urso outlines the same process in the more technical language of natural
philosophy. He explains that when we sense something pleasurable, the mind's
attention turns toward it, and the *spiritus* moves to the 'instrument of the
fantasy,' which is the first cell of the brain where imagination is localized.
Immediately imagination moves us to conceive the pleasurable effects of the
sensed thing 'with a thirsting appetite.' Once the imagination of the potential
pleasures has been completed, the *spiritus*, with the mind's attention as a
guide, is drawn to that member which has been designated as the instrument to
achieve such effects. Fortunately, Urso clarifies this involuted process with an
example. A husband, admiring the beauty of his wife and revolving her form
in his mind, is excited further with desire. So that his burning libido may be
satisfied when the imagination is complete, the *spiritus*, led by the mental
intention, races to the virile member to achieve the effect comprehended by the
imagination.[22] For both Andreas and Urso, then, the imagination's creative
representation of possible pleasures generates the desire that links perception
and action.

A great deal of *De amore*, however, chronicles thwarted desire rather than
triumphant progression to action. Although the suitors in the dialogues are
constantly rebuffed by the resourcefully argumentative women, they refuse to
take 'NO' for an answer. Urso and Master Alan rationalize such perseverance
in the face of obstacles when they explain the workings of obsessive imagination. Both ask: 'Why do we strive for what is forbidden'? In Urso's more
elaborate account, desire for the forbidden or the unobtainable, whether books,
knowledge, food, or illicit pleasure, leads to overestimation of its value as well

---

[22] 'Aliquotiens per sensum concupiscendo ad ymaginanda sensibilia incitamur, utpote
cum aliquae delectabilia sensu percipiamus, intentione mentis ad haec deflexa, spiritu recur-
rente ad fantasiae instrumentum et incitante virtutem fantasticam, statim ad concipiendos
effectus rei sensae et cum sitienti appetitu per ymaginationem movemur et ymaginatione
completa animae intentione duce spiritus ad illa membra trahitur, quae membra utpote
instrumenta ad tales effectus perficiendos sunt deputata, ut membrorum natura per spiritum
mota hos conceptos effectus percipiat. . . . Sic et sponsus sponsae pulchritudinem admirans,
ipsius formam mente revolvens in eius concupiscentiam amplius incitatur, unde ut ardor
libidinis satisfaciat expleta ymaginatione spiritus intentione duce ad virilia membra decur-
runt, ut eorum virtutem excitent ad persequendum effectum ymaginatione comprehensum'
(Creutz 51–52).

as to anxiety, physical debility, and ultimately to madness if the desire is not satisfied.[23] In addition, Urso repeatedly stresses the anxiety that accompanies the cogitation or imagination of the unobtainable.[24]

Like Urso, Andreas also highlights the relation of anxiety or fear to desire. Immediately following the definition of love, Andreas explains why it is a *passio*. Significantly, Andreas' definition of *amor* as a *passio* (rather than, say, as a *morbus*) allows him to exploit the broad semantic range of *passio* in his extended definition of love in a way that reveals its affinity with Urso's psy-

---

[23] Urso investigates the topic in Aphorisms 84 and 85 and their glosses (Creutz 118–20). Aphorism 84: 'Perfectione rei excogitatae natura quiescit, et dum eam perficere nequit diuturniori motu conata defatigat.' Aphorism 85: 'Quae autem ex se concipit aliquis dimittit facile, et quae ex alio per prohibitionem diutius servat.' The gloss to Aph. 84 reads: 'Nota quod iuxta formarum presentationem anima ad sui actionem exsurgit, et quiescit si actio excogitata completur. Sicuti alicui volenti studere in libris aliquibus eorum detur copia habendi, completo desiderio anima illico requiescit. Sed si quis unum ex his, ne inspiciat, prohibeat, iam quid in eo contineatur cogitat et quia ea prohibita ob magnam utilitatem aestimat, saltem nocere cogitatione attenta. Sed si eam rem saepius replicat nec investigatione ea scire valet, *anxiatur non modice*, ad cuius laboris remedium rem quam ratione nequit investigare multo violentius impulsus nititur comprehendere, cum ea sensu non cognita a sollicitudine cognitionis non valeat quiescere.' Another version of the same gloss begins: 'Hinc solvitur quaestio quare nititur in vetito anima.' The relevant portion of gloss 85 is: 'Et hac ratione nititur in vetitum, quia tanto diutius *anxiamur per cogitationem*, quanto diutius res desiderata cognosci sensu vel cognitione vel intellectu a sensu vel investigatione subtrahitur, et unde quia cum res per quam quis ad cognitionem incitatur, nulla cognitione comprehenditur, motui animae [unleserlich] non infigitur, propter quod animal magis ac magis *angustatur*. Unde philosophali ratione per animam imperantem ad hoc ostendendum sibi consulitur, ubi ne amplius defatigetur rem sensu cognoscere, quam vel ad modicum comprehendere nulla ratione valebat. Simili modo res ex alio cognita vel per se nota sensus complemensione placita desiderata et tamen prohibita, cum haberi non posset habendi desiderium amplius excrescit, nec concupiscentiae ardor sedatur, nisi abjectione rei sititae, utpote humore, extinguatur. Nam et cibus desideranter appetitur, qui nisi animali procuretur, amplius in non habendo *anxiatur*. Nam nisi sensualitas corporis incitativa [?] membrum per calorem membrum dissolvendo depascit et secundo consumendo ad interitum. Similiter omnis vis imaginaria, quae virtus est animae appetitiva, per spiritum ad aliquid detestabile imaginandum movetur, cum videat quae concupiscuntur haberi nequeat, ut desiderium compleatur ad movendum spiritum amplius incitatur, quo motu intercluso sic spiritus calefit et subtiliatur, ut suae motionis impetu occulta substantia aduratur vel substantialis humiditas penitus aduratur et propter hoc exsiccatione cerebri non modica illiciti amantes sequuntur mente desiderata volentes; cum ea habere nequeant, sollicita et sedula cogitatione maniaci vel melancolici seu ethici efficiuntur, qua causa nitimur in vetitum cupimus semper quae negata' (emphasis mine).

[24] Emphasized in the previous note. Alfred Karnein, '*Amor est passio* — A Definition of Courtly Love?,' in *Court and Poet*, ed. Glynn Burgess (Liverpool 1981) 215–21 quotes Aelred of Rievaulx on the anxiety resulting from concupiscence.

chology.[25] Fear (one of the traditional *passiones animae*) rather than the symptoms one might expect were he alluding to love as a sickness (pallor, insomnia, unstable pulse, etc.) characterizes the lover: he fears failure, wasted effort, gossip, poverty, parsimony; indeed, his fears are innumerable (1.1.2–8). Therefore, Andreas concludes, this sort of love is suffering: 'Est igitur amor ille passio.'[26] At the root of the anxiety, just as Urso explains, is the excessively high value attributed to what is desired: 'in the opinion of the lover, nothing compares with the act of love' (1.2.3).

Natural philosophers explicitly discussed the case of lovers who strive for the forbidden. Master Alan, who may be identical with Alain de Lille, notes in the *Prose Salernitan Questions* that imagination, which is warm and dry, is the appetite of the soul. 'The imagination of and appetite for a thing occur with pleasure,' he continues. 'Because of excessive pleasure, the *spiritus* is moved more greatly and more frequently and immoderately, as is the imagination, whence the first cell [of the brain, where imagination is located] grows warmer and dries out, whence greater imagination follows, and greater appetite. Whence we see lovers sometimes become maniacs because of excessive thought and imagination. Thus it is necessary to grant the desired things, or destruction follows, or severe damage.'[27] Imagination and excessive thought are thus

---

[25] See Karnein, '*Amor est passio*' and DE AMORE *in volkssprachlicher Literatur: Untersuchungen zur Andreas-Capellanus-Rezeption* (Heidelberg 1985) 59–71. On the semantic range of *passio*, see Erich Auerbach, 'Passio als Leidenschaft,' *Publications of the Modern Language Association of America* 56 (1941) 1179–96 and Eric D'Arcy's discussion of *passiones animae* in Aquinas, *Summa theologiae* XIX (London 1967) xxi–xxxii.

[26] Recent scholars have detected in Andreas' definition of love as *passio* echoes of a medical tradition of lovesickness (*amor hereos*) that entered the Latin West around 1070–80 with Constantine the African's translations of Arabic medical works (Rüdiger Schnell [n14] 159–65 and Paolo Cerchi, 'Andreas' De amore: Its Unity and Polemical Origin,' in *Andrea Cappelano i trovatori e altri temi romanzi* [Rome 1979] 83–111). Given the limitations of the medical tradition of lovesickness in the late twelfth century, however, I find it unlikely that it provided Andreas with sufficient material for his portrait of the workings of the erotic imagination. The few medical works on the subject available in the 1180s (Constantine's *Viaticum* and the *Pantegni*; the *Canon* of Avicenna is less likely) do not systematically analyze the operations of the imagination in relation to sexual desire. Not until around 1230, when Gerardus Bituricensis composed his widely-circulated gloss on the *Viaticum* did physicians include imagination in the psychology of *amor eros* (*hereos*) or *ilisci*, and not until the second half of the thirteenth century did imagination become a standard feature of such analyses.

[27] Lawn, *Prose Questions*, N 1 (275–76): 'Fit alicuis rei imaginatio et appetitus cum delectatione. Propter nimiam delectationem spiritus magis, et frequenter, et immoderate moventur, et imaginatio, unde plus calefit et desiccatur cellula, et spiritus magis subtiliantur. Subtiliati magis moventur, unde maior sequitur imaginatio, et magis rem appetitam imitatur. Unde videmus amantes quandoque maniacos fieri propter nimiam cogitationem et imaginationem. Unde oportet appetita prebere, vel ipsius rei sequitur destructio vel vehemens lesio.' Lawn xviii discusses the possibility that 'Master Alan' is Alain de Lille, whose work Andreas seems to have known: see Walsh, index, s.v. Alain de Lille.

equated in a destructive, enclosed cycle of desire and frustration leading to physical collapse.

The phrase 'we strive for the forbidden,' which occasions both Urso's and Alan's inquiries into imagination, is from Ovid's *Amores* (3.4.17): 'nitimur in uetitum semper cupimusque negata,' a line Andreas quotes twice. In discussing how love is acquired, Andreas remarks that some simple lovers fall in love because of external beauty of the beloved. But because these lovers are not able to keep their love hidden, evil rumors arise and they lose all opportunity of speaking together or meeting. 'In such ones,' says Andreas, 'love which is not able to seize its solaces increases immoderately and leads lovers into laments of monstrous suffering, for: "We seek the forbidden, and always desire what is denied."'[28] Although Ovid's line was a commonplace in the twelfth century, its association with the obstruction of imaginative desire in both Andreas and the Salernitan writers strengthens the probability that the former drew upon the latter for his theory of the erotic imagination.[29]

II

Andreas may have found the Salernitan theories of imagination and desire particularly useful because they integrated erotic desire with eloquence through the creative powers of the imagination. At the simplest level, the threat of madness and physical destruction provides the male lovers with a *topos* that they use with varying degrees of subtlety to persuade the unwilling women to grant their solaces. In one dialogue, the noble man says to the plebeian woman: 'If you send me away without hope of your love, you will condemn me to an immediate death, after which your remedies will be of no use and thus you will be called a homicide' (1.6.192).[30] In another conversation, the lover makes the same point in a less threatening, but no less manipulative fashion. Comparing himself to a sick man whose wise physician indulges him with food or medicine normally withheld, he concludes: 'Therefore the pains and continual suffering that regularly threaten me with bitter death as I languish for

---

[28] 1.6.7: 'In talibus amor, quum non possit sua solatia capere, immoderata suscipit incrementa et in immanium lamenta poenarum deducit amantes, quia "Nitimur in vetitum cupimus semperque negatum."'

[29] Hans Walther, *Proverbia sententiaeque latinitatis medii aevi* (Göttingen 1963) 170–71. Elsewhere in *De amore* Andreas mentions the intensification of love in the face of obstacles (1.6.361–64; 2.2.1).

[30] 'Morosa namque dilatio pereuntis solet amoris indicare praesagia, et modica consuevit mora eventus mutare fortunae; si me igitur tui amoris spe frustratum dimiseris me protinus mortem subire compellis, cui tua postea nullatenus poterit prodesse medela, et ita poteris homicida vocari.'

love of you forcefully drive me to request — irregularly and importunately
— remedies for this death.'[31]

More generally, striving for the 'forbidden,' or at least the unattainable,
initiates some of the copious rhetoric of the dialogues, just as it intensifies the
imaginative fixation of sexual desire. The *platea ymaginacionis*, as the later,
thirteenth-century anonymous author of *De vero amore* (based on Andreas'
De amore) calls it, is a place where multiple aspects of imagination dwell and
interact; it is both the storehouse of images and the space where images are
clothed with speech.[32] In *De amore*, imagination first generates erotic desire,
and then, anticipating the possible pleasurable or fearful outcomes, becomes
the locus of invention for rhetorical stratagems designed to fulfill that desire.
In the dialogues, the women's resistance, anticipated or actual, to the men's
postulations generates their ingenious, imaginative, and not wholly consistent
attempts to persuade. Eloquence, such as it is in the mouths of these men,
has its birth in imagination's unsatisfied desire. Paradoxically, then, the lover's
imagination is potentially both physically destructive and rhetorically productive. If its inventions are successful, physical destruction can be averted
through the fulfillment of all love's mandates. The dialogues of *De amore* thus
dramatize how erotic imagination can give rise to poetic imagination.

The opening speeches of several dialogues illustrate the varying ways in
which the lovers attempt to transmute their obsessive thoughts and images of
the beloved into *copiosa sermonis facundia*. The plebeian man who addresses a
noble woman in the second dialogue struggles to invent and deliver a request
for love that expresses what his mind has conceived. He clears the way for his
suit by appealing to a topic provided by chapter 1.5.1, which begins: 'Est nunc
videre quae sint aptae personae ad amoris arma ferenda.' The commoner asserts that since love follows nature (as it does in 1.5.2–8), a woman need only
consider 'an aliquis sit aptus ad amoris arma ferenda.' Having established to
his satisfaction that his class is therefore no impediment to their relationship

---

[31] 'Aegroto cui finalia videntur imminere praeludia assueta non debet ciborum diaeta
servari vel medicina regularis adiungi; sed quidquid eius desiderat appetitus assumere, quam-
vis regulariter sit eius infirmitati contrarium, misericorditer tamen hoc sibi sapiens consuevit
medicus indulgere. Poenae igitur continuique dolores, qui pro vestro mihi amore languenti
mortem regulariter minantur amaram, me violenter cogunt huius mortis irregulariter et im-
portune remedia postulare' (1.6.522).

[32] Massa, *De libero amore* 2.28: 'Carnalis autem amor, qui solum causa fornicacionis ortus
est, quia nunquam ad illud triclinium cordis ingreditur set in platea ymaginacionis moratur,
ideo faciliter ad ymaginandas formas corporeas amantium ca[r]naliter v[er]titur.' On imagination and eloquence, see Trimpi, *Muses* 289–90; Douglas Kelly, 'Topical Invention in
Medieval French Literature,' in *Medieval Eloquence*, ed. James J. Murphy (Berkeley 1979)
231–36 and 'Obscurity and Eloquence: Sources for Invention in Medieval French Literature,'
in *Vernacular Poetics in the Middle Ages*, ed. Lois Ebin (Kalamazoo, Mich. 1984) 33–37;
Frances Yates, *The Art of Memory* (Chicago 1966) 31–32.

('hac ergo invincibili ratione munitus'), he proceeds to his main point, though not without misgivings about her reaction. Should she contest his words, he says, it would be an 'intolerabile malum et omnium causa dolorum.' Struck by the arrow of love, he has tried to hide the wound, since the sight of her face so terrifies and confuses his mind that he forgets his carefully worked-out ideas.[33] In the strategy of this dialogue, then, the commoner's shaken *ingenium* not only testifies to his love, but also excuses the tenuity of his eloquence. But he bravely presses on: he has concealed his wound, but the pain has only intensified. His plea culminates: 'Vos quidem estis mei causa doloris et mortalis poenae remedium; meam namque simul cum morte vitam tenetis vestro pugno reclusam.' Finally, he concludes with the double irony of an unaffected modesty topos: 'I cannot reveal to you the individual points my mind has invented (*concepit*) to relate to you, but God himself knows what words the mute wishes to express.'[34] His rhetorical helplessness, his failure to translate imaginative inventions into effective language, bars him from finding solace for his erotic desires: the woman consistently demolishes his arguments. At the end of the dialogue, the lover nonetheless persists, still striving for the forbidden and hoping that at some point the woman will grant him a remedy for his pains.

The nobleman in dialogue E uses the contrast between outer and inner vision, sight and imagination, as a *locus* for his argumentation. His assiduous cogitation about the beloved, his treasure, constantly keeps her present before him. His fear ('For whoever desires single-mindedly always fears lest an adverse outcome thwart him' 1.6.198) recalls 1.1.2–8 and Urso's psychology of anxiety for the highly valued but unobtainable object of desire.[35] The intensity of the nobleman's mental preoccupation then leads him into an inexpressibility topos (199), and this in turn ends in an offer of service (200). But service deserves reward, and in formulating his request for grace, the lover returns to the topic of outer and inner vision. Although he now rejoices in her presence, in her absence only the delusive images of sleep give him solace for his pains (202). He desires to replace the deceptive consolation of dream images and obsessive

---

[33] 1.6.74–75: 'Visus enim vestri aspectus adeo meum perterret ingenium mentemque perturbat quod eorum etiam quae mente attente conceperam penitus obliviosus existo. Merito ergo meum studebam celare dolorem; quanto tamen magis meum conabar tegere vulnus, tanto magis mihi crescebat poena doloris.'

[34] 1.6.77: 'Singula quidem quae meus anima narranda concepit vobis aperire non possum, sed Deus ipse novit quos sermones velit exprimere mutus.'

[35] 1.6.198: 'Licet me raro corporaliter vestro repraesentem aspectui, corde tamen et animo a vestra nunquam abscedo praesentia; assidua namque de vobis habita cogitatio saepe saepius me vobis praesentem constituit et illum thesaurum, circa quem mea versatur intentio, cordis me facit oculis semper aspicere poenasque mihi affert et solatia multa. Nam, quod quis toto mentis affectu desiderat, semper timet ne adverso turbetur eventu.'

thought with more substantial pleasures, lest 'mortuo . . . frustra medicina porrigitur'; so noble a woman would not allow him to fall victim to his sufferings.[36]

Less crudely formulated than the commoner's, the nobleman's plea is also more effective, since the lady grants him face-to-face sight of her in order to prevent the charge of homicide.[37] The humor of the scene depends on recognizing that her compliance actually falls far short of his real desire. And this in turn depends on their different conceptions of what was at stake with the nobleman's images. Her answer — you may look at me — grants him outer vision to replace mental images. But, of course, his mental images, as his next speech makes clear, were not only of a noblewoman sitting decorously in public and conversing. His next speech therefore attempts to bring her to yield to his imaginative desires. To do this he returns to the topic of death from denied love, working it to the fullest. A second attack of sickness is worse than the first, and drives men to a harder death; it is more bitter to lose what we thought was granted to us than to love what desire alone hopes for. Although gazing at her will preserve him for a while, she must 'open the unknown road to the performance of all good deeds' or reveal to him the path of death (206–8).[38] This time she understands: she will never submit herself to the servitude of Venus (210). Her resistance to love then stimulates the full scope of the nobleman's invention as he relates his long allegorical vision of the Garden of Love.

---

[36] 1.6.201–3: 'Quando vero vos non possum corporali visu aspicere nec super vos constitum aërem deprehendere, undique contra me cuncta incipiunt elementa consurgere, et varia me poenarum incipiunt allidere genera, nullo possum gaudere solatio, nisi quantum falsa mihi demonstratione dormienti somni sopor adducit. Sed licet falsa me somnus quandoque largitione decipiat, nihilominus tamen ei affectuosas offero grates, quod tam dulci atque nobili me voluit deceptione frustrare. Talis namque somniculosa largitio mihi vivendi viam modumque conservat mortisve defendit ab ira, quod maximum munus mihi videtur atque praecipuum. Mortuo namque frustra medicina porrigitur. . . . Credo namque et plenariam gero fiduciam quod tam nobilis tantaeque femina probitatis non diu permittet me poenis subiacere tam gravibus, sed a cunctis me relevabit angustiis.'

[37] 1.6.205: 'Praeterea nolo ut solius sis aëris inspectione contentus, sed nostra specie poteris corporali visione potiri et opposita me facie intueri. Malo etenim ad vitae tibi conservanda gubernacula laborare quam mortis praestare causam vel homicidii incurrere crimen.'

[38] 1.6.207–8: 'Gravius enim recidivus quam initialis videtur affligere morbus, et duriori cogit hominem morte deficere, et acrius amittitur quod spe aliqua videtur possideri largita quam quod nuda voluntate speratur. Potius ergo eligerem momentaneo perire interitu quam multas poenales angustias mortis subiacere periculis. Deliberet ergo prudentia vestra et indagatione subtili perquirat quid vestro magis expedire videatur honori, utrumne spem amanti largiri et ab ira ipsum mortis eripere eique ad omnia peragenda bona viam aperire incognitam, an hoc denegando cunctorum bonorum praecludere viam et mortis semitam aperire.'

Andreas' vision of imagination as the nexus between sexuality and language is manifestly akin to the figure of Genius in Alain de Lille's *De planctu Naturae*, who mediates between the physical and intellectual levels of man's creativity.[39] Imagination in *De amore* is also broadly related to the Chartrian notion of *ingenium*, not surprisingly, since both Andreas — if I am correct — and the Chartrian poets assimilated the 'new science' emerging from the activity at Salerno, drawing particularly upon its psychology.[40] Such literary use of the scientific discourses beginning to penetrate clerical culture helps to shape *De amore* as 'an intellectually controlled, witty, and often satiric analysis of sexual love itself.'[41]

The alliance of medicine and vernacular literature on the subject of love was not, however, fully forged when Andreas wrote in the late twelfth century. This is clear in the rejection of the language of medicine as a suitable vehicle for discoursing on love (e.g., 1.6.458); in the refusal to pursue arguments depending on medicine (e.g., 2.7.48); and in Andreas' apparent reluctance to refer to the medical tradition of lovesickness.[42] *De amore* nonetheless begins to secularize the theological language that was the only vehicle available for discussing love abstractly; the treatise initiates a blurring of discourses that became typical in love literature of the later Middle Ages.[43] Its integration of eros and eloquence through Salernitan theories of imagination may well have paved the way for the later synthesis of literary traditions of love with medical traditions of lovesickness. That such a cross-fertilization has taken place by the late thirteenth century is apparent on the medical side in Arnald of Villanova's *Tractatus de amore heroico* and on the literary in such works as Cavalcanti's 'Donna me prega' and in Dante's *Vita nuova*.[44]

Gerard of Berry (Gerardus Bituricensis), a Parisian physician who wrote one of the most influential commentaries on the *Viaticum* of Constantine the African sometime before 1236/7, may have benefited from Andreas' collocation of medical ideas of erotic preoccupation with vernacular literary notions of love.

---

[39] Winthrop Wetherbee, *Platonism and Poetry in the Twelfth Century* (Princeton 1972) 202–11.

[40] Heinrich Schipperges, 'Die Schulen von Chartres unter dem Einfluss des Arabismus,' *Sudhoffs Archiv* 40 (1956) 193–210 and *Assimilation* 111–23; Wetherbee, *Platonism* 70; Eduard Seidler, *Die Heilkunde des ausgehenden Mittelalters in Paris*, Sudhoffs Archiv, Beiheft 8 (Wiesbaden 1967) 46.

[41] R. E. Kaske, 'Chaucer and Medieval Allegory,' *ELH* 30 (1963) 191.

[42] See *n*26 above and Karnein, *De amore* 59–71.

[43] Karnein, '*Amor est passio*' 217 and *De amore* 59–71; Ciavolella, *Malattia* 103–7. On the blurring of discourses, see Lee Patterson, 'Ambiguity and Interpretation: A Fifteenth-Century Reading of *Troilus and Criseyde*,' *Speculum* 54 (1979) 297–330.

[44] Ed. Michael McVaugh, Opera Arnaldi omnia, III (Barcelona 1985). On Cavalcanti and Dante, see Bruno Nardi, 'L'amore e i medici medioevale,' in *Studi in onore di Angelo Monteverdi* (Modena 1959) II 517–42; Ciavolella, *Malattia* 137–40.

Gerard's chapter on lovesickness (*amor hereos*) seems to betray knowledge of *De amore*. One of the symptoms of lovesickness listed in Gerard's treatise but not found in earlier works is the patient's inattention to anything but talk of his beloved. Andreas notes this same characteristic in the third book of *De amore*.[45] Moreover, in describing how the mind is disturbed in lovesickness, Gerard introduces a formulation destined to a long afterlife in medical writing on *amor hereos*. The patient's overestimation of the beloved leads him to think her more noble, better, and more desirable than the rest. Later medical writers, while adopting the general formulation from Gerard, tend to substitute 'more beautiful' for 'more noble.'[46] Andreas, however, in keeping with his preoccupation with class differences, insists that love not only makes an ugly woman beautiful, but also a low-born one noble in the sight of the lover.[47] Interest in the relation between love and nobility links Andreas and Gerard in another way as well. Gerard is the first medical writer to classify love as a disease of the nobility, recalling Andreas' discussion in 1.6.13–15, in which the nobility derived from moral excellence is considered the best reason for loving.[48]

---

[45] Gerard's commentary, *Glosule* (*Notule*) *super Viaticum* is available in the Venice 1505 edition of Gerard de Solo's *Opera*. For biographical information, see Ernest Wickersheimer, *Dictionnaire biographique des médecins français du moyen âge*, Hautes Études Médiévales et Modernes 34.1 (Geneva 1979) I 203 and Danielle Jacquart's *Supplément*, Hautes Études Médiévales et Modernes 35 (Geneva 1979) 92–93. The symptom in question in Gerard's treatise is formulated as follows: 'Ex parte anime sunt profunde cogitationes et sollicitudines ut si aliquis de alio [*var*. aliquo, aliqua re] loquatur, vix intelliget; si autem de eodem, statim movetur' (quoted from Basel D.III.6, fol. 24ᵛ, the earliest dated MS [1236]). Compare *De amore* 3.36–37: 'Si aliquis ei de quocunque facto loquatur, ipsius dictis intentas adhibet aures, nec precantis solet ad plenum verba percipere, nisi aliquid de suo referendo amore. Tunc etenim si continuo secum uno mense loquatur non unum iota de omni fabulatione dimitteret. Tanta namque aviditate suscipit verba de coamante relata quod assiduitate quoque multa loquendi eius nunquam fatigatur auditus.' The relation between Gerard's chapter on *amor heros* and imaginative literature will be treated at greater length in my forthcoming book, *Lovesickness in the Middle Ages*.

[46] 'Causa huius passionis est error virtutis estimative que inducitur per intentiones sensatas ad apprehendenda accidencia non sensata, que forte non sunt in persona. Unde credit aliquam mulierem esse nobiliorem et meliorem et magis appetendam omnibus aliis' (quoted from GonC 97, fol. 18 since Basel D.III.6 is corrupt here). Later writers who adopt the notion of overestimation but substitute 'beauty' for 'nobility' include Peter of Spain, *Questiones super Viaticum*; Bernard de Gordon, *Lilium medicinae*; and Gerard de Solo, *Commentum super nono Almansoris*.

[47] 1.6.181: 'Amor enim personam saepe degenerem et deformem tanquam nobilem et formosam repraesentet amanti, et facit eam plus quam omnes alias nobilem atque pulcherrimam deputari.'

[48] 'Heroes [glossing *amor heros*] dicuntur viri nobiles qui propter divitias et mollitiem <vite> tali laborant potius passione' (Basel D.III.6, fol. 24ᵛ). On the problem of nobility in medieval lyric (with brief discussion of Andreas), see Erich Köhler, 'Zur Diskussion der Adelsfrage bei den Trobadors,' in *Medium aevum vivum: Festschrift für Walther Bulst*, edd. H. R. Jauss and Dieter Schaller (Heidelberg 1960) 161–78.

Granted that Gerard's and Andreas' definitions of 'nobility' differ (socio-economic *vs.* ethical), the authors are nonetheless united by their localization of passionate love in a social or moral elite.

Since Gerard wrote in the same intellectual context of early Parisian scholasticism as Andreas, it is possible that he drew upon the chaplain's compendium for his amplifications of the *Viaticum*. It may also be the case, however, that Gerard looked to Andreas' sources, both Latin and vernacular, rather than to *De amore* itself. Either way, Gerard's *Glosule super Viaticum* show that within several decades of *De amore*, literary and medical ideas of *amor* had begun to converge, a development that may well have been spurred by Andreas' use of Salernitan ideas in his anatomy of love.[49]

Stanford University

---

[49] An early version of this paper was read at the convention of the Modern Language Association in Washington, D.C., December 1984. A grant from the American Council of Learned Societies and fellowship support from the Stanford Humanities Center aided the completion of this article. I would like to thank Theodore Andersson, Susan Aronstein, Nancy Benjamin, Steven Kruger, Thomas Moser, Jr., Roger Smith, and Winthrop Wetherbee for commenting on earlier drafts.

PERCEVAL AND PARZIVAL DISCOVER KNIGHTHOOD

BY ARTHUR GROOS

Salimbene of Parma, one of the most interesting commentators on the protean career of the emperor Frederick II, relates with obvious disapprobation a variety of *superstitiones* tested on human subjects by that inquisitive ruler, including the following experiment in the behavioral sciences. Frederick wished to discover what language and what mode of speech children would have if they grew up without hearing or speaking to anyone, 'cuiusmodi linguam et loquelam haberent pueri, cum adolevissent, si cum nemine loquerentur.'[1] He commanded the guardians of an unspecified test group to suckle and bathe their charges, but not to caress or speak to them, hoping thereby to ascertain whether they would speak Hebrew, Greek, Latin, Arabic, or the language of their natural parents. Unfortunately, the experiment failed, for the children were unable to live without the clapping of hands, the gestures, the silly faces, and the endearments of their wet-nurses: 'Non enim vivere possent sine aplausu et gestu et letitia faciei et blanditiis baiularum et nutricum suarum.' Commentators on this investigation usually cite an experiment of Pharaoh Psamtik referred to by Herodotus (2.2) or a later attempt attributed to James IV of Scotland; one could also include the extensive discussion from classical antiquity on, about natural language and 'wild' children.[2]

But it is equally interesting to repress such diachronic urges and investigate the medieval context of Frederick's experiment. To be sure, the attempt to verify a proposition by actual experimentation, a characteristic feature of his unique scientific mind, remains an exception. Nonetheless, interest in whether 'nurture' or 'nature' is ultimately more important, whether acquired learning or innate ability predominates in child development, is a frequent concern during the renaissance of the twelfth century, particularly in literature, where the communal and defensive focus of the heroic epic shifts to a new interest in the individual and his development in courtly romance.[3] Writers of the new

---

[1] *Cronica Fratris Salimbene de Adam Ordinis Minorum*, ed. O. Holder-Egger, MGH SS XXXII 350. For a recent survey of the larger context of Frederick's experiments, see Thomas Curtis Van Cleve, *The Emperor Frederick II of Hohenstaufen* (Oxford 1972) 317.

[2] See Roger Shattuck, *The Forbidden Experiment: The Story of the Wild Boy of Aveyron* (New York 1980) 41–46 for analogues, and Richard Bernheimer, *Wild Men in the Middle Ages* (Cambridge, Mass. 1952).

[3] See R. W. Southern, 'From Epic to Romance,' *The Making of the Middle Ages* (New Haven and London 1953) 219–57; R. W. Hanning, *The Individual in Twelfth-Century Romance* (New Haven and London 1977).

genre designed a fictional experiment similar to Frederick's, but less extreme in conception and outcome: a noble youth is raised by a loving mother in isolation from society, information about his name and background is withheld, and he is denied the education appropriate to his station and heritage. The situation raises basic questions in the nurture/nature controversy: What will happen when the youth comes in contact with courtly society? How far can he develop on his own?

This description epitomizes a common experiment of Arthurian romance, whose characteristic activity, the knightly quest, lends itself to presentations of the hero's search for his true identity and proper place in the chivalric world.[4] The most prevalent version of this type of experiment seems to be that of the Fair Unknown (*Le Bel Inconnu*), usually the adolescent son of a fairy (in the medieval sense) and an absentee knight (often Gauwain, the playboy of the Arthurian world), who leaves the fairy realm in order to discover his knightly identity and destiny. The 'sources' of the story are still debated, as are the relationships between the extant texts: Renaut de Beaujeu's *Le Bel Inconnu* (ca. 1200), Wirnt von Gravenberg's *Wigalois* (ca. 1210), the Middle English *Libeaus Desconus* (ca. 1350), the Italian *Carduino* (ca. 1375), and a variety of late medieval redactions.[5] Other Arthurian heroes experience a similarly isolated childhood, for example in Ulrich von Zatzikhoven's *Lanzelet* (ca. 1210) or the Old French and Middle High German prose *Lancelot* (ca. 1230).

The most famous — and probably earliest — version of this theme, however, is that of the Grail hero, whose mother retires from courtly society after her husband dies in knightly combat, hoping thereby to prevent her infant son from suffering an identical fate. Withdrawing to an isolated forest, she establishes a non-courtly 'alternative' community based on farming and hunting, and forbids her vassals to mention knighthood to her son, lest he be tempted to follow in his father's spursteps. When the inevitable happens and the youth accidentally encounters a group of knights, the meeting and ensuing exchange of

---

[4] See Friedrich Ohly, 'Die Suche in Dichtungen des Mittelalters,' *Zeitschrift für deutsches Altertum* 94 (1965) 171–84; Anthony van der Lee, *Zum literarischen Motiv der Vatersuche*, Verhand. d. Konink. Nederlandse Akad. v. Wetenschappen, Afd. Letterkunde, NS 63.3 (Amsterdam 1957).

[5] See the still basic studies of A. Menung, *Der BEL INCONNU des Renaut de Beaujeu in seinem Verhältnis zum LYBEAUS DISCONUS, CARDUINO und WIGALOIS* (Halle/Saale 1890) and W. H. Schofield, *Studies on the LIBEAUS DESCONUS*, Harvard Studies and Notes in Philology and Literature 4 (Boston 1895). The attempt of D. D. R. Owen, 'The Development of the Perceval Story,' *Romania* 80 (1959) 473–92, to derive the Fair Unknown stories from a Celtic source and *Perceval* from it, provides a typical example of extrapolations based on imagination. For a more reasoned analysis of the problem of 'sources,' see Christoph Cormeau, *WIGALOIS und DIU CRÔNE: Zwei Kapitel zur Gattungsgeschichte des nachklassischen Aventiureromans*, Münchener Texte und Untersuchungen 57 (Munich 1977) 68–103.

information trigger in him an irresistible desire to realize his knightly potential, and the hero immediately sets out for King Arthur's court. This, briefly stated, comprises the beginning of the Grail hero's career, left incomplete about 1190 by the death of Chrétien de Troyes, the brilliant founder of written Arthurian romance, and adapted in the early thirteenth century by Wolfram von Eschenbach, the creator of the genre's masterpiece.

Although the story apparently derives from widespread folktale types,[6] both authors experiment with the basic episode in remarkably different ways.[7] Chrétien renders the underprivileged hero's discovery of knighthood as a paradigmatic treatment of 'nurture,' i.e., the role of socialization in character development; Wolfram emphasizes instead the inborn 'nature,' i.e., the innate ability of his hero. At the same time, however, this reversal of focus is subsumed by a larger and more fundamental opposition, the hierarchical relationship between salvation history and individual development, between God and the world, *got unde werlt*.

I

Chrétien's romance begins with a carefully delineated introductory scene, in which the unnamed 'filz a la veve dame / De la gaste forest soutainne' (74–75) leaves his mother's manor one morning to visit her harrowers, whom he eventually encounters laboring at the high wood of Valdone (295ff.).[8] The course of true narrative, however, never did run true, and this scene is no exception. The hero's sojourn is interrupted by a posse of five knights; and his seemingly irrelevant responses to their questions interrupt in turn their hot pursuit of several fugitives.[9] The scene comprises three sections, each with a different focus: [1] the hero's departure and reaction to the approach of armed knights (69–158), [2] the moment of their actual encounter (159–81), and [3]

---

[6] See Wolfgang Mohr, 'Parzival und die Ritter: Von einfacher Form zum Ritterepos,' *Fabula* 1 (1958) 201–13; Dennis Green, 'Parzival's Departure — Folktale and Romance,' *Frühmittelalterliche Studien* 14 (1980) 352–409.

[7] In addition to the works cited in n5, see Karl Bertau, 'Versuch über den späten Chrestien und die Anfänge Wolframs,' in *Probleme mittelhochdeutscher Erzählformen*, edd. Peter Ganz and Werner Schröder (Berlin 1972) 85–106; rpt. in Bertau, *Wolfram von Eschenbach: Neun Versuche* (Munich 1983) 24–59, esp. 40–47. More specialized work and earlier approaches to the comparison are cited in the notes to all three essays.

[8] Cited from the ed. of Alfons Hilka, *Der Percevalroman (Li Contes del Graal)*, Christian von Troyes sämtliche erhaltene Werke 5 (Halle/Saale 1932).

[9] On this scene, see esp. Peter Haidu, *Aesthetic Distance in Chrétien de Troyes: Irony and Comedy in* CLIGÈS *and* PERCEVAL (Geneva 1968) 113–26; Rupert T. Pickens, *The Welsh Knight: Paradoxicality in Chrétien's* CONTE DEL GRAAL, French Forum Monographs 6 (Lexington, Ky. 1977) 71–88.

the lengthy mutual interrogation that finally concludes with the continuation of their respective journeys (182–361/64).

The action of the romance commences with a *Natureingang* or nature-introduction describing the joys of a spring morning,

> Ce fu au tans qu'arbre florissent,
> Fuellent boschage, pré verdissent
> Et cil oisel an lor latin
> Doucemant chantent au matin
> Et tote riens de joie anflame . . .   (69–73)

to which the youth responds spontaneously:

> Et maintenant li cuers del vantre
> Por le douz tans li resjoï,
> Et por le chant que il oï
> Des oisiaus qui joie feisoient:
> Totes cez choses li pleisoient.   (86–90)

The close verbal parallels between external and internal, between the objective natural setting, '*Et tote riens* de joie anflame' (73) and a subjective reaction to it, '*Totes cez choses* li pleisoient' (90), implies a pre-conscious state of wholeness in which the nameless hero is a still undifferentiated member of the natural world. At the same time, the similarity of this *Natureingang* to common motifs of the courtly love lyric (such as the expansive heart) draws attention to the larger range of social and corresponding literary expectations that will be raised during the course of this scene. The introductory pastoral mode foreshadows the world of courtly romance into which Perceval will soon be assimilated.[10]

The simpler, pastoral harmony of this world is immediately disturbed by a 'mout grant noise' (103), a cacophony of unfamiliar knightly artifacts intruding upon the joyful sounds of spring. Knightly society impinges upon the natural scene in two parallel and increasingly detailed stages. Each proceeds from a description of external action to the youth's responses, emphasizing the interruption of Perceval's forest journey and focusing our attention on his reactions, first to hearing and then to seeing armed knights on horseback for the first time. The whole is a masterpiece of rhetorical brilliance which reflects Chrétien's clerical delight in manipulating his material.[11]

The first of these two stages (100–24) begins by identifying the source of the intrusion, five armed knights (101–2), and the hero's mode of perception, 'il oï' (100). In accordance with the rapid approach of the intruders and its vivid impression on the youth, the ensuing lines dilate upon this initial description

---

[10] In fact, subsequent revelations by the narrative suggest a political significance to the mother's domain that is far from primitive. See Pickens 71–73.

[11] Cf. Bertau 40–42, 48–49.

by means of the rhetorical technique of progressive amplification. The narrator explains the noise in general terms as emanating from the arms of the approaching figures, 'Et mout grant noise demenoient / Les armes de çaus qui venoient' (103–4). He then becomes more precise, specifying the oaks and hornbeams against which those arms resound, 'Car sovant hurtoient as armes / Li rain des chasnes et des charmes' (105–6), before identifying the particular components of knightly equipment — lances, shields, and hauberks (leitmotifs of the entire scene, as we shall see) — and the noises particular to them:

> Les lances as escuz hurtoient,
> Et tuit li hauberc fremilloient;
> Sonoit li fuz, sonoit li fers
> Et des escuz et des haubers.   (107–10)

A further reference to the hero's incomplete sensory perceptions, 'li vaslez ot et ne voit pas' (111), introduces his inaccurate subjective response in an interior monologue, which proceeds deductively from his mother's instructions to associate these sounds with devils (115).

When the knights finally come into view, the narrator repeats the entire process of progressive amplification and subjective response, which is now based on sight. This second stage of the process (125–59) begins again with a general reference to the intruders and the hero's perception, 'il les veïst' (126). It also becomes more specific, 'il les vit an apert / Que del bois furent descovert' (127–28), proceeding to catalogue ('et') precisely what the hero sees ('et vit' . . . 'et vit') — the lances, shields, and hauberks that he has just heard, as well as the colors particular to them:

> Et vit les haubers fremianz
> Et les hiaumes clers et luisanz
> Et les lances et les escuz
> Que onques mes n'avoit veüz,
> Et vit le vert et le vermoil
> Reluire contre le soloil
> Et l'or et l'azur et l'arjant . . .   (129–35)

The description of Perceval's response again introduces an interior monologue that deductively associates his sensory perceptions with the instruction of his mother. In accordance with the rhetorical drama of this scene as well as with the narrative's emphasis on the hero's ignorance of external reality, the monologue expands through two deliberations, the first (137–45) identifying what he now sees with the opposite of what he heard,[12] 'Ce sont ange que je voi ci' (138), the second (146–54) escalating this assessment to include the supreme being: 'Ci voi je Damedeu' (146). Both provide a

---

[12] The opposite associations via sound and sight are not gratuitous: much medieval folklore associates the devil with noise and angels with luminescence.

further example of Perceval's inability to associate unfamiliar things or forms of behavior with their meaning.

The actual meeting between Perceval and the knights — a medieval 'close encounter of the third kind' — narrows the focus on the *folie* of the hero and prepares for the social comedy of their mutual interrogation. Having misassociated unfamiliar *signantia* with unknown *signata*, sounds and sights with the extremes of creation, with devils and angels as well as God, the youth proceeds to misapply the ultimate conclusion to a received form of behavior, throwing himself to the ground and reciting *all* the creed and prayers he knows (156–58). This extreme form of behavior in turn causes a misapprehension by the knights, who assume that the youth might die of fright. Their first exchange initiates a process of mutual correction in which the assumptions of the one are negated by the other: the knights' assumption of Perceval's fear by his 'Non ai je [peor]' (172), his 'Estes vos Deus?' by their emphatic 'Nenil' (174). The open-ended reformulation and positive response in one lapidary line, '"Qui estes dons?" — "Chevaliers sui"' (175), narrows the cosmic confusion to a courtly comedy of errors.

The implications of this process extend not only into the hilarious exchange that follows, but reverberate throughout the entire romance. Chrétien's dialectic of humor initially plays both sides off against each other, revealing the hero's total ignorance of knightly society as well as the knights' unexamined assumptions about it. The narrator provides us first with a preliminary but partial understanding of Perceval's misconception of the approaching knights (132), which the hero soon confirms: he has neither seen nor heard of them before: '"ne nul *n'an vi* / N'onques mes parler *n'an oï*"' (177–78). We now understand the constant emphasis on the hero's sensory perceptions. According to a widespread medieval theory of psychology, perception depends primarily upon the action of external sensory impressions on the mind, which stimulate it to match them with images stored in the memory.[13] Having no courtly *imaginatio*, i.e., no already acquired store of externally received images to match with what he perceives, the hero can only engage in free association. Perceval's development therefore begins by establishing a repository of images that enable him to function in knightly society — hence the importance of things and their names, such as the lances, shields, and hauberks that have already been introduced as leitmotifs of the encounter. The fact that the

---

[13] The basic classical and patristic sources for this idea are Boethius, *De consolatio Philosophiae* 5. Met. 4.33–40: 'Cum uel lux oculos ferit / uel uox auribus instrepit: / Tum mentis uigor excitus / quas intus species tenet / ad motus similes uocans / notis applicat exteris / introrsumque reconditis / formis miscet imagines' (CCL 94.98–99), and St. Augustine, *De Trinitate*, Book 11 (CCL 50.332–55). For a survey, see E. Ruth Harvey, *The Inward Wits: Psychological Theory in the Middle Ages and the Renaissance* (London 1975).

knights themselves are also uncertain about the true relationship between signifiers and things in turn calls into question the ontological grounding of courtly society. To be sure, Perceval will — as this scene reveals — rapidly become socialized in their culture, but this preliminary success will soon be found wanting at the Grail castle. The religious confusion that began his encounter with knights ultimately proves to have introduced the determining factor in his career.

The final and longest segment of the encounter between Perceval and the knights, a delightful mutual interrogation, introduces us to the course of these developments. Its humor can be related theoretically to Henri Bergson's category of comedy designated as the 'interférence des series' as well as generically to a variety of analogues in medieval *Schwank* literature and folk-tales.[14] In this particular version of that structure, Perceval frustrates the knight's request for information by responding with a question about the knight's armor instead. In spite of the knight's repetition of his question in four subsequent and increasingly insistent attempts to force Perceval's attention back to his request, ranging from 'mes . . . me respont' or 'di moi' (209 and 255) to 'mais *or* me *redi*' (291), the hero does not desist from his own questions until his single-minded curiosity is satisfied. The broad humor of this frustrating exchange of non sequiturs soon proves to be subversive as well. Although the knight and Perceval assume a relationship of authority and subservience that is maintained in their forms of address, 'vaslez' or 'tu' and 'sir' or 'vos' respectively, the course of the conversation actually questions this relationship. Whereas the *vaslez'* incongruous questions seem ignorant or foolish (200, 245–48), they gradually reveal a wily self-interest, eliciting information about knightly weapons that enables him to judge their effectiveness and potential threat to his way of life (202–7, 273–76). At the same time, the knight's superior knowledge and condescending responses to Perceval's questions gradually reveal a touch of foolishness in his pompous restating of the obvious (195–97, 236–41).

The exchange reveals the hero to be literal-minded and the knight to be metaphorically inclined. Perceval's literalness conflates the relationship between things and names, which leads to the assumption that his interlocutor's name is 'Knight' (190) and that one can be 'made' (181, 333) or transformed (285) into a knight like some artifact. It also reveals that the relationship between signifiers and things signified in any society is often arbitrary and based on conventions which are not entirely free of incongruity. Chrétien illustrates the point three times with the now familiar three pieces of knightly equipment, beginning with the lance. Since Perceval is an expert at throwing

14 On the comedy, see Haidu (*n*8) 120ff.; on Schwank-motifs, see Mohr (*n*5) 203–4.

('lancier' 95) a javelot, which the narrator emphasizes at the outset of his journey by a series of warm-up tosses in rhetorically complete but impractical directions ('*lançant* / Une ore arriere et autre avant, / Une ore an bas et autre an haut' 97–99), he is surprised to discover that a lance is not thrown but used to strike a blow. The knight, who has apparently never thought about the etymology of his weapon (a rather striking anomaly in a culture whose basic encyclopedia is Isidore of Seville's *Etymologiae*), is equally surprised to discover that anyone would assume that a lance should be *lancee*, a discrepancy that Chrétien emphasizes by means of *annominatio*:

> 'Jel te dirai: ce est ma *lance.*'
> 'Dites vos' fet il, 'qu'an la *lance*
> Si con je faz mes javeloz?'
> 'Nenil, vaslez, tu es toz soz,
> Einz an fiert an tot demanois.'   (197–201)

Similarly, the fact that what a knight carries in his hand 'is called' a shield, 'Escuz a non ce que je port' (224), causes Perceval to question the separation of the name from the thing, 'Escuz a non?' (225), and the knight to dissociate its significance entirely from the thing, embarking on a flight of feudal allegory that attributes to the shield the 'bone foi' and 'servises' of a trusty vassal (227–30). Finally, the knight transfers his metaphorical inclinations from the feudal to the futile, bathetically asserting that a hauberk is as heavy as iron because it is made of iron, i.e., making a meaningless comparison of a thing with itself: 'Vaslez, c'est mes haubers, / S'est aussi pesanz come fers, / Qu'il est de fer' (263–65).[15]

This playful dialectic between the literal and the metaphorical frames the beginning of Perceval's career, illustrating the gap between the hero's un-cultured ignorance, which makes him appear less than human, even beast-like, to condescending courtly observers (244–48), and the knight's unexamined familiarity with the arbitrary *lois* that govern all societal activity from the names of things to the manners of human interaction. The knightly socializa-tion of Perceval will gradually bridge this gap, and it has in fact already begun. Perceval's first three questions — not surprisingly — concern the lance, shield, and hauberk, the three pieces of knightly equipment whose unfamiliar sight and sound initially led to his misidentification of knights. Now that his heredi-tary sphere of interest has been revealed, these same pieces of equipment also illustrate his progress in learning about the realia of knightly society. The hero initially inquires only what the lance is, 'Que est ice que vos tenez?' (191),

---

[15] The majority of MSS have this reading, rather than the more reductive variant spoken by Perceval, 'de fer est il?,' which Hilka 12 chooses for his critical ed.

but then asks about the shield as well as its purpose, 'Ce que est et de quoi vos sert?' (214), and finally demands to know what the hauberk is, what the knight does with it, and what use it has: 'Qu'est ce que vos avez vestu? / . . . Qu'an feites vos et que vos vaut?' (261–68).

Furthermore, the knight's responses to these progressively more complicated and inclusive questions elicit a series of three responses from Perceval which compare the natural world with the chivalric world and reveal his growing interest in the latter. Perceval's first response rejects the lance in favor of a javelin because the latter can be thrown to kill animals at a greater distance (202–8). The next response, also comparing his pastoral world with the knightly world, again ignores the chivalric use of armor in order to apply it to the hunting situation with which he is familiar, but indirectly acknowledges the superiority of the strange weapon (273–76). The third response of the hero, a series of questions rather than a defensive value judgment, probes the basic difference between his natural state and the social state of the knights. Knights are not born, but made:

> Li dist: 'Fustes vos einsi nez?'
> 'Nenil, vaslez, ce ne puet estre
> Que nule riens puisse einsi nestre.'
> 'Qui vos atorna donc einsi?'   (282–85)

By the conclusion of the encounter, the initial difference between the ignorant *vaslez* and the knowledgeable *chevaliers* has narrowed appreciably. We see this particularly in the changing relationship between the two, in the increasing affinity of the knight for the youth to whom he initially condescends, 'biaus douz amis' (194), but whom he quickly comes to like (223) and is loath to leave (250–52), and whom he finally calls 'biaus frere' (299). The two are indeed related. The *seignor* of the knights is not that different from the *seignor* of the manor. Indeed, the young knight, who was dubbed only five days previously (288) and still fills his new role somewhat awkwardly, is but a slightly older version of Perceval, whom Gornemant will knight in turn a few days hence. Perceval's series of questions, which progressed from realia to the general social system underlying knighthood, now assumes the insistent tone of the knights' earlier questions of him, concluding with the request for precise information that will launch his own knightly career:

> 'Mes or me redites noveles
> Del roi que les chevaliers fet
> Et le leu ou il plus se tret.'   (332–34)

The implicit process of Perceval's socialization now becomes the explicit goal of his adventures.

II

The encounter between the hero and knights in Wolfram von Eschenbach's *Parzival* is considerably shorter than that of his source. The difference is substantial: Chrétien's scene extends for 292 lines (69–361), Wolfram's for only 169 (120.11–125.30). This is a surprising anomaly, given the general tendency of medieval adaptations — including Wolfram's romance as a whole — to be longer than their sources. Earlier scholarship explained this tendency either by the loss of Gallic charm or by the infusion of *deutsche Tiefe*, depending upon the side of the Rhine on which it originated. Recent work suggests that the medieval attitude toward translation/adaptation differed markedly from ours, requiring fidelity to the sense (i.e., content and actions) of a story, but allowing greater freedom in presenting character and motivation as well as in choosing the words and style of expression.[16] In most instances, there results what we might call a commenting translation, except when the adaptor does not agree with the import of his source — as is the case with Wolfram, 'von Troys meister Christjân / disem maere hât unreht getân' (827.1–2). This basic disagreement explains Wolfram's drastic reduction and rearrangement of Chrétien's scene.

The most obvious difference between the two romances stems from their differing points of departure.[17] Since Chrétien's narrative begins with this scene, the audience shares Perceval's ignorance of his heritage while it observes his responses to hearing, seeing, and talking to armed knights for the first time, and it must gradually be informed by the development of the story as well as by narrative asides. In Wolfram's narrative, however, the audience already knows the background history of Parzival's parents from Books I and II, and it has already learned from the first 125 lines of Book III much of what must be intimated or revealed during the course of Chrétien's scene.

The most consequential result of placing Parzival's encounter with the knights in this larger context is that the beginning of Book III can raise the question of Parzival's development *before* he has any contact with the outside chivalric world. Although he is not yet *versunnen* (117.19, 161.7) and is deprived of his kingly heritage (118.2), Parzival develops nonetheless. And he develops not through any process of socialization, as is the case with Chrétien's hero, but through the emergence of characteristics and interests inherited from his

---

[16] See esp. Carl Lofmark, 'Der höfische Dichter als Übersetzer,' in *Probleme* (*n*6) 40–62. In following Lofmark, I distance myself as strongly as possible from the reductive methods of Michel Huby, 'Wolframs Bearbeitungstechnik in "Parzival" (Buch III),' *Wolfram-Studien* 3 (1975) 40–51.

[17] See Green (*n*5) 379–80.

parents. To put it in terms of the modern slogan: innate nature (MHG *art*),[18] not external nurture, predominates in Wolfram's scene.

The paternal influence emerges first, as the narrator emphasizes with an introductory reference to the hero as 'Gahmuretes kint' (117.15) at the beginning of Book III. Parzival initially learns to fashion a bow and arrow for shooting birds 'mit sîn selbes hand' (118.5); he soon progresses to larger game with a javelin, a more lethal but still unknightly weapon, bringing home stags on his shoulders, since — unlike Chrétien's *vaslez* — he does not even seem to have been taught to ride a horse. A second characteristic emerges as soon as Parzival listens to birdsong while hunting: 'die süeze in sîn herze dranc: / daz erstracte im sîniu brüstelîn' (118.17–18). When the watchful Herzeloyde notices the effect on Parzival, she immediately associates it with both his inborn nature and his own inclination: 'si wart wol innen daz zeswal / von der stimme ir kindes brust. / des twanc in art und sîn gelust' (118.26–28). She is entirely correct, since a similar swelling of the breast — described in a similar fashion with identical rhyme — characterizes Gahmuret's own definition of his innate striving for knightly renown and love:

> 'mîn herze iedoch nâch hoehe strebet:
> ine weiz war umbez alsus lebet,
> daz mir swillet sus mîn winster brust.
> owê war jaget mich mîn gelust?'   (9.23–26)

Such actions and emotions clearly reveal that in spite of his extensive deprivation, he is very much the son of his father. In contrast to Chrétien's pastoral hero, Parzival already evinces the innate natural capacity for knightly deeds and love that characterizes the traditional romance hero.

The emergence of Herzeloyde's heritage in the young Parzival is less easy to document, partly because her influence emerges throughout the romance and partly because that influence is initially detrimental. The beginning of her *Waldleben* raises all the genre expectations of a saint's life, a life which negates her previous courtly existence (117.3–13), giving up 'der erden rihtuom' for the sake of 'des himeles ruom' (116.23–24).[19] Strangely enough, although Herzeloyde thereby deprives her son of his worldly education, she does not concern herself with his spiritual training either. Unlike Perceval, who already knows the creed and a series of prayers by heart (156–58) and receives detailed

---

[18] See Julius Schwietering, 'Natur und *art*,' *Zeitschrift für deutsches Altertum* 91 (1961–62) 108–37.

[19] The saint's life and the romance are closely related, as Max Wehrli, *Formen mittelalterlicher Erzählung* (Zürich and Freiburg i. Br. 1969) 155–76, has demonstrated. Wolfram's play with the expectations of both genres in Books III and XVI (with its clear allusion to the legend of St. Silvester) establishes a situation that begins with the antithesis between these genres and concludes with their successful co-ordination in the synthesis of God and world achieved by the hero.

instructions about behavior in churches and minsters, Parzival is deprived in this regard also and will not begin to learn socially acceptable norms of religious behavior until Gurnemanz takes him into his care at the end of Book III (169.16–20).

Fortunately, Parzival is not the complete *tabula rasa* religiously that he is socially, since the *imago Dei* in every human being (Genesis 1.26) enables him to respond instinctively to the word 'God.' In accordance with Wolfram's shift of emphasis from nurture to nature, the epistemological model of this response is not based on *intromission*, but on *extramission*:[20] whereas Chrétien's hero attempts to understand unfamiliar external sensory impressions, Wolfram's Parzival intuitively yearns to understand an innate idea before he begins to experience the world. Parzival's inquiry proceeds from a question about Herzeloyde's slaughter of the birds (119.10) to one about God, ' "ôwê muoter, waz ist got?" ' (119.17), establishing a larger concern about the relationship between creatures and their creator that hovers over his entire knightly career and will be raised again with the revelation of his failure at the Grail castle, ' "wê, waz ist got?" ' (332.1).

Herzeloyde's answer to Parzival's first innocent posing of that question characteristically has little to do with socialization and social forms:

> 'ôwê muoter, waz ist got?'
> 'sun, ich sage dirz âne spot.
> er ist noch liehter denne der tac,
> der antlitzes sich bewac
> nâch menschen antlitze.
> sun, merke eine witze,
> und flêhe in umbe dîne nôt:
> sîn triwe der werlde ie helfe bôt.
> sô heizet einr der helle wirt:
> der ist swarz, untriwe in niht verbirt.
> von dem kêr dîne gedanke,
> und och von zwîvels wanke.'   (119.17–28)

Her instruction is neither heretical nor misleading, as scholars have occasionally claimed;[21] rather, she reduces religion to its basic elements:[22] the antithesis

---

[20] For a brief survey of classical theories of intromission and extramission, and their combination in medieval concepts of vision, see David C. Lindberg, 'Alhazen's Theory of Vision and Its Reception in the West,' *Isis* 58 (1967) 321–41, esp. 321–22.

[21] See Walter Johannes Schröder, *Die Soltane-Erzählung in Wolframs* PARZIVAL, Germanische Bibliothek 3 (Heidelberg 1963); Alois Haas, *Parzivals 'tumpheit' bei Wolfram von Eschenbach*, Philologische Studien und Quellen 21 (Berlin 1964) esp. 56–71; Gertrud Jaron Lewis, 'Die unheilige Herzeloyde: Ein ikonoklastischer Versuch,' *Journal of English and Germanic Philology* 74 (1975) 465–85.

[22] On this passage as a 'winziges Religionskompendium' in accord with Biblical imagery and dogma, see Benedikt Mockenhaupt, *Die Frömmigkeit im* PARZIVAL *Wolframs von Eschenbach*, 2nd ed. (Darmstadt 1968) 63.

between light and dark as well as between God and the devil, the incarnation of the word, and the right and wrong relationships respectively between man and God or man and the devil. In keeping with her withdrawal from the world, Herzeloyde practices a faith independently of any social situation or social forms. Although this extreme solution ultimately proves satisfactory for her, it remains to be seen whether Parzival's career can accommodate his dual heritage from Herzeloyde and Gahmuret, reconciling the apparently conflicting demands of *got unde werlt*, isolation from and involvement in society, saint's life and chivalric romance.

Parzival's meeting with the knights illustrates in paradigmatic fashion the difficulty of this synthesis. In accordance with his reversal of emphasis from 'nurture' to 'nature,' Wolfram reduces the beginning of the encounter, eliminating the rhetorical amplification of Perceval's sensory perceptions in order to de-emphasize his rapid socialization. Thus, when Wolfram's hero embarks on his hunt, he is not already attuned to the joyful sounds of the world around him, but concerns himself with making his own music: 'er brach durch blates stimme ein zwîc' (120.13). And when the knights interrupt Parzival's progress a few moments later, there is no increasingly precise description of the weapons that he hears, but merely the simple observation, 'dâ hôrter schal von huofslegen' (120.15), before he associates these hoofbeats with the devil (120.17–23). Furthermore, there is no corresponding repetition to describe how Parzival sees the approaching knights. What comprises the first 89 lines of Chrétien's scene (69–158) takes only 12 in Wolfram's (120.11–23).

The reduction of the conclusion to this episode is even more revealing. Wolfram's inquisitive knight, Karnahkarnanz, requests information from the hero about the fugitives only once (122.15–20), eliminating Chrétien's humorous series of five questions and non-sequitur responses. And whereas Perceval asks a series of progressively more complicated questions about knightly equipment and makes a progressively more positive comparison of the chivalric world with his own, Parzival seems to regress into *tumpheit*. After asking first about knighthood ('"du nennest ritter: waz ist daz?"' 123.4) and knighting ('"sô sage mir, wer gît ritterschaft?"' 123.6), he gradually disappoints Karnahkarnanz' assumption that he may be of knightly 'art' (123.10) by simpering over the chain-mail skin of his interlocutor, '"waz mahtu sîn? / du hâst sus manec vingerlîn / an dînen lîp gebunden"' (123.21–23). The knight's reply describes the use of sword and chain-mail as offensive and defensive weapons in the give-and-take of combat (124.5–10), which Parzival, still thinking of chain-mail as skin, uncomprehendingly reduces to the hunting situation familiar to him:

> 'ob die hirze trüegen sus ir vel,
> so verwunt ir niht mîn gabylôt.
> der vellet manger vor mir tôt.'   (124.12–14)

The cumulative effect of this exchange does not reveal the hero's progressive adaptation to knightly society, but rather underscores the persistence of his foolishness. It is not surprising that the narrator calls Parzival *tump* for the first time at this juncture (124.16), or that the knights depart, admiring his beauty but lamenting his foolishness:

> 'ôwî wan waer dîn schoene mîn!
> dir hete got den wunsch gegebn,
> ob du mit witzen soldest lebn.'   (124.18–20)

At this point, we seem faced with an unexpected contradiction: Wolfram's placement of this scene in a larger context and his reduction of its length appear first to emphasize Parzival's natural progress independently of any socialization, and then to emphasize his foolishness once he comes into contact with the outside world. Why should he first reveal the hero's innate ability and then deny it? The answer lies in the intervening section of text, which is not part of this scene's folkloric archetype and seems to represent Wolfram's main interest:[23] Parzival's confusion of knights with God. In Chrétien's version, this event comprises a brief transition of only 22 lines (159–81); in Wolfram's revision it becomes tripled in length (120.24–123.2), forming the central event of the entire encounter.

The most obvious indicator is the restructuring of the narrative. In Chrétien's presentation, Perceval's confusion of knights with God forms a brief interlude between two longer passages, emphasized by amplification and repetition respectively. Wolfram inverts this structure, creating a large central section with doubling and amplification, flanked by a brief introduction and conclusion. The doubling of the central episode is caused by the separation of three knights from their leader, so that we observe Parzival confuse knights with God in two successive and increasingly detailed encounters (120.24–121.12 and 121.13–123.1). The first encounter, with three unnamed knights, proceeds rapidly from the narrator's description of Parzival's confusion, 'der knappe wânde sunder spot, / daz ies[l]îcher waere ein got' (120.27–28), to his prayer for help, which — not incidentally, as we shall see — invokes the three in the second person singular like the Trinity:[24] 'lûte rief der knappe sân, / "hilf, got: du maht wol helfe hân"' (121.1–2). The inappropriateness of this reaction is confirmed by the knights' annoyance with 'dirre toersche Waleise' (121.6) and by the narrator's aside about doltish Bavarians (121.7–12).

---

[23] This scene comprises the bulk of the passages without folklore parallels listed by Green (n5) 384; on its centrality see Mohr (n5) 208–10.

[24] The model for this playful motif is Abraham's address of the three angels as God in the second person singular (Genesis 18.2–3). With Augustine's *De Trinitate* 2.10–11, the Trinitarian interpretation becomes standard (CCL 50.105–7).

The second encounter unfolds in a parallel, but much more detailed manner. Whereas the three knights merely come galloping along (120.24), the narrator describes Karnahkarnanz' arrival and explains the reasons for his haste (121. 12–27). And whereas the knights are armed 'from the feet up' (120.5), the narrator itemizes Karnahkarnanz' almost dandyish equipment in lavish detail, beginning with the hem of his surcoat and proceeding upward (122.1–12). In accordance with its importance and the emphasis on his perceptions, Parzival's ensuing confusion of Karnahkarnanz with God is described several times.[25] The introductory reference merely evokes his reaction, 'den dûhter als ein got getân' (121.30), and provides a brief explanation, 'ern hete sô liehtes niht erkant' (122.1). The second reference, with an expanded description and explanation, further emphasizes Parzival's mistake by using the same key words and even the same rhyme (got/spot) as his confusion of the three knights with God (120.27–28):

> der knappe wânde, swaz er [Karnahkarnanz] sprach,
> es waere got, als im verjach
> frou Herzeloyd diu künegîn,
> do sim underschiet den liehten schîn.
> dô rief er lûte sunder spot
> 'nû hilf mir, hilferîcher got.'   (122.21–26)

As the narrator makes clear, Parzival's confusion stems ultimately from the misapplication of his mother's instruction, which it follows point for point in the association of God with light and human form (119.17–21) and the belief in His help (119.24). Even the rhyme at the transition from indirect to direct discourse, got/spot, is identical with that introducing her comments ('"ôwê muoter, waz ist got?"' / '"sun, ich sage dirz âne spot."' 119.17–19).

Wolfram's emphasis on this particular moment extends beyond Parzival's repeated confusion of the knights with God. Such confusion also occurs throughout the romance,[26] usually characterizing heathen attitudes. Among the potential candidates from the Old Testament, Wolfram — using the familiar got/spot rhyme — singles out Nebuchadnezzar, who 'solde selber sîn ein got. / daz waere nû der liute spot' (102.7–8), to exemplify the ludicrousness of such an attitude. Flegetanis, the first of two main 'sources' for the Grail story, succumbs to the devil's temptation to elevate creatures above their Creator,

---

[25] On the perceptual levels involved in the encounter, see D. H. Green, *The Art of Recognition in Wolfram's* PARZIVAL (Cambridge 1982) 62–65. That Wolfram's emphasis concerns Parzival's religious confusion is suggested by the detailed allusion to this moment in *Willehalm* 271.16–26.

[26] From a Christian perspective, the confusion of human beings with deities characterizes heathen idolatry. Several passages in Acts (10.25, 14.11–18, and 28.6) describe the phenomenon in New Testament times. See Gerd Wolfgang Weber, 'Irreligiosität und Heldenzeitalter: Zum Mythencharakter der altisländischen Literatur,' in *Speculum norroenum: Norse Studies in Memory of Gabriel Turville-Petre* (Odense 1981) 474–505, esp. 489n42.

praying to a calf, 'als op ez waer sîn got. / wie mac der tievel selhen spot / gefüegen an sô wîser diet . . . ?' (454.3–5). Even Parzival's father becomes the object of religious veneration in the service of the *baruc*: ' "ez betent heiden sunder spot / an in als an ir werden got" ' (107.19–20).

Viewed in this context, Parzival's confusion of men with gods ceases to be merely comic. Karnahkarnanz' response to the hero's adoration immediately introduces the correct perspective, 'der fürste sprach "ich pin niht got, / ich leiste ab gerne sîn gebot" ' (122.29–30), simultaneously denying the implication of the prayer and asserting his own subservience to the commandments of God, which explicitly forbid idolatry and demand obedience to Him alone (Exodus 20.1–6). The hero's insistence that his knights are nonetheless 'noch liehter danne got getân' (126.10) suggests overtones of a lingering 'heathen' or 'idolatrous' attitude toward chivalry. It is thus not surprising that the armor taken from the murdered Ither, which becomes the hero's identifying feature and the mark of his single-minded pursuit of knighthood, is of heathen provenance (679.8),[27] or that Parzival's advice to Gawan at the end of Book VI (332.9–16) recapitulates the attitude of heathen *Minneritter*.[28] Similar motifs continue throughout Book IX.[29]

As Wolfram's discussion of Flegetanis suggests, the devil's temptation of man often causes such idolatry, and it is not surprising that Parzival's confusion of knights and God also resembles this archetypal pattern. In direct disobedience to his mother's instruction to turn his thoughts from the devil (119.27), Parzival eagerly hopes to combat him when he hears the knights approaching (120.17–20),[30] but instead finds armored knights whose bright radiance makes him confuse them with gods: 'der knappe wânde sunder spot / daz ieslîcher waere ein got' (120.27–28). Even after being informed to the contrary by his 'ritter-got' or 'knight-god' (123.21),[31] he still insists to his mother that he has seen

---

[27] See Arthur Groos, 'Parzival's *swertleite*,' *Germanic Review* 40 (1975) 245–59, esp. 258.

[28] Cf. the attitude expressed by Feirefiz (768.26–30) and *Willehalm* 338.13–14; also the comments by Joachim Bumke, *Wolframs* WILLEHALM: *Studien zur Epenstruktur und zum Heiligkeitsbegriff der ausgehenden Blütezeit* (Heidelberg 1959) 169–75, esp. 173–74.

[29] When Parzival arrogantly appears in his armor on Good Friday, in defiance of the *truga Dei*, the pilgrim immediately assumes that he is a heathen (448.19–20). The motif continues in the discussion with Trevrizent, beginning with the paradox of the earth as Adam's virgin ancestor (463.24ff.) — a paradox used by St. Silvester in debates to convert heathens — and continuing with the discussion of love service, a heathen's quest for the Grail, and the turning around or 'converting' of Parzival's priorities.

[30] On the importance of *striten*, see Martin H. Jones, 'Parzival's Fighting and his Election to the Grail,' *Wolfram-Studien* 3 (1975) 52–71.

[31] 'ritter-got' is the reading in a majority of MSS (Ddgg), although Lachmann has taken the *lectio facilior*, 'ritter guot' (MSS Ggg), for his critical edition. In this instance, however, the more difficult reading is also the more appropriate: 'ritter-got' expresses quite precisely Parzival's confusion and the reversal of priorities, according to which chivalric rather than religious concerns determine his actions.

knights brighter than God. This emphatic and lasting confusion, reversing the proper relationship between the Creator and His creatures, and the priorities of God and world, humorously but insistently reminds us of the primal drama of the temptation of man by Lucifer ('the light bearer'), the temptation namely that 'eritis sicut dii' (Gen. 3.5), and of man's consequential acquiescence and fall. The narrator observes rather pointedly at this juncture — crediting his source with something it does not contain — that the foolish Parzival is the handsomest man since the time of Adam:

> von der âventiure ich daz nim,
> diu mich mit wârheit des beschiet,
> nie mannes varwe baz geriet
> vor im sît Adâmes zît.   (123.14–18)[32]

Given these reminiscences of the Fall, it is entirely appropriate that Parzival is called foolish or stupid for the first time during this episode, first by one of the knights whom he confuses with God (121.5), and then by the narrator (124.16). This seems rather late, given Parzival's extensive ignorance of society revealed at the beginning of Book III. But it is important to differentiate between several types of ignorance — a differentiation often overlooked in the debate over the 'foolishness' of a hero defined as 'traeclîche wîs' (4.18).[33] [1] One type is the lack of experience stemming from the fact that Parzival is deprived of his aristocratic heritage (118.2). This ignorance does cause difficulties on the hero's way to Arthur's court in Book III (the endangering of Jeschute, Kay's beating of Cunneware and Antenor), but these difficulties are rectified by the further knightly adventures which lead Parzival back to court in Book VI. [2] A second and more consequential type of ignorance is the moral deficiency which is ineluctably present in every human being as a result of the Fall. This type of ignorance leads the hero in his inordinate pursuit of knighthood, involving him in a series of irremedial sins against kin (the death of his mother, the murder of Ither, and the failure to redeem Anfortas), the consequences of

---

[32] On the problem of Parzival's beauty, see L. P. Johnson, 'Parzival's Beauty,' in Dennis Howard Green and Leslie Peter Johnson, *Approaches to Wolfram von Eschenbach*, Mikrokosmos 5 (Bern–Frankfurt/Main–Las Vegas 1978) 273–94; Ingrid Hahn, 'Parzivals Schönheit: Zum Problem des Erkennens und Verkennens im *Parzival*,' in *Verbum et signum*, edd. Hans Fromm *et al.* (Munich 1978) II 203–32.

[33] The monograph of Alois Haas (n19), which attempts to impose a four-fold meaning of *stultitia* on the work, leads rather far astray from the genre expectations of romance and the concerns of the text, although the analysis of the present scene quite properly emphasizes Parzival's Adamic nature (64, 67). The more text-oriented study of Heinz Rupp, 'Die Funktion des Wortes *tump* im *Parzival* Wolframs von Eschenbach,' *Germanisch-romanische Monatsschrift* 38 (1957) 97–106 delineates a differentiation between worldly and religious ignorance through the varying distribution of the word *tump*, especially in Books III and IX.

which, as we see in Book IX, can be accommodated only within the context of salvation history.

That Parzival's confusion of knights with God derives from this second type of ignorance is suggested by one tradition relating man's post-lapsarian deficiencies with the disobedience of Adam and Eve in the Garden of Eden. The explicit punishment inflicted on the transgressors by God in Genesis 3.16–19 involves physical hardship and the loss of immortality. But the immediate result of their transgression, described in the devil's promise that in becoming gods 'aperientur oculi vestri' (Gen. 3.5), becomes associated early in the history of Biblical exegesis with the opening of man's physical eyes to sin, and thus with a 'darkening' or 'clouding' of his spiritual eyes or original mental capacities.[34] The *Vorauer Genesis*, a work that Wolfram may have known, reminds us that the devil cast man into a prison called 'ignorantia,' and in this benighted state,

> do wurden in dev ougen
> des neist nechein lovgen
> zallen sunden ûf getan.
> dev inneren ûz getan.
> ir uirnunft wart plint.
> same wurden ellev ir kint.[35]

This moment is frequently characterized metaphorically in terms of light imagery as the confusion of a lesser radiance with the divine light. According to Boethius' *De consolatio Philosophiae* (5. Pr. 2.10), for example, man's choice of vice turns his eyes from the sovereign light to inferior obscurities, blinding him with ignorance:

> Nam ubi oculos a summae luce ueritatis ad inferiora et tenebrosa deiecerint, mox inscitiae nube caligant, perniciosis turbantur affectibus, quibus accedendo consentiendoque quam inuexere sibi adiuuant seruitutem et sunt quodam modo propria libertate captiuae. (CCSL 94.90)

Parzival similarly confuses knights with God because of their shining armor and continues to marvel at the divine radiance of his knightly interlocutors even after being explicitly informed of their true nature, '"muoter, ich sach vier man / noch liehter danne got getân"' (126.10–11). In terms of the psycho-

---

[34] St. Augustine provides the basis for this tradition: see the discussion of ignorance in fallen man by Joseph Mausbach, *Die Ethik des heiligen Augustinus* (Freiburg i. Br. 1909) II 226–40.

[35] Ed. Joseph Diemer, *Deutsche Gedichte des elften und zwölften Jahrhunderts* (Vienna 1849; rpt. Darmstadt 1968) 8. For a discussion of this pattern in early MHG religious literature and its exegetical background, see Brian Murdoch, *The Fall of Man in the Early Middle High German Biblical Epic*, Göppinger Arbeiten zur Germanistik 58 (Göppingen 1972) 96–105.

logical model handed down to the Middle Ages by St. Augustine's *De Trinitate*, the *imago Dei* in man, a reflection — among other attributes — of the Trinity's wisdom, becomes perverted by Adam's turn toward himself. Ignorance is thus a primary result of the Fall ('primus homo propter peccatum in ignorantiam ceciderat'), and it is further repeated by such idolatrous acts as the adoration of human beings as gods.[36] Wolfram's playful allusion to the Trinity in Parzival's invocation of the three knights as one deity (121.2) and the ensuing description of his *tumpheit* intimates his familiarity with this commonplace psychological system.

This is not to suggest that Parzival is reducible to an allegory of Adam. Quite the contrary: Parzival is Parzival, the son of Gahmuret and Herzeloyde, and has a lengthy and precise fictional genealogy extending over generations. But he is also, as are all men, a descendant of Adam, a fact that Wolfram emphasizes by giving the name Mazadan, i.e., *mac Adam* ('relative of Adam'), to Parzival's great-great-great-grandfather. As a result, the Biblical figure and the romance hero, though not identical, remain homologous or analogous. Just as the immediate consequence of the Fall is the clouding of man's interior eye by ignorance, so that he must find his way in the world by external sensory perceptions, so Parzival immediately discovers that he is *unversunnen*, unable to act according to his senses, 'mit witzen leben' (124.20). Like Adam, who is expelled from a timeless state of immortality to a state of mortality subject to time, Parzival becomes separated from a natural idyll marked only by the eternal pattern of the seasons (120.5) on the first particularized day of his career ('eins tages' 120.11), beginning a quest with a clearly delineated chronological and liturgical background into which he is ultimately integrated.[37] And just as Adam's sin results in the murder of Abel by Cain for the sake of paltry possessions ('umb krankez guot' 464.17), Parzival will soon kill Ither — to whom he is related by their common ancestry with Mazadan — in pursuit of

---

[36] On ignorance as a result of the Fall, see St. Thomas Aquinas, *Summa theologiae* I.–II.85.3, and the discussion of his predecessors in Odon Lottin, *Psychologie et morale aux XIIe et XIIIe siècles*, III (Louvain and Gembloux 1949) 12–18. On ignorance as a perversion of the Trinitarian *imago Dei*, see Robert Javelet, *Image et ressemblance au douzième siècle* (Paris 1967) I 251, 314; II 215n65, 224–25n178, 226n181, 227–28n207, 234n290, 235n308, 240n 374. On idolatry as a continuation of this pattern, see I 261–62 and II 222.

[37] See Hermann J. Weigand, 'Die epischen Zeitverhältnisse in den Graldichtungen Chrestiens und Wolframs,' *Publications of the Modern Language Association of America* 53 (1938) 917–50, rev. in *Wolfram's* PARZIVAL: *Five Essays with an Introduction*, ed. Ursula Hoffmann (Ithaca 1969) 18–74; Arthur Groos, 'Time Reference and the Liturgical Calendar in Wolfram von Eschenbach's *Parzival*,' *Deutsche Vierteljahrsschrift für Literaturwissenschaft und Geistesgeschichte* 49 (1975) 43–65; Margret Sauer, *Parzival auf der Suche nach der verlorenen Zeit*, Göppinger Arbeiten zur Germanistik 323 (Göppingen 1981).

knightly armor, simultaneously recapitulating the deed of Cain.[38] Parzival, like all men, is burdened by 'der sünde wagen' (465.5), the 'wagon-load of sin' bequeathed to us by the first man. The ontogeny of sin recapitulates the phylogeny of sin.

III

Like all men, however, the Grail hero is also capable of redemption, and the treatment of this ultimate success reveals the significance of Perceval's and Parzival's differing introductions to knighthood. For Chrétien, the confusion of knights with God is a humorous but not otherwise consequential example of worldly inexperience, even if the larger context of the scene may imply the inadequate ontological grounding of knightly culture. Only with Perceval's heartless departure from his mother does he initiate the concatenation of sin leading to his failure at the Grail castle. In accordance with this *Schuldautomatismus*,[39] Perceval cannot remedy the consequences of his misdeeds by himself — the solution must be provided by the appropriate social context. What Perceval has committed in the pursuit of his legitimate role in chivalric society can be remedied only by adherence to the proper forms of religious life in the Good Friday scene. After suddenly experiencing the pangs of contrition, Perceval is shriven by the hermit in accordance with twelfth-century practice and given a penance of fasting and daily attendance at Mass.[40] And there the matter ends, as far as we can tell: knightly socialization becomes subsumed by religious socialization.

Wolfram's romance resolves the problem differently. Parzival's confusion of knights with God is consequential, since it marks the beginning of his unconscious *superbia*, reversing the proper relationship between *got* and *werlt* as well as the priorities they represent. This confused attitude explains the pursuit of knighthood above all else, which leads to the deaths of Herzeloyde and Ither as well as the failure at the Grail castle, and it is not surprising that the portrayal of the hero in Books III through VI continually emphasizes the epistemological confusion of his adventures. As a result, the goal of Wolfram's Good Friday scene is not ritual socialization by penance, but a lengthy dialogue devoted to rectifying Parzival's moral ignorance and its consequences, beginning with a conversion or 'turning around' of his 'heathen' attitude. For if the goal of

---

[38] See Wolfgang Mohr, 'Parzivals ritterliche Schuld,' *Wirkendes Wort* 2 (1951–52) 148–60.

[39] See Wilhelm Kellermann, *Aufbaustil und Weltbild Chrestiens von Troyes im Percevalroman*, Zeitschrift für romanische Philologie, Beiheft 88 (Halle 1936) 109 and 120–21.

[40] See Bonnie Buettner, 'The Good Friday Scene in Chrétien de Troyes' *Perceval*,' *Traditio* 36 (1980) 415–26.

human endeavor defined in the epilogue is a life which is 'so concluded that God is not robbed of the soul through fault of the body and which nonetheless can worthily retain the favor of the world,'

> swes lebn sich sô verendet,
> daz got niht wirt gepfendet
> der sêle durch des lîbes schulde,
> und der doch der werlde hulde
> behalten kan mit werdekeit,
> daz ist ein nütziu arbeit.   (827.19–24)[41]

then Parzival has acted under a consequential reversal of these priorities, placing knightly renown in this life ahead of paradise for the soul:

> 'Mac rîterschaft des lîbes prîs
> und doch der sêle pardîs
> bejagen mit schilt und ouch mit sper,
> sô was ie rîterschaft mîn ger.'   (472.1–4)

Trevrizent's instruction reverses these priorities, so that he can absolve the hero of his sins and still encourage him to pursue his knightly quest,

> wand in der wirt von sünden schiet
> und im doch rîterlîchen riet.   (501.17–18)

resolving the catastrophic results of his confusion of men with God on the day on which God does indeed become man. Only then is Parzival capable of fulfilling the hierarchical goal of Wolfram's Christian humanism, that of satisfying the demands of revelation and socialization, God and world.

Cornell University

---

[41] Cf. Mockenhaupt 25–32.

WILLIAM OF ORANGE IN THE 'CANSO DE LA CROSADA'

By ALICE M. COLBY-HALL

It is well known that a brief passage in the Occitan *Canso de la Crosada*
provides valuable evidence for the existence of a lost epic concerning the siege
of Orange that should logically follow the events recounted in the *Prise d'Orange*, but the reference to William in this passage deserves closer scrutiny than
it has heretofore received. The lines in question do not appear in the first
part of the poem, which was composed by Guillaume de Tudèle between 1212
and 1213,[1] but rather in the anonymous continuation, which, in all probability,
was begun in 1228 and finished soon thereafter.[2] Here Régnier de Chauderon
encourages the crusaders who are besieged in the castle of Beaucaire by urging
them to recall William's endurance in similar circumstances: 'Senhors, remem-
bre vos Guilhelmet al cort nes, / Co al seti d'Aurenca suffri tans desturbiers.'[3]
This exhortation can be translated as follows: 'Lords, remember Billy Short-
nose, how he endured such great trials at the siege of Orange.'
    Léon Gautier, in his monumental study of the medieval French epic, makes
the following comment about the form used by the continuator for William's
name: 'Il y a bien *al cort nés*, qui rime avec *desturbiers*, non pas *al cort nas*.
Ces vers, qui ont été remarqués avant nous par M. Jonckbloet, prouvent net-
tement que les mots *Guillelme* [sic] *al cort nés* ne faisaient plus qu'un seul et
même vocable, importé et popularisé dans le Midi par nos jongleurs français.'[4]
Jonckbloet himself is less categorical when he says: 'Le surnom a ici une physio-
nomie toute septentrionale, qui semble prouver que si Guillaume vivait encore
dans les souvenirs du peuple, il n'était le héros d'aucune production littéraire.'[5]
At first glance, conclusions such as these seem fully justified, since one could
easily be led to suppose that *cort nes* ('short nose') was inserted here because
William was so popular in northern France that the first epics written about

---

[1] Jean-Marie D'Heur, 'Sur la date, la composition et la destination de la *Chanson de la
Croisade albigeoise* de Guillaume de Tudèle,' in *Mélanges d'histoire littéraire, de linguistique
et de philologie romane offerts à Charles Rostaing*, edd. Jacques De Caluwé, Jean-Marie
d'Heur, and René Dumas (Liège 1974) I 240–59.

[2] Eugène Martin-Chabot, ed. and trans., *La Chanson de la Croisade albigeoise*, II: *Le Poème
de l'auteur anonyme (1ère partie)*, Les Classiques de l'Histoire de France au Moyen Âge 24
(Paris 1957) xiv–xv.

[3] *La Chanson de la Croisade albigeoise*, ed. and trans. Martin-Chabot, II, laisse 159, verses
49–50.

[4] *Les Epopées françaises*, 2nd ed., IV (Paris 1882) 10.

[5] Willem J. A. Jonckbloet, *Guillaume d'Orange: Chansons de geste des XIe et XIIe siècles*
(The Hague 1854) II 191.

him were composed in French, and that the epithet attached to his name by
northern poets traveled south and was adopted by Occitan writers at a later
date. However, from the prosodic standpoint, *cort nes* does not belong in the
seventy-eight–line laisse where it occurs in the sole surviving manuscript of the
Canso de la Crosada. This laisse rhymes in *-iers*, although the scribe's spelling
does not always indicate the yod that precedes *-ers*. In other words, the rhyme
nes : *desturbiers*, which, according to Gautier, proves the authenticity of
French *nes* as opposed to Occitan *nas*, is in fact false. In this line, *nes* should
obviously be *niers*.

If *nes* is really *niers*, what then is the sense of *al cort niers*? It would seem
that further emendation is in order; and this time the key to the enigma can
be found in the Occitan epic known as the *Roman d'Arles*, which dates from the
end of the thirteenth century or the first half of the fourteenth,[6] and also in the
Franco-Italian manuscript of *Aliscans*, a French epic that was probably written
between 1185 and 1200.[7] In the *Roman d'Arles*, our hero is regularly referred
to as *Guilhenmes* or *Guilhermes al Cor Nier*;[8] and *Giellmes au Cor Nier* appears
at the rhyme in one line of the Franco-Italian *Aliscans*,[9] which Madeleine
Tyssens has shown to be the best of the *Aliscans* manuscripts in terms of its
closeness to the lost *Chanson de Rainouart*,[10] the text that can be posited as the
common source of *Aliscans* and Part II of the *Chanson de Guillaume*.[11]

In my view, Camille Chabaneau, the nineteenth-century editor of the *Roman
d'Arles*, was in error when he treated *cornier* as a single word and also as a
borrowing from French.[12] In Old French, *cornier* may mean 'cornel tree,' as in
Old Occitan, or 'corner'; but, since William has no known connection with
either of these, *cornier* makes little sense unless one divides it into two perfectly
normal Old Occitan words, *cor*, meaning 'horn'[13] or 'heart,' and *nier*, meaning
'black.'

---

[6] Mario Roques, 'Le *Roman d'Arles*,' *Histoire Littéraire de la France* 38 (1949) 639.

[7] Jean Frappier, *Les Chansons de geste du cycle de Guillaume d'Orange*, 2nd ed. (Paris 1967) I 240–41.

[8] Camille Chabaneau, ed., 'Le *Roman d'Arles*,' *Revue des Langues Romanes* 32 (1888) 473–542, lines 963, 999, 1009, 1048–49, and 1055 of the partially prosified verse.

[9] Venice, Biblioteca Marciana, Fr. VIII (= 252), fol. 35ʳ, line 24.

[10] *La Geste de Guillaume d'Orange dans les manuscrits cycliques*, Publications de la Faculté de Philosophie et Lettres de l'Université de Liège 178 (Paris 1967) 249, 263–64.

[11] Frappier, *Les Chansons de geste* I 145–48.

[12] 'Le *Roman d'Arles*' 479.

[13] *Corn* is the usual medieval spelling when this word means 'horn'; but *cor* is also attested. See François J. Raynouard, *Lexique roman ou dictionnaire de la langue des troubadours*, II (Paris 1836), s.v. *corn*. Additional examples of *cor* can be found in the *Roman d'Arles*, ed. Chabaneau, line 878, and in *Roland à Saragosse*, ed. Mario Roques, Les Classiques Français du Moyen Âge 83 (Paris 1956), verse 253. Moreover, it is unlikely that speakers of Old Occitan made a special effort to articulate a double *n* when pronouncing *corn* followed by *nier*.

Al cor nier, signifying 'with the black horn,' would seem to be the medieval Occitan equivalent of *au cornet* 'with the little horn,' the French epithet frequently attached to William's name in present-day Orange. The curved hunting horn which appears on the escutcheon of the city of Orange is traditionally regarded as representing the horn of Guillaume au Cornet[14] and is first attested in 1184 on the seal of Guillaume de Baux, prince of Orange.[15] This heraldic horn is now blue, but it is shown as black in the Bellenville armorial, which dates from the second half of the fourteenth century,[16] and in the Uffenbach armorial,[17] which was completed about 1440.[18] Since a blue horn is also attested for Orange in armorials that are contemporary with these,[19] it is possible that some members of the house of Orange practiced heraldic differencing in order to be recognized on the battlefield.[20] Furthermore, in view of the fact that the author of the Bellenville armorial sometimes drew information from sources that were too old for the period in which he was working,[21] the black horn in this compilation is quite possibly that of Prince Raymond IV, who died in 1340, or that of one of his predecessors.[22] Whatever the answer may be, it is likely that the horn of Guillaume de Baux was black rather than blue since, as Michel Pastoureau has demonstrated, sable was much more common than azure on twelfth- and thirteenth-century escutcheons. According to Pastoureau, azure does not begin to occupy an important place in coats of arms until the middle

---

[14] See especially Joseph de la Pise, *Tableau de l'histoire des princes et principauté d'Orange* (The Hague 1640) 51, and Joseph Bastet, *Histoire de la ville et de la principauté d'Orange* (Orange 1856; rpt. Marseilles 1977) 23–28.

[15] Alice M. Colby-Hall, 'In Search of the Lost Epics of the Lower Rhône Valley,' *Olifant* 8 (1981 [1983]) 342–44.

[16] Léon Jéquier, ed., 'L'Armorial Bellenville,' *Cahiers d'Héraldique* 5 (1983) 31, 52 (fol. 1ᵛ no. 17).

[17] Fol. 88ᵛᵉ, described by Léon Jéquier, 'Tables héraldiques de dix-neuf armoriaux du moyen âge,' *Cahiers d'Héraldique* 1 (1974) 81. Cf. Jéquier, 'L'Armorial Bellenville' 47, 52.

[18] Jéquier, 'Tables héraldiques' xli.

[19] Paul Adam-Even, ed., *L'Armorial universel du héraut Gelre (1370–1395)* (Tirage à part des *Archives Héraldiques Suisses*; Neuchâtel 1971) 6–7 and 56 no. 738; Louis-Claude Douët-d'Arcq, ed., 'Armorial de France de la fin du xivᵉ siècle,' *Le Cabinet Historique* 5.1 (1859) 11 and 252 no. 601; and Jan Raneke, *Bergshammarvapenboken: En medeltidsheraldisk studie* (Lund 1975) I 164; II 270 no. 1620. On the date of the armorial edited by Douët-d'Arcq, see Max Prinet, 'Recherches sur la date du plus ancien armorial français,' *Bulletin Archéologique du Comité des Travaux Historiques et Scientifiques* (1915) 171–80. This armorial was compiled by a herald called Navarre.

[20] On differencing, see, for example, Donald Lindsay Galbraith, *Manuel du blason*, 2nd ed., rev. Léon Jéquier (Lausanne 1977) 235–40.

[21] Jéquier, 'L'Armorial Bellenville' 17.

[22] For a more detailed discussion of the heraldic material presented here, see Alice M. Colby-Hall, 'Du nouveau sur le cornet de Guillaume au Court Nez,' *Bulletin des Amis d'Orange* 26 no. 100 (1985) 16–19, 23–24.

of the thirteenth century.[23] Moreover, as I have shown elsewhere, the heraldic *cor nier* was probably intended to suggest, both physically and phonetically, the curved nose that is attested for William at an earlier date than the well-known short nose.[24]

The hero praised in the *Canso de la Crosada* is almost certainly William Blackhorn, but the ambiguity of *cor nier* must not be forgotten. As I mentioned earlier, it can refer to a black heart as well as to a black horn; and Joseph Bastet, in the history of Orange that he published in 1856, recounts a vague legend according to which the village of Châteauneuf-de-Gadagne near Avignon was conquered from the Saracens by a certain Guillaume au Cœur Noir.[25] In Bastet's time, this story was still in circulation; but he does not tell us what language was normally used for narrating this event in William's life. One strongly suspects that it was Provençal; in Modern Provençal, the noun *cor* is just as ambiguous as it was in the language of the troubadours.[26] William's *cœur noir* is probably based on a misunderstanding of *cor nier*; but since a black heart, in medieval French and Occitan texts, is a sign of melancholy rather than malevolence and does befit William's state of mind in many of the situations he encounters, the ambiguity of the epithet may be intentional. William Blackhorn and William Sadheart are not mutually exclusive.

On the basis of the foregoing evidence, it is now possible to eliminate the *t* of *cort* in *al cort niers*. The ungrammatical *s* added to *nier* presents no difficulty, since the continuator often uses a flectional *s* without any grammatical function in order to obtain a perfect rhyme. Inasmuch as this writer prefers to deform the ends of words in various ways rather than produce inexact rhymes, it is most unlikely that *cort nes* is the correct reading for the line in question. This kind of poetic license is completely foreign to the habits of the continuator.

'Lords, remember Billy Blackhorn,' says Régnier de Chauderon. It is important to notice who is speaking in this passage. The anonymous continuator, who is an ardent supporter of the counts of Toulouse in their struggle against Simon de Montfort, puts these words into the mouth of a crusader from the North, which may well explain why someone saw fit to substitute a northern

---

[23] 'Vogue et perception des couleurs dans l'Occident médiéval: Le témoignage des armoiries,' *L'Hermine et le sinople: Études d'héraldique médiévale* (Paris 1982) 140–41.

[24] Colby-Hall, 'Du nouveau sur le cornet' 15–16, 18–19, 23–24, and 'From *curb niés* to *cor nier*: The Linguistic Metamorphoses of William's Epic Nose,' in *The Tenth LACUS Forum 1983*, edd. Alan Manning, Pierre Martin, and Kim McCalla (Columbia, S.C. 1984) 505–15 In the LACUS Forum article, I analyze various possible connections between the curved or short nose of William and the *cor nier* of Orange.

[25] *Histoire de la ville et de la principauté d'Orange* 24. Cf. 'Canton de l'Isle,' *Annuaire de Vaucluse* (1838) 187.

[26] See Frédéric Mistral, *Lou Tresor dóu Felibrige* (Aix-en-Provence 1879–87) I, s.v. *cor* 'heart' and *cor* 'horn.'

epithet for a southern one in the text that has come down to us. Such linguistic realism is actually out of place in this part of the *Crosada* poem, where everyone, by convention, speaks the language of Toulouse, the city in which the continuator appears to have resided and may have been born.[27] We must, however, ask ourselves why a crusader, rather than an opponent of Simon de Montfort, is portrayed as citing the example of William and even referring to him familiarly as *Guilhelmet*. To the best of my knowledge, this is the only attestation we have of William's name in its diminutivized form, a form which expresses the kind of affection and admiration that Americans are likely to feel for Billy the Kid or Davy Crockett. This nuance has unfortunately been neglected by the three editors of the poem, all of whom treat 'Guillaume' as an adequate translation of *Guilhelmet*.[28] Régnier's attitude is not particularly difficult to explain if one meditates for a moment on the parallels between William's situation during the siege of Orange and that of the crusaders trapped inside Beaucaire. Like William, Simon's followers must defend a town which was formerly in the hands of their adversaries.[29] Like William, they are engaged in a holy war; and their opponents, whether heretical in their beliefs or merely tolerant of heresy, bear a strong resemblance to William's Saracens, who likewise were enemies of the faith and whom medieval theologians would, in general, have considered to be heretics.[30] As Gerard Brault has shown, Turpin was not unjustified when he said of Abisme: 'That Saracen looks like a great heretic to me.'[31]

Such similarities do not, however, create bonds between William and Simon's chief opponent, Raymond VI, count of Toulouse. There is no reason for Raymond VI, his son Raymond, or their allies to extol a hero who could be viewed as an enemy *avant la lettre*. Any Christian, whether heretical or not, who fell victim to the crusading zeal of other Christians would find it difficult to admire William. In addition, it is worthy of note that Guillaume de Tudèle,

---

[27] Martin-Chabot, ed. and trans., *La Chanson de la Croisade albigeoise* II xxix–xxxi.

[28] Claude Fauriel, ed. and trans., *Histoire de la Croisade contre les hérétiques albigeois* (Paris 1837) 289; Paul Meyer, ed. and trans., *La Chanson de la Croisade contre les Albigeois*, II (Paris 1879) 221; and Martin-Chabot, ed. and trans., *La Chanson de la Croisade albigeoise* II 127.

[29] William took Orange by force, according to epic tradition, whereas Simon de Montfort acquired Beaucaire by an infeudation of dubious legality. On this investiture, see Martin-Chabot, ed. and trans., *La Chanson de la Croisade albigeoise* II 86–87n2.

[30] On heresy and Islam in the Old French epic, see Paul Bancourt, *Les Musulmans dans les chansons de geste du Cycle du Roi* (Marseilles 1982) I 343–46. Cf. Philippe Sénac, *L'Image de l'autre: Histoire de l'Occident médiéval face à l'Islam* (Paris 1983) 56–57.

[31] Gerard J. Brault, ed. and trans., THE SONG OF ROLAND: *An Analytical Edition* (University Park, Pa. 1978) I 208–9; II verse 1645 (1485 in other editions). I have used Brault's translation of this line.

who sides with the crusaders, praises his patron for being equal to Roland and Oliver in feats of arms;[32] whereas the continuator, who is a partisan of Raymond VI, regards Oliver as a model of courage[33] and yet has a northerner criticize both Roland and Oliver by claiming that they died 'per l'orgolh de Fransa e pels faitz menudiers' ('for the pride of France and for exploits without great value').[34] It is a bit simplistic, I feel, to place all of the blame upon Roland here, as Paul Meyer and Eugène Martin-Chabot have done in the notes to their editions of the text.[35] The speaker, Robert de Picquigny, seems to regard the two knights as both participants in, and victims of, the pride and ambition of the North. All of this goes to show that, at the time of the Albigensian Crusade, the residents of both northern and southern France could have negative reactions to the content of certain epics.

In fact, Raymond VI would have had special justification for disliking an epic hero who was said to have become the ruler of Orange after wresting it from the hands of the Saracens. Guillaume de Baux, the reigning prince of Orange during the first ten years of the Crusade, supported the cause of the Church;[36] and so did the consuls and councilmen of Orange, who with Guillaume's consent swore to the papal legate on June 25, 1209, that they would not allow their men or their allies to aid Raymond VI, should the latter resume his opposition to the Church.[37] Guillaume's loyalty to the Church cost him

---

[32] *La Chanson de la Croisade albigeoise*, ed. and trans. Eugène Martin-Chabot, I: *La Chanson de Guillaume de Tudèle*, Les Classiques de l'Histoire de France au Moyen Âge 13 (Paris 1931), laisse 72, verses 9–10.

[33] *La Chanson de la Croisade albigeoise*, ed. and trans. Martin-Chabot, II, laisse 183, verses 6–7.

[34] *La Chanson de la Croisade albigeoise*, ed. and trans. Eugène Martin-Chabot, III: *Le Poème de l'auteur anonyme (2ᵉ partie)*, Les Classiques de l'Histoire de France au Moyen Âge 25 (Paris 1961), laisse 192, verse 74.

[35] Meyer, ed. and trans., *La Chanson de la Croisade contre les Albigeois* II 352n1; and Martin-Chabot, ed. and trans., *La Chanson de la Croisade albigeoise* III 69n5.

[36] Innocent III, *Opera omnia*, PL 216.95–96 no. 10; 96 no. 11 (= Louis Barthélemy, *Inventaire chronologique et analytique des chartes de la maison de Baux* [Marseilles 1882] no. 139); and 96 no. 12 (= Barthélemy no. 137); 128–29 no. 2 (= Barthélemy no. 140). No. 146 in Barthélemy's inventory seems to be a misdated duplicate of no. 140. An additional document revealing Guillaume's favorable attitude toward the Church can be found in *Delectus ex epistolarum Honorii papae III libris decem, de rebus Francicis, regnantibus Philippo Augusto et Ludovico VIII*, ed. Michel-Jean-Joseph Brial, in *Recueil des historiens des Gaules et de la France*, new ed. under the direction of Léopold Delisle, XIX (Paris 1880) 649. Concerning Guillaume's conduct at the time of the Crusade, see also Paul Meyer, ed. and trans., *La Chanson de la Croisade contre les Albigeois* II 203–4n2; Paul Fournier, *Le Royaume d'Arles et de Vienne (1138–1378)* (Paris 1891) 114–15; and Martin-Chabot, ed. and trans., *La Chanson de la Croisade albigeoise* II 99n4.

[37] Innocent III, *Opera omnia*, PL 216.130–31 no. 5 (= Barthélemy no. 142). No. 147 in this inventory seems to be a misdated duplicate of no. 142. Cf. *La Chanson de la Croisade albigeoise*, ed. and trans. Martin-Chabot, II, laisse 154, verses 65–66.

his life in 1218, when — according to contemporary accounts — he was skinned alive and cut into pieces by the people of Avignon,[38] who were staunch supporters of Raymond's son, the future Raymond VII.[39] Like the besieged crusaders at Beaucaire in 1216, Guillaume de Baux and his followers would quite logically have felt no hostility or resentment toward William of Orange. On the contrary, one would fully expect them to enjoy listening to any jongleur who was singing the praises of Guilhelmet al Cor Nier, especially since Guillaume de Baux's equestrian seal shows that he had a hunting horn on the shield that he would have carried into battle.[40] To judge by the literary and heraldic evidence at our disposal, the prince was a veritable reincarnation of William Blackhorn.

It is worthwhile to remember that the chief, if not the only, historical prototype for the epic hero known as William of Orange is Saint William of Gellone, who, as count of Toulouse, fought against the Saracens in Spain and southern France. Toward the end of his life, he withdrew from worldly affairs to become a monk and founded the Abbey of Gellone, which now appropriately bears the name of Saint-Guilhem-le-Désert. This William can hardly be viewed as favorable to heresy; and, what is more, during the Inquisition that followed the Albigensian Crusade, the Abbey of Saint-Guilhem was one of the places to which repentant heretics could be required to make a humiliating pilgrimage in order to do penance for their waywardness.[41] Raymond VI seized

---

[38] Alexandre Teulet, ed., *Layettes du Trésor des Chartes*, I (Paris 1863) 466 no. 1301 (bull of Pope Honorius III dated July 30, 1218 [= Barthélemy no. 188]); and Nicolas de Bray, *Gesta Ludovici VIII*, ed. Michel-Jean-Joseph Brial, in *Recueil des historiens des Gaules et de la France*, new ed. under the direction of Léopold Delisle, XVII (Paris 1878) 339, verses 1555–60. Cf. Claude Devic and Joseph Vaissète, *Histoire générale de Languedoc*, 2nd ed., VI, rev. Auguste Molinier (Toulouse 1879) 522. Devic and Vaissète mention the papal bull edited by Teulet and a document of August 11, 1218, excerpted in the *Annales ecclesiastici* of Odorico Rinaldi (rpt. in Caesar Baronius [Cesare Baronio], Odoricus Raynaldus [Odorico Rinaldi], and Jacobus Laderchius [Giacomo Laderchi], *Annales ecclesiastici*, rev. Augustinus Theiner [Augustin Theiner], XX [Bar-le-Duc 1870] 403–4 no. 55). These seem to be two slightly different versions of the same bull, but they contain the same information about Guillaume de Baux. Cf. Petrus Pressutti [Pietro Pressutti], ed., *Regesta Honorii papae III*, I (Rome 1888; rpt. Hildesheim 1978) no. 1577. In two bulls dated June 2 and June 3, 1221 (Pressutti, *Regesta*, I nos. 3421 and 3424 [= Barthélemy, 2nd Suppl. nos. 37–38]), Hugues de Baux is also reported as having mentioned the cruel death of his brother in his request for papal support and reparations (Honorius III, *Honorii III Romani pontificis Opera omnia*, ed. César-Auguste Horoy, Medii Aevi Bibliotheca Patristica 3 [Paris 1879], no. 408 [June 2] col. 829, and no. 407 [June 3, misdated as June 2] col. 828).

[39] Concerning Avignon's loyalty to Raymond VII from 1216 to 1227, see Léon-Honoré Labande, *Avignon au XIIIᵉ siècle* (Paris 1908; rpt. Marseilles 1975) 21–31.

[40] Colby-Hall, 'In Search of the Lost Epics' 342–43 and 349 fig. 1.

[41] Bernardus Guidonis [Bernard Gui], *Practica inquisitionis heretice pravitatis*, ed. Célestin Douais (Paris 1886) 37–39, 94–98.

the possessions of William's abbey at some point prior to his temporary reconciliation with the Church at Saint-Gilles-du-Gard on June 18, 1209; and he was
still holding them unjustly when he made his public confession to the papal
legate on that day.[42]   Though he must have relinquished these possessions
without delay if he kept the promises he made before and after his absolution,[43] one cannot credit him with great devotion to William.

In short, the name of William was clearly associated with Orange and with
orthodoxy. Prior to the ravages of Simon de Montfort and Raymond VI,
William's exploits could have had wide appeal throughout southern France,
but the divisiveness of the Albigensian Crusade may well have decreased the
popularity of any Occitan poems, whether epics or ballads, that dealt with
Guilhelmet al Cor Nier. The William passage in the *Canso de la Crosada*
reveals the presence of local traditions regarding this semi-legendary leader
and, at the same time, adumbrates a plausible explanation for their almost
complete disappearance from Occitan culture.[44]

Cornell University

---

[42] Innocent III, *Opera omnia*, PL 216.89–91 no. 2.

[43] Innocent III, *Opera omnia*, PL 216.89 no. 1; 89–91 no. 2; 93 no. 6.

[44] This article is a slightly revised version of a paper presented on May 10, 1985, at the
Symposium on the Romance Epic sponsored by the Société Rencesvals, American-Canadian
Branch, at the Twentieth International Congress on Medieval Studies held at Western
Michigan University in Kalamazoo, Michigan. The writer acknowledges with gratitude that
an important part of the research for the article was completed with the aid of a Fellowship
for Independent Study and Research from the National Endowment for the Humanities in
1984–85.

THE LIGHT OF VENUS AND THE POETRY OF DANTE

By GIUSEPPE MAZZOTTA*

My title refers to the passage in the *Convivio* in which Dante classifies the seven liberal arts according to a conventional hierarchy of knowledge. Grammar, dialectic, rhetoric, music, geometry, arithmetic, and astronomy are the disciplines of the *trivium* and *quadrivium*, and each of them is linked to one of the planets in the Ptolemaic cosmology.[1] Venus is the planet identified with Rhetoric because the attributes of Venus, like those of rhetoric, are

> la chiarezza del suo aspetto, che è soavissima a vedere più che altra stella; l'altra sì è la sua apparenza, ora da mane ora da sera. E queste due proprietadi sono ne la Rettorica: chè la Rettorica è soavissima di tutte le altre scienze, però che a ciò principalmente intende; e appare da mane, quando dinanzi al viso de l'uditore lo rettorico parla, appare da sera, cioè retro, quando da lettera, per la parte remota, si parla per lo rettorico.[2]

The definition alludes, as is generally acknowledged, to the traditional double function of rhetoric, oratory and the *ars dictaminis* or letter-writing.[3]

---

* All quotations from the *Divine Comedy*, unless otherwise stated, are from *La* DIVINA COMMEDIA *secondo l'antica vulgata*, ed. G. Petrocchi, 4 vols., Società Dantesca Italiana (Milan 1966–67).

[1] The passage occurs in the *Convivio* 2.12.7–8, edd. G. Busnelli and G. Vandelli, 2nd ed., ed. A. E. Quaglio, 2 vols. (Florence 1964).

[2] *Convivio* 2.13.13–14.

[3] Brunetto Latini, *La rettorica*, ed. F. Maggini (Florence 1915), defines rhetoric as follows: 'Rettorica èe scienzia di due maniere: una la quale insegna dire, e di questa tratta Tulio nel suo libro; l'altra insegna dittare, e di questa, perciò che esso non ne trattò così del tutto apertamente, si nne tratterà lo sponitore nel processo del libro, in suo luogo e suo tempo come si converrà' (3). General studies on rhetoric include C. E. Baldwin, *Medieval Rhetoric and Poetic* (New York 1928) and James R. Murphy, *Rhetoric in the Middle Ages* (Berkeley 1974). On the *ars dictaminis*, see P. O. Kristeller, 'Un' "Ars dictaminis" di Giovanni del Virgilio,' *Italia medioevale e umanistica* 4 (1961) 181–200; Helene Wieruszowski, 'Ars Dictaminis in the Time of Dante,' *Medievalia et humanistica* 1 (1943) 95–108, rpt. in *Politics and Culture in Medieval Spain and Italy* (Rome 1971) 359–77; Charles H. Haskins, *The Renaissance of the Twelfth Century* (Cambridge 1927) 138–50, which surveys the revival of 'oratio' in the Roman political and judicial fields as well as the renewed importance of the epistolary style in the Middle Ages. This art of drafting official letters and documents, identified in the Bolognese *dictatores*, finds its authority in Alberic of Monte Cassino, *Breviarium de dictamine*, and Boncompagno of Signa, *Antiqua rhetorica*. See C. H. Haskins, 'The Early *Artes Dictandi* in Italy,' in *Studies in Medieval Culture* (Oxford 1929) 170–92; also Robert L. Benson, 'Proto-humanism and Narrative Technique in Early Thirteenth-Century Italian "Ars Dictaminis,"' in *Boccaccio: Secoli di vita*. Atti del Convegno internazionale Boccaccio 1975, edd. M. Cottino-

What the definition also contains is the notion of the *ornatus*, the techniques of style or ornamentation whereby rhetoric is said to be the art that produces beautiful appearances.[4] The term 'chiarezza,' one might add, translates *claritas*, the light that St. Thomas Aquinas conceives to be the substance of beauty and the means of its disclosure.[5]

In the *Convivio*, Dante does not really worry about the issue of the beautiful as an autonomous aesthetic category. Although the beautiful can be an attribute of philosophy (Dante speaks, for instance, of 'la bellissima Filosofia')[6] or the synonym of morality,[7] the importance of both the beautiful and rhetoric is decisively circumscribed in this speculative text of moral philosophy. To grasp the reduced value conferred on rhetoric in the *Convivio*, where it is made to provide decorative imagery, one should only remember its centrality in the *De vulgari eloquentia*. The treatise, which straddles medieval poetics and rhetoric, was written with the explicit aim of teaching those poets who have so far versified 'casualiter' to compose 'regulariter' by the observance of rules and by the imitation of the great poets of antiquity.[8] This aim reverses,

---

Jones and E. F. Tuttle (Ravenna 1977) 31–48; Ronald Witt, 'Medieval "Ars Dictaminis" and the Beginnings of Humanism: A New Construction of the Problem,' *Renaissance Quarterly* 35 (1982) 1–35.

[4] Brunetto Latini writes (4): 'Et ee rettorica una scienza di bene dire, ciò è rettorica quella scienza per la quale noi sapemo ornatamente dire e dittare.' The quote echoes the conventional definition of rhetoric. Cf. Isidore of Seville, 'Rhetorica est bene dicendi scientia in civilibus quaestionibus, ad persuadendam iusta et bona,' *Etymologiae* 2.1.1, ed. W. M. Lindsay (Oxford 1966); also Martianus Capella, *De nuptiis Philologiae et Mercurii*, ed. A. Dick (Leipzig 1925) 5. The theory of the *ornatus* in Dante is tied to the principle of linguistic *convenientia*. Cf. *De vulgari eloquentia* 2.1.2–10 ed. A. Marigo, rev. P. G. Ricci (Florence 1968). See Francesco Tateo, '*Retorica*' e '*Poetica*' *fra Medioevo e Rinascimento* (Bari 1960) 209–11. For the *ornatus* and degrees of style, see Geoffrey of Vinsauf, *Poetria nova*, in *Les Arts poétiques du XIIᵉ siècle*, ed. E. Faral (Paris 1923) lines 830ff. Cf. Matthew of Vendôme, *Ars versificatoria* 2.9–10, also in *Les Arts poétiques*. For the *colores rhetorici*, see Brunetto Latini, *Li Livres dou tresor* 3.10.3, ed. F. J. Carmody (Geneva 1975). Cf. *Vita nuova* 25.7 and 10. Useful are the remarks by C. Grayson, 'Dante e la prosa volgare,' *Il verri* 9 (1963) 6–26, and A. Schiaffini, *Tradizione e poesia nella prosa d'arte italiana dalla latinità medievale al Boccaccio* (Rome 1969).

[5] 'Ad pulchritudinem tria requiruntur. Primo quidem *integritas* sive perfectio: quae enim diminuta sunt, hoc ipso turpia sunt. Et debita *proportio* sive consonantia. Et iterum *claritas*; unde quae habent colorem nitidum, pulchra esse dicuntur.' *Summa theologiae* 1.39.8. Cf. Edgar De Bruyne, *Études d'esthétique médiévale*, 3 vols. (Brugge 1946).

[6] *Convivio* 2.12.9.

[7] 'Quella cosa dice l'uomo essere bella cui le parti debitamente si rispondono per che de la loro armonia resulta piacimento. Onde pare l'uomo essere bello, quando le sue membra debitamente si rispondono; dicemo bello lo canto, quando le voci di quello, secondo debito de l'arte, sono intra sè rispondenti' (*Convivio* 1.5.13).

[8] *De vulgari eloquentia* 2.4.1–3. The same disapproval of those who compose without awareness of rules is expressed in *Vita nuova* 25.5 and 10.

may I suggest in passing, Matthew of Vendôme's judgment. In his *Ars versificatoria*, Matthew dismisses the lore of the ancient poets, their rhetorical figures and metaphors as useless and unworthy of emulation: 'hoc autem modernis non licet.'[9] But for Dante rhetoric, which begins with the Greeks, is the very equivalent of poetry, or as he puts it, 'fictio rhetorica musicaque poita.'[10] The concern with style and taste, which occupy a large portion of the *De vulgari eloquentia*, dramatizes the identification of rhetoric and poetry. At the same time, as the art of discourse, the art of pleading political or juridical causes, rhetoric is also in the *De vulgari eloquentia* the tool for the establishment of political, legal, and moral authority. In this sense, Dante's notion of rhetoric re-enacts the concerns of a cultural tradition that ranges from Cicero to Brunetto Latini.[11]

It comes as something of a surprise that scholars, who have been remarkably zealous in mapping the complex implications of rhetoric in the *De vulgari eloquentia*, have not given equal attention to its role in Dante's other major works. In the case of the other texts, rhetoric is treated as a repertory of figures, but not as a category of knowledge with unique claims about authority and power. The statement, in truth, ought to be tempered somewhat in the light of the extensive debates to which the question of allegory in both the *Convivio* and the *Divine Comedy* has been subjected.[12] Yet even then the relationship between rhetoric and the other arts or the way in which rhetoric engenders reliable knowledge and may even dissimulate its strategies is not always ade-

---

[9] *Ars versificatoria* 4.5.

[10] The definition occurs in *De vulgari eloquentia* 2.4.2–3. The importance of music, an art from the *quadrivium*, and its conjunction with rhetoric and the art of language will be discussed elsewhere. On Dante's understanding of poetry, see A. Schiaffini, ' "Poesis" e "poeta" in Dante,' *Studia philologica et litteraria in honorem L. Spitzer* (Bern 1958) 379–89; August Buck, 'Gli studi sulla poetica e sulla retorica di Dante e del suo tempo,' in *Atti del Congresso internazionale di studi danteschi* (Florence 1965) I 249–78. More generally, see R. McKeon, 'Poetry and Philosophy in the Twelfth Century: The Renaissance of Rhetoric,' in *Critics and Criticism, Ancient and Modern*, ed. R. S. Crane (Chicago 1954) 297–318; G. Barberi-Squarotti, 'Le poetiche del Trecento in Italia,' in *Momenti e problemi di storia dell'estetica* (Milan 1959) I 255–91.

[11] 'Rettorica è scienza d'usare piena e perfetta eloquenzia nelle pubbliche cause e nelle private.' Brunetto Latini, *Rettorica* 4. Cf. also *Li Livres dou tresor* 3.1–2 and Cicero's *De inventione* 1.1–2 for the power of eloquence in the city. More generally, see A. Galletti, *L'eloquenza (dalle origini al XVI secolo): Storia dei generi letterari* (Milan 1938). Cf. *De vulgari eloquentia* 1.17.1 for the complex senses in which language is envisioned as 'illustre, cardinale, aulicum et curiale.'

[12] G. Paparelli, '*Fictio*: La definizione dantesca della poesia,' in *Ideologia e poesia di Dante* (Florence 1975) 53–138, views allegorical poetry in rhetorical terms. For a review of the theological understanding of allegory, see Jean Pèpin, *Dante et la tradition de l'allégorie* (Montreal 1970).

quately probed.[13] It is not my intention to review here the research that scholars
such as Schiaffini, Pazzaglia, Tateo, Baldwin, and others have carried out on
the various influences on Dante's thinking about rhetoric, or their systematic
analyses of the places in Dante's *œuvre* where rhetoric is explicitly mentioned.[14]
I shall focus instead on the *Convivio*, the *Vita nuova*, and *Inferno* 27 to show
how rhetoric works itself out in these texts, but I will also submit new evidence
that might shed light on Dante's position in the liberal arts, namely, thirteenth-
century polemics involving the secular masters of theology at the University
of Paris and the anti-academicism of the early Franciscans.

There is no significant trace of this polemic in the *Convivio*. The point of
departure for this unfinished treatise, and the principle that shapes its articula-
tion, is the authority of Aristotle, who in his *Metaphysics*, which Dante calls
'la Prima Filosofia,' states that 'tutti li uomini naturalmente desiderano di
sapere.'[15] The reference to Aristotle may well be an enactment of the technique
of the exordium which rhetorical conventions prescribe. But the reference also
announces what turns out to be the central preoccupation of the four books:
namely, that knowledge is made available by and through the light of natural
reason. This recognition of man's rationality allows Dante to argue that it
can be the choice of man to pursue the way to achieve the good life on this
earth. In spite of the initial *sententia*, the *Convivio* is explicitly modeled not on
Aristotle's *Metaphysics*, which deals with pure theoretical knowledge such as
the knowledge of spiritual entities, but on Aristotle's *Ethics*. This is, as Isidore
of Seville refers to it, the practical 'ars bene vivendi,' which casts man in the
here and now of his historical existence and which demands that man exercise
the choices (without which no ethics can be conceived) appropriate to a moral
agent.[16]

It is this philosophical optimism about human rationality that accounts for
the thematic configuration of the *Convivio*. The narrative is punctuated, for

---

[13] The tension between the liberal arts — and rhetoric chief among them — has been
neglected by Dante studies, although medieval scholarship has probed the issue. See, for
instance, P. Delhaye, 'Grammatica et Ethica au xiie siècle,' *Recherches de théologie ancienne
et médiévale* 25 (1958) 59–110; H. de Lubac, 'St. Grégoire et la grammaire,' *Recherches de
science religieuse* 48 (1960) 185–226; J. A. Weisheipl, 'Classification of the Sciences in Medieval
Thought,' *Medieval Studies* 27 (1965) 55–90.

[14] A convenient summary is available in the *Enciclopedia dantesca*, ed. U. Bosco (Rome
1978) IV 892–93.

[15] *Convivio* 1.1.1.

[16] 'Philosophiae species tripertita est: una naturalis, quae Graece Physica appellatur...
altera moralis, quae Graece Ethica dicitur, in qua de moribus agitur: tertia rationalis, quae
Graece vocabulo Logica appellatur. . . . In Physica igitur causa quaerendi, in Ethica ordo
vivendi, in Logica ratio intellegendi versatur. . . . Ethicam Socrates primus ad corrigendos
conponendosque mores instituit, atque omne studium eius ad bene vivendi disputationem
perduxit' (*Etym.* 2.24.3–5).

instance, with references to one's own natural language as preferable to Latin, which is at some remove from one's own life; it is clustered with insistent discussions of the moral virtues and whether or not nobility is contingent on birth, wealth, or customs; it focuses on the value of political life and the justice which the Roman Empire, a product of human history, managed to establish in the world.[17] What sustains the textual movement is above all a belief in the allegory of poets as a technique that affords the thorough interpretability of the indirections of poetic language.[18] Running parallel to the notion that poetry can be the object of a full philosophical investigation, there is an insistence on the knowability of the moral and rational operations of man.

This acceptance of the natural order is the principle that lies at the heart of two related and crucial gestures which shape the intellectual structure of the *Convivio*. The first, as Gilson has argued,[19] is the revolutionary re-arrangement, within the confines of the *Convivio*, of the dignity of aims: ethics rather than metaphysics is placed as the *summum bonum*. The second is the subordination of rhetoric to ethics. This statement needs clarification. The first treatise actually begins by explaining Dante's own shift away from the *Vita nuova* to the *Convivio*:

> Non si concede per li retorici alcuno di sè medesimo sanza necessaria cagione parlare, e da ciò è l'uomo rimosso perchè parlare d'alcuno non si può che il parladore non lodi o non biasimi quelli di cui elli parla: . . . Veramente . . . per necessarie cagioni lo parlare di sè è conceduto: . . . L'una è quando sanza ragionare di sè grande infamia o pericolo, non si può cessare; . . . E questa necessitate mosse Boezio di sè medesimo parlare, acciò che sotto pretesto di consolazione escusasse la perpetuale infamia del suo essilio. . . . L'altra è quando, per ragionare di sè, grandissima utilitade ne segue altrui per via di dottrina; e questa ragione mosse Agustino ne le sue Confessioni a parlare di sè, chè per lo processo de la sua vita, . . . ne diede essemplo e dottrina. . . .[20]

The passage is primarily a dismissal of what is known as epideictic rhetoric, one of the three classical divisions — along with the deliberative and the forensic — of rhetoric proper. Epideictic rhetoric, says Cicero in *De inventione*, is the

---

[17] Cf. *Convivio* 4.4.

[18] 'Onde, sì come dice lo Filosofo nel primo de la Fisica, la natura vuole che ordinatamente si proceda ne la nostra conoscenza, cioè procedendo da quello che conoscemo meglio in quello che conoscemo non così bene: dico che la natura vuole, in quanto questa via di conoscere è in noi naturalmente innata. . . . Io adunque, per queste ragioni, tuttavia sopra ciascuna canzone ragionerò prima la litterale sentenza, e appresso di quello ragionerò la sua allegoria, cioè la nascosa veritade' (*Convivio* 2.1.13–15). The passage is the conclusion of Dante's treatment of the allegory of poets.

[19] Étienne Gilson, 'Philosophy in the *Banquet*,' in *Dante and Philosophy*, trans. D. Moore (New York 1963) 83–161. But see the review by Bruno Nardi, 'Dante e la Filosofia,' in *Nel mondo di Dante* (Rome 1944) 209–45.

[20] *Convivio* 1.2.12.

branch of oratory 'quod tribuitur in alicuius certae personae laudem aut vituperationem.'[21] This epideictic mode, quite clearly, is identified with the autobiographical writing of Boethius and St. Augustine. But for all the acknowledgment of the utility and exemplariness of the *Confessions*, Dante's passage is overtly anti-Augustinian: the point of the *Convivio* is that the natural order, of which St. Augustine had too narrow an appreciation ,is the locus of a possible moral-social project. More importantly, the passage marks an anti-Augustinian phase in Dante because it signals the limitations of autobiographical writing in favor of a philosophical discourse that would transcend private concerns and squarely grapple, as the *Convivio* will do, with the issue of the authority of intellectual knowledge and its relationship to political power.

The departure from the *Confessions* is in reality Dante's way of distancing himself from his own Augustinian text, the *Vita nuova*, and its rhetoric. It could be pointed out that in the *Vita nuova* there is an occasional resistance to the excesses of self-staging: 'converrebbe essere me laudatore di me medesimo, la quale cosa è al postutto biasimevole a chi lo fae.'[22] Yet the rhetoric of the self remains the path through which the poet's own imaginative search is carried out. The exordium of the *Vita nuova* consistently stresses the autobiographical boundaries of the experiences about to be related:

> In quella parte del libro de la mia memoria dinanzi a la quale poco si potrebbe leggere, si trova una rubrica la quale dice: *Incipit vita nova*. Sotto la quale rubrica io trovo scritte le parole le quali è mio intendimento d'assemplare in questo libello; e se non tutte, almeno la loro sentenzia.[23]

The exordium is a proem, as Dante will call it later in the narrative, in the technical sense of a *captatio benevolentiae*.[24] One could also point out the

---

[21] 'Aristoteles autem . . . tribus in generibus rerum versari, rhetoris officium putavit, demonstrativo, deliberativo, iudiciali. Demonstrativum est quod tribuitur in alicuius certae personae laudem aut vituperationem; deliberativum, quod positum in disceptatione civili habet in se sententiae dictionem; iudiciale, quod positum in iudicio habet in se accusationem et defensionem aut petitionem et recusationem.' *De inventione* 1.5.7, ed. H. M. Hubbel (Cambridge 1976).

[22] Quoted from the *Vita nuova* 28.2, ed. D. de Robertis (Milan–Naples 1980).

[23] *Vita nuova* 1.1.

[24] In chapter 28.2, Dante writes: 'E avvegna che forse piacerebbe a presente trattare alquanto de la sua partita da noi, non è lo mio intendimento di trattarne qui per tre ragioni: la prima è che ciò non è del presente proposito, se volemo guardare nel proemio che precede questo libello.' De Robertis (*Vita nuova* 27) rightly refers to the Epistle to Cangrande (13.44) for the sense of proem: 'proemium est principium in oratione rhetorica sicut prologus in poetica et preludium in fistulatione.' The quotation, which is from Aristotle's *Rhetoric* 3.14, introduces Dante's own distinction between rhetoric and poetry which is central to our discussion: 'Est etiam prenotandum, quod prenuntiatio ista, que comuniter exordium dici potest, aliter fit a poetis, aliter fit a rhetoribus. Rhetores enim concessere prelibare dicenda ut animum comparent auditoris; sed poete non solum hoc faciunt, quin ymo post hec invoca-

technical resonance of the term 'sententia.' Although the *Glossarium* of Du Cange refers only to the juridical sense of the word and neglects the meaning of moral lesson, which one can find in the *Rhetorica ad Herennium*, it hints that the text is also a plea for oneself in the presence of one's beloved. But what is central in the proem is the textual presence, which has gone unnoticed by the editors, of Guido Cavalcanti's 'Donna me prega.'

As is well known, Cavalcanti wrote his poem in response to the physician Guido Orlandi's query about the origin of love. Orlandi's sonnet 'Onde si move e donde nasce amore?' proceeds to ask where love dwells, whether it is *sustanzia*, *accidente*, or *memora*, and what feeds love; it climaxes with a series of questions as to whether love has its own figural representation or whether it goes around disguised.[25] Cavalcanti replies that love takes its dwelling place in that part where memory is, 'in quella parte dove sta memora / prende suo stato,' a formulation which Dante's exordium, 'in quella parte del libro de la mia memoria,' unequivocally echoes.

The echo compels us to place the *Vita nuova* as conceived from the start in the shadow of Cavalcanti's poetry, but it does not mean that the two texts are telling the same story. The most fundamental difference between them is their antithetical views of rhetoric and the nature of the aesthetic experience. For Guido, memory — which is in the sensitive faculty of the soul — is the place where love literally resides. In his skeptical materialism there is no room for a vision that might relieve one's dark desires.[26] The deeper truth — so runs Cavalcanti's argument — is imageless, and Guido's steady effort in the poem is to unsettle any possible bonds between poetic images and love, or love and the order of the rational soul. The scientism of 'Donna me prega' literalizes desire and makes it part of the night: its poetry, with its overt anti-metaphysical strains, paradoxically turns against poetry and assigns truth to the idealized realm of philosophical speculation.

For Dante, on the contrary, the truth of love is to be the child of time — as Venus is — and hence under the sway of mutability and death. The tem-

---

tionem quandam emittunt. Et hoc est eis conveniens, quia multa invocatione opus est eis, cum aliquid contra comunem modum hominum a superioribus substantiis petendum est, quasi divinum quoddam munas.' The quotation from the Epistle to Cangrande is taken from *The Letters of Dante* 13.44–48, ed. Paget Toynbee, 2nd ed. (Oxford 1966).

[25] See the remarks by Gianfranco Contini, *Poeti del Duecento* (Milan–Naples 1960) II 522–23.

[26] Here are the main bibliographical items on Cavalcanti's poem: Mario Casella, 'La canzone d'amore di Guido Cavalcanti,' *Studi di filologia italiana* 7 (1944) 97–160; J. E. Shaw, *Guido Cavalcanti's Theory of Love: The Canzone d'Amore and Other Related Problems* (Toronto 1949); B. Nardi, 'L'averroismo del "primo amico" di Dante,' in *Dante e la cultura medievale*, 2nd ed. (Bari 1949) 93–129; see also by Nardi, 'Dante e Guido Cavalcanti,' and 'L'amore e i medici medievali,' in *Saggi e note di critica dantesca* (Milan–Naples 1966) 190–219 and 238–67; Maria Corti, 'Guido Cavalcanti e una diagnosi dell'amore,' in *La felicità mentale: Nuove prospettive per Cavalcanti e Dante* (Turin 1983) 3–37.

porality of desire links it unavoidably to memory, but memory is here — and this is the main departure from Cavalcanti — a book or the 'memoria artificialis,' which is one of the five parts of rhetoric. The parts are usually identified as *inventio, dispositio, elocutio, memoria*, and *pronuntiatio*; memory is defined as 'firma animi rerum ac verborum perceptio.'[27] The rhetoricity of memory turns the quest of the *Vita nuova* into an interrogation of the value of figures. More precisely, memory is not the refuge of a deluded self, the *a priori* recognition of appearances as illusive shapes, the way Cavalcanti would have it. For Dante, memory is the visionary faculty, the imagination through which the poet can question the phenomena of natural existence and urge them to release their hidden secrets. It can be said that Cavalcanti makes of memory a sepulcher and of death the cutting edge of vision: he broods over the severance death entails, and it thwarts his imagination. He is too much of a realist, too much of a philosopher to be able to soar above the dark abyss into which, nonetheless, he stares.

But the poet of the *Vita nuova* is impatient with this skepticism, this dead literalism, and from the start he seeks to rescue vision from the platitudes of the materialists. The figures of love are not irrelevant shadows or insubstantial phantoms in the theater of one's own mind, as Cavalcanti thinks when he ceaselessly beckons Dante to join him on the plain where the light of ideas endures. Nor are women part of an infinite metaphorization, always replaceable (hence never necessary), as the physician Dante da Maiano believes, who tells Dante that his dream of love is only lust that a good bath can cure.[28]

The contrivance of the lady of the screen, related in chapter four, which literally makes a woman the screen on which the lover projects and displaces his own desires, is rejected because it casts doubt on Beatrice's own uniqueness. At the same time, chapter eight, which tells of the death of one of Beatrice's friends, allows Dante's sense of poetry in the *Vita nuova* to surface. The passage is undoubtedly meant to prefigure Beatrice's own future death. Retrospectively, however, it is also another put-down of the materialists' belief that love is reducible to the mere materiality of bodies. Dante refers to the dead woman as a body without a soul — she is one 'lo cui corpo io vidi giacere sanza l'anima.' The poem he then proceeds to write is 'Piangete, amanti, poi che piange Amore,' which turns out to be, quite appropriately, a lament over the dead figure, 'la morta imagine.' But this poet can glance heavenward, 'ove

[27] *De inventione* 1.7.9.

[28] The reference is to the first sonnet of the *Vita nuova* ('A ciascun'alma presa e gentil core'), which produced poetic responses by Cavalcanti, Cino da Pistoia ('Naturalmente chere ogni amadore'), and Dante da Maiano ('Da ciò che stato sei dimandatore'). Cf. my 'The Language of Poetry in the *Vita nuova*,' *Rivista di studi italiani* 1 (1983) 3–14.

l'alma gentile già locata era.'[29] In short, Dante installs his poetry at the point
where Cavalcanti's poetry — where most poetry, for that matter — stops:
between the dead body and the soul's existence. Images are not *a priori*,
mere simulacra of death, and the 'stilo de la loda,' which re-enacts the
principles of epideictic rhetoric, strives for a definition of Beatrice's felt but
unknown essence.

This concern with metaphysics, with the links between rhetoric and the soul,
emerges in chapter twenty-five, where metaphor is said to be the trope that
animates the face of the world. The meditation on metaphor, which is the
burden of the chapter, is carried out as an attempt to grasp the nature of love.
Here we see why Venus should be coupled to rhetoric. The question Dante
raises has a stunning simplicity: is love a divinity, as the Notaro suggests, or is
it a mere rhetorical figure, as Guido Cavalcanti states in his *pastorella*, 'In un
boschetto'?[30] Dante defines love in only partial agreement with Cavalcanti,
for whom love is 'un accidente — che sovente — è fero,' as 'accidente in sustanzia.'[31] The metaphoricity of Love is then discussed in terms of a movement
from the animate to the inanimate and vice versa:

> Onde, con ciò sia cosa che a li poete sia conceduta maggiore licenza di parlare
> che a li prosaici dittatori, e quei dicitori per rima non siano altro che poete
> volgari, degno e ragionevole è che a loro sia maggiore licenzia largita di
> parlare che a li altri parlatori volgari: onde se alcuna figura o colore rettorico
> è conceduto a li poete, conceduto è a li rimatori. Dunque, se noi vedemo che
> li poete hanno parlato a le cose inanimate, sì come se avessero senso e ragione,
> e fattele parlare insieme; e non solamente cose vere, ma cose non vere, cioè
> che detto hanno, di cose le quali non sono, che parlano, e detto che molti
> accidenti parlano, sì come fossero sustanzie e uomini; degno è lo dicitore
> per rima di fare lo somigliante, ma non sanza ragione alcuna, ma con ragione
> la quale poi sia possibile d'aprire per prosa. . . . Per questo medesimo poeta
> parla la cosa che non è animata e le cose animate, nel terzo de lo Eneida,
> quivi: *Dardanide duri.* Per Lucano parla la cosa animata a la cosa inani-
> mata . . . per Ovidio parla Amore, sì come fosse persona umana. . . .[32]

It could be mentioned that 'dicitori per rime' and 'prosaici dittatori' are
phrases that find their gloss in Brunetto Latini's *Rettorica*, which is defined as

---

29 'Audite quanto Amor le fece orranza, / ch'io 'l vidi lamentare in forma vera / sovra la
morta imagine avvenente; / e riguarda ver lo ciel sovente, / ove l'alma gentil già locata era, /
che donna fu di sì gaia sembianza' (*Vita nuova* 8.6).

30 The divinity and/or rhetoricity of the god of love is a commonplace of love poetry.
Cf. Cavalcanti's jocular pose: 'Per man mi prese, d'amorosa voglia, / e disse che donato
m'avea il core; / menommi sott'una freschetta foglia, / là dov'e' vidi fior' d'ogni colore; /
e tanto vi sentiò gioia e dolzore, / che 'l die d'amore — mi parea vedere.' On this problem see
Thomas Hyde, *The Poetic Theology of Love: Cupid in Renaissance Literature* (Newark, Del.
1986).

31 *Vita nuova* 25.1–2.

32 *Vita nuova* 25.7–10.

the science of two aims, one of which 'insegna dire' and the other 'insegna dittare.'[33] More to the point, metaphor is given in the guise of προσωποποιία, the orphic fiction whereby that which is dead is given a voice or, more correctly, a face.

With the actual death of Beatrice, related from chapter twenty-eight on, the fiction that poetry is capable of providing a simulation of life is no longer sufficient. To be sure, Beatrice was described as the living figure of love, but now that she is physically dead, the metaphors for her seem to be another empty fiction. If the question while Beatrice was alive was whether she is and how she is unique, now that she is dead the question is finding the sense of metaphors that recall her. Dante's imaginative dead-end at this point (it induces tears, but Dante records no poetry) narrows in the prose to a vast image of general darkness, the death of Christ. An analogy is established between Beatrice and Christ in an effort to invest the memory of Beatrice with a glow of material substantiality. Charles Singleton views this analogy as the exegetical principle of the *Vita nuova*, the aim of which is to portray the lover's growing awareness of the providentiality of Beatrice's presence in his life.[34]

But the tension between the Christological language, the status of which depends on the coincidence between the image and its essence, and the poetic imagination, which in this text comes forth in the shifting forms of memory and desire, is problematic. There is no doubt that the poetic imagination aspires to achieve an absolute stability which only the foundation of theology (which has its own visionariness) can provide. But Dante marks with great clarity the differences between his own private world and the common theological quest. The penultimate sonnet of the *Vita nuova* addresses exactly this predicament:

> Deh peregrini che pensosi andate,
> forse di cosa che non v'è presente.
> venite voi da sì lontana gente,
> com'a la vista voi ne dimostrate,
> che non piangete quando voi passate
> per lo suo mezzo la città dolente
> come quelle persone che neente
> par che 'ntendesser la sua gravitate?
> Se voi restaste per volerlo audire,
> certo lo cor de'sospiri mi dice
> che lagrimando n'uscireste pui.
> Ell'ha perduta la sua beatrice;
> e le parole ch'om dilei pò dire
> hanno vertù di far pianger altrui.

---

[33] *Rettorica* 8.
[34] Charles S. Singleton, *An Essay on the 'Vita nuova'* (Cambridge, Mass. 1949) 20–24.

The sonnet is an apostrophe to the pilgrims who are going to Rome to see the true image — literally a prosopopoeia — Christ left on the veil of Veronica. The pilgrims are unaware of the lover's own heart-sickness, and the poet's mythology of love — that Beatrice is an analogy of Christ — comes forth as too private a concern. More precisely, the sonnet is built on a series of symmetrical correspondences: the pilgrims are going to see Christ's image and are caught in an empty space between nostalgia and expectation, away from their homes and not quite at their destination; the lover is in his own native place, but, like the pilgrims, away from his beatitude. But there is another contrast in the sonnet which unsettles the symmetries: the motion of the pilgrims, who are on their way, is in sharp contrast to the poet's invitation that they stop to hear the story of his grief. In the canzone 'Donne ch'avete intelletto d'amore,' the heavens vie with the lover to have Beatrice; now the terms are reversed: the lover seeks to waylay the pilgrims, begs them to stop for a while, a gesture that is bound to remind us of the repeated temptations the pilgrim himself eventually will experience in *Purgatorio*.

The vision of the pilgrims' journey to Rome triggers the last sonnet, 'Oltre la spera,' which tells of the poet's own pilgrimage. This is an imaginative journey to the separate souls which the intellect cannot grasp, for the intellect stands to those souls, Dante says, 'sì come l'occhio debole a lo sole: e ciò dice lo Filosofo nel secondo de la Metafisica.' At the moment when a revelation is at hand in this most visionary text, the eye is dazzled by the sun and the essences remain hidden behind their own inapproachable light. The perplexing quality of the image is heightened by the fact that it was used by both Averroës and Aquinas to describe the separate souls. Doctrinally, the text evokes and is poised between two opposite metaphysical systems.[35] More poignantly, the phrase "'l sospir ch'esce del mio core' echoes 'sospiri, / che nascon de' penser che son nel core,' which in turn is patterned on Cavalcanti's 'Se mercè fosse amica a' miei disiri.'[36] Cavalcanti restates the absolute separation of desire and its aim; Dante yokes rhetoric to metaphysics, makes of rhetoric the privileged imaginative path to metaphysics, though rhetoric can never yield the spiritual essence it gropes for.

The *Convivio* picks at the very start the reference to Aristotle's *Metaphysics* on which the *Vita nuova* comes to a close. But Dante challenges, as hinted earlier, the traditional primacy of metaphysics and replaces it with ethics.

---

[35] G. Salvadori, *Sulla vita giovanile di Dante* (Rome 1906) 113–14, remarks that the comparison derives from St. Thomas Aquinas (*Summa contra gentiles* 3.43), who quotes Aristotle. St. Thomas actually gets it from Averroës' commentary on the *Metaphysics*.

[36] 'i miei sospiri, / che nascon della mente ov'è Amore / e vanno sol ragionando dolore / e non trovan persona che li miri, / giriano agli occhi con tanta vertute, / che 'l forte e 'l duro lagrimar che fanno / ritornebbe in allegrezza e 'n gioia.'

The move is so radical that Dante dramatizes the shift to ethics in the first song, 'Voi che 'ntendendo il terzo ciel movete.' Written in the form of a *tenso*, a battle of thoughts within the self, and addressed to the angelic intelligences that move Venus, the planet of rhetoric, the poem tells the triumph of the 'donna gentile' — Philosophy — over Beatrice. With the enthronement of Philosophy, rhetoric is reduced to an ancillary status: it is a technique of persuasion, the cover that wraps the underlying morality within its seductive folds. The *envoi* explicitly confronts this issue:

> Canzone, io credo che saranno radi
> color che tua ragione intendan bene,
> tanto la parli faticosa e forte.
> Onde, se per ventura elli addivien
> che tu dinanzi da persone vadi
> che non ti paian d'essa bene accorte,
> allor ti priego che ti riconforte,
> dicendo lor, diletta mia novella:
> 'Ponete mente almen com'io son bella!'

The confinement of rhetoric to a decorative role in philosophical discourse is not unusual. From Cicero to Brunetto Latini rhetoricians are asked to link rhetoric to ethics because of rhetoric's inherent shiftiness, its power to argue contradictory aspects of the same question.[37] In a way, it is possible to suggest that the voice of Dante in the *Convivio* is a Boethian voice, for like Boethius, who in his *De consolatione Philosophiae* banishes the meretricious muses of poetry to make room for Lady Philosophy, under whose aegis poetry is possible, Dante, too, makes of poetry the dress of Philosophy.

This analogy with the Boethian text stops here, for unlike Boethius, Dante does not seek consolation for too long. Philosophy, says Isidore of Seville, is 'meditatio mortis.'[38] Dante has no intention of being trapped in the grief that the shadow of Beatrice's death caused in him. He turns his back on the past in the *Convivio* and ponders ethics, which is not the land of the dead, but the 'ars bene vivendi.'[39] As a matter of fact, his voice is that of the intellectual,

---

[37] 'La sentenzia d'Aristotile fece cotale, che rettorica è arte, ma rea, per ciò che per eloquenzia parea che fosse avenuto più male che bene a' comuni e a' divisi. Onde Tullio... conclude che noi dovemo studiare in rettorica, recando a cciò molti argomenti, li quali muovono d'onesto e d'utile e possibile e necessario' (*Rettorica* 7); cf. also p. 16 on how the eloquent and wise man establishes cities and justice. More generally see my 'Rhetoric and History,' in *Dante, Poet of the Desert: History and Allegory in the* DIVINE COMEDY (Princeton 1979) 66–106.

[38] 'Philosophia est divinarum humanarumque rerum, in quantum homini possibile est, probabilis scientia. Aliter: Philosophia est ars artium et disciplina disciplinarum. Rursus: Philosophia est meditatio mortis, quod magis convenit Christianis qui, saeculi ambitione calcata, conversatione disciplinabili, similitudine futurae patriae vivunt' (*Etym.* 2.24.9).

[39] *Etym.* 2.24.5.

who, exiled and dispossessed, asserts the authority of his knowledge and seeks power by virtue of that knowledge.[40] This claim for power by an intellectual obviously does not start with Dante. Its origin lies in the revival of another sphere of rhetoric, the *artes dictaminis* elaborated by Alberic of Monte Cassino and the Bologna school of law and rhetoric, where intellectuals shaped and argued the political issues of the day.[41]

Yet Dante's project in the *Convivio* to cast the philosopher as the adviser of the emperor fails utterly. Many reasons have been suggested by Nardi, Leo, and others as to why the project collapsed.[42] The various reasons essentially boil down to Dante's awareness that a text expounding a system of values cannot be written unless it is accompanied by a theory of being. The text that attempts the synthesis is the *Divine Comedy*.

The point of departure of the poem is the encounter with Vergil, whose 'parola ornata' (an allusion to the *ornatus* of rhetoric) has the power, in Beatrice's language, to aid the pilgrim in his quest.[43] But if rhetoric is unavoidably the very stuff of the text, rhetoric's implications and links with the other disciplines of the encyclopedia are explicitly thematized in a number of places. One need only mention *Inferno* 15, where rhetoric, politics, grammar, law, and their underlying theory of nature are all drawn within the circle of knowledge; or *Inferno* 13, the canto which features the fate of Pier delle Vigne, the counselor at the court of Frederick II, whose failure can be gauged by Brunetto Latini's reference to him in *La rettorica* as a master in the art of 'dire et in dittare sopra le questioni opposte.'[44]

---

[40] 'E io adunque, che non seggio a la beata mensa . . . intendo fare un generale convivio . . . vegna qua qualunque è [per cura familiare o civile] ne la umana fame rimaso, e ad una mensa con li altri simili impediti s'assetti . . . e quelli e questi prendono la mia vivando col pane, che la farà loro e gustare e patire' (*Convivio* 1.1.10–14).

[41] H. Wieruszowski, '*Ars dictaminis* in the Time of Dante,' *Medievalia et humanistica* 1 (1943) 95–108; Charles T. Davis, 'Education in Dante's Florence,' *Speculum* 40 (1965) 415–35, rpt. in *Dante's Italy* (Philadelphia 1984) 137–65. Cf. also G. Vecchi, *Il magistero delle 'artes' latine a Bologna nel medioevo* (Bologna 1958).

[42] Ulrich Leo, 'The Unfinished *Convivio* and Dante's Rereading of the *Aeneid*,' *Medieval Studies* 13 (1951) 41–64; Bruno Nardi, 'Tre momenti dell'incontro di Dante con Virgilio' in *Saggi e note di critica dantesca* 220–37.

[43] See my *Dante, Poet of the Desert* 157–58.

[44] *Rettorica* 5. On Brunetto, cf. Helene Wieruszowski, 'Rhetoric and the Classics in Italian Education,' *Studia Gratiana* 2 (1967) 169–208, rpt. in *Politics and Culture in Medieval Spain and Italy* (Rome 1971) 589–627; cf. also Giancarlo Alessio, 'Brunetto Latini e Cicerone (e i dettatori),' *Italia medievale e umanistica* 22 (1979) 123–69. More generally, see Charles T. Davis, 'Brunetto Latini and Dante,' in *Dante's Italy* 166–97. For Pier della Vigna, see Ettore Paratore, 'Analisi "retorica" del canto di Pier della Vigna,' in *Tradizione e struttura in Dante* (Florence 1968) 178–220; William Stephany, 'Pier della Vigna's Self-Fulfilling Prophecies: The "Eulogy" of Frederick II and *Inferno* 13,' *Traditio* 38 (1982) 193–212.

I shall focus, however, on *Inferno* 27 because this is a canto that inscribes Dante's text within the boundaries of the thirteenth-century debate on the liberal arts and, more precisely, on the Franciscan attack against logic and speculative grammar. The canto is usually read in conjunction with the story of Ulysses that precedes it.[45] The dramatic connections between the two narratives, however superficial they may be, are certainly real. It can easily be granted that *Inferno* 27 is the parodic counter to *Inferno* 26 and its myth of style. In the *De vulgari eloquentia*, in the wake of Horace's *Ars poetica* and the *Rhetorica ad Herennium*, Dante classifies the tragic, elegiac, and comical styles in terms of fixed categories of a subject matter that is judged to be sublime, plain, or low.[46] In the canto of Ulysses, with its 'verba polita,' to use Matthew of Vendôme's phrase,[47] moral aphorisms and grandiloquence stage the language of the epic hero whose interlocutor is the epic poet Virgil.[48] Ulysses' is a high style, making his story a tragic text, for Ulysses is, like all tragic heroes, an overstater and hyperbole is his figure: he is one who has staked everything and has lost everything for seeking everything.

As we move into *Inferno* 27, there is a deliberate diminution of Ulysses' grandeur. His smooth talk is replaced by hypothetical sentences ('S'i' credesse che mia risposta fosse' or 'Se non fosse il gran prete' 61–70), parenthetical remarks ('s'i' odo il vero' 65), swearing, colloquialisms, and crude idioms. From the start, Guido's speech draws the exchange between Virgil and Ulysses within the confines of dialect:

> . . . . 'O tu, a cu' io drizzo
> la voce, e che parlavi mo Lombardo
> dicendo: "istra ten va, più non t'adizzo,"'   (19–21)

Virgil allows Dante to speak to Guido, 'Parla tu, questi è latino' (33), because Virgil, too, observes the rhetorical rules of stylistic hierarchy. There is a great deal of irony in shifting from Ulysses' high ground to the specifics of the Tuscan Apennines or Urbino and Ravenna. But from Dante's viewpoint the irony is vaster: degrees of style are illusory values, and Ulysses and Guido, for all their stylistic differences, are damned to the same punishment of being enveloped in tongues of fire in the area of fraud among the evil counselors. Even though the image of the Sicilian bull within which its maker perishes (7–9) conveys the sense that we are witnessing the fate of contrivers trapped by their own contrivances, it also harks back to Ulysses' artifact, the Trojan horse.

---

[45] Cf. James G. Truscott, 'Ulysses and Guido: *Inferno* XXVI–XXVII,' *Dante Studies* 91 (1973) 47–72. Louis R. Rossi, 'The Fox Outfoxed (*Inferno* XXVII),' *Cesare Barbieri Courier* 7 (Spring 1965) 13–23, focuses on the logical argument of the canto.

[46] *De vulgari eloquentia* 2.4.5–7. Cf. also *Rhetorica ad Herennium* 4.8; *Ars versificatoria* 2.5–8.

[47] *Ars versificatoria* 2.9.

[48] See *Dante, Poet of the Desert* 66–106.

It could be said that Guido is the truth, as it were, of Ulysses. If the pairing
of their voices, however, can be construed as a confrontation between the epic
and the mock-heroic, style is not just a technique of characterizing their
respective moral visions. Guido's municipal particularity of style introduces
us to the question of political rhetoric — the rhetoric by which cities are
established or destroyed — which is featured in the canto. What we are
shown, to be sure, is an obsessive element of Dante's political thought: Guido
da Montefeltro, the adviser of Pope Boniface VIII, counseled him how to
capture the city of Palestrina, and this advice is placed within the reality of the
temporal power of the papacy. From this standpoint *Inferno* 27 prefigures
St. Peter's invective in *Paradiso* 27, and it also echoes *Inferno* 19, the ditch
of the Simonists where Pope Boniface is expected.

As in *Inferno* 19, we are given the cause of the general sickness: just as
Constantine sought out Pope Sylvester to cure his leprosy (94–99), so did
Boniface VIII seek Guido da Montefeltro to cure his pride. If leprosy suggests
the rotting away of the body politic, pride is the fever of the mystical body;
the origin of both is the Donation of Constantine. The chiasmus that the
comparison draws (Boniface is equated with Constantine) points to the unholy
mingling of the spiritual and secular orders and to the role-reversal of the
pope and his adviser.[49]

But there is in the canto an attention to political discourse that goes beyond
this level of generality. In a way, just as there was a theology of style, we are
now allowed to face the politics of theology. We are led, more precisely, into
the council chamber — behind the scenes, as it were — where 'li accorgimenti
e le coperte vie' (76), the art of wielding naked political power, is shown. Here
big deals are struck, so big that they focus on the destruction of cities and the
salvation of souls. These are the terms of the transaction: by virtue of his
absolute sovereignty (an authority that depends on the argument of the two
keys, 'Lo ciel poss'io serrare e diserrare, / come tu sai; però son due le chiavi /
che 'l mio antecessor non ebbe care' [103–5]), the pope promises absolution for
Guido's misdeed.[50] Guido's advice is simply to make promises without planning
to keep them, 'lunga promessa con l'attender corto / ti farà triunfar ne l'alto
seggio' (110–11).

This advice, I would suggest, textually repeats and reverses Brunetto Latini's formulation in *La rettorica*. Commenting on Cicero's statement that the
stability of a city is contingent on keeping faith, on observing laws and prac-

---

[49] An extensive bibliography of the canto is available in Gian Luigi Berardi, 'Dante
Inferno XIX,' in *Letteratura e critica: Studi in onore di Natalino Sapegno* (Rome 1975) II
93–147.

[50] 'E poi ridisse: "Tuo cuor non sospetti; / finor t'assolvo, e tu m'insegna fare / sì come
Penestrino in terra getti"' (*Inferno* 27.100–2).

ticing obedience to one another, Brunetto adds that to keep faith means to be loyal to one's commitments and to keep one's word: 'e dice la legge che fede è quella che promette l'uno e l'altro l'attende.'[51] The deliberate violation of the ethical perspective, which alone, as Brunetto fully knows, can neutralize the dangerous simulations that rhetoric affords, brings to a focus what the canto of Ulysses unveils: that ethics is the set of values rhetoric manipulates at will.[52] From Dante's viewpoint, however, the arrangement between the pope and his counselor is charged with heavy ironies that disrupt the utilitarian calculus of the principals.

The pope begins by taking literally what is known as his *plenitudo potestatis*, the fullness of spiritual and temporal powers given to him by God, yet he is powerless to act and seize a town. He believes in the performative power of his words, that by virtue of his office his words are a sacramental pledge. Yet he takes advice to say words that do not measure up to his actions. There is irony even in Dante's use of the word 'officio' — a term which for Cicero means moral duty; its appearance in line 91 only stresses the dereliction of duty. On the other hand, there is Guido, who knows that in the tough political games men play there is a gap between words and reality. Yet he believes in the pope's 'argomenti gravi' (106) — a word that designates probable demonstration according to logical rules — [53] without recognizing that the pope does not deliver what he promises, which — after all — was exactly Guido's advice to him.

The point of these ironies is that Boniface and Guido thoroughly resemble and deserve each other. Both believe in compromises, practical gains, and moral adjustments, as if God's grace could be made adaptable to their calculus and to the narrow stage of everyday politics. And both are sophists of the kind St. Augustine finds especially odious in *De doctrina Christiana*,[54] those who

---

[51] The whole passage reads: 'Di questa parola [sc. fede] intendo che coloro ànno fede che non ingannano altrui e che non vogliono che lite nè discordia sia nella cittadi, e se vi fosse si la mettono in pace. Et fede, sì come dice un savio, è lla speranza della cosa promessa; e dice la legge che fede è quella che promette l'uno e l'altro l'attende. Ma Tulio medesimo dice in un altro libro *delli offici* che fede è fondamento di giustizia, veritade in parlare e fermezza delle promesse; e questa èe quella virtude ch'è appellata lealtade.' *Rettorica* 19.

[52] Cf. *Dante, Poet of the Desert* 78–81.

[53] 'E queste due proprietadi sono ne la Dialettica: chè la Dialettica è minore in suo corpo che null'altra scienza, chè perfettamente è compilata e terminata in quello tanto testo che ne l'Arte vecchia e ne la Nuove si trova; e va più velata che nulla scienza, in quanto procede con più sofistici e probabili argomenti più che altra.' *Convivio* 2.13.12.

[54] 'There are, moreover, many false conclusions of the reasoning process called sophisms, and frequently they so imitate true conclusions that they mislead not only those who are slow but also the ingenious when they do not pay close attention.' St. Augustine, *On Christian Doctrine* 2.31, trans. D. W. Robertson, Jr. (Indianapolis–New York 1958).

transform the world of political action to a world of carefully spoken words. As a sophist, Boniface entertains the illusion that he can control the discourse of others and ends up controlling Guido while at the same time being controlled by him. As a sophist, Guido is the character who is always drawing the wrong logical inference from his actions: he mistakenly believes Dante is dead because he has heard that nobody ever came alive from the depths of Hell (61–66); he becomes a friar, believing that thus girt he could make amends for his past (66–69).

What exactly does it mean to suggest, as I am doing, that Guido is portrayed as if he were a logician? And how does it square with the fact (to the best of my knowledge it has not been investigated by commentators) that he is a Franciscan, or, as he calls himself, a 'cordigliero' (67)? The fact that Guido is a Franciscan has far-reaching implications for the dramatic and intellectual structure of the canto. The tongues of fire in which the sinners are wrapped are an emblem more appropriate to a Franciscan like Guido than to Ulysses. The tongues of fire are usually explained as a parody of the Pentecostal gift of prophecy that descended on the apostles at the time of the origin of the Church. It happens, however, that the Constitution of the Franciscans established that the friars should convene at the Porziuncola every four years on Pentecost.[55] The reason for this ritual is to be found in the Franciscans' conscious vision of themselves as the new apostles, capable of reforming the world.

Guido's language perverts the Pentecostal gift, and the perversion puts him in touch with the fierce enemies of the Franciscans, the logicians. The possibility for this textual connection is suggested by the canto itself. At Guido's death there is a *disputatio* between one of the 'neri cherubini' and St. Francis over Guido's soul (112–17). The devil wins the debate and speaks of himself as a 'loico' (123). The debate between a devil and St. Francis is not much of a surprise, for as a fallen angel — one of the cherubim — the devil is the direct antagonist of Francis, who is commonly described in his hagiographies as 'the angel coming from the east, with the seal of the living God.'[56] Furthermore, the reference to the devil as one of the cherubim, which means 'plenitudo

---

[55] The link is made by St. Bonaventure, *Legenda duae de vita S. Francisci seraphici* (Quaracchi 1923) 3.21–22. Cf. also Thomas of Celano, *Vita prima*, ed. M. Bihl in *Analecta franciscana* 10 (1941) Ch. 9, par. 22. Celano writes that while preaching, St. Francis spoke with such 'fervor' (an overt metaphor of fiery spirituality) that he 'made a tongue of his whole body.' Guido da Montefeltro, a Franciscan, is now, ironically, trapped in a tongue of fire. Cf. *Vita prima* 1.27.73. The importance of Franciscan prophecy and the Joachistic extension of it in Dante has been magisterially illustrated by R. E. Kaske, 'Dante's "DXV" and "Veltro,"' *Traditio* 17 (1961) 185–254. More generally, see Marjorie Reeves, *The Influence of Prophecy in the Later Middle Ages: A Study in Joachism* (Oxford 1969) 135–228.

[56] The phrase is from Rev. 7.12. The scriptural phrase is used by St. Bonaventure, *Legenda maior* preface. *Omnibus* 632.

scientiae' and is the attribute of the Dominicans,[57] seems to be involved obliquely in Dante's representation of both orders of friars. But this is not the hidden allegory of a *quaestio disputata* between Dominicans and Franciscans. What is at stake, on the contrary, is the long debate in which the two fraternal orders were engaged in the thirteenth century — and in which they end up on the side of their opponents, as Dante implies.[58] The debate centered on the value of the liberal arts at the University of Paris.[59]

In historical terms, the debate saw the preachers and the mendicants opposed by the secular masters of theology. The Dominicans, to be sure, adapted quickly to the pressures of university circles because they were founded with the explicit intellectual aim of combating heresies. The Franciscans, on the other hand, in response to the call for evangelical practice, believed that their homiletics had to retrieve the essence of the good news without any sophistry.[60] St. Francis is an 'idiota,' given to the cult of *simplicitas*; Paris, the city of learning, is made to appear the enemy of Assisi.[61]

This stress on simplicity did not mean that the Franciscans kept away for too long from the world of learning. There is in effect a strong Augustinian strand

---

[57] 'L'un fu tutto serafico in ardore; / l'altro per sapienza in terra fue / di cherubica luce uno splendore' (*Par.* 11.37–39); 'Cherubin interpretatur plenitudo scientiae' (*Summa theologiae* 1.63.7).

[58] The debate has been much examined. See Maurice Perrod, *Maître Guillaume de Saint-Amour, l'Université de Paris et les ordres mendiants au XIIIe siècle* (Paris 1895); Christine Thouzellier, 'La place du "Periculis" de Guillaume de Saint-Amour dans les polémiques universitaires du xiiie siècle,' *Revue historique* 156 (1927) 69–83; Decima L. Douie, *The Conflict Between the Seculars and the Mendicants at the University of Paris in the Thirteenth Century*, Aquinas Paper 23 (London 1954); Yves M.-J. Congar, 'Aspects ecclésiologiques de la querelle entre mendiants et séculiers dans la seconde moitié du xiiie siècle et le début du xive,' *Archives d'histoire doctrinale et littéraire du moyen âge*, Année 36 Tome 28 (1961) 35–151. For a brilliant literary understanding of the question, see Penn R. Szittya, 'The Antifraternal Tradition in Middle English Literature,' *Speculum* 52 (1977) 287–317.

[59] See L. J. Paetow, *The Arts Course at the Mediaeval Universities with Special Reference to Grammar and Rhetoric* (Champaign, Ill. 1910); P. Glorieux, 'La Faculté de théologie de Paris et ses principaux docteurs au xiiie siècle,' *Revue d'histoire de l'église de France* 32 (1946) 241–64; C. H. Haskins, *The Rise of the Universities* (Ithaca 1957); J. Le Goff, *Les Intellectuels au moyen âge* (Paris 1957); Gordon Leff, *Paris and Oxford Universities in the Thirteenth and Fourteenth Centuries* (New York 1968).

[60] I am indebted to the following studies: A. Lecoy de la Marche, *La Chaire française au moyen âge* (Paris 1886); G. R. Owst, *Preaching in Medieval England*, 2nd ed. (Oxford 1961); cf. also Anscar Zwart, 'The History of Franciscan Preaching and of Franciscan Preachers (1209–1927): A Bio-bibliographical Study,' *The Franciscan Education Conference* 9 (1927) 247–587; and John V. Fleming, *An Introduction to the Franciscan Literature of the Middle Ages* (Chicago 1977).

[61] 'Tale qual è, tal è; non ci è relione. / Mal vedemo Parisi, che ane destrutt' Asisi: / co la lor lettoria messo l'ò en mala via.' Iacopone da Todi, *Laude*, ed. F. Mancini (Bari 1980) 293.

in their attitude toward academic knowledge. St. Augustine, it will be remembered, encourages Christians in *De doctrina Christiana* to make good use of pagan rhetoric in order to communicate the message of the Revelation effectively. Secular wisdom, which is crystallized in the liberal arts and which St. Augustine rejected in the *Confessions*, is now viewed as a treasure to be plundered by Christians the way the Hebrews plundered the 'Egyptian gold.'[62]

The Franciscans, figures such as Alexander of Hales, St. Bonaventure, and Duns Scotus, did move into the universities, but by virtue of their voluntarism they adhered to an essential anti-Aristotelianism. The formal edifice of Aristotelian logic was severely challenged, both as a theory of abstract reasoning and as a doctrine that the universe is a logical system of numbers and mathematically measurable order.[63] In *Inferno* 27, as the devil is identified as a logician, logic comes forth as the art that deals with judgments about the consistency or contradictions within the structure of an argument, but radically lacks an ethical perspective. Appropriately, Guido, who has betrayed his Franciscan principles, is now claimed by one of the very logicians the Franciscans opposed.

But the debate between Franciscans and the secular masters is not left entirely on this academic level in the canto. There are political ramifications which Dante absorbs in his representation. Guillaume de Saint-Amour, a leader of the secular masters, had unleashed an attack in his *De periculis novissimorum temporum* against the Franciscans as the pseudo-apostles and heralds of the anti-Christ; in their purely formal observance of the externals of faith they are identified as the new pharisees, who connive with popes under the habit of holiness to deceive the believers.[64] As Y. M.-J. Congar suggests, the polemic was a clear attempt to contain the power of the pope, for the mendicants, by being under the pope's direct jurisdiction, weakened the *potestas officii* of the

---

[62] 'Just as the Egyptians had not only idols and grave burdens which the people of Israel detested and avoided, so also they had vases and ornaments of gold and silver and clothing which the Israelites took with them secretly when they fled. . . . In the same way all the teachings of the pagans contain not only simulated and superstitious imaginings . . . but also liberal disciplines. . . . These are, as it were, their gold and silver. . . . When the Christian separates himself in spirit from their miserable society, he should take this treasure with him for the just use of teaching the gospel.' *On Christian Doctrine* 2.40, trans. Robertson 75.

[63] An eloquent opposition to the use of logic in theological discourse is voiced by St. Bonaventure, *In Hexaemeron* 6.2–4; 5.360–61.

[64] The attack against the Pharisees depends on the authority of Matthew 23.15, 'Vae vobis scribae et pharisaei.' For the attack against the Franciscans, see William of St. Amour, *De periculis* in Ortwin Gratius, *Fasciculum rerum expetendarum*, ed. Edward Brown (London 1690) 2.18–41. Cf. also *Le Roman de la Rose*, ed. E. Langlois (Paris 1914–24) 11605–36. Cf. also Rutebeuf, 'Du *Pharisien* ou C'est d'Hypocrisie,' in Edmond Faral and Julia Bastin, *Œuvres complètes de Rutebeuf, Romance Philology* 17 (1963/64) 391–402.

local bishops.[65] Largely at stake was the issue of confessions, a source of controversy between local priests and friars, which ironically was given a firm solution in the bull *Super cathedram* by Boniface VIII.[66]

In *Inferno* 27, Boniface is 'lo principe d'i novi Farisei' (85); he makes a mockery of confession, 'tuo cuor non sospetti; / finor t'assolvo' (100–1), and his *potestas* appears as only temporal power. By the same token, Guido, who as a Franciscan should believe in the power of confession, settles for a pharisaic formula, 'Padre, da che tu mi lavi / di quel peccato ov'io mo cader deggio' (108–9), and seeks absolution before the commission of sin — an act that makes a mockery of his prior contrition and confession (83). And finally, he is the pope's conniver throughout.

In effect, Guido da Montefeltro never changed in his life. The emblem he uses for himself, 'l'opere mie / non furon leonine, ma di volpe' (74–75), gives him away. The animal images, to begin with, are consistent with the unredeemed vision of the natural world in terms of mastiff, claws, and young lion (45–50). More to the point, the metaphor of the lion and the fox echoes Cicero's *De officiis* (1.13.41), and it may be construed in this context as a degraded variant of the τόπος of *sapientia et fortitudo*.[67] But the fox, Guido's attribute, has other symbolic resonances. In the *Roman de Reynard*, the fox goes into a lengthy confession of his sin and then relapses into his old ways; for Jacques de Vitry, more generally, the fox is the emblem of confession without moral rebirth. More important for *Inferno* 27 is the fact that Rutebeuf, who wrote two poems in support of Guillaume de Saint-Amour, uses the fox as the symbol of the friars; in *Renart le nouvel* the fox is a treacherous Franciscan.[68]

These historical events and symbols are brought to an imaginative focus in the digression on the deceits of False Seeming in the *Roman de la Rose* of Jean de Meung. Absorbing the anti-fraternal satire of Guillaume, Jean presents

---

[65] Yves Congar, 'Aspects ecclésiologiques,' *Archives d'histoire doctrinale et littéraire du moyen âge* 28 (1961) 35–151.

[66] See Alfonso M. Stickler, *Il giubileo di Bonifacio VIII: Aspetti giuridico-pastorali* (Rome 1977).

[67] The medieval recurrence of the τόπος has been investigated by R. E. Kaske in his classic article '*Sapientia et Fortitudo* as a Controlling Theme in *Beowulf*,' *Studies in Philology* 55 (1958) 423–57. Cf. also E. R. Curtius, *European Literature and the Latin Middle Ages*, trans. W. R. Trask (New York 1963) 178ff.

[68] For the τόπος of the fox, see St. Gregory, *Expositio super Cantica Canticorum* (PL 79.500); see also PL 114.283, 168.870, 191.773; Ernst Martin, *Le Roman de Renart* (Strasburg 1882) I 13; *The Exempla of Jacques de Vitry*, ed. T. F. Crane (London 1890) 125; *Roman du Renart*, ed. D. M. Méon (Paris 1826) IV 125–461. More generally, see P. Glorieux, 'Prélats français contre religieux mendiants,' *Revue d'histoire de l'Église en France* 11 (1925) 480–81; cf. also Rutebeuf, *Poèmes concernant 'université de Paris*, ed. H. H. Lucas (Manchester 1952).

Faussemblant as a friar, a 'cordelier,'[69] who has abandoned the evangelical ideals of St. Francis and lives on fraud. Reversing Joachim of Flora's hope that the fraternal orders were providentially established so that history would hasten to a close, Jean sees the mendicants as symptoms of decay: 'fallacious is the logic of their claim: religious garment makes religious man.'[70] This sense of the friars' deceptiveness ('now a Franciscan, now a Dominican,' as Jean says)[71] reappears in *Il fiore*, where Falsembiante's steady practice of simulation comes forth as metaphoric foxiness:

> 'I' sì so ben per cuor ogne linguaggio,
> le vite d'esto mondo i' ho provate;
> ch'un or divento prete, un'altra frate,
> or prinze, or cavaliere, or fante, or paggio.
> Secondo ched i' veggio mi vantaggio.
> Un'altra or son prelato, un'altra abate:
> molto mi piaccion gente regolate,
> chè co llor cuopro meglio il mi' volpaggio.'[72]

If 'ogni linguaggio' hints at and perverts the apostles' knowledge of all tongues under the power of the Spirit, the sonnet also conveys Jean's insight: namely, that the only fixed principle in False Seeming's shifty play of concealment (which the technique of enumeration and the iterative adverbs of time mime in the sonnet) is falsification itself.

To turn to the anti-fraternal satirists such as Guillaume and Jean is not equivalent, from Dante's viewpoint, to granting assent to their statement or even giving them the seal of a privileged authority. In *Inferno* 27, Dante endorses the anti-fraternal rhetoric, for Guido da Montefeltro has clearly betrayed the paradigm of Franciscan piety. But Dante also challenges, as the Franciscan intellectuals did, the logicians' categories of knowledge. When the devil, at the triumphant conclusion of his dispute with St. Francis, appeals to

---

[69] *Le Roman de la Rose* 11200. Dante echoes the word which refers to the Franciscans as Guido da Montefeltro describes himself, 'Io fui uom d'arme, e poi fui cordigliero' (*Inferno* 27.67).

[70] The whole passage reads: 'Il font un argument au monde / Ou conclusion a honteuse: / Cist a robe religieuse, / Donques est il religieuse / . . . La robe ne fait pas le moine.' *Le Roman de la Rose* 11052–59. The translation is taken from *The Romance of the Rose*, trans. Harry W. Robbins (New York 1962) 225.

[71] The passage reads: 'Car Protheiis, qui se soulait / Muer en tout quanqu'il voulait, / Ne sot one tant barat ne guile / Con Je faz . . . / Or sui chevaliers, or sui moines, / Or sui prelaz, or sui chanoines, / Or sui clers, autre eure sui prestres, / E sai par cueur trestouz langages, / . . . Or cordeliers, or Jacobins' (*Le Roman de la Rose* 11181–200). This is the passage that Dante will echo in *Il fiore* (see n72).

[72] This is sonnet 101 from *Il fiore*, ed. E. G. Parodi in the *Enciclopedia dantesca*. Cf. also sonnet 92 for references to William of St. Amour (and Siger of Brabant) and links between preachers and False Seeming.

logic's principle of non-contradiction ('nè pentere e volere insieme puossi / per la contradizion che nol consente' 119–20), he is using logic only rhetorically: it is a sophistic refutation by which he sways the opponent. But logical conceptualizations, as has been argued earlier, are delusive because they are not moored to the realities of life and because they establish a *de facto* discontinuity between the order of discourse and the order of reality. More importantly, the devil is claiming Guido da Montefeltro as his own, whose very experience in the canto unveils exactly how the principle of non-contradiction is a fictitious abstraction: like Faux-Semblant, the pope, and the devil himself, Guido is Proteus-like (to use Jean de Meung's metaphor for the friars), shifty, and always unlike himself.

This rotation of figures and categories of knowledge is the substance of a canto in which, as this paper has shown, prophecy is twisted into rhetoric, theology is manipulated for political ends, politics and ethics are masks of the desire for power, and logic is deployed rhetorically. From this perception of how tangled the forms of discourse are comes Dante's own moral voice, both here and in his attacks against the sophistry of syllogisms immediately after the Dominican St. Thomas Aquinas celebrates the life of St. Francis.[73]

Because of this movement from theory to practice and back again to theory, and from one order of knowledge to another, it appears that the liberal arts can never be fixed in a self-enclosed autonomous sphere: each art unavoidably entails the other in a ceaseless pattern of displacement. Ironically, what Dante condemns in Guido da Montefeltro from a moral point of view becomes, in Dante's own poetic handling, the essence of knowledge itself, whereby the various disciplines are forever intermingled. The idea that the arts cannot be arranged in categorical definitions is not only a poet's awareness of how arbitrary boundaries turn out to be. Medieval textbooks and compendia are consistent, so to speak, in betraying the difficulty of treating each of the liberal arts as crystallized entities. If Isidore views dialectic as logic, John of Salisbury's *Metalogicon* considers *logica* an encompassing term for 'grammatica' and 'ratio disserendi,' which in turn contains dialectic and rhetoric.[74] For

---

[73] 'O insensata cura de' mortali, / quanto son difettivi sillogismi / quei che ti fanno in basso batter l'ali' (*Paradiso* 11.1–3).

[74] The sense of how unstable is the definition of each art is conveyed by Paul Abelson, *The Seven Liberal Arts: A Study in Mediaeval Culture* (New York 1906). Cf. also the definition of dialectics given by Isidore of Seville: 'Dialectica est disciplina ad discernendas rerum causas inventa. Ipsa est philosophiae species, quae Logica dicitur, id est rationalis, definiendi, quaerendi et disserendi potens. Docet enim in pluribus generibus quaestionum quemadmodum disputando vera et falso diiudicentur' (*Etym.* 2.22.1); cf. also John of Salisbury, *Metalogicon* 2.4, ed. C. C. J. Webb (Oxford 1929); Hugh of St. Victor, *Didascalion* 1.11, trans. J. Taylor (New York 1968).

Hugh of St. Victor, who follows St. Augustine's *City of God*, *logica* is the name for the *trivium*.

These references are valuable only if we are ready to recognize that what is largely a technical debate never loses sight of the spiritual destination of the liberal arts. What the technicians may sense but never face, however, is that which rhetoricians and poets always know: that knowledge may be counterfeited. Small wonder that in the *Convivio* Dante would repress rhetoric — in vain. But in the *Vita nuova* and the *Divine Comedy*, we are left with the disclosure that rhetoric, in spite of its dangerous status and, ironically, because of its dangerousness, is the only possible path the poet must tread on the way to metaphysics and theology respectively. Whether or not the poet delivers genuine metaphysical and theological knowledge or dazzles us with luminous disguises is a question which lies at the heart of Dante's poetry.

Yale University

DANTE'S BEARD: SIC ET NON ('PURGATORIO' 31.68)

By R. A. SHOAF

The question whether Dante wore a beard or not is one of that class of questions that raises in the general public already suspicious of the ways in which scholars spend their time (and money) the arched eyebrow and dismissive harumph. Happily, I can affirm right away that it is no concern of mine here whether the historical person Dante Alighieri actually wore a beard or not.[1] Indeed, the answer to this question is probably not historically decidable (and to this extent the general public is vindicated). But there is another closely related though slightly different question whose answer definitely is decidable, and this question is very much a concern of mine. This is the question why the text says, at *Purgatorio*, canto 31, line 68, in the speech of Beatrice, that Dante the pilgrim possesses a beard.[2]

For, of course, the text does say just that: '"alza la barba"' indisputably says that the pilgrim, in some sense, possesses a beard. Of course, the real question is: in what sense? *This* is the question I would like to try to answer.

The question so put touches, I should note before going any further, on a much larger issue of literature and literary theory — namely, the issue of truth in fiction. The text, precisely because it is a lie, never lies. If the text says that Dante the pilgrim possesses a beard, then Dante the pilgrim possesses a beard. It is the privilege of the text to make us wonder what this means, where 'meaning' is as much the work of wonderment as it is the work of annotation. Our duty, by wonder and by scholarship equally, is, taking the lie of the text, to discover the truth of the lie. And, I might add here, we have all had (I especially) an important model of fulfilling this duty to literature and literary criticism in the man to whom this volume of essays is dedicated.

We can begin our work by first admitting that the question — in what sense does Dante the pilgrim possess a beard? — has a variety of true answers, each of which participates in the truth of the lie. The first of these we might style

---

[1] See the article by Luigi Peirone on 'barba' in the *Enciclopedia dantesca* I 514 and the bibliography cited there for various positions on the matter. Consult also Robert Hollander, *Allegory in Dante's* COMEDY (Princeton 1969) 125, on Cato's beard (*Purg.* 1.34–36) and the figuration of Moses; and also G. Barone, 'I capelli e la barba nella *Divina Commedia*,' *Giornale dantesco* 14 (1906) 262–77, esp. 268.

[2] The text of the *Commedia* cited throughout this paper is that prepared by Giorgio Petrocchi for the Società Dantesca Italiana, *La* COMMEDIA *secondo l'antica vulgata* (Milan 1966–67); the translation used is that by Charles Singleton, *The Divine Comedy*, Bollingen Series 80 (Princeton 1970–75).

the physiological answer. Dante the pilgrim possesses a beard in the sense
in which any adult male with normally functioning hormones grows facial
hair, one of his secondary sex characteristics; furthermore, we must be careful
to note that even if he shaves daily, he still possesses a beard — though he does
not wear one. Next there is the idiomatic answer, so to speak. This answer
Francesco Mazzoni, in his excellent edition of the *Purgatorio*, helpfully summarizes:

> A 68, quanto a *barba* . . . in questo luogo vale semplicemente 'mento' (e
> sarà un generico settentrionalismo); il *velen de l'argomento* si fonda sull'an-
> cipite presenza di un secondo significato, primario per Dante ('onor del
> mento', dell'area toscana). L'alterità di significato, appresa da Dante nei
> suoi contatti coi dialetti del Nord Italia, deve averlo colpito e indotto a
> questo sottile giuoco intelletuale.
> [At line 68, as regards *barba* . . . in this place, it means simply 'chin' (and
> is a northernism); the phrase *il velen de l'argomento* {which of course is the
> phrase Dante uses to record Beatrice's disdain and disgust as she calls to
> him and upbraids him} is founded on the simultaneous presence of a second
> significance, primary for Dante, namely 'the honor of the chin' (which is a
> Tuscan idiom). The difference of signification, which Dante learned through
> his contacts with the north of Italy, must have struck him and led to this
> subtle intellectual play.][3]

This answer, we can observe, amounts in effect to *sic et non*: in this answer
Dante both does and does not have a beard.

The final answer to the question, and the one in which I am most interested,
is different from the first two though certainly consonant with them, in particular resembling the second in that it amounts to *sic et non*. This answer I
will call the figural-exegetical, and the bulk of my remarks will demonstrate
its applicability and validity.

It will help at this point to recall the scene. In canto 31 of *Purgatorio*,
Dante the pilgrim confesses, under relentless probing by Beatrice, to his
betrayal of her. Repeatedly, the text emphasizes the nearly insupportable
grief and shame under which the pilgrim labors. At one point in her accusation,
Beatrice berates the pilgrim for having succumbed to a '"pargoletta / o altra
novità"' ('young damsel or other novelty' 59–60) as if he were a fledgling
rather than a full-grown bird ('"pennuti"' — '"full-fledged"' 62). Dante
stands under this withering indictment 'quali fanciulli, vergognando, muti /
con li occhi a terra' ('like children, ashamed and dumb, with eyes on the
ground' 64–65). But even now Beatrice refuses to relent:

---

[3] Dante Alighieri, *La Divina Commedia*, con i commenti di Tommaso Casini, Silvio Adrasto
Barbi e di Attilio Momigliano, *Purgatorio* (Florence 1977) 733.

'Quando
per udir se' dolente, alza la barba,
e prenderai più doglia riguardando.'
(Purg. 31.67–69)

['Since you are grieved through hearing, lift up your
beard and you will receive more grief through seeing.']

The pilgrim's response to this stunning command the poet records as follows:

Con men di resistenza si dibarba
robusto cerro, o vero al nostral vento
o vero a quel de la terra di Iarba,
   ch'io non levai al suo commando il mento,
e quando per la barba il viso chiese,
ben conobbi il velen de l'argomento.   (Purg. 31.70–75)

[With less resistance is the sturdy oak uprooted, whether by wind of ours
or by that which blows from Iarbas' land, than at her command I raised
my chin; and when by the beard she asked for my face, well I knew the
venom of the argument.]

So ends this movement of the scene — a scene notable for many intriguing
allusions, not the least of which is the one to the pilgrim's beard.

Dante the pilgrim possesses a beard in a sense, among the several other
senses, that descends ultimately from Leviticus 14.9 and its tradition of exegesis.
Chapter 14 of Leviticus is concerned with the rites of cleansing for a leper,
who is about to re-enter society; verse 9 prescribes that

On the seventh day he shall shave the hair of his head, and his beard and
his eyebrows, and the hair of all his body.

Beginning with Origen, this chapter in general and the verse in particular are
applied to the Christian penitent, cleansing himself of the (so to speak) leprosy
of sin.[4] Origen on Leviticus, of course, was translated by Rufinus, before A.D.
410, and was thus available to the later Middle Ages, which received his comment, at least on this chapter and verse, as normative.[5] On verse 9, Origen
writes:

In barba vero, ut memineret se virilis aetatis deposuisse peccata, et con-
versus fiat sicut infans.
[He includes shaving the beard, however, in order that the penitent might
know that a man of virile age is to cast aside his sins, and become through
his conversion like an infant again.][6]

---

[4] On this important figure, see Saul N. Brody, The Disease of the Soul: Leprosy in Medieval
Literature (Ithaca 1974) esp. 107–47.

[5] See PG 12.395 for data on Rufinus' translation; consult also The Oxford Dictionary of the
Christian Church, s.v. Rufinus (1207).

[6] Homilia in Leviticum 8.11 (PG 12.506A). Comments similar to Origen's or clearly deriving
from his can also be found in Hesychius, In Leviticum, ed. Marguerin de La Bigne, Maxima
bibliotheca veterum patrum (Lyons 1677) XII 108; the Venerable Bede, In Pentateuchum

I think the relevance to the scene in *Purgatorio* of both verse and comment is immediately evident; moreover, we can quickly confirm it by noting that Dante's son Pietro, in his comment on the poem, uses a very similar argument:

> Et intellexit auctor argumentum de barba elevanda, ut dicit; qua rasa, homo debet puerilia et lasciva deponere cum ea, nam non ita postea excusatur.
> [And as far as the argument about lifting the beard is concerned, it is to be understood this way: when he begins shaving a man ought to cast aside childish and lustful distractions, for after this point, youth is no excuse.][7]

Both comments, we should be careful to observe, clearly entail the assumption of shaving — as does, of course, the verse in Leviticus 14. In other words, the figural-exegetical significance of the beard resides in the shaving of it — in the erasure of it. We would conclude from this much that the pilgrim, within the fiction, does not *wear* a beard but has a beard which he should have been shaving for some time now.

This conclusion is important. In the *Convivio*, Dante dwells at length on the beard as a sign of the philosopher. In particular, he cites wearing a beard as an emblem of the philosopher's disdain of all worldly goods in comparison with wisdom:

> Per che li filosofi eccellentissimi ne li loro atti apertamente lo ne dimostraro, per li quali sapemo essi tutte l'altre cose, fuori che la sapienza, avere messe a non calere. Onde Democrito, de la propria persona non curando, ne barba ne capelli ne unghie si togliea.
> [Hence the most excellent philosophers openly show by their behavior their love of wisdom, and in this way we know that they cared for nothing in

---

commentarii — *Leviticus* (PL 91.349); Rhabanus Maurus, *Expositiones in Leviticum* 4.6 (PL 108.393); Rupert of Deutz, *De Trinitate et operibus ejus libri XLII — In Leviticum* 2.25 (PL 167.812–13); *Glossa ordinaria in Biblia Latina* (Basel 1498), *loc. cit.*; Pierre Bersuire, *Reductorium morale super totam Bibliam*, in *Opera omnia* (Cologne 1712) I 51–52; and Santus Pagninus, *Isagoge ad mysticos Sacrae Scripturae sensus* 9.26 (Lyons 1536) 468.

A different tradition of commentary on Leviticus 14.9, deriving from Gregory the Great (see, e.g., *Moralia in Iob* 1.36.52 [PL 75.551]), also contributes to an understanding of Dante's 'barba,' though less directly so than the tradition deriving from Origen. Gregory's contribution is the argument that 'barbam quippe radunt qui sibi de propriis viribus fiduciam subtrahunt' ('They are shaving, so to speak, who are withdrawing faith in their own powers from themselves' [i.e., who are not trusting in their own powers]). Clearly in this sense also, Dante should have been shaving, should not have had a 'barba' by which Beatrice could summon him to lift his face to her, should not have been trusting in his own powers, especially his philosophical powers, after her death. This tradition is also represented in the important commentary on Leviticus by Raoul de Flavigny: *Libri viginti super Leviticum Moysi*, ed. Marguerin de La Bigne, Maxima Bibliotheca Veterum Patrum XVII 144.

[7] Petrus Alighieri, *Super Dantis ipsius genitoris* COMOEDIAM *commentarium*, ed. Vincentio Nannucci (Florence 1845) 519–20.

this world except wisdom. Thus, for example, Democritus, caring nought for his own person, did not cut his beard, nor his hair, nor his nails.][8]

Moreover, Busnelli and Vandelli note that 'wearing a beard was a characteristic custom of philosophers,' and they cite several ancient sources to this effect.[9]

Gradually, Beatrice's allusion to the pilgrim's beard is assuming weighty importance indeed. For, as we know, the 'pargoletta' to whom she accuses Dante of having succumbed was in all likelihood Lady Philosophy.[10] Hence if in the very next breath after that accusation she alludes to Dante's *beard*, she may be pointing again, with extraordinary but in the circumstances very justifiable irony, to the *philosopher* who betrayed her. He who let himself be ensnared by the 'pargoletta' of Philosophy still shows the beard, whether or not he is wearing one, of philosophers; he is still the traitor and will be until his confession and penitence are finished. Hence, 'il velen de l'argomento' is indeed venomous, doubly venomous in fact: not only is there the venom of the shame at being an adult who has behaved like an adolescent, there is also the venom of the shame at being a poet who has behaved like a philosopher.

This argument finds further justification from later exegesis of Leviticus 14.9 to which we can now turn. Rupert of Deutz, in his comment on the verse, though clearly in the tradition of Origen, is much more detailed:

> Haec namque perfectio est reformationis in eo qui barbatus et veternosus haereticus fuerat, si ex toto ad infantiam innocentiae redeat, si deposita philosophia et inani fallacia . . . tota exspoliatione corporis carnis reflorescat, quod est capillos capitis . . . barbamque virilem ac superbiae supercilia cum totius corporis pilis radere, ut totus homo novus incedat.
>
> (*In Leviticum* 2.25 [PL 167.812–13])
>
> [For this cleansing and perfection is that of reformation in the one who had been bearded and an inveterate heretic — namely, if he returns entirely to the infancy of innocence, if, *having cast aside philosophy and all empty fallacies* . . . he blooms again in the complete pruning of the demands of this flesh, which is to shave the hair of the head . . . and the beard and the eyebrows and indeed of the whole body, *so that he might go forward entirely a new man* {my emphasis}.]

Here exegesis almost literally predicts Dante's text — 'si deposita philosophia et inani fallaci' ('if having cast aside philosophy and all vain fallacies'). The shaving of the beard is the putting away of philosophy. It is the cleansing of the soul that prepares it for the return 'ad infantiam innocentiae . . . ut totus homo novus incedat' ('to the infancy of innocence . . . so that he might go forward

---

[8] *Il Convivio* 3.14.7–8, edd. G. Busnelli and G. Vandelli (Florence 1934–37) II 422.

[9] See II 422 and see also Barone 263.

[10] See R. A. Shoaf, 'Dante's *colombi* and the Figuralism of Hope in the *Divine Comedy*,' *Dante Studies* 93 (1975) 27–59, esp. 43–44.

entirely a new man'). And, of course, when Beatrice has in a sense cut away the pilgrim's beard by making him confess and repent his apostasy, the next thing that happens to him is his cleansing immersion in Lethe (*Purg.* 31.85–105) — he is reborn, 'ad infantiam innocentiae . . . ut totus homo novus incedat.'

If I have glossed the Christian, scriptural dimensions of the allusion to the beard, I have not as yet addressed the pagan, literary dimensions. Dante, we know, combines the Christian and the pagan in his poem when occasion affords, out of his conviction of their final harmony. When the pilgrim hears Beatrice summon his countenance by his beard, he looks up, but

> Con men di resistenza si dibarba
> robusto cerro, o vero al nostral vento
> o vero a quel de la terra di Iarba,
>   ch'io non levai al suo commando il mento.

(Purg. 31.70–73)

> [With less resistance is the sturdy oak uprooted, whether by wind of ours or by that which blows from Iarbas' land, than at her command I raised my chin.]

The allusion through Iarbas to *Aeneid* 4 and the story of Dido and Aeneas is unmistakable, and we must work out all its implications for the scene of Dante's confession to Beatrice.

It is Iarbas of course who precipitates the crisis in the love-affair between Dido and Aeneas: he prays to Jupiter for justice against Dido, and Jupiter proceeds to send Mercury to command Aeneas to leave Carthage and finish his great task.[11] Obviously, Dante the poet, just when Dante the pilgrim is being reprimanded for his apostasy, is alluding to the occasion of Aeneas' greatest apostasy too, and the implied similarity between the pilgrim and Aeneas is, I assume, largely self-explanatory.

However, in one respect it does need explanation. The allusion to *Aeneid* 4 and the story of Dido and Aeneas lies not only through the mention of Iarbas but also through the simile of the oak. This simile is a direct quotation of *Aeneid* 4 at that moment just before Aeneas' departure from Carthage when he is wavering under Dido's hapless pleading with him to stay:

>   sed nullis ille movetur
>   fletibus, aut voces ullas tractabilis audit,
>   fata obstant, placidasque viri deus obstruit auris.
>   ac velut annoso validam cum robore quercum
>   Alpini Boreae nunc hinc nunc flatibus illinc
>   cruere inter se certant, it stridor, et altae

---

[11] *Aeneid* 4.196–278 — the text of the *Aeneid* cited in this paper is that of the Loeb Classical Library, trans. H. Rushton Fairclough (Cambridge, Mass. 1974).

consternunt terram concusso stipite frondes,
ipsa haeret scopulis et, quantum vertice ad auras
aetherias, tantum radice in Tartara tendit:
haud secus adsiduis hinc atque hinc vocibus heros
tunditur, et magno persentit pectore curas,
mens immota manet, lacrimae volvuntur inanes.

Aeneid 4.438–49 (Loeb 425–26)

[But by no tearful pleas is he moved, nor in yielding mood pays he heed to
any words. Fate withstands and heaven seals his kindly, mortal ears. Even
as when northern Alpine winds, blowing now hence, now thence, emulously
strive to uproot an oak strong with the strength of years, there comes a
roar, the stem quivers and the high leafage thickly strews the ground, but
the oak clings to the crag, and as far as it lifts its top to the airs of heaven
so far it strikes its roots down towards hell — even so with ceaseless appeals, from this side and from that, the hero is buffeted.]

Immediately noticeable when we compare the two similes is the striking difference: Aeneas is *not* uprooted; he remains fixed in his resolve to seek out
Italy and found the empire. Dante, on the other hand, is — so to speak —
uprooted: though his roots have just been literally in 'Tartara,' in Hell, he
does lift his countenance to Beatrice who commands it.

I think we hardly need doubt that this variation between the two similes
serves principally to emphasize the difference between Dido and Beatrice:
Beatrice is incomparably more powerful than Dido — she is divine as well as
human love — and if the pilgrim resists her with more force than that with
which an oak resists its uprooting, in the end his roots are finally pulled up,
pulled up from Hell. Unlike Aeneas, Dante enters the promised land with no
regrets, no lingering mortal attachments either to a Dido or to a Lady Philosophy.[12]

The University of Florida

---

[12] I would like to thank the National Endowment for the Humanities for a Fellowship in
the academic year 1982–83 which enabled me to pursue my research for this and other studies
in Rome.

   A briefer version of this paper was read at one of the Dante sessions of the Annual Meeting
of the American Association of University Professors of Italian, in Bloomington, Indiana,
in April 1984. I would like to thank the many participants who responded with helpful
comments, especially Professors Robert Hollander and Maristella Lorch.

EPICUREAN SECULARISM IN DANTE AND BOCCACCIO: ATHENIAN ROOTS AND FLORENTINE REVIVAL

By EMERSON BROWN, JR.*

The word 'secularism,' as we all know, derives from the Latin *saeculum*, a word of obscure origin meaning a lifetime, generation, or age. Thus it would be etymologically correct to think of secularity as *timeness*, living in time, in contrast to living in or with regard to eternity. As Augustine and Boethius discovered (with some help from the Platonists), eternity differs from time not because it is endless but because it is outside of time. Eternity grasps all of time in a timeless now. As Boethius stated definitively, 'Eternity is the whole, simultaneous and perfect possession of endless life' ('interminabilis vitae tota

---

* An essay on Epicureanism in medieval literature may seem a curious way to honor Robert Kaske, a scholar who has been so successful in interpreting difficult medieval literary texts through the use of Christian traditions. Yet Professor Kaske would surely agree that the obligation of the literary scholar is not to find Christian themes wherever possible but to use any material, Christian or otherwise, that may be valuable in clarifying a text on its own terms. For more than a century, literary scholars have productively explored three great sources of medieval thought and literature: European paganism, the main currents of classical Latin culture, and — enriched in recent decades by such sensitive use of patristic exegesis as Robert Kaske's — Latin Christianity. Less important but of interest because it has been almost entirely overlooked is a system of thought that originated in Greek antiquity, that throve for several hundred years of the Christian era, and that was revived in the high Middle Ages. In its fundamental assumptions, that thought system provided the most coherent and appealing alternative both to the main lines of classical pagan thought and to the Hebrew–Christian tradition. In general terms, it might be described as philosophical secularism. Its most influential, enduring, and — to both pagan and Christian opponents — misguided and dangerous form is Epicureanism.

In progress is a study of Epicurean thought from classical antiquity through the Middle Ages. In print is an essay that will become one of the middle chapters and gives some idea of the scope of the whole: 'Epicurus and Voluptas in Late Antiquity: The Curious Testimony of Martianus Capella,' *Traditio* 38 (1982) 75–106. After completing that essay, I realized that an adequate treatment of Epicureanism in late antiquity and the Middle Ages would have to begin not with those classical Latin texts known in the Middle Ages — as I had originally intended — but with the roots of philosophical materialism in ancient Greece. Chapters now completed on the period from the Pre-Socratics through Lucretius may appear as a separate volume.

The following essay briefly explores the role of Epicurean secularism in Dante's *Commedia* and Boccaccio's *Decameron*. It began as a paper for the 1985 Sewanee Medieval Colloquium, 'Secularism in the Middle Ages.' At this stage in my research I must offer it to Robert Kaske more as a report on work in progress than as the comprehensive treatment of its subject that the model of his scholarly achievement would demand.

simul et perfecta possessio' *Consolatio* 5. Pr. 6). Secular man, then, lives in time, as we all do, but he thrives in time and does not long to escape. To those theologians who display their condemnation of secularism in such arenas of intellectual discourse as the letters to the editor section of the Nashville *Tennessean*, 'secular humanism' is the generic sin of our age. But what is wrong with time?

The trouble with time, as Augustine discovered, is not only that we live our wretchedly sensual and sinful lives in it and are doomed to die in it, but that the present time seems little more than an illusion.[1] In his great meditation on time in the *Confessions*, Augustine observes that with the past over and the future yet to come, the only temporal reality is the present. But this line of thinking forces the present into that mysterious space between the past and the future, a space Augustine found difficult to locate, as Plato and Aristotle had already observed.[2] 'How,' he asks, 'can we say that even the present *is*?' For 'the present does not take up any space' ('praesens autem nullum habet spatium' 11.15). Reality must lie elsewhere than in that nonexistent space between past and future. Reality must be unchanging, out of time as we experience time. Augustine recognized that the rejection of time and this world could go too far. Greek anti-materialism without Hebrew–Christian historicity could lead to a bodiless Christianity, as with the Gnostics, whose tendency to slip out of time and materiality led them to misunderstand the Incarnation and the positive value of human history. But we must seek our ultimate values and the goal of our existence outside of the endless flux of our *saeculum*. Mere travelers, *homines viatores* all, for us this world should be a

---

[1] Time remains a difficult philosophical and scientific concept. The entry on Time in *The Encyclopedia of Philosophy* provides a quick introduction to the problem and some valuable bibliography. More extensive, and for the medievalist more valuable, are the entries on Time and Eternity in the *New Catholic Encyclopedia*. For discussions of time from the point of view of contemporary physics, see Paul Davies, *God and the New Physics* (New York 1983), chapter 9 and the works listed in the bibliography (241–42), and the many references to time (well indexed) in Ilya Prigogine and Isabelle Stengers, *Order Out of Chaos* (New York 1984).

[2] Seeking a space for the instant between a state of rest and a state of motion, Plato found himself facing a similar paradox: 'But there is no time during which a thing can be at once neither in motion nor at rest. . . . this queer thing, the instant, is situated between the motion and the rest; it occupies no time at all' (*Parmenides* 156cᴅ). Aristotle begins his discussion of time in *Physics* 4.10–14 with a similar observation. Does time exist? 'The following considerations would make one suspect that it either does not exist at all or barely, and in the obscure way. One part of it has been and is not, while the other is going to be and is not yet. Yet time — both infinite time and any time you like to take — is made up of these. One would naturally suppose that what is made up of things which do not exist could have no share in reality.'

temporary road to an eternal goal.[3] Thus, we might define 'secularism in the Middle Ages' as 'interest in the time-bound things of this world during a period which, at least putatively, differs from the ages before and after it in its widespread concern with the time-less things of eternal existence and only with those things of this world that signify eternity or propel us toward it.'

Medieval folk have left us much evidence of that sort of secular interest. In paintings, songs, and stories they proclaim that this world, though fleeting, nonetheless has its joys. The joys of their secular world are much like the joys of ours: song and story, food and drink, sport, spring, intellectual discourse, friends, and — of course — love. There is nothing surprising about such manifestations of the secular spirit in a world whose attentions were supposedly focused on eternity. Even those observers who persist in desiring to see the Middle Ages as the ideal 'Age of Faith' against which we should measure our own dismally secular age are rarely so naïve as to claim that the 'Age of Faith' was an age of universal piety and goodness. The medieval secularism under investigation here is of a different sort, though — not the heedless secularism of fallen, ignorant, and sensual humankind, but a philosophical secularism, a secularism that consciously opposes the most fundamental notions of Platonism and Christianity concerning time, human behavior, and the nature of reality.

The greatest proponent of philosophical secularism was Epicurus, the ancient Greek thinker most radically opposed to Plato and most effective in establishing a radical and enduring alternative to Platonism. Of course, Aristotle also opposes Plato in important ways, and much of the time he is as unabashedly secular as Epicurus. Indeed, with no more concern for an afterlife than Epicurus displays and with far more emphasis on the importance of good fortune and material comfort in achieving human happiness in this life, Aristotle may be more bound to the material things of this world. But medieval Christians were able to transform Aristotle into 'The Philosopher,' the most valuable and reliable ancient thinker and the one most nearly in tune with Christianity. Although from time to time important Christian thinkers, Abelard among them, tried tentatively to Christianize Epicurus, he remained throughout the Middle Ages the ancient philosopher whose ideas were most irreconcilable with Christian beliefs. In basing his physics on the atomism of Plato's contemporary and greatest philosophical rival, Democritus, Epicurus developed a philosophy

---

[3] Concerning the medieval concept of man as *viator*, wayfarer, 'wanderer between two worlds,' see Gerhart B. Ladner, '*Homo Viator*: Mediaeval Ideas on Alienation and Order,' *Speculum* 42 (1967) 233–59.

that was irreducibly materialist.[4] In the Epicurean view of reality there is nothing but atoms and void. Not only the obviously material things of this world, but our thoughts and dreams, our souls, and even the gods are composed of only atoms and void. The gods are remote from us and care nothing about us, as Epicurus announced in the first of his *Principal Doctrines* (Κύριαι δόξαι): 'A blessed and immortal being is not troubled itself, nor does it trouble another [Τὸ μαχάριον καὶ ἄφθαρτον οὔτε αὐτὸ πράγματα ἔχει οὔτε ἄλλῳ παρέχει]. As a result, it is not affected by anger or favor, for these belong to weakness.'[5] For us there is no eternal realm in which we may seek permanent values and our permanent home. There is only this world and countless other worlds. All these worlds have come into being by the chance collision of atoms, and these worlds will eventually break apart and die, and their atoms will form new worlds. This process will continue, time without beginning, time without end. Time, the great horror to the Platonists and Christians, is, to Epicurus, an accidental property of the chance confluence of atoms and void: 'We associate time with days and nights and their parts, and in the same way with changes in our own feelings and with motion and rest, recognizing that the very thing we call time is in its turn a special sort of accident of these accidents' (DL 10.73). We ourselves are chance confluences of atoms and void. We live in time. And yet, in this most secular of secular thought systems, our secularity is no cause for lamentation. With little effort we can free ourselves from pain and anxiety and enjoy the pleasure such freedom provides. We are not victims of time. We do not experience death. We can live as the immortals.

This latter point is likely to seem paradoxical if not simply muddle-headed. If all things perish, including our bodies and souls, how can we avoid experi-

---

[4] Scandalous as such a thought is, there is a certain plausibility to the ancient charge that Plato wanted to burn all the writings of Democritus that he could lay hands on, a story Diogenes Laertius attributes to the *Historical Notes* of Aristoxenus, a pupil of Aristotle's. Writing in the second century C.E., Diogenes, himself favoring Epicurean thought above all other systems, finds 'clear evidence' for the book-burning charge 'in the fact that Plato, who mentions almost all the early philosophers, never once alludes to Democritus, not even where it would be necessary to controvert him, obviously because he knew that he would have to match himself against the prince of philosophers' (*Lives of the Philosophers* 9.40).

[5] The best edition of the complete works of Epicurus (Greek with Italian translation) is *Epicuro: Opere*, ed. Graziano Arrighetti, 2nd ed. (Turin 1973). The few Greek words cited here are from this edition. Although Epicurus was a prolific writer, few of his works have come down to us. The most important are preserved in Diogenes Laertius, *Lives of the Philosophers* (Book 10). The most accessible edition and translation of Diogenes Laertius is the Loeb Classical Library edition by R. D. Hicks. A handy edition of the most important works of Epicurus (omitting the extensive fragments and some other material) is Russell M. Geer, *Epicurus: Letters, Principal Doctrines, and Vatican Sayings* (Indianapolis 1964), whose translations, with a few adjustments, I use here. The following abbreviations will be used in citations: KD (= Principal Doctrines), DL (= Diogenes Laertius).

encing death? How can we live as the immortal gods? Epicurus explains: we do not experience death because at the moment of death we no longer exist to experience it. In our final illness or injury we may be in pain and we may be aware that our end is near, but death itself we do not experience; for at death the soul breaks into the atoms of which it was composed, and only the soul can experience anything. While to Aristotle 'death is the most terrible of all things' (*Nicomachean Ethics* 3.6), to Epicurus 'death is nothing to us ['Ο θάνατος οὐδὲν πρὸς ἡμᾶς]; for what has been dissolved has no sensation, and what has no sensation is nothing to us' (KD 2, DL 10.139). If mortality means experiencing death, then we are free from mortality. For us, no less than for the immortal gods, death is simply, and forever, beyond our experience.

We can be similar to the immortal gods in other ways. To Epicurus, the gods were remote from human life in their divine dissociation from the pain and anxiety of human existence, but they were accessible as models for what we might, with proper philosophical training, become. Their blessedness consists not in existing out of time and materiality, like the gods of Augustine and Boethius, but in living properly in time. As they live, so can we.

The 'blessed and eternal' being of Epicurus' first maxim is 'blessed' because he neither experiences nor causes pain and anxiety. Freedom from pain and anxiety is what the greatest good, pleasure, is all about. Epicurus believes that we can find pleasure in this world. And in this we are exactly as the immortals are. We experience the pleasure of this moment, in time. Our *saeculum*, long or short, provides all the time we need. Follow my precepts, Epicurus writes, and you will 'live like a god among men [ζήσῃ δὲ ὡς θεὸς ἐν ἀνθρώποις]; for life amid immortal blessings is in no way like the life of a mere mortal' (DL 10.135).

Epicurus' own thoughts on time contrast sharply with those of such self-styled Epicureans as Horace and the 'Epicurean' voice of Ecclesiastes, who lament the brevity of earthly life and urge us to gather our rosebuds while we may. In voicing such sentiments such writers may produce great poetry, and they put themselves in respectable company, for even Aristotle thought that the 'human good' of 'activity of the soul in conformity with excellence' was only possible in a long life: 'a short time does not make a man blessed and happy' (*Nic. Eth.* 1.7). But pseudo-Epicureans of Horace's variety miss Epicurus' point. To Epicurus the brevity of earthly life is irrelevant: 'Time that is unlimited and time that is limited afford equal pleasure, if one measures pleasure's extent by reason' (KD 10, DL 10.145).[6]

---

[6] The following maxim continues: 'The flesh believes that pleasure is limitless and that it requires unlimited time; but the mind, understanding the end and limit of the flesh and ridding itself of fears of the future, secures a complete life and has no longer any need for unlimited

Medieval writers allude to Epicurus from time to time, but how much of his authentic thought was available to them? Specifically, for present purposes, how do Epicurean ideas get from ancient Athens to the Florence of Guido Cavalcanti, Dante, and Boccaccio? Conventional wisdom has it that Epicureanism 'died' around the time of Augustine, if not earlier, was misunderstood and condemned in the Middle Ages when it was noticed at all, and was not resurrected until the fifteenth century. With some interesting exceptions, the Church Fathers did harshly condemn Epicurus.[7] But conventional wisdom is wrong concerning the 'death' of Epicureanism at the time of Augustine, as Augustine himself, in spite of himself, reveals.[8] Epicureanism was probably not finally silenced until 529, when, weary of attempting to defeat pagan falsehood by means of Christian truth alone, Justinian simply banned the teaching of all pagan philosophy. But it is true that Epicurus' own writings were not available in Western Christendom from late antiquity to the fifteenth century. The work of his great Roman disciple, Lucretius, though copied in the ninth century, had virtually no circulation we can detect and little if any influence. Yet hints of the survival or re-creation of philosophical materialism turn up in curious places, even among humble folk. Among the heresies uncovered by the meticulous inquisitor Jacques Fournier in a small region of the Pyrenees in the early fourteenth century are several beliefs entirely compatible with classical Epicureanism: the beliefs, for example, that nothing exists apart from the

---

time. It does not, however, avoid pleasure; and when circumstances bring on the end of life' it does not depart as if it still lacked any portion of the good life' (KD 20). Nothing could be farther from authentic Epicurean belief than the plea to 'eat, drink, and be merry, for tomorrow we may die.' On this important point, see Philip Merlan, 'Epicureanism and Horace,' *Journal of the History of Ideas* 10 (1949) 445–51; Merlan concludes: 'if it is necessary to keep the term "Epicureanism" for a type of philosophy represented by Horace, let there be a clear understanding that this is a kind of whining Epicureanism if we compare it to the true and virile Epicureanism.... only this true and virile Epicureanism has a liberating effect. The one who lives in a certain way because he is influenced by his thinking of death, far from being an Epicurean, has not understood the meaning of the message of Epicurus' (451).

[7] 'Epicurus' is a popular term in Jerome's carefully nurtured vocabulary of abuse, but perhaps the grossest distortion of Epicurean thought among the early Christians is found in Theophilus of Antioch, who accused Epicurus not only of advocating atheism (a standard charge) but of teaching incest and sodomy as well (*Ad Autolycum* 3.6). Richard Paul Jungkuntz provides a summary of the anti-Epicurean tradition in 'Fathers, Heretics, and Epicureans,' *Journal of Ecclesiastical History* 17 (1966) 3–10 and of the more positive tradition in 'Christian Approval of Epicureanism,' *Church History* 31 (1962) 279–93.

[8] This is a subject that requires further study. For some evidence of the continuing vitality of Epicurus past the lifetime of Augustine, see for now 'Epicurus and Voluptas' (above n*).

material world and that the soul is material and perishes with the body.[9]
As Fournier's editor observes, 'chose singulière les milieux les plus atteints
par l'albigéisme donnent, par contre, sous une forme grossière, l'exemple d'un
matérialisme et d'un esprit critique qui jettent dans la crédulité et le fanatisme
de l'époque une note, sinon moderne, du moins discordante.'[10] I suppose it is
possible that this materialism and critical spirit derive in some obscure way
from the secular philosophy of late antiquity, though it seems more likely that
they were rediscovered by skeptical folk unwilling to accept the dogmas of
either Christian orthodoxy or Christian heresy. Whatever the source, these
beliefs are incompatible with Christianity in any form, orthodox or heretical,
and they were surely not limited to the few people whose ideas happened to be
preserved in Fournier's records.

The sources of more obviously learned secular philosophy are easier to track
down. Key elements of Epicurean thought were preserved in the Latin classics and picked up by important thinkers in the Middle Ages, as I expect to
show in detail elsewhere. For the moment, though, I shall have to be content
to look at Epicurus' appearance in three texts from the high Middle Ages:
Vincent of Beauvais' encyclopedia, Dante's *Inferno*, and Boccaccio's *Decameron*.

Vincent notes that Epicurus opposed the pleasures of the body, and he cites
several of Epicurus' praiseworthy sayings, drawn from Seneca. These are ir-
reproachable moral banalities, such as his famous advice to one who wished to
become wealthy: 'Si vis divitem facere, non pecuniae adjiciendum, sed cupi-
ditati detrahendum est.' He also lets Epicurus' own words give further
evidence of the inaccuracy of the popular view of him as a promoter of sensual
living: 'Non potationes, non commessationes, nec copulae feminarum, nec
copia piscium, et aliorum hujus modi, quae splendido usu parantur convivii,
suavem vitam faciunt, sed sobria disputatio.' But then Vincent balances

---

[9] *Le registre d'Inquisition de Jacques Fournier, Évêque de Pamiers (1317–1325)*, ed. Jean
Duvernoy, Bibliothèque Méridionale, 2nd series 41.1–3 (Toulouse 1965); French translation,
also by Jean Duvernoy (Paris 1978). From the wealth of material contained in this register,
Emmanuel LeRoy Ladurie prepared his *Montaillou, Village Occitan de 1294 à 1324* (Paris
1975); English trans., *Montaillou: The Promised Land of Error* (New York 1978). Fascinating
as *Montaillou* is, one should be cautious about its methodology and accuracy. Concerning the
accuracy of the English translation and concerning Duvernoy's edition as well, see Leonard E.
Boyle, o.p., 'Montaillou Revisited: *Mentalité* and Methodology,' in *Pathways to Medieval
Peasants*, ed. J. A. Raftis, Papers in Medieval Studies 2 (Toronto 1981) 119–40. I would like
to thank Father Boyle for sending me a copy of this essay in typescript. For testimony concerning some ideas of which Epicurus would approve, see particularly the following deposi-
tions (numbers are of the order in the edition of the Latin text, with numbers of the French
translation in parentheses): 5 (14), 6 (15, 68), 12 (19), 44 (51), 63 (62), 73 (74), and 80 (61).

[10] Duvernoy (1965) I 30.

this surprisingly positive view of Epicurus with the sort of observation one might anticipate from a medieval Christian: Epicurus 'erred in many things more than the other philosophers, for he thought that God does not care about human affairs but is lazy and does nothing, and he said that pleasure is the greatest good, and that the souls die with the bodies.'[11] None of those beliefs could be expected to endear Epicurus to medieval Christians, but it was the second — the idea that the soul dies with the body — that was the most horrifying and that inspired Dante to create one of his most memorable episodes.

To Dante the essence of Epicureanism and the most abominable of philosophical errors is just that proposition: the soul dies with the body. Even in the *Convivio*, where Dante is more natural philosopher than Christian theologian, he finds that idea appalling: 'Dico che intra tutte le bestialitadi quella è stoltissima, vilissima e dannosissima, chi crede dopo questa vita non essere altra vita' (2.8.8). This idea, central to Epicurean philosophy, would be an abomination to Christian heretics of virtually all persuasions, certainly to the most important heretical movements from the early Christian centuries up to the Albigensians of Dante's time. Yet Dante makes this idea the essence of all heresy. Concerning the sixth circle of Hell, the abode of the heretics, he writes:

> Suo cimitero da questa parte hanno
> con Epicuro tutti suoi seguaci
> che l'anima col corpo morta fanno.
>
> (*Inf*. 10.13–15)
>
> [Here, with Epicurus, all of his followers have their cemetery,
> those who hold that the soul dies with the body.]

As Anthony Cassell and Robert Durling have recently demonstrated, in depicting the Epicurean heretics Farinata degli Uberti and Cavalcante de' Cavalcanti rising from their infernal tomb, Dante draws on the general tradition of the resurrection of the dead and the specific iconographical motif of the 'imago pietatis,' the tradition of Christ as the 'Man of Sorrows,' rising from His tomb. Far from living as the immortals, the Epicureans in Dante's Hell will at the Last Judgment be forever imprisoned in the tombs from which they can now rise only in grotesque and futile parody of the Resurrection of Christ (10.10–12).[12] So terrifying to Dante is the idea of the soul's mortality that he

---

[11] 'Erravit autem in multis plusquam omnes philosophi, nam putavit Deum res humanas non curare, sed ociosum esse, & nihil agere, dixitque voluptatem summum bonum esse, & animas cum corporibus interire' (*Speculum historiale* 4.41 [Douai 1624] 128).

[12] Anthony K. Cassell, 'Dante's Farinata and the Image of the Arca,' *Yale Italian Studies* 1 (1977) 335–70; Robert M. Durling, 'Farinata and the Body of Christ,' *Stanford Italian Review* 2 (1981) 5–35. I am grateful to Professor Durling for allowing me to consult his work in typescript and for some stimulating and valuable conversation.

condemns to an eternity of torture the Greek philosopher most associated with
that philosophical error — no matter if the heretic died three hundred years
before the orthodoxy from which he veered was even established.[13]

Still among the living at the time of Dante's pilgrimage through Hell,
Cavalcante's son Guido nonetheless plays a prominent, perhaps central, role in
this canto. The fate of Farinata and Cavalcante is fixed for eternity. In subtle
ways discussed in several fine critical studies, Dante leads us to ponder the
fate of their son and son-in-law Guido, a fate somehow hinted at in his famous
and controversial 'disdegno' (10.63). Is Guido to suffer the same fate as his
Epicurean father and father-in-law? This question would be far more vital
to Dante's immediate public if, as there may be reason to believe, Guido was
prominent in a group of sophisticated and daring thinkers who toyed with
non-Christian philosophy and who liked to think of themselves, at least half
seriously, as Epicureans. Detailed information about Epicurean thought was
readily available in thirteenth-century Florence, mainly through several of
Cicero's philosophical works. An example of a free-thinking philosophical
circle — and perhaps an influence on Guido and his companions — was the
court of the Emperor Frederick II, who is another occupant of the circle of the

---

[13] A quick introduction to the scholarly effort to cope with Dante's curious decision to
transform an ancient Greek philosopher into a Christian heretic can be found in the *Enciclopedia dantesca*, ss.vv. Epicurei, Epicuro, Cavalcanti, and Farinata. An important recent
study of the canto is Giuseppe Mazzotta, *Dante, Poet of the Desert: History and Allegory in the
DIVINE COMEDY* (Princeton 1979) 275–318. But even Professor Mazzotta's brilliant analysis
leaves Dante's choice of Epicurus as the archheretic inadequately explained. 'Heresy,'
Mazzotta asserts, is 'a sin that for Dante involves the failure of understanding and imagination, and which he equates with the madness of those who produce poetic and philosophical
discourses but have no faith in God' (279). But Epicurus claimed to believe in the gods (as
seen in KD 1), and the error of Dante's Epicureans is not that they lack faith in God but that
they deny the immortality of the soul, an error shared by Democritus and most likely by
Aristotle, who — far from being condemned as heretics — reside with other noble pagans in
the comfortable environment of Limbo (*Inferno*, canto 4). If Dante 'gives an essentially
Thomistic account of heresy' (284) and if Thomas defines heresy as 'a corruption of the
Christian faith' (283n), how was Epicurus (341–270 B.C.) able to corrupt the Christian faith?
Of course, Cain sinned before Moses brought down the Ten Commandments, and one can
imagine Dante thinking of some sort of 'natural law' of the immortality of the soul, a law
accessible to the ancients. Some such reasoning as this seems reflected in C. S. Singleton's
gloss on *Inf.* 10.14–15: 'Disbelief in this basic idea [personal immortality] was traditionally
characterized as Epicurean; it was also, of course, heretical. In the Christian view, then,
Epicurus can be seen as an archheretic' (C. S. Singleton, ed., THE DIVINE COMEDY, INFERNO 2.
Commentary [Princeton 1970] 146). Even if the Church did believe that pre-Christian thinkers
could be treated as heretics, it may be asking a good deal of Epicurus to expect him to respond
to Christ's empty tomb, even more to respond as an orthodox Christian: 'In the case of
Epicurus, who is blind to the fact that Christ's empty tomb is a sign of his resurrection from
the dead, philosophy goes mad' (Mazzotta 288–89).

Epicureans in Dante's Hell ('qua dentro e'l secondo Federico' 10.119). Whether or not Frederick really was an Epicurean, Dante was not alone in so characterizing him. Salimbene da Parma records that 'erat enim Epycurus, et ideo quicquid poterat invenire in divina Scriptura per se et per sapientes suos, quod faceret ad ostendendum quod non esset alia vita post mortem, totum inveniebat,' and a *sirventes* of Ugo di Sain Circ reveals the same view: 'Ni vida apres mort ni paradis non cre: / E dis c'om es nienz despueis que pert l'ale.'[14] Evidence of Dante's Epicurean sympathies may be found in the tolerant attitude toward Epicurus he displays in the *Convivio*: 'Per le quali tre virtudi [fede, speranza, caritade] si sale a filosofare a quelle Atene celestiale, dove li Stoici e Peripatetici e Epicurii, per la l[uc]e de la veritate etterna, in uno volere concordevolemente concorrono' (3.14.15).

Guido's own philosophical position is highly controversial. Scholars seeking to establish and define his philosophical heterodoxy have concentrated on his famous, exciting, but occasionally murky and textually confused *canzone* 'Donna me prega' and on a detailed near-contemporary gloss on it by the Florentine physician Dino del Garbo.[15] For Bruno Nardi, Guido reveals himself to be an Averroist, and this opinion has become something of a critical commonplace in our time.[16] Not all agree, however, and I fear that Guido's own writings as we have them provide an inadequate basis for persuasive assertions about his beliefs.[17] Still, there is something to Ezra Pound's suspicion that Guido is less orthodox, more of a free-thinker, than Dante: 'the tone of his mind is infinitely more "modern" than Dante's.'[18] Farinata and his wife,

---

[14] Quoted from C. S. Singleton, Inferno *Commentary* 159.

[15] Text of 'Donna me prega' and of Dino's gloss in Guido Cavalcanti, *Le Rime*, ed. Guido Favati (Milan 1957). Text of gloss also included in O. Bird, 'The Canzone d'Amore of Cavalcanti According to the Commentary of Dino del Garbo,' *Medieval Studies* 2 (1940) 150–203, 3 (1941) 117–60.

[16] Bruno Nardi, 'L'averroismo del "primo amico" di Dante,' *Studi danteschi* 25 (1940) 43–80; 'Di un nuovo commento alle canzone del Cavalcanti sull'amore,' *Cultura Neolatina* 6–7 (1946–47), 123–35; 'Noterella polemica sull'averroismo di Guido Cavalcanti,' *Rassegna di filosofia* 3 (1954) 47–71.

[17] Denying Guido's Averroism is G. Favati, 'La glossa latina di Dino del Garbo a "Dona me prega" del Cavalcanti,' in *Annali Scuola Normale Superiore di Pisa*, NS 21 (1952) 70–103; Nardi responded to the 'giovane critico' Favati in 'Noterella' (n16), which Favati answered in 'Guido Cavalcanti, Dino del Garbo, e l'averroismo di Bruno Nardi,' *Filologia romanza* 2 (1955) 67–83.

[18] David Anderson, ed., *Pound's Cavalcanti* (Princeton 1983) 211. In trying to ascertain Guido's philosophical and theological position on the basis of a handful of lyric poems, Pound finds himself relying on hunches: Guido reveals 'no open "atheism," indeed no direct attack on any church dogma, but there is probably a sense of briskness; I mean it would not have been comforting to lovers of quiet. . . . I may be wrong, but I cannot believe that Guido "swallowed" Aquinas' (211).

Guido's father-in-law and mother-in-law, were condemned posthumously as heretics in 1283.[19] And, as we shall see shortly, in the *Decameron* Boccaccio presents Guido with the reputation of holding somewhat 'della opinione degli epicuri.'

Although chroniclers carry on about the evil presence of Epicureans, the term often appears to have been little more than an abusive epithet, like 'communist' or 'secular humanist' in our time. Thus, on present evidence it may not be possible to make a strong case for the existence of a circle of self-styled Epicureans in the Florence of Dante's youth. It seems to me, though, that Dante's treatment of Epicurus, the Florentine Epicureans, and his 'primo amico' Guido reveals a passion difficult to account for without some personal involvement in Epicureanism on the part of Dante himself, especially when seen in contrast to the favorable treatment given Democritus and Aristotle. It is tempting to speculate that Dante himself felt the lure of Epicureanism as an appealing alternative to the terror of death and damnation. But whatever the facts concerning Dante's connection with a perhaps imaginary circle of Epicureans, canto 10 of *Inferno* is among the most powerful and harshest treatments of Epicurus and of Epicurean philosophical secularity in Western thought.

If Dante of the *Commedia* provides the greatest medieval affirmation of eternal values and goals, the Boccaccio of the *Decameron*, at least in some of his moods, offers the most self-conscious affirmation of an opposing secular spirit.[20] Dante presented Farinata and Cavalcante as Epicureans in a scene of

---

[19] Niccolò Ottokar, 'La condanna postuma di Farinata degli Uberti,' *Archivio storico italiano* 77.6 (1919 [1921]) 155–63.

[20] Not too long ago the secular spirit of the *Decameron* seemed a well-established certainty of literary criticism. But with that secular spirit occasionally romanticized into an adolescent affirmation of the 'religion of love' on the one hand and denied by a newly discovered Christian allegory on the other, the *Decameron* now takes its place beside the *Canterbury Tales* as one of the most problematic and controversial of medieval literary masterpieces. The problematic nature of much late medieval literature may be intentional, and it may become less foreign to us as we become more comfortable with late medieval philosophy. Still, I acknowledge that a Boccaccio of the extreme secularity proposed here does not easily harmonize with the Boccaccio of many learned and imaginative studies of the *Decameron*. However, concerning Boccaccio's attitude toward sexual passion (and the attitude of Guido and Dino del Garbo as well), there may not be as much difference between pagan secular thought and medieval Christianity as one might suppose. Even if Professor Hollander's impressively argued theory concerning Boccaccio's early and continuing endorsement of Guido Cavalcanti's antipathy to sexual love becomes generally accepted, such opposition would not reduce the possibility that Guido or Boccaccio embraced in some way a thought system like that of Epicurus (cf. Robert Hollander, *Boccaccio's Two Venuses* [New York 1977]). Not constrained by miraculous events at the Marriage of Cana, the ancients could oppose sexuality with even more exhuberance than the Christians. Epicurus was no more in favor of human sexuality than Paul or Jerome ('a man never gets any good from sexual

tombs. In the ninth tale of the sixth day of the *Decameron*, Boccaccio presents their son and son-in-law, Dante's friend Guido Cavalcante, also as an Epicurean, also in a scene of tombs. Betto Brunelleschi has been trying to lure Guido, an 'ottimo filosofo naturale,' to join his company, a group devoted to high living, particularly to giving and attending banquets:

> Ma a messer Betto non era mai potuto venir fatto d'averlo, e credeva egli co' suoi compagni che ciò avvenisse per ciò che Guido alcuna volta speculando molto abstratto dagli uomini divenia; e per ciò che egli alquanto tenea della oppinione degli epicuri, si diceva tralla gente volgare che queste sue speculazioni erano solo in cercare se trovar si potesse che Iddio non fosse.
>
> Ora avvenne un giorno che, essendo Guido partito d'Orto San Michele e venutosene per lo Corso degli Adimari infino a San Giovanni, il quale spesse volte era suo cammino, essendo arche grandi di marmo, che oggi sono in Santa Reparata, e molte altre dintorno a San Giovanni, e egli essendo tralle colonne del porfido che vi sono e quelle arche e la porta di San Giovanni, che serrata era, messer Betto con sua brigata a caval venendo su per la piazza di Santa Reparata, vedendo Guido là tra quelle sepolture, dissero: 'Andiamo a dargli briga'; e spronati i cavalli, a guisa d'uno assalto sollazzevole gli furono, quasi prima che egli se ne avvedesse, sopra e cominciarongli a dire: 'Guido, tu rifiuti d'esser di nostra brigata; ma ecco, quando tu avrai trovato che Idio non sia, che avrai fatto?'
>
> A' quali Guido, da lor veggendosi chiuso, prestamente disse: 'Signori, voi mi potete dire a casa vostra ciò che vi piace'; e posta la mano sopra una di quelle arche, che grandi erano, sì come colui che leggerissimo era, prese un salto e fusi gittato dall'altra parte, e sviluppatosi da loro se n'andò.
>
> Costoro rimaser tutti guatando l'un l'altro, e cominciarono a dire che egli era uno smemorato e che quello che egli aveva risposto non veniva a dir nulla, con ciò fosse cosa che quivi dove erano non avevano essi a fare più che tutti gli altri cittadini, né Guido meno che alcun di loro.
>
> Alli quali messer Betto rivolto, disse: 'Gli smemorati siete voi, se voi non l'avete inteso: egli ci ha onestamente e in poche parole detta la maggior villania del mondo, per ciò che, se voi riguarderete bene, queste arche sono le case de' morti, per ciò che in esse si pongono e dimorano i morti; le quali egli dice che son nostra casa, a dimostrarci che noi e gli altri uomini idioti e non letterati siamo, a comparazion di lui e degli altri uomini scienziati, peggio che uomini morti, e per ciò, qui essendo, noi siamo a casa nostra.'
>
> Allora ciascuno intese quello che Guido aveva voluto dire e vergognossi, né mai più gli diedero briga, e tennero per innanzi messer Betto sottile e intendente cavaliere.[21]

passion, and he is fortunate if he does not receive harm' Vatican Sayings 51); Lucretius, if possible, less so. Over the centuries Christian laymen have proposed a compromise involving acceptance of the positive value of marital sexuality, even when it is neither procreative nor undertaken to pay the marriage debt and/or avoid worse sin, a compromise the Church seems from time to time almost willing to entertain.

[21] *Decameron*, ed. Vittore Branca (Florence 1976). For convenience I include John Payne's translation revised by Charles S. Singleton (Berkeley 1982) 470–71:

But Messer Betto had never been able to succeed in getting him, and he and his companions believed that this was because Guido, being sometimes engaged in speculation, became all

Here, in one of the great intertextual moments in medieval literature, Boccaccio confronts his master Dante.[22] At first, Boccaccio's insistent symbolism seems to affirm Dante's values and judgments and to promise a fate for the Epicurean son like that of the Epicurean father. Guido stands between the church, eternal salvation, and the tombs, eternal damnation. If this were all, we might conclude that his fate is undecided, that — poised between the church and the tombs — Guido still has a choice between salvation through Christianity and damnation through heresy. But from the outset, the door of the church is shut (*serrata*). Apparently, only the tombs, the fate of his heretical father and father-in-law, remain. Were the novella to end here, it would

---

abstracted from humankind; and because he was inclined somewhat to the opinion of the Epicureans, it was reported among the common folk that these his speculations consisted only in seeking if it might be discovered that God was not.

It chanced one day that Guido set out from Orto San Michele and came by way of the Corso degli Adimari, which was oftentimes his road, to San Giovanni, round about which there were at that time divers great marble tombs (which are nowadays at Santa Reparata) and many others. As he was between the columns of porphyry there and the tombs in question and the door of the church, which was shut, Messer Betto and his company, coming on horseback along the Piazza di Santa Reparata, espied him among the tombs and said, 'Let us go plague him.' Accordingly, spurring their horses, they charged all down upon him in sport and coming upon him before he was aware of them, said to him, 'Guido, you refuse to be of our company: but look, when you will have found that God is not, what will you have accomplished?' Guido, seeing himself hemmed in by them, answered promptly, 'Gentlemen, you may say what you will to me in your own house'; then, laying his hand on one of the great tombs aforesaid and being very nimble of body, he took a spring and alighting on the other side, made off, having thus rid himself of them.

The gentlemen abode looking one upon another and fell to saying that he was a crackbrain and that this that he had answered them amounted to nought, seeing that there where they were they had no more to do than all the other citizens, nor Guido himself less than any of themselves. But Messer Betto turned to them and said, 'It is you who are the crackbrains, if you have not apprehended him. He has courteously and in a few words given us the sharpest rebuke in the world; for, if you consider aright, these tombs are the houses of the dead, seeing they are laid and abide therein, and these, says he, are our house, meaning thus to show us that we and other ignorant and unlettered men are, compared with him and other men of learning, worse than dead folk; wherefore, being here, we are in our own house.' Thereupon each understood what Guido had meant to say and was abashed nor ever plagued him more, but held Messer Betto thenceforward a gentleman of a subtle and understanding wit.

[22] A recent study of this intertextuality is Robert M. Durling, 'Boccaccio on Interpretation: Guido's Escape (*Decameron* VI.9),' in *Dante, Petrarch, Boccaccio: Studies in the Italian Trecento in Honor of Charles S. Singleton*, edd. Aldo S. Bernardo and Anthony L. Pellegrini, Medieval and Renaissance Texts and Studies 22 (Binghamton 1983) 273–304. Although our interpretations differ, Professor Durling's essay is rich in learning and insight and is probably the most up-to-date guide to the extensive commentary on this *novella*.

provide strong evidence to support interpretations of the *Decameron* that treat it as an orthodox (if clever and, of course, ironic) Augustinian Christian work.[23] Strengthening such interpretations might be the fact that Dante and his public knew that Guido was buried at Santa Reparata, now the home, Boccaccio notes, of the 'arche grandi di marmo' where Betto's 'Brigata' confronts him. But then, suddenly, in an act that astonishes the reader as much as it does Guido's playful antagonists, Guido taunts Betto and his comrades with being at home in the abode of the dead, lightly vaults over the tombs, and escapes. Like the Epicurean wise man, death is nothing to him. One might even infer that in spurning the social life so forcefully offered by compatriots like Betto, Guido spurns the sensual Epicureanism of popular misconception. From the point of view of genuine Epicureanism, such search for the sensual pleasures of this world is a kind of death, and in the cemetery the young revelers are indeed in their 'own house.' As Lucretius puts it, 'Hell is right here, the work of foolish men' ('hic Acherusia fit stultorum denique vita' 3.1023).

As Boccaccio grew older, he grew more orthodox (or if the Christian allegorists are correct, more *openly* orthodox), and, as we might expect, his opinion of the Epicureans grew more (openly) orthodox, too, as Dante's did. In the *Genealogy of the Gods*, he speaks of the Cynics and Epicureans, 'who having got themselves tangled up in unspeakable errors ['qui infandis erroribus involuti'], proceeded in various ways to defame [Philosophy] more like enemies than supporters' (14.19).[24] But in a moment of youthful brilliance and iconoclasm,

---

[23] One effort to find a controlling moral allegory in the *Decameron* is Joan M. Ferrante, 'The Frame Characters of the *Decameron*: A Progression of Virtues,' *Romance Philology* 19 (1965) 212–26, but she concentrates almost entirely on the frame story.

[24] Even toward the end of his life, however, Boccaccio can acknowledge Epicurus' virtues while condemning his errors:

Epicuro fu solennissimo filosofo e molto morale e venerabile uomo a' tempi di Filippo, re di Macedonia e padre d'Alessandro. È il vero che egli ebbe alcune perverse e detestabili oppinioni. . . . Ed estiman molti che questo filosofo fosse ghiotissimo uomo; la quale estimazione non è vera, per ciò che nessun altro fu più sobrio di lui; ma, acciò che egli sentisse quello diletto, nel quale poneva che era il sommo bene, sosteneva lungamente la fame, o vogliam più tosto dire il disiderio del mangiare, il qual, molto portato, adoperava che non che'l pane, ma le radici dell'erbe salvatiche maravigliosamente piacevano e con disiderio si mangiavano; e così, sostenuta lungamente la sete, non che i deboli vini, ma l'acqua, e ancora la non pura, piaceva e appetitosamente si beveva; e similmente di ciascuna altra cosa avveniva. E perciò non fu ghiotto, come molti credono; né fu perciò la sua sobrietà laudevole, in quanto a laudevol fine non l'usava. Adunque per queste oppinioni, separate del tutto dalla verità, sì come eretico mostra l'autore lui in questo luogo esser dannato, e con lui tutti coloro li quali le sue oppinioni seguitarono (*Esposizioni sopra la* COMEDIA *di Dante*, ed. Giorgio Padoan [Verona 1965] 515–16).

he gave us the picture of Epicurean Guido nimbly leaping over the tomb in which orthodoxy would imprison him. Rising above death, *in time*, is, after all, the essence of Epicurean secularity.

Qualified if not repudiated elsewhere in Boccaccio, even in the *Decameron*, Guido's defiance of the fate assigned his father and father-in-law and threatening him is a stunning example of the possibility for playful, audacious, and iconoclastic secularity in the 'Age of Faith.'

Vanderbilt University

THE 'LUUE-RON' OF THOMAS OF HALES

By JAMES W. EARL

A poem called a 'love-rune' is not likely to be transparent. Even if 'rune' no longer meant magic, mystery, profundity, or complexity in the thirteenth century, as a word meaning 'poem' it still connoted the magical, mysterious, profound, and complex aspects of poetry. At first sight, the 'Luue-Ron'[1] appears to be a conventional call to chastity in a highly spiritualized language of courtly love, presenting Christ as the ideal courtly lover. But the transformation of courtly values into their exact opposites requires some sleight of hand on the part of the poet; after all, he must answer the girl's desires only to subvert and destroy them. He is only *pretending* to write her a love-poem. In fact, he answers her request with its complete opposite, a sermon on the contempt of the world, which he follows with a vision of Christ in glory, couched in the most worldly metaphors imaginable, then bids the girl vow chastity for His love. Even as he is denying them, the poet reveals the girl's untransformed desires as rich metaphors for the spiritual life. Like a few other Middle English lyrics which play with the Christ–lover conceit, such as 'Quia amore langueo,' the 'Luue-Ron' is clever enough in its manipulation of Christian imagery and the reader's desires to qualify fully as a *rune*, something other than it seems.

Until recently, the poem received no serious study. It is commonly used to illustrate the *ubi sunt qui ante nos* theme in the Middle English lyric;[2] a short note by Wells points out the poem's similarity to 'Clene Maydenhod' of the Vernon MS, though it establishes no connection between the two poems and comes to no conclusion; Hill investigates the authorship of the poem; and the few pregnant remarks by Manning, Woolf, Kane, and Gray do not hint at the poem's complexity.[3] Although Thomas of Hales is 'de ordine fratrum Mino-

---

[1] All references to the poem are to the edition of Bruce Dickens and R. M. Wilson, *Early Middle English Texts* (New York 1964) 104–9; it can also be found in the editions of Richard Morris, *An Old English Miscellany*, EETS 49 (London 1872) 93–99, and Carleton Brown, *English Lyrics of the XIIIth Century* (Oxford 1932) 68–74.

[2] Albert Baugh, 'The Middle English Period,' in *A Literary History of England*, edd. Baugh et al. (New York 1948) 123; David M. Zesmer, *Guide to English Literature from* BEOWULF *to Chaucer and Medieval Drama* (New York 1961) 144; Dickens and Wilson 103.

[3] John Edwin Wells, '"A Luue Ron" and "Of Clene Meidenhad,"' *Modern Language Review* 9 (1914) 236–37; Betty Hill, 'The "Luue-Ron" and Thomas de Hales,' *Modern Language Review* 59 (1964) 321–30; Stephen Manning, *Wisdom and Number* (Lincoln 1962) 122–24; Rosemary Woolf, *The English Religious Lyric in the Middle Ages* (Oxford 1968) 61–67; George Kane, *Middle English Literature* (London 1957) 117; Douglas Gray, *Themes and Images in the Middle English Lyric* (London 1972) 186–87.

rum,' Jeffrey does not treat the poem in his *Early English Lyric and Franciscan Spirituality*, except to say that it is 'a fair précis of St. Francis' ideal for
preaching, covering typically Franciscan points,' and that it is in a Franciscan
MS, Jesus College Oxford 29.[4]

It would seem that scholars have considered it a clear, uncomplicated, and
self-explanatory example of a popular medieval literary theme. But it is
certainly not that: the *ubi sunt* theme occupies only one-tenth of the poem's
two hundred and ten lines, and the rest abounds in unexplored difficulties.
The task of unraveling and explicating them has been begun by Rogers in an
essay on which some of the following arguments are built.[5]

Most of the difficulties are problems of unity which arise in a first reading
of the poem. For example: what business does a 'mayde Crystes' ('puella
deo dicata') have in asking for a 'love-rune' in the first place? How are we
to understand her desire for '*on-oper* soþ lefmon'? What is the relationship
between the theme of mortality, which occupies a very large portion of the
poem, and the exhortation to purity and the love of Christ? What is the
significance of the many allusions to the concluding chapters of the Apocalypse? And finally, what of the gem of maidenhood, the central metaphor of
the poem, a complex symbol which demands interpretation? When these and
other problems are examined, the poem appears quite different from what its
casual traditional interpretation assumes.

The way the poet weaves together his many themes makes the poem a small
tour de force. After stating the initial theme by contrasting earthly and heavenly love, the poem modulates into meditations upon mortality, mutability,
the Heavenly City, the love of Christ, salvation, and chastity. As early as the
third stanza, the poem becomes not simply a renunciation of an earthly lover,
but a renunciation of earthly matters altogether. Of the first eighty-six lines —
that is, until the introduction of Christ as lover — over forty concern death,
with only the slightest reference to love at all. By the eighth stanza it is clear
that the poet's intention is greater than simply to 'wurche a luue-ron,' for he
then launches into a discussion of the folly of riches. His dark conclusion,
'Al deþ hit wile from him take' (64), supersedes (or transcends) what appeared
to be the theme to that point — that there is no earthly lover 'þat her may
beon studeuest' (18). The ninth stanza, the popular *ubi sunt* passage, illustrates the subtle shift of emphasis which is taking place: where are, the
poet asks, those earthly lovers *Paris* and *Heleyne*, *Amadas* and *Ideyne*, *Tristram* and *Yseude*? But the catalogue continues with the addition of *Ector* and

---

[4] David L. Jeffrey, *The Early English Lyric and Franciscan Spirituality* (Lincoln, Neb.
1975) 177, 210–11.
[5] William E. Rogers, *Image and Abstraction*, Anglistica 18 (Copenhagen 1972) 22–40.

Cesar, who are certainly not being remembered as lovers; as two of the pagan members of the Nine Worthies, they are examples of human greatness in a general sense, having little or no relation to the theme of the earthly lover in the poem.[6] The problem of love has been utterly transformed by the time the poet says

>þus is þes world of false fere—
>Fol hi is þe on hire is bold.   (79–80)

At this point Christ is introduced, ostensibly as an alternative to the earthly lover, but more generally — and more importantly — as an alternative to earthliness itself: He is not only 'studeuest,' but also eternal and immutable. Christ as lover is presented in the traditional courtly imagery of secular love — He is handsome, rich, powerful, genteel, generous, etc.; but even as His qualities are being enumerated, the poet is constructing a greater argument, that He is also our salvation and thus the remedy for our mortality. The poet builds his argument with an extended allusion to the Apocalypse, which expands the theme of the poem to the limits of the Christian concept of love.

The Apocalyptic allusion is most evident in the four stanzas dealing with the Heavenly City (113–44). An ambiguous reference to Solomon's 'bolde' accomplishes the transition from the worldly level of the argument to the transcendent:

>Hwat spekestu of eny bolde
>þat wrouhte þe wise Salomon
>Of iaspe, of saphir, of merede golde,
>And of mony on-oþer ston?   (113–16)

The Temple of Solomon is the most obvious meaning, but it was built of wood, not stone, and there is no mention in Scripture of jewels or gold. Clearly what the poet means to evoke is the anti-type of the Temple, the New Jerusalem as it is described in Apocalypse 21–22. By deliberately confusing the earthly Temple with the Heavenly City in accordance with common exegetical tradition, the poet quietly refers the courtly Christ–lover image to the most elevated of its allegorical significances.

---

[6] Gray, in his discussion of the *ubi sunt* theme (186–87), says of these lines, 'Hector and Caesar, from the traditional "Nine Worthies," are a less happy choice. There is a sort of continuity between these exemplary figures and earlier remarks on wealth, and on the instability of the world in general, but it is hard to avoid a sense of imprecision here, a sense that the poet is following a set theme rather mechanically.' But the inclusion of these figures broadens the theme of the transience of earthly love to that of transience itself; and they are a particularly pregnant choice, since they are pagans who cannot enjoy even the possibility of salvation.

This 'confusion' of the earthly and celestial Temples is not really clarified
for us in the verses which immediately follow:

> Hit is feyrure of feole-volde
> More þan iche eu telle con,
> This bold, mayde, þe is bihote
> If þat þu bist His leouemon.   (117–20)

Our reading of these lines depends on how we understand the first word, 'hit';
does it refer back to Solomon's 'bold,' or ahead to 'þis bold' of line 119, or are
the two in fact identical? The phrase 'þe is bihote' is also ambiguous. It may
be understood as 'which is promised,' which would establish a *contrast* between
the two temples. Read this way, the whole stanza might be paraphrased:
'What do you say of a temple built by Solomon, of jasper and other stones?
The temple which is promised to you if you will be His lover is many times
fairer.' This reading would account for the possibly derogatory tone in the
phrase 'hwat spekestu of' (which might be translated 'why do you talk
about . . .?'), the vagueness of the word 'eny' in line 113, and the comparative
'feyrure' in line 117. Morris, in his edition of the poem, glosses these two
stanzas in this way: 'His dwelling is fairer than any Solomon ever wrought.'[7]

But recent editors punctuate the passage in a way that precludes this reading.
Carleton Brown, Dickens and Wilson, and Rogers put a semicolon after line
118, which forces us to read 'þe is bihote' as 'is promised to thee,' in which
case the two temples are *identified*: 'What do you say of a temple built by
Solomon? It is fairer, more than I can tell you, and is promised to you, if
you will be His lover.' This reading makes the description of the jeweled
Temple more understandable, since it is identical with the jeweled City. It
also makes line 119 syntactically parallel with line 127, 'þis bold, mayde, is
þe bihote,' which happens to occur in the same position in the next stanza—
a parallel which must have struck the poet, since he sacrifices his rhyme for the
effect. But the second reading makes the comparative 'feyrure' somewhat
awkward; also, it would be odd for the poet to promise the girl Solomon's
Temple, and it would be stretching even the elastic language of typology to
say that Solomon built the Heavenly City. The difficulty of these lines cannot
really be resolved; the ambiguity is such that both readings are to some extent
necessary for the coherence of the image.

None of the poem's several editors and commentators has felt it necessary
to explore such allegorical–typological mechanisms as this one of the Temple
and the City, which unify the poem's many themes. The studied ambiguity of
these lines provides a transition from the worldly level of the poem to the
otherworldly, as it passes from the negative significance of earthly riches,

---

[7] Morris 96; he does not punctuate the poem, except with the pointing of the MS.

which the poem has been stressing, to the significance *in bono* of the lavish heavenly riches; and it incidentally prepares for the 'ymston' which later becomes the central image of the poem.

The description of 'þis bold' proceeds in the next stanza in accordance with the description of the City in the Apocalypse. We are told that 'Hit stont vppon a treowe mote' (121), which is one of many scriptural details:

> Et sustulit me in spiritu in montem magnum at altum, et ostendit mihi civitatem sanctam Jerusalem, descendentem de caelo a Deo, habentem claritatem Dei, et lumen ejus simile lapidi pretioso tanquam lapidi iaspidis.
> (Apoc. 21.10–11)

The repeated mention of the 'grundwal' in the next few lines derives from the jeweled foundations of the City in Apoc. 21.19–20. The unusual image we find in lines 153–54,

> Hit is ymston of feor iboren,
> Nys non betere vnder heoene grund,

should not evoke the Miltonic image of celestial mining, and certainly does not mean, as Dickens and Wilson suggest, 'beneath the lowest part of heaven,'[8] but rather refers to the many jewels which make up the foundations of the Heavenly City. And the description of Christ in line 142, 'He is day wyþ-ute nyhte,' is a clear reference to Apoc. 21.23, 'Et civitas non eget sole, neque luna, ut luceant in ea: nam claritas Dei illuminavit eam, et lucerna ejus est Agnus,' and also 25.5, 'Et nox ultra non erit,' etc.

Allusions to the Apocalypse are not confined to the description of the City. Another series of references occurs in the last two stanzas of the poem. When the poet says

> þis rym, made, ich þe sende
> Open and wiþe-ute sel   (193–94)

we should be reminded of St. John's epilogue, 'Et dicit mihi: ne signaveris verba prophetiae libri hijus' (Apoc. 22.10). And the poet's exhortation to the maiden to read and learn the poem by heart, to teach it and to say it aloud, recalls the end of the Apocalypse, 'Beatus qui custodit verba prophetiae libri hujus' (22.7), and 'Beatus qui legit et audit verba prophetiae hujus, et servat ea quae in ea scripta sunt' (1.3). Most especially, we should note the last quatrain,

> To þe He haueþ send one gretynge;
> God almyhti þe beo myd,
> And leue cumen to His brudþinge
> Heye in heouene þer He sit.
>
>   (205–8)

---

8 Dickens and Wilson 219.

which brings to mind not only the Annunciation, but also the closing verses of the Apocalypse, 'Et spiritus, et sponsa dicunt: Veni. Et qui audit, dicat: Veni. Et qui sitit, veniat; et qui vult, accipiat aquam vitae gratis' (22.17).

The precise nature of the 'brudþinge' in these lines and in the Apocalypse largely determines the poem's meaning. It might be assumed from the echo of the angel's words to the Virgin that the poet is exhorting the maiden to become a 'bride of Christ' in the sense derived from Canticles and often associated with the convent. Brown certainly implies this in his notes to the poem, when he refers to 'the familiar *Sponsus* theme of medieval allegory,'[9] and cites as a source a passage from the *Ancrene Riwle* 'in which Christ is represented as wooing "his deore spuse, þet is . . . þe clene soule."' But although this implication cannot be denied, the poem nowhere speaks of the *sponsa Christi*; it speaks of Christ only as 'lefmon.' This detail accords with the use of courtly love imagery, which does not often propose marriage, and the use of Apocalyptic imagery, in which the *sponsa* is not the individual soul, as in Canticles, but is the City itself. The only mention of brideship in the poem is in line 207, and the invitation to the 'brudþinge' there certainly does not imply that the maiden of the poem is to be the bride; rather, the image fits neatly into the symbolism of the Apocalypse, where Christ takes as His bride the New Jerusalem. Thus the extended reference to the City is not mere ornament. At the end of the poem, as at the end of Scripture, the Spirit (Christ) and the Bride (the City) — both transcendental figures — say 'Come,' and the maiden and the reader are asked to respond.

The *virgines*, although they appear several chapters before the *sponsa Agni* is introduced into the Apocalyptic narrative, are traditionally included in the 'brudþinge.' Bede, for example, commenting on the procession of virgins singing to Christ in Apoc. 14.35, says, 'Vos affertis ad nuptias Agni canticum novem, quod cantabitis in citharis vestris.'[10] This association also illuminates the last stanza of our poem, in which the maiden is enjoined 'mid swete stephne þu hit singe' as she is invited to the heavenly bridal. We might also note that the *virgines* are characterized in Apoc. 14.5 as *sine macula*, a phrase commonly translated in Middle English 'wiþute wemme,' as the maiden is described in line 165. In the Middle English sermon 'Hali Meidenhad,' which is addressed to young women with the same general purpose as our poem, the explanation of the 'canticum novum' of the virgins is very similar:

> Ne moten nane but heo hoppen ne singen, for þat is ai hare song, þonken godd, and herien, þat he on ham se muche grace ȝef of him seluen, þat ha forsoken for him euch eorðlich mon, and helden ham cleane ai fra fleschliche

---

[9] Brown 199.
[10] Bede, *Explanatio Apocalypsis* 2.14 (PL 93.173–74).

ful en ibodi and ibreoste, and i stude of man of lam, token liues lauerd, þe
king of þe hehe blisse, for hwi he menske ham se muchel biforen alle þe
oðre, as þe brudgume deð his weddede spuse. Þe song he maken nane bute
heo singen.[11]

So the poet's request that the maiden *sing* his poem is especially significant in
the Apocalyptic framework.

The typology of the *patria coelestis* need not be expounded here at length.
For our purposes it may be illustrated (somewhat in reverse) by the significance
commonly given to the Temple, upon which the imagery of the poem builds.
Allegorically the Temple represents the Church; tropologically it is the *viri
sancti*, or the soul (thus implying the allegory of Canticles), or the body (in
discussions of chastity);[12] and anagogically it is the Heavenly City. This typology is virtually the same as Origen's classic example of the meanings of Jerusalem. These levels overlap and flow together in exegesis, of course, and also in
our poem: the poet's moral exhortation to chaste love has an anagogical
meaning, which is the rationale for the poem's Apocalyptic imagery.

Once we have established an extended allusion to the Apocalypse, other
details of the poem can be seen as part of the pattern. This quatrain is an
example:

> Henri, king of Engelonde,
>   Of Hym he halt and to Hym buhþ.
> Mayde, to þe He send His sonde
>   And wilneþ for to beo þe cuþ.   (101–4)

The last two lines fit easily into the Apocalyptic context (cf. Apoc. 1.9ff.;
22.6, 16); and the reference to Henry echoes 21.23–25, where the kings of the
earth present themselves before Christ, and 1.5, where Christ is called 'princeps
regum terrae.' It might also be noted that in the catalogue of stones in the
twenty-second stanza (169–76), nine of the ten jewels listed are those of the
foundations of the City in 21.19–20.[13]

If the description of Christ as lover in the last half of the 'Luue-Ron' is in
Apocalyptic terms, it is a dramatic and reasonable contrast to the earthly lover
of the first half; but the real significance of the Apocalyptic reference is that it
makes salvation central to the poem's meaning, in response to the themes of
mortality and mutability which are developed simultaneously with (and somewhat independently of) the discussion of earthly love. The distinction the
poet is making is not simply between an earthly lover and Christ, but between
what Augustine would call death-in-life and life-in-death.

---

[11] *Hali Meidenhad*, ed. Oswald Cockayne, EETS ns 18 (London 1886) 21–23.

[12] Rogers 34–35 documents this typology fully, especially the relation of the Temple and
the chaste body.

[13] Rogers 30 explains the extra jewel from lapidary tradition.

What, in the end, is the poet's advice to the girl? Is it simply to choose
Christ as lover and live in chastity? The Apocalyptic metaphor implies more:
the paradox of the poem is not just that the highest love is found in chastity,
but that it is found in salvation after death, for which chastity is a symbol.
One cannot literally join the procession of virgins in Heaven by making a
commitment or being chaste; these are in anticipation of that final reward, with
which the poet is equally concerned. However, the life of chastity and devotion
does enlist the maiden allegorically in the heavenly train. Just as the poet
carefully glosses over the distinction between type and anti-type in speaking
of the Temple and the Heavenly City, he explores simultaneously the literal,
allegorical, and anagogical meanings of virginity and the love of Christ.

There is a traditional significance of the City developed especially in reference
to the monastic life: Jerusalem is 'illos, qui in hoc saeculo vitam ducunt reli-
giosam, mores supernae illius Jerusalem conversatione honesta et ordinata
pro viribus imitantes.'[14] St. Bernard defines monasticism in this context:
monachus et Ierosolymita. Dom Jean Leclercq analyzes the 'eschatological
tendency' in monastic life and literature, describing the monastery as 'a
Jerusalem in anticipation, a place of waiting and desire, of preparation for that
holy city.' Monastic theology places great emphasis on this typology:

> Those who participate in God are all citizens of one and the same Church,
> in Heaven and on earth. The 'type' which serves to evoke it is, not the
> Jerusalem of the flesh whose Temple was material, but the spiritual Jeru-
> salem of which St. Paul spoke to the Galatians and of which the earthly
> Jerusalem was merely a figure. Those who are united with God form a
> single community: Heaven and the Church. It is simply given one name;
> to it is applied what the Bible said of the Holy City, in the description of the
> Prophets or of Revelation.[15]

And he summarizes the concept which might be considered the cornerstone
of monastic practice, in a passage which could very well serve, with the lines
above, as a summary of the method, themes, and imagery of the 'Luue-Ron':

> The task we face is, really, to subsitute the concupiscence of the spirit for
> that of the flesh. A parallel is established between them in which the role of
> spiritual concupiscence is to comfort the weary soul with hope of future
> glory. But instead of placing emphasis on the negative aspect of asceticism,
> that is to say on suppression of desire, this mode of expression accentuates
> the positive side: the soaring toward God, the inclination toward the End
> of man which is God possessed fully and eternally.[16]

---

[14] PL 183.1045; cited by Jean Leclercq, *The Love of Learning and the Desire for God,*
trans. Catharine Misrahi, 3rd ed. (New York 1982) 55.

[15] Leclercq 56.

[16] Leclercq 58.

We can recognize in this outline the conception and the mode of expression which mark our poem: the call for the sublimation, or transcendence, of physical desire in terms at once moral and eschatological. In the poem, Christ is described in the language of courtly love, but is to be found in the Heavenly Jerusalem — which is symbolized on earth by the chastity of monastic life.[17] Although Thomas of Hales was not a monk but a friar, the poem concerns the virtues of the convent, virtues as relevant to a Franciscan as to any cloistered woman. When we read the poem it is easy to forget sometimes, caught as we are in the spell of the courtly imagery, that we are not just reading moral advice to a girl, but to a 'mayde Crystes,' a novice, *deo dicata*, whose renunciation of worldly love is meant to be complete and irrevocable. The poet intends to reinforce a *total* transformation of desire.

In the Franciscan context it is hard not to think of St. Clare, whose teen-age supplication was answered by Francis with an alternate bridal ceremony (for she was already betrothed) and a ride to a local Benedictine convent. Perhaps this evocation helps us understand the girl's desire in our poem for 'on-oþer soþ lefmon.'

The way the poet effects this transformation of desire can be seen in his manipulation of the poem's central symbol, the gem of maidenhood. The 'tresur,' which is introduced in line 145, is first identified with a bower, and then a castle:

> He haueþ bi-tauht þe o tresur
> > þat is betere þan gold oþer pel,
> And bit þe luke þine bur,
> > And wilneþ þu hit wyte wel,
> Wyþ þeoues, wiþ reueres, wiþ lechurs,
> > þu most beo waker and snel;
> þu art swetture þane eny flur
> > Hwile þu witest þene kastel.   (145–52)

Immediately afterward, the poet announces that 'Hit is ymston of feor iboren.' One stanza later we are finally told that 'Mayden-hod i-cleoped is.' Maidenhood, then, is 'þe ymston of þi bur' (178); and in the lines which follow, the bower itself is finally associated with the Heavenly City, an extension of that image which complements our earlier remarks concerning the eschatological character of the cloister. The bower-castle is associated with maidenhood and the New Jerusalem in 'Hali Maidenhad' too:

> Ah heo [the virgin] stont þurh heh lif iþe tur of ierusalem; Nawt of lah on eorðe, ah of þe hehe tur in heouene, þat is bitacned þurh þis . . . þah ha

---

licomliche wunie up on eorðe. And is as in sion þe hehe tur of hevene. . . .[18]

But then we learn that this new and puzzling metaphor of the heavenly
bower-castle has as its tenor not just maidenhood, but Christ too. The entire
next stanza is ambiguous:

> He is i-don in heouene golde
> And is ful of fyn amur.
> All þat myhte hine wite scholde,
> He schyneþ so bryht in heouene bur.
>
> (181–84)

We note the consistent use of 'he,' though 'hit' was frequently used earlier
(both are appropriate to ME *gim*, masc.); we note too that line 182 is less appropriate to a gem than to Christ. Ambiguous too is the word 'wite,' which
could mean either 'to guard' or 'to know'; both senses appear in the poem (6,
62, 148, 152, 158, 167). The former meaning is given by Dickens and Wilson;
read in this way, the line repeats the obvious advice about maidenhood, i.e.,
guard it. The latter meaning, however, makes more sense in the context of the
whole sentence: 'All who might should know Him, He shines so bright in
heaven's bower.' These lines, then, refer not only to the maintenance of
chastity, but to the vision of Christ in glory which is the object of the con-
templative life in the mystical tradition, as described by Rolle, Hilton, Juliana
of Norwich, and others, and to a degree in the *Ancrene Riwle*.

In the five stanzas devoted to the 'tresur,' then, the bower, castle, Heaven,
the gemstone, maidenhood, and Christ are all bound up in a protean symbol
which becomes richer and more widely significant in its development from a
simple exhortation to chastity to an image of Christ mystically perceived
within the chaste life. The vehicle of this symbolism is the gem of maidenhood,
which can be identified as the pearl. Many lines point to this identification,
which clarifies the use of the symbol in the poem, and explains some puzzling
details.

We are told that 'Hit is ymston of feor iboren,' which is the peculiar case
of the orient pearl; it is also said that 'Of all oþre he berþ þat pris,' perhaps
recalling the 'pearl of great price' (Matt. 13.45–46), a parable echoed also in the
line 'He is to-fore alle oþre i-coren'; the comparison of the gem to the others
'in heore colur' implies that it is clear or white; and of course the association of
the pearl with chastity is a well-developed medieval tradition, especially in the
legends of St. Margaret and the *Pearl*.[19] As *Pearl* indicates, there is also a well-

---

[18] *Hali Meidenhad* 5; the connections between the Temple, the body, the castle-bower,
and the Heavenly City are developed and documented by Rogers 34–38.

[19] For the pearl as an image of the Virgin, see Anselm Salzer, *Die Sinnbilder und Beiworte
Mariens* (1886–94; rpt. Darmstadt 1967) 243–48; for the traditions linking the pearl and

developed tradition of anagogical interpretation: the pearl's association with
the Heavenly City is derived from the fact that the gates of the City in the
Apocalypse are pearls (Apoc. 21.21); and the pearl is commonly interpreted
as Heaven in both the parable of the pearl of great price and the comment that
pearls should not be thrown before swine (Matt. 7.6). Even one of the pearl's
traditional qualities from the lapidary may be relevant: Jacobus de Voragine
mentions in the introduction to the life of St. Margaret in the *Legenda aurea*,
'Virtus autem hujus lapidus dicitur esse contra cordis passionem, et ad spiritus
confortationem.'[20] Perhaps this notion helps clarify the line 'He heleþ alle
luue wunde' (156), which is clear enough as it refers to Christ, but also applies
to the particular gemstone which is the vehicle of the metaphor.

The joy of the pearl symbol in this poem, as in *Pearl*, is its great flexibility.
An extraordinary amount of lore and exegesis is attached to the pearl, and it
commonly symbolizes either virginity or Christ, especially in their eschatological aspects in relation to the Heavenly City. The pearl is thus a perfect
symbol for drawing together the various typologically related themes of the
poem. Why the poet describes the gem of maidenhood and explicates its
symbolism without naming it directly is not a question for scholarship but
literary intuition. It seems right. Like virginity itself, it is something withheld; it remains a mystery, a crucial bit of knowledge held privately by the
girl and the reader, in restraint and silence.

These remarks should reveal at least that this seemingly simple poem is a
complex weaving-together of several religious and literary themes, united in
the conception of the religious life. It is also a little gem of our literature, which
can be included with the best Middle English religious poetry. Among the
other Middle English lyrics, the 'Luue-Ron' stands out not so much for its
technical mastery as for its unique personal tone. The poet addresses an innocent girl with the sternest possible teaching — *think on your mortality* —
but with a fatherly understanding of her adolescent desires. He accommodates
and capitalizes on her worldliness, in order to lead her to a God she can accept
as the complete fulfillment of her young and still innocent feelings of love.
He teases her with this accommodation, with fear and desire; teases her out of
her childhood innocence and into the innocence of Christian womanhood;
shows her, in the Franciscan manner, that the road of renunciation is in fact a
joyful road.

Fordham University

---

virginity, C. A. Luttrell, 'The Medieval Tradition of the Pearl Virginity,' *Medium Aevum*
31 (1962) 194–200; and James W. Earl, 'Saint Margaret and the Pearl Maiden,' *Modern
Philology* 70 (1972) 1–8.
   [20] Jacobus de Varagine, *Legenda aurea*, ed. J. G. Theodor Graesse (1890; rpt. Osnabrück
1965) 260.

THE TRINITY IN LANGLAND AND ABELARD

By PENN R. SZITTYA

In the midst of his account of Man's creation in *Piers Plowman*, Passus 9, Wit pauses to offer a puzzling metaphor for the Creator in action:

> Right as a lord sholde make lettres; if hym lakked parchemyn,
> Thouȝ he wiste to write neuer so wel, and he hadde a penne,
> The lettre for all þe lordshipe, I leue, were neuere ymaked.
>
> (9.39–41)[1]

The writing lord and his letters clearly represent the creating God and his new creation, Man, but the parchment and the pen have no obvious or easy relevance. In fact, the difficulty of the passage has provoked considerable discussion in recent years, along with some justifiable grumbling about the analogy, which has been called 'not a particularly happy one,' 'rather forced,' and 'unsatisfactory.'[2] We are not, however, without clues to a certain precision and appropriateness in the metaphor.

In a long discussion about the Trinity in Passus 16, there is a difficult passage about a lord whose resemblance to the writing lord of Passus 9 has gone unremarked:

> So þre bilongeþ for a lord þat lordshipe claymeþ:
> Might and a mene his owene myȝte to knowe,
> Of hymself and of his seruaunt, and what suffreþ hem boþe.
>
> (16.191–93)

As in Passus 9, the metaphor compares God to a lord. As in 9, there seem to be three things necessary to this lord: the power of writing, a pen, and parchment; here (apparently) might, a means to know his own might, and suffering. The 'might' of this lord recalls not only the power of writing mentioned in 9, but also the line that introduces the letter-writing lord: ' "my myȝt moot helpe forþ wiþ my speche." / Right as a lord sholde make lettres . . .' (9.38–

---

[1] All quotations from *Piers Plowman* are from the edition of the B text by George Kane and E. Talbot Donaldson (London 1975), unless otherwise noted.

[2] J. F. Goodridge, *Piers the Plowman* (Harmondsworth 1966) 282n5; Ruth Ames, *The Fulfillment of the Scriptures* (Evanston, Ill. 1970) 82; A. V. C. Schmidt, ed., *The Vision of Piers Plowman* (London 1978) 327–28; Daniel Murtaugh, PIERS PLOWMAN *and the Image of God* (Gainesville, Fla. 1978) 17, 21–22; M. N. K. Mander, 'Grammatical Analogy in Langland and Alan of Lille,' *Notes and Queries* NS 16 (1970) 501–4; A. V. C. Schmidt, 'Langland's Pen/Parchment Analogy in *Piers Plowman*, B.IX, 38–40,' *Notes and Queries* NS 27 (1980) 538–39.

39). Unfortunately, these tantalizing similarities do not immediately clarify either passage; the exact meanings of the 'mene' and of the joint suffering in Passus 16 are just as obscure as the parchment and pen of Passus 9.

The context of the passage in 16, however, offers an interesting lead which may enable us to resolve these difficulties. The lord who claims lordship is introduced in Passus 16 specifically as a metaphor for the one God in the three Persons of the Trinity. The First Person is said to be the *Pater* who has *myȝt* and majesty and is maker of all things (16.184–85); the Second is the *Filius* who is *Sothfastnesse*, the *Wardeyn* of all who have Wit, i.e., Wisdom (16.186–87); the Third is the Holy Spirit, the light of all that has life, from whom comes all 'blisse' (16.188–90). The lord who claims lordship here is a metaphor in some way for this Trinity of *myȝt*, *Wit*, and *blisse*, corresponding to the Father, Son, and Holy Spirit.

This is not the only place in the poem where such terms are used for the Trinity. As Passus 16 opens, Piers names the three staves that support the Tree of Charity: *Potentia-Dei-Patris*; *Sapientia-Dei-Patris*, which is the passion and power of Christ; and third, 'grace and help of þe holy goost' (16.30–52). In Passus 17 this Trinitarian vocabulary appears again, this time in connection with a strange metaphor (17.141–205). The Trinity is like a hand. The Father is like its fist, symbol of the 'myȝt' of God in the making of all things. The Son is like a finger put forth from the fist, to serve the hand, to touch and to teach, to portray and to paint, to point out the works of God and the way to him. Thus the finger is a symbol of the science or knowledge of God. The Holy Spirit is like the palm, which perceives what is profitable to feel and puts forth the fingers and the fist to do their office, to receive what the fingers reach. The palm thus symbolizes the Holy Spirit in its aspect as the will of God.

These Trinitarian references provide a pattern that can help us resolve the two problematic passages in Passus 9 and 16, and can lead us, if not to Langland's very source, at least to the tradition within which he was working. In the twelfth century for the first time, the Trinity of Father, Son, and Holy Spirit began to be associated with the triad of *Potentia*, *Sapientia*, and *Benignitas* respectively.[3] These terms came to be called in theological parlance

---

[3] Earlier theologians identified one or another of these attributes with God, or with individual members of the Trinity, but the identification of the Trinity specifically with *Potentia, Sapientia*, and *Benignitas* does not appear until the twelfth century. More common were the triads of St. Hilary (*Aeternitas, Species, Usus*) and Augustine (*Unitas, Aequalitas, Concordia; Unitas, Species, Ordo*, and others in *De Trinitate*). For the evolution of the concept of appropriations and the triad of *Potentia, Sapientia, Benignitas* in the twelfth century down to the time of Aquinas, see Jean Châtillon, 'Unitas, Aequalitas, Concordia vel Connexio: Recherches sur les origines de la théorie Thomiste des Appropriations (*Sum. Theol.*, I.q.39, art. 7–8)' in *St. Thomas Aquinas 1274–1974: Commemorative Studies* (Toronto 1974) I

the appropriated names or simply appropriations of the Trinity, to be distinguished from the proper names, such as *Pater, Filius,* and *Spiritus Sanctus.* The proper names are exclusive, but the appropriated names are not. They appropriate, or make proper, to one Person an aspect which is shared by all three. Although the Father is primarily associated with *Potentia,* there is nonetheless power in the Son and in the Holy Spirit.[4] The appropriations should not be thought of as real but only convenient and instructive distinctions.

The Victorines, especially Richard and Hugh, are largely responsible for the entry of this terminology into the mainstream of Catholic theology.[5] Since we know that Langland was influenced by them in other matters, it seems reasonable to think that he might have been in this.[6] But his language in fact is much closer to that of the man who seems to have been the first to relate *Potentia* explicitly to the Father, *Sapientia* to the Son, and *Benignitas* to the Holy Spirit: Peter Abelard.[7]

For Abelard the necessity for appropriated names arises from the insufficiency of human language to describe the mysteries of the Trinity. Since

---

337–79. Châtillon traces the triad from its origins in Peter Abelard through Robert of Melun, Peter Lombard, Hugh and Richard of St. Victor, Alain of Lille, Simon of Tournai, the authors of commentaries on the *Sententiae* of the Lombard, and the authors of several thirteenth-century *Summae.* Lawrence M. Clopper, in a useful article, points out the importance of the appropriated names in Langland, but mistakenly attributes the concept of appropriations and the *Potentia* triad to Augustine and other early patristic writers: 'Langland's Trinitarian Analogies as Key to Meaning and Structure,' *Medievalia et Humanistica* NS 9 (1979) 87–89.

[4] For the definition of appropriations, see Aquinas, *Summa theologiae* I.39.7–8; *Dictionnaire de Théologie Catholique* ss.vv. 'appropriations' I 1708–17, 'noms divins' XI 790–91.

[5] See particularly Hugh of St. Victor, *De sacramentis* 1.2.5–13, 1.3.28–29, PL 176.208–11; Richard of St. Victor, *De Trinitate* 6.15, ed. Gaston Salet, Sources Chrétiennes 63 (Paris 1959) 416–20; *De tribus appropriatis personis in Trinitate,* PL 196.991–94.

[6] H. S. V. Jones, 'Imaginatif in *Piers Plowman,*' *Journal of English and Germanic Philology* 13 (1914) 583–88; Randolf Quirk, 'Vis Imaginativa,' *Journal of English and Germanic Philology* 53 (1954) 81–83; Joseph S. Wittig, '"Piers Plowman" B, Passus IX–XII: Elements in the Design of the Inward Journey,' *Traditio* 28 (1972) 211–80, esp. 264ff.; A. V. C. Schmidt, 'A Note on the Text of *Piers Plowman* X.91–94,' *Notes and Queries* NS 14 (1967) 365–66.

[7] See the works of Abelard in E. M. Buytaert, ed., *Opera theologica* II, CCCM 12 (Turnhout 1969), particularly *Theologia Christiana* 1.1–7, 4.48–49, 55, 86–91, 5.17; pp. 72–75, 286–87, 289, 306–9, 354, and *Theologia scholarium* 38–75, pp. 416–32. Other references and recent scholarship in Châtillon, '*Unitas*' 359n98. It used to be thought that Abelard's ideas about appropriations had little influence in the later Middle Ages because of the charges of heresy brought against him by St. Bernard, resulting in the condemnation of 1140. That assessment is changing, particularly because of the work of scholars like D. E. Luscombe, *The School of Abelard: The Influence of Abelard's Thought in the Early Scholastic Period* (Cambridge 1969), and E. M. Buytaert, 'Abelard's Trinitarian Doctrine,' in *Peter Abelard,* Mediaevalia Lovaniensia, Series I: Studia 2 (Louvain 1974) 127–52.

we cannot describe truth itself, we can describe only something similar to truth; we speak in similes whether we will or not.[8] About God we can know only like from like, the Creator from his creation. As Abelard says, 'pro qualitate operum quae videntur, absentis artificis industriam diiudicamus.'[9] Hence our understanding of the Trinity should be carried out through examples and similitudes from the created world. The appropriated terms *Potentia, Sapientia,* and *Benignitas* are themselves taken from the created world of man and serve the purpose of similitude; they help to make intelligible the interrelationships among the divine Persons.[10]

Those interrelationships are usually described by Abelard and his contemporaries with the terms generation and procession. The Father is from no one; the Son is generated from the Father; but the Holy Spirit proceeds from them both, *ab utroque.*[11] The procession of the Holy Spirit *ab utroque,* from both of the other two Persons, is the crucial point; it is often expressed in medieval iconography by a pictorial 'spiration,' a breathing forth, in which the Spirit is depicted as the intermingled breath of the Father and Son.[12] In theological terms their intermingled breath, their conjoint action, is called grace or will or love.[13] The Holy Spirit is God's love, and proceeds from the love of the Father and Son for each other and their creation.

The procession of love which is the Spirit takes place under two aspects, according to Abelard: *secundum effecta* and *secundum affectum.* The Affect is God's eternal love within the Trinity; the effects are God's love manifest in the created world. The Affect is the eternal, effects the temporal manifestation of the divine love. *Benignitas,* Abelard's appropriated name for the Holy Spirit, is a synonym, then, not only for God's affection but also for its effect in the

---

[8] *Introductio ad theologiam* (a mistaken title: actually the longer redaction of *Theol. schol.,* of which Buytaert prints the shorter) PL 178.1040, 1065, 1059–63.

[9] *Theol. Christ.* 5.3–4, pp. 347–48.

[10] See Aquinas, *Summa Theologiae* 1.39.7: 'Possunt autem manifestari personae divinae per essentialia attributa dupliciter. Uno modo per viam similitudinis, sicut ea quae pertinent ad intellectum appropriantur Filio, qui procedit per modum intellectus ut Verbum. Alio modo per modum dissimilitudinis, sicut potentia appropriatur Patri, ut Augustinus dicit, quia apud nos patres solent esse propter senectutem infirmi, ne tale aliquid suspicemur in Deo.

'Ad primum ergo dicendum quod essentialia attributa non sic appropriantur personis ut eis esse propria asserantur, sed ad manifestandum personas per viam similitudinis vel dissimilitudinis, ut dictum est.'

[11] *Theol. Christ.* 4.82–115, 116–53, pp. 303–22, 323–42.

[12] Louis Réau, *Iconographie de l'art chrétien* II (Paris 1956) 25.

[13] *Theol. Christ.* 4.114, pp. 321–22; also 1.32–34, pp. 85–86, and *Theol. schol.* 47, 50, 71–74, pp. 419, 420, 429–31.

works of creation and grace.[14] *Benignitas* can be said to be the effect of God's love in time, its manifestations among God's creatures.[15] God's affective love *is*; his effective *Benignitas* acts. It bestows grace and gifts, like the Holy Spirit in Passus 19 of *Piers Plowman*; it regenerates and restores. It is God's action in the world; and, to use Abelard's appropriated names, it proceeds *ab utroque*, from the conjoint action of *Potentia* and *Sapientia*, Power and Wisdom, Father and Son.

Abelard's insistence on similitude in our language about God bears fruit in several striking similes and analogies for the processions of the Trinity. One of them, the *Deus artifex*, is drawn directly from Plato's *Timaeus*. God is like an artisan who has, first, the power to make and create, like God the Father. He secondly conceives a plan beforehand, a Divine Idea, by which the work is to be providentially guided, and this idea is like the Son, who is the thought and wisdom of God. And third, the work is put into effect. The work itself is *ab utroque*, the product of the creative power and the manifestation in time of the plan, as the Spirit and its *effecta* proceed from the *Potentia* and *Sapientia* of the Father and the Son.[16]

Another simile for these processions is a seal made of bronze. When wax is sealed with this bronze seal, there are three things of one substance: the bronze, the bronze seal, and the image sealed in the wax. The metal seal in a sense proceeds from the bronze as the Son from the Father, though they are of one substance. And the image in the wax proceeds *ab utroque*, from the bronze and the seal both.[17]

The simile which can take us back to *Piers Plowman*, however, is that of the lute-player. When an artist plays a lute, says Abelard, three things come to-

---

[14] *Theol. Christ.* 4.145–51, pp. 337–41; 4.117–19, pp. 323–25; *Intro. ad theol.* PL 178.1073; Heinrich Ostendler, ed., *Theologia summi boni*, Beiträge zur Geschichte der Philosophie und Theologie des Mittelalters 35.2–3 (Münster 1939) 3.3.102–3, 3.4.105–7. See also related passages in *Theol. Christ.* 1.32, p. 85; 4.138–39, pp. 335–36; *Theol. schol.* 71–74, pp. 429–31; *Intro. ad theol.* PL 178.990–91, 1072.

[15] *Theol. Christ.* 4.148–51 (esp. 150–1), pp. 338–41; *Theol. summi boni* 3.3.104, 4.105–7. '. . . videbit Spiritum Sanctum ex Filio quoque siue per Filium recte procedere, cum ex ratione sapientiae uniuersa Dei opera administrentur et ita quodammodo conceptus diuinae mentis in effectum per operationem prodeat. Effectus autem ad Spiritum pertinent, qui ex bonitate conditoris eueniunt, quia Spiritus ipse bonitas est.

'Dicamus itaque Spiritum ex Filio quoque procedere, cum ratio diuinae prouidentiae ad effectum benignitatis perducitur, et quod ab aeterno faciendum prouiderit, temporaliter quando uult facit' (*Theol. Christ.* 4.138–39, pp. 335–36).

[16] *Theol. Christ.* 4.138–42, pp. 335–36; *Theol. summi boni* 3.3–4, pp. 104–5; *Intro. ad theol.* PL 178.1080.

[17] *Intro. ad theol.* PL 178.1068–75; *Epitome theologiae Christianae*, PL 178.1715, 1720. This image ('horrenda similitudo de sigillo aereo') was made notorious by the *Capitula haeresum* against Abelard, printed in Buytaert, ed., *Opera theologica* II 473. For the recurrence of the image after Abelard, see Luscombe 148, 160, 249, 254, 255, 286.

gether as one to make music: art, hand, and strings. Art, the power of playing,
corresponds to the Father's *Potentia*; the hand, the instrumental agent which
puts art into action, corresponds to the Son's *Sapientia*, the Word which gives
expression to God's thought; and the sounding strings, which produce the
musical effects of art and hands working together, correspond to the *effecta*
of the Spirit, the manifestation of God's love through his works.[18]

These Trinitarian similitudes are not those of *Piers Plowman*, but they provide
a paradigm of the relationships Langland was trying to express in the two
problematic passages we have been examining. In Passus 16, the lord who
claims lordship is introduced as a metaphor for the Trinity, which has just been
described in Abelard's vocabulary of appropriations:

> The firste haþ myȝt and maiestee, makere of alle þynges;
> *Pater* is his propre name, a persone by hymselue.
> The secounde of þat sire is Sothfastnesse *filius*,
> Wardeyn of þat wit haþ; was euere wiþouten gynnyng.
> The þridde highte þe holi goost, a persone by hymselue,
> The light of al þat lif haþ a londe and a watre,
> Confortour of creatures; of hym comeþ alle blisse.   (16.184–90)

This outline of the *Potentia, Sapientia,* and *Benignitas secundum effecta* in
the Trinity is followed immediately by the metaphor of the lord:

> So þre bilongeþ for a lord þat lordshipe cleymeþ:
> Might and a mene his owene myȝte to knowe,
> Of hymself and of his seruaunt, and what suffreþ hem boþe.
>   (16.191–93)

The 'might' (192) of the lord who claims lordship is surely identical with the
'myȝt' (184) of the Father, Abelard's *Potencia dei patris*. What we are to
identify with the Son and the Holy Spirit in the lordship metaphor is a little
more difficult to see. Following the syntactical sequence, most commentators
take the three things that 'bilongeþ' to a lord to be might, a means to know it,
and 'what suffreþ hem boþe.' Since this trio is clearly intended as a metaphor
for the Trinity, most commentators identify them with the Father, Son, and
Holy Spirit respectively. But there are obvious difficulties with such a reading
that its proponents acknowledge.[19] How is the Son 'a mene his owene myȝte to

---

[18] *Theol. Christ.* 4.82, p. 303. This image was also taken up by several of Abelard's followers, including Robert of Melun and Roland Bandinelli (Luscombe 249, 285).

[19] See, for example, Derek Pearsall, ed., *Piers Plowman* (Berkeley 1979), Passus 18.202–3n,
commenting on the corresponding passage in the C text: ' "Power, and a mediator to recognize
[read *shewe* for *se* ? B has *knowe*] his own power in operation [i.e. an executive instrument of his
power], as it has to do with himself and his servant, and (thirdly) what allows mutual existence
to them both [viz. Love]". This reading treats the lines as a threefold analogy to the activity
of the Trinity (as is more explicitly stated in B), though it is clearly meaningful in neither
original nor transferred sense.'

knowe'? To what does 'of hymself and of his seruaunt' refer? How is the Spirit 'what suffreþ hem boþe'?

These difficulties seem to be capable of resolution if one recognizes the Abelardian concept of the Trinity introduced just before the lordship metaphor. The verb 'knowen' has a well-attested sense, 'to make known, to show, to manifest.' Therefore, when Langland says a lord who claims lordship requires 'a mene his owene myȝte to knowe,' a likely reading is that God requires a 'means to make his own might known.'[20] So construed, the phrase describes with some precision Abelard's conception of the Holy Spirit as the effects of God's power (*Benignitas secundum effecta*), the 'means' by which God makes known his power and wisdom and love in the world. God's 'means,' says Langland, springs 'of hymself and of his seruaunt, and what suffreþ hem boþe.' Only two lines later, God's servant is specifically identified as Christ: 'So God . . . sente forþ his sone as for seruaunt' (193–95). Therefore the 'means' that makes known God's might and that comes 'of hymself and of his seruaunt, and what suffreþ hem boþe' is Abelard's Holy Spirit, sprung *ab utroque*, from the Father and the Son both, and from what they both 'suffre.'[21] Suffering, with its multiplicity of senses, has been an important concept throughout the poem, embodied on the human level by Patience and on the divine by Christ, the *seruaunt* of God, whose Passion is the supreme example of 'suffraunce' or 'patientia.' 'Suffraunce is a souerayn vertue,' says Reson: 'Who suffreþ moore þan god?' (11.379–80). God's 'suffraunce,' his patience and his Passion for mankind, is his love, and it is from that love that the Spirit springs. The three things that belong to the lord who claims lordship, then, are — contrary to the syntactical order — might (associated with the Father), a 'seruaunt' (the Son), and a means to make known that might (the Spirit *secundum effecta*), sprung from them both and from their love. The pattern resembles that in Abelard's metaphor of the lute-player. The lute-player's art, hand, and the musical effect of both working together are here paralleled by the lord's power, his servant, and the manifestation of his power through himself and his servant. Such a reading of the lordship metaphor, with its em-

---

[20] See *Middle English Dictionary*, ed. Hans Kurath (Ann Arbor 1956 —) s.v. 'knouen' 7 (a): 'to make (sth.) known, tell or say (sth.); teach (sb.; sth.); reveal (oneself), show (sth.).' *Piers Plowman* A.8.91, 'I wol construe vch a clause and knowen [vrr. kenne, teche, telle] hit in English.' A. V. C. Schmidt ed. 263*n*193 suggests this meaning for 'knowe,' though otherwise he construes lines 193–94 differently from what is offered here.

[21] 'What suffreþ hem boþe' is the reading of MSS R and F (Kane–Donaldson ed.), called the α sub-archetype by Schmidt, and is confirmed by the best MSS of the C text; see Derek Pearsall's edition, C.18.201–3. But as Schmidt points out, 'No impersonal use of *suffre* is recorded and *hem boþe* may be no more than a version of *þei boþe*' (*Piers Plowman* 16.193, textual *n*, p. 293). 'Þei suffre' is found in 11 MSS of the B text (Schmidt's β sub-archetype), including Kane–Donaldson's base MS, Trinity College, Cambridge, B.15.17.

phasis on the Spirit *ab utroque*, seems reinforced by the analogy for the Trinity
which follows it a few lines later:

> Adam [was] oure aller fader. Eue was of hymselue,
> And þe issue þat þei hadde it was of hem boþe,
> And eiþer is oþeres ioye in þre sondry persones,
> And in heuene and here oon singuler name.   (16.205–8)

Adam sprang from no one. Eve sprang 'of hymselue,' that is, from Adam
alone. Their children, however, sprang 'of hem boþe.' The wording seems
intentionally to echo the lordship metaphor, and hence to reinforce the description of the Spirit as 'of hymself and of his seruaunt . . . boþe' (193), *ab utroque*.

The Abelardian explanation of the lord who claims lordship helps in turn
with the lord who makes letters in Passus 9. He too is introduced as a metaphor for God, in a context that is also Trinitarian, though less explicitly so:

> For he was synguler hymself and seide *faciamus*
> As who seiþ, 'moore moot herto þan my word oone;
> My myȝt moot helpe forþ wiþ my speche.'
> Right as a lord sholde make lettres; if hym lakked parchemyn,
> Thouȝ he wiste to write neuer so wel, and he hadde a penne,
> The lettre, for al þe lordshipe, I leue, were neuere ymaked.
>   (9.36–41)

Faciamus is from Genesis 1.26 where, on the sixth day of creation, God says:
'Faciamus hominem ad imaginem et similitudinem nostram.' Medieval commentators frequently take the plural verb to indicate the involvement of the
entire Trinity in the creation of man and to reveal that man, the *imago Dei*, is
created in the image of the Trinity.[22] If so, Langland's lord who makes letters
is surely a metaphor for the Trinity in creation, and related particularly to
Abelard's metaphors of the *Deus artifex* and the lute-player.[23] The power of

---

[22] See Abelard, PL 178.760, 990; Remigius of Auxerre, PL 167.247; Bede, PL 91.28–29;
De spiritu et anima, PL 40.805–6, 809; *Meditationes piissimae*, PL 184.487; Peter Comestor,
PL 198.1063; Rupert of Deutz, PL 167.247–50; Bruno of Asti, PL 164.157; Hugh of St.
Victor, PL 175.37; *Biblia Sacra cum Glossa ordinaria* (Douai 1617) I 30–2 (Gen. 1.26); Diony-
sius the Carthusian, *Opera omnia* (Montreuil-sur-Mer 1896–1935) I 51–52; Hugh of St. Cher,
Opera omnia in universum Vetus et Novum Testamentum (Lyons 1645) on Gen. 1.26.

[23] A. V. C. Schmidt (*Piers Plowman* 327–28n35) argues correctly that there is an emphasis
here on the contrast between creation by action (*faciamus*) and by command (*dixit et facta
sunt*). The contrast is a common one in patristic tradition after Gregory the Great, whose
formulation is widely quoted by later writers: 'non per jussionis vocem, sed per dignitatem
operationis existeret, qui ad conditoris imaginem fiebat' (PL 75.900). On the other hand,
the contrast between *faciamus* and *dixit et facta sunt* does not contradict, as Schmidt suggests,
a Trinitarian theme as well. Gregory in the same passage emphasizes that *faciamus* means
that man was created by 'counsel.' Bede quotes Gregory's distinction between creation by
command and by work, and immediately introduces the Trinity: 'non per jussionem vocis,
sed per dignitatem operationis existeret, quia ad Conditoris imaginem fiebat. Cum autem

writing ('he wiste to write neuer so wel') corresponds to the art of the musician and hence to the creative power of the *Deus artifex*, both of which Abelard says pertain to the Father. The pen, the agency which can put the art of writing into action, corresponds to the hand of the lute-player and to the plan of the *artifex*, which in Abelard pertain to the *Sapientia* of the Son. The parchment with letters on it, that is, the effect of the combined action of the pen and the power of writing, corresponds to the sounding strings, to the works of the *Deus artifex*, and so to the *Benignitas secundum effecta* of the Spirit, which proceeds from the Father and the Son, *ab utroque*.[24] Consequently the three things necessary to the letter-making lord closely resemble the three that pertain to the lord who claims lordship in Passus 16: the power of writing for the former parallels the *myȝt* of the latter; the pen parallels the *seruaunt*, the agency that can put power into action; and the parchment with letters parallels what Passus 16 calls the Spirit, a means to make known the power of God and his servant, Christ, a means sprung from the lord and his servant *ab utroque*.

It is worth noting briefly that like the two Trinitarian metaphors discussed here, all of the lengthy discussions of the Trinity in the B text do not appear in the A text.[25] Langland seems to have launched a concerted effort to give the Trinity a larger role in B. Furthermore, all the new Trinitarian passages in the B text are related to the tradition of Abelard, particularly in the appropriations of *Potentia, Sapientia,* and *Benignitas,* in the doctrine of the Spirit's procession *ab utroque*, and in the use of similitudes as a path to understanding the divine mysteries. How Langland came across these Abelardian ideas in the interval between the A and B versions we of course do not know. We do know that Abelard was read in England; one of the four surviving twelfth-century manuscripts of the *Theologia Christiana* has been in the Library of Durham Cathedral since it was written.[26] The *Theologia scholarium*, also important for Abelard's

---

dicitur, *faciamus hominem ad imaginem et similitudinem nostram*, unitas sanctae Trinitatis aperte commendatur. . . . *Faciamus*, una ostenditur trium personarum operatio' (PL 91.28–29). See also Rhabanus Maurus, PL 107.459.

[24] See Abelard on the procession of 'bonus effectus faciendi aliquid' from power and knowledge: 'Ex Patre autem et Filio procedere Spiritus habet, quia bonus ipse affectus siue effectus faciendi aliquid ex potentia ipsius et sapientia prouenit, cum ideo uelit Deus et faciat, quia et potest illud adimplere et sollerter efficere. Nisi enim posset aliquid, frustra illud uellet quia efficacia carceret, et nisi sollerter sciret illud efficere, non haberet egregium effectum. Constat etiam nihil eum posse uelle nisi optimum, nec rationabiliter aliquid uelit facere et optime, oportet eum et hoc posse et ante cognoscere quae faciat et scire optime facere' (*Theol. Christ.* 4.119, p. 325).

[25] 10.240–52, 16.23–63, 16.181–224, 17.140–288.

[26] MS A.IV.15. This MS contains only the first book of the *Theologia Christiana*, but it also has a 'capitula librorum' of all the five books. For comments on this and the other three MSS see the edition of Buytaert 7–23.

Trinitarian doctrine, exists in two manuscripts (saec. xiii–xiv) of English provenance.[27] And some of the works of Abelard's followers who helped to disseminate his ideas about the Trinity can also be found in English manuscripts, as D. E. Luscombe has shown in his *The School of Peter Abelard*. The *Ysagoge in theologiam*, for example, is found (whether in whole or in part) in manuscripts associated with Cerne Abbey in Dorset, Buildwas Abbey near Shrewsbury, and Rochester Priory.[28] It seems therefore that further study of Abelardian writers, like those discussed by Luscombe, might well be profitable for *Piers Plowman*. An assessment of Abelard's full significance for the poem would have to await such study, but since Langland's emphasis on the divine Trinity in the B text is clearly related to the newly expanded moral trinity of Dowel, Dobet, and Dobest, it seems not unreasonable to hope that more extensive exploration of Abelard and his school may yet unlock other trinities in *Piers Plowman*.

Georgetown University

---

[27] BL MS Royal 8.A.I, fols. 3ʳ–69ʳ; Balliol College, Oxford, MS 296.

[28] Trinity College, Cambridge, MS B.14.33; BL MS Harley 3038, fols. 3ʳ–7ᵛ; BL MS Royal 10.A.XII, fols. 117ᵛ–123ʳ. On these and other English manuscripts, see Luscombe, *School of Peter Abelard* 90–93.

THE MIDDLE ENGLISH 'ABSOLUTE INFINITIVE' AND 'THE SPEECH OF BOOK'

By JOSEPH S. WITTIG

In 1959 R. E. Kaske proposed an interpretation of 'the Speech of Book' in Passus 18 of *Piers Plowman*.[1] His interpretation gave rise to a debate about the grammar and translation of a crucial part of that speech (lines 255–60),[2] and the ultimate object of this essay is to address the meaning of those lines. Before such a discussion can proceed, however, a preliminary topic must be confronted, and in some detail. For it has been asserted that attempts to deal with the difficulties of Book's speech have erred largely because they failed to recognize in it the relatively unusual 'absolute infinitive' construction.[3] In order to evaluate such an assertion, one must understand the 'absolute infinitive'—a construction which has not been defined and described in such a way as to make understanding easy. The term 'absolute' has been variously used, definitions have been at odds, and the rationale of the construction, especially its syntax, has not been very well served. Part I of this essay will therefore endeavor to come to terms with the construction itself, so that we may then reasonably gauge its relevance to a particular line of text; Part II will return to Book's speech and the problems which its reading presents.

I

We might best begin with an overview of the variety of constructions which have been called 'independent' or 'absolute' infinitives. F. Th. Visser's *Historical Syntax of the English Language* lists, under that heading, the following types:[4]

---

[1] R. E. Kaske, 'The Speech of "Book" in *Piers Plowman*,' *Anglia* 77 (1959) 117–44.

[2] All references (hereafter *PP*) are to *Piers Plowman: The B Version*, edd. George Kane and E. Talbot Donaldson (London 1975). Earlier discussions of this passage refer to it by Skeat's line numbers, viz. 252–57.

[3] E. Talbot Donaldson, 'The Grammar of Book's Speech in "Piers Plowman,"' *Studies in Language and Literature in Honor of Margaret Schlauch*, edd. Mieczyław Brahmer, Stanisław Helsztynski, and Julian Krzyzanowski (Warsaw 1966) 103–9.

[4] *An Historical Syntax of the English Language.* Part Two: *Syntactical Units with One Verb*, II (Leiden 1966) 1045–61. The examples are listed with Visser's paragraph numbers and semantic sub-classifications. Types for which he gives no ME citation have been omitted.

Visser

§ 983	Interrogative	'For al my wille, my lust holly Ys turned; but yet, *what to doone*?'[5]
§ 984	Exclamatory	'Allas! *to bidde* a woman goon by nyghte . . .' (Chaucer *LGW* 838)
§ 985	as above, but with subject expressed	'A kynges *sone*, and ek a knyght,' quod she, / '*To ben* my servaunt . . .!' (Chaucer *LGW* 2080–81)
§§ 987–90	Parenthetical[6]	And *shortly to concluden*, swich a place Was noon in erthe . . . (Chaucer *CT* A1895–96)
§§ 992–93	Wills, ordinances, etc.	Y will þat John Edmund [have] þe kechyn þat stont in forneys, he *to paie* þerfor as it is worthy.[7]
§ 995	as above, but subject not expressed	Heere i. ȝelde me to þi as þi boonde-man and þi prisoner, and þi perpetuel seruant, and . . . neuer *to departe* from þi seruyce.[8]
§ 996	as above, but introduced by *that*	[Kynde] is þe pies patron and putteþ it in hir ere / *That* þere þe þorn is þikkest *to buylden and brede*. (*PP* 12.227–28)
§ 997	Imperative	Nowe chiritree *to graffe*, and peches wilde And plumtree eree in gumme it goo with childe.[9]
§ 998	Historical[10]	. . . ek men ben so untrewe, That, right anon as cessed is hire lest, So ceeseth love, and forth *to love* a newe. (Chaucer *T&C* 2.786–88)
§ 999	as above, but with subject expressed	'By God,' quod he, 'I hoppe alwey by-hynde!' / And *she to laughe* . . . (Chaucer *T&C* 2.1107–8)

---

[5] Chaucer, *BD* 688–89. All quotations are from the 2nd ed. of *The Works* by F. N. Robinson (Boston 1957).

[6] The example given illustrates §987. The other types are the same infinitive preceded by *for to*, 'shortly for to seyn' (§988); preceded by *as (for) to*, 'as (for) to speken in comune' (§989); and the bare infinitive without introductory *and* or any adjunct, 'to wisse' (§990).

[7] Thus in Visser. Although the grammar remains unaffected, John's bequest is rather more modest: 'Also y will þat John Edmund [have] al þe led þat light in þe stuys, & þe sesterne þat longeþ to the stuys, and þe bordes & þe gaudron in the kechyn þat stont in forneys, he to paie . . . ' *A Book of London English, 1384–1425* (hereafter *BLE*), edd. R. W. Chambers and Marjorie Daunt (Oxford 1931) 210.28–31. Visser §993 is the same construction preceded by *and*; sometimes *for to* rather than *to* marks the infinitive.

[8] 'A ful good meditacion for oon to seie by him-self al-oone,' *Yorkshire Writers*, ed. C. Horstmann (London 1896) II 443.

[9] *Palladius on husbondrie* 2.398–99, ed. Barton Lodge, EETS es 52 (London 1873). Visser cites the passage from M. Liddel's ed. (Berlin 1896).

[10] Visser applies the term 'historical infinitive' only to §999, but says it is 'the same idiom as that dealt with' in §998.

A much more restricted meaning is given to 'absolute infinitive' in the standard handbook, Tauno F. Mustanoja's *A Middle English Syntax*, which identifies just two types. The first is the parenthetical (Visser §§ 987–90). The second is 'a construction with a nominative subject, occasionally used to express futurity, expectation, purpose, even command.'[11] Mustanoja gives the following examples:

1. He het men to ȝyue hem mede
   If þei coude hit riȝtly rede
   And *þei to ȝyue* þe same aȝeyn . . .[12]
2. Glotonye he gyueþ hem ek . . .
   And al day to drynken . . .
   'And *þei to haue and to holde* . . .' (*PP* 2.93–94, 102)
3. . . . that I frely may
   . . . do yow laughe or smerte,
   And nevere *ye to grucche* it, nyght ne day . . . (Chaucer *CT* E352–54)
4. I dar the bettre aske of yow a space
   Of audience, to shewen oure requeste,
   And *ye*, my lord, *to doon* right as yow leste. (Chaucer *CT* E103–5)
5. Oure lord wolde for resoun þilke
   Be fed of a maydenes mylke
   So hir *maydenhede to be* hid . . . (*CM* 10795–98)[13]
6. and heere auȝten proude men of this world, but principalli prelates and prestis, be sore ashamed to see her lord and maister, whom they schulde principalli suen, ride in thus pore aray, as I saide bifore, and *they to ride* so proudeli in gai gult sadeles with gingelinge brideles . . . (BL Add. MS 41321 fol. 1, cited from Owst).

The treatments of Visser and Mustanoja show how widely the use of the term 'absolute infinitive' varies. Yet all the types of Visser, along with the examples just cited from Mustanoja, share certain characteristics. Formally, the infinitives are most often marked by *to*;[14] if they appear with expressed subject pronouns, these are in the nominative case. Syntactically, though they are non-finite forms, these infinitives usually seem to have no clear function *within* a clause: they are not recognized as its subject, object, or verb complement; nor are they consistently recognized as modifiers of the clause's elements.

---

[11] *A Middle English Syntax*. Part I: *Parts of Speech* (Helsinki 1960) 542. Mustanoja is not enthusiastic about the designation, saying that it applies 'more or less appropriately.' He considers the exclamatory and historical infinitives under 'infinitive for finite verb' (538–39).

[12] *Cursor Mundi* (hereafter *CM*), ed. Richard Morris, EETS 57, 59, 62, 66, 68 (London 1874–86) 1721–23. All citations are from the Trinity MS in this ed.

[13] In this example the case is not marked, and it might be better to describe it as Subject + *to* + Inf. This matter will be discussed below.

[14] In Visser's types, *to* can be absent in the interrogative, the exclamatory, and the historical infinitives, the infinitive then being marked by the suffix *-en*.

Having observed that all these constructions have common features, this discussion will now reduce its scope sharply, limiting itself to just a few of the 'absolute' infinitives Visser lists. The interrogative, exclamatory, parenthetical, imperative, and historical infinitive can (for obvious reasons of context) have no bearing on the lines of *Piers Plowman* ultimately in question, and they will be discussed only to the extent required by that main concern.

What follows will focus on those constructions included in Visser §§ 992–96 (wills, ordinances, etc.) and in Mustanoja's second type of 'absolute infinitive.' As one looks to grammarians for an elucidation of those constructions, one discovers that extending the terms 'absolute' or 'independent' to them, though it has a long tradition, nevertheless obscures as much as it illuminates.[15]

Writing in 1885, Eduard Mätzner uses the designation 'unabhängig' to describe an infinitive 'wenn er sich an kein Satzglied oder an keinen Satz anschliesst.' He then treats, as 'unabhängig,' the exclamatory (Visser § 985) and parenthetical (Visser §§ 987–90) infinitives. Most grammarians follow him in classifying these two as 'absolute.'[16] Toward the end of his discussion he adds a few examples of the historical infinitive (Visser § 999), and, finally, a few instances of infinitives which, he rightly says, function as 'Verkürzungen von Nebensätzen' (54). But to call even a reduced subordinate clause 'independent' of a main clause seems to describe it in terms both partial and confusing.[17] Baldwin uses the term 'absolute' for an infinitive 'disconnected

---

[15] For the following discussion, I have taken into consideration all examples cited by Visser §§992–93 and 995–96 (citations up to 1500); Eugen Einenkel, *Streifzüge durch die mittelenglische Syntax* (Münster 1885) 80–82; *idem, Geschichte der englischen Sprache.* II: *Historische Syntax*, 3rd ed. (Strasburg 1916) 18–22; J. S. Kenyon, *The Syntax of the Infinitive in Chaucer* (London 1909) 137–40; Mustanoja 542; *Caxton's* BLANCHARDYN AND EGLANTINE, ed. Leon Kellner, EETS ES 58 (London 1890) lxv–lxx; C. S. Baldwin, *The Inflexions and Syntax of the* MORTE D'ARTHUR (Boston 1894) 77–79; J. Zeitlin, *The Accusative with Infinitive and Some Kindred Constructions in English* (New York 1908) 141–66; B. Trnka, *On the Syntax of the English Verb from Caxton to Dryden* (Prague 1930) 82–84; A. Dekker, *Some Facts Concerning the Syntax of Malory's* MORTE DARTHUR (Amsterdam 1932) 35, 142–46; U. Ohlander, *Studies in Coordinate Expressions in Middle English* (Lund 1936) 121–38; Broder Carstensen, 'Die Testationsformel,' *Anglia* 80 (1962) 63–88. I have also examined E. Scholz, *Der absolute Infinitiv bei Shakespeare* (Berlin 1908); Herman Druve, *Der absolute Infinitiv in den Dramen der Vorgänger Shakespeares* (Kiel 1910); and George O. Curme, *A Grammar of the English Language.* III: *Syntax* (Boston 1931) 158, 191–93, 457. These works give a *corpusculum* of more than two hundred pre-1500 citations, whose contexts have also been examined.

[16] *Englische Grammatik* (Berlin 1885) III 52–53. Carstensen (75) urges that 'absolute' be restricted to these two uses, citing — somewhat longingly — a linguistic dictionary. One wonders if the term is necessary at all, since the more specific 'parenthetical' and 'exclamatory' are widely current.

[17] Two decades later Scholz adopts Mätzner's definition and extends it to a wide array of subordinate clauses: see his types II–VII. Druve adopts Scholz's types in turn. Cf. Kellner, who suggests that 'absolute' infinitive constructions were 'more or less governed by, or at

from the construction of the rest of the sentence' (78n); as 'absolute' he considers the exclamatory infinitive and 'the absolute infinitive of condition,'
of which his first example is: 'for hym thought no worship to have a knyght
at such an avayle, *he to be* on horsebacke and hys adversary on foote.'[18] Zeitlin
(163–66) defines the construction as 'the use of a nominative and infinitive in
place of a clause, to express an idea parenthetically or loosely joined to the
principal idea of a sentence.' His first example is: 'And all the remenauntys
of my godys, y wyll they be preysyd & partyd in thre: *on part for to be don*
for my soule, & that other part to my wyfe.'[19] Both Baldwin and Zeitlin are
responding to a fact of syntax: these infinitives function as if they were finite
verbs; but calling them 'absolute' encourages further loose, semantic classification. 'Condition' seems almost whimsical when applied to Baldwin's example; and one wonders if Zeitlin meant to imply that there is something
'parenthetical' about the *idea* that part of the testee's goods is to go for the
repose of his soul.[20]

Other grammarians minimize or altogether avoid the term 'absolute' when
designating some of these constructions (Visser §§ 985, 992–93, 996, 999);
instead they concentrate on their form, characterizing them as 'Nom. + Inf.'
Thus Einenkel writes: 'Wie der einfache Infinitiv, so löst sich auch dieser
Nominativus cum Infinitivo leicht aus seiner Umgebung los und wird daher
oft absolut gebraucht.'[21] In his later *Geschichte*, Einenkel discusses various
notional uses to which the Nom. + Inf. is put, noting particularly purpose
clauses, wills and ordinances, and the historical infinitive.[22] But while the
designation 'Nom. + Inf.' is more concrete than 'absolute infinitive,' it does
not cover two cases which seem syntactically and semantically very similar:
that in which the subject of the infinitive, clear in the context, is unexpressed
(Visser § 995); and that in which a noun subject (as opposed to a pronoun)
is expressed but is unmarked as to case (see example 5 above, and the passage
just quoted from Zeitlin). Nor does Nom. + Inf. do much to describe the
construction's syntactic relationship to its context.

---

least in connection with, the finite verb of the main sentence' (lxix–lxx). The term seems at
odds with the facts observed.

[18] *The Works of Sir Thomas Malory*, ed. Eugène Vinaver, 2nd ed. (Oxford 1967) 50.19–21.
All citations of Malory are from this ed. by page and line.

[19] *The Fifty Earliest English Wills* (hereafter *EEW*), ed. F. J. Furnivall, EETS 78 (London
1882) 13.19–21.

[20] Similarly, Dekker 142–46 gives examples of parenthetical infinitives along with infinitives
used as 'adverbial clauses.'

[21] *Streifzüge* 81. Einenkel is speaking here of the usage of Chaucer and calls this the 'auf-
fälligste der make-shift-Constructionen' (82). Cf. Kenyon 137–40; Trnka 82; O. Jespersen,
A Modern English Grammar (Copenhagen 1909–49) V 306–7 and 321–22.

[22] *Geschichte* 19–20. Cf. Kenyon; Jespersen V 321–22; and E. Krusinga, *A Handbook of
Present-Day English* (Utrecht 1922) 207–8.

In a very full discussion of two of these infinitive structures (Visser §§ 992–93), Carstensen rejects both 'absolute' and 'Nom. + Inf.' in favor of the designation 'Testationsformel.' He acknowledges that these constructions are by no means confined to wills and ordinances, but employs the term because it reflects their chief semantic locus (68). He describes them as follows: a Nom. + *to* + Inf., where the infinitive is sometimes semantically modal, but more often future, the latter especially when the infinitive phrase is introduced by *then* or *else* (73). Useful as Carstensen's discussion is, it too raises a problem about how to deal with these constructions. Although his identification of the 'Testationsformel' proceeds according to clear criteria, the approach seems finally to obscure its fundamental relationships with similar constructions. Consider the following examples which Carstensen expressly excludes from the class he wishes to establish:[23]

> 7. ... all ages smack of this vice; and *he*
>   *To die* for 't! (Shakespeare *Measure for Measure* 2.2.5–6)
> 8. ... *thou to ly* by oure modir is to muche shame for us to suffir. (Malory 612.25–26)
> 9. A heavier task could not have been impos'd
>   Than *I to speak* my griefs unspeakable ... (Shakespeare *Comedy of Errors* 1.1.32–33)
> 10. For if a preest be foul, on whom we truste,
>   No wonder is a lewed *man to ruste* ... (Chaucer *CT* A501–2)
> 11. Til it dawed to day and *sunne to vp-rise*.[24]
> 12. Keep your word, Phebe, that you'll marry me,
>   Or else, refusing me, *to wed* this shepherd ... (Shakespeare *As You Like It* 5.4.22–23).

Of these examples, 7–9 show Nom. + *to* + Inf. All except 11 can easily be seen to imply some sort of modality/futurity.[25] And the fact that 7 implies exclamation, or that in 8 the Nom. + *to* + Inf. precedes the main verb, or that in 12 the subject is to be understood from the immediate context, does not seem to make these infinitives (with the exception of 11) fundamentally distinct from the 'Testationsformel.'

---

[23] Carstensen 67. The numbers at the left carry on from Mustanoja's examples and will be continued in sequence hereafter.

[24] *The Romance of William of Palerne*, ed. W. W. Skeat, EETS es 1 (London 1867) 1791.

[25] 7 futurity/obligation; 8 futurity/possibility; 9 futurity/obligation/possibility; 10 futurity/necessity/probability; 12 futurity. The problem of specifying the senses of English modal auxiliaries is a notorious one and not crucial here. Hereafter I will use the term 'modality' in the broad sense employed by modern grammarians, including that whole range of meanings beyond plain statement of fact embraced by the modern English 'modals': will/would, shall/should, may/might, can/could, must. See, for example, Randolf Quirk, Sidney Greenbaum, Geoffrey Leech, and Jan Svartvik, *A Grammar of Contemporary English* (New York 1972) III 28, 43–53.

In spite of differences in emphasis and terminology, however, the studies of the grammarians and the examples they cite lead to some clear conclusions. The infinitive under discussion (Visser §§ 992–96 and Mustanoja's second type) can be considered as one construction. Formally it is characterized by the marker *to* (sometimes *for to*) and, should the infinitive have an expressed pronoun subject, that pronoun is nominative. Semantically the infinitive has a modal sense. Syntactically, the name 'absolute' reflects the fact that the infinitive, though it is not a finite verb, functions not within the main clause but as the verb of a subordinate clause. An attempt to define the construction any more precisely — to say, for instance, in what form it must appear, how it can be used, or what it can 'mean' — leads to some further considerations.

There is, first, the matter of this infinitive's modality. Visser, Mustanoja, and Carstensen all justly acknowledge this characteristic, and it is manifest in the examples they and others cite. But attempting to define this construction by specifying what the modal sense of the infinitive must be, by saying that it must mean 'futurity' or 'obligation' or anything else, seems both unnecessary and impossible. For an 'infinitive' is non-finite, i.e., non-specified as regards mood (just as it is in tense, person, and number). Careful consideration of the examples will show how the modal sense of the infinitive arises, not from the infinitive clause itself, but from a modality of context: an infinitive's mood and tense are precisely contextual mood and tense. One could suggest that the historical infinitive differs from the construction here described not because it is an entirely different structure, but simply because, in the case of the historical infinitive, contextual 'past, indicative' dominates (so that if one were to supply an auxiliary for the infinitive it would be something like *gan*); in the latter case, on the other hand, some contextual modality (for instance exhortation or volition) dominates (so that one would supply something like *will/wolde* or *shall/sholde*).

In connection with contextual modality, the characteristic marker *to* merits consideration. Its appearance with infinitives is increasingly common in Middle English,[26] but it is worth noting that *to* is particularly characteristic of infinitives when they are separated from an auxiliary (including a modal). This could occur when an infinitive preceded the auxiliary:

13. *To deyen* in the peyne I *coulde* nought! (Chaucer *T&C* 3.1502)[27]

It could also occur when a phrase intervened between the auxiliary and the infinitive, especially if the infinitive was the second of two:

---

[26] Mustanoja 514.
[27] See Visser 3 §1728.

14. For euery cristene creature *sholde* be kynde til ooþer,
    And siþen heþen *to helpe* in hope of amendement. (*PP* 10.368–69)[28]

Such an occurrence of *to* might easily give rise to the structure S(ubject) + *to* + Inf. if the second of two infinitives, dependent upon a previously stated modal, is given a new subject:

15. Out of the erth herbys *shal* spryng
    Trees to florish and frute furth bryng.[29]

It is clear, then, that modality supplied from earlier context is not unique to the *to* + Inf. of 'absolute' constructions. That the occurrence of *to* + Inf. in cases where the infinitive was separated from an auxiliary might have contributed to the development of 'absolute' constructions is plausible, though it could not be claimed as a fact without more extensive data;[30] but certainly recognizing the similarity of the two cases helps better understand the 'absolute' infinitive.

Finally, it should be observed that contextual modality is not limited to statements which contain an explicitly modal auxiliary. Consider the following three examples:

16. All-so I *woll* that Iane Newmarch have CC mark in gold, And *I to bere* all Costes as for her bryngynge yn-to seynt Katrens . . . (*EEW* 118.14–16)

17.   . . . thy brother
    Ysworn ful depe, and ech of us til oother,
    That nevere, for to dyen in the peyne
    Til that the deeth departe shal us tweyne,
    Neither of us in love *to hyndre* oother . . . (Chaucer *CT* A1131–35)

18. But the custom was suche amonge them that none of the kyngys wolde helpe other, but *all the felyshyp* of every standard *to helpe* other as they myght. (Malory 734.25–27)

---

[28] See Visser 3 §§1729–34; cf. Mustanoja 522. Even these infinitives have occasionally been labeled 'absolute'; thus Kellner lxvii–lxix and Dekker, 'absolute infinitive without subject' 145–46.

[29] *The Towneley Plays*, ed. Alfred W. Pollard, EETS es 71 (London 1897) 2.43–44.

[30] The stages might be: separation of an infinitive from a modal; use of *to* to mark separated infinitive; occasional introduction of a new subject for that infinitive. Sometimes an infinitive can be very widely separated from a modal. Consider the following examples, in which a new subject is not introduced: 'Also hit is ordeyned that what man of the same Craft that cometh vnto the seide Cite . . . and he sette vp a shoppe . . . he *shall* make fyne or pay to the Maysters of the seide craft xx s, or elles withein the summe as the maysters & he may accorde; and yif they mow not acorde then *to be demed & demened* be the meire' (*The Coventry Leet Book*, ed. Mary Dormer Harris, EETS 134 [London 1907] 225); 'the persones so accused . . . *shalle* be called in the yeld halle of the seid cite to answere to the seid accusement; and yf h[e] appere not in propre persone, ne by attorney, at eny of the seid courts, then *to be disfraunchised*' ('Ordinances of Worcester,' *English Gilds*, ed. Toulmin Smith, EETS 40 [London 1870] 402–3).

In the first of these, 'I woll' establishes the mood. In the second it is established by the past participle 'ysworn,' with its consequences of futurity and obligation. In the last, one could argue whether it arises from the explicit 'wolde' (volition, perhaps shading into habitual futurity) or from the implications of 'custom' (obligation, propriety). The ability of the non-finite form to reflect whatever modality is appropriate to a context makes it an efficient and convenient verbal for a subordinate clause. It obviates the need to repeat an auxiliary if that is in any way awkward. It allows an apt modal sense to be understood when specification of *one* modal auxiliary might seem inadequate; either because a particular modal is becoming ambiguous (is *will* volitional or future?) or because more than one modal is pertinent (e.g., 'will and intend,' 'will and ought,' 'will and can'). Since the modality which gives this infinitive construction its special character is the modality of context,[31] the only way to specify the 'meaning' of the *construction* would be to list all the contexts in which the construction appears. Handbook definitions of that meaning, like the one offered by Mustanoja, can do no more than offer a limited description of *typical* meanings; it would not be legitimate to use such definitions of meaning, by themselves, either to identify an infinitive as belonging to the construction or to exclude it.

Consideration of the 'absolute' infinitive's subject might also help toward a clearer grasp of the construction. It has already been suggested that non-expression of a subject should not lead one to overlook essentially similar syntax. The 'deletion' of 'equivalent noun phrases' is modern terminology for what has always been recognized: the subject of an infinitive need not be expressed when it is clear in the context.[32] If a noun, instead of a pronoun, appears as the infinitive's subject, that is a result of meaning, context, and the grammar, not of this particular construction, but of the language in general. As for the nominative case shown by pronoun subjects in the construction, it might be useful to contrast this with what we see in the 'Acc. + Inf.':

19. Wher as I se my lady stonde. . . .[33]

In the example above, no one would deny that the object of 'se' is the 'sentence,' or what Jespersen calls the 'nexus,'[34] whose subject is 'lady' and whose verb is 'stonde.' It is also clear that, were the subject of the infinitive a

[31] For a discussion of examples where a modal main clause is merely implicit, see below, ex. 43–49.

[32] Einenkel, *Streifzüge,* has a brief but lucid discussion of the expression or non-expression of the subject of an infinitive (145); cf. Mustanoja 527–28. As examples of the 'absolute' construction without expressed subject, see examples 34, 36 below, and cf. n30.

[33] John Gower, *Confessio Amantis*, ed. G. C. Macaulay, EETS es 81 (London 1900) 1.563.

[34] *A Modern English Grammar* V 9ff.

pronoun instead of a noun, it would appear in the accusative case; it, as well as the whole 'sentence,' would be sensed as object of the verb 'se.' Consider another instance of the Acc. + Inf., this one in the form Acc. + *to* + Inf.:

> 20. And we haue founde *you* our trewe lieges and subgitz of good wille at all tymes, *to do* al thing þat might do vs worship and ese. . . . (*BLE* 73.6–7)[35]

One wonders how the language arrived at the nominative which distinguishes the 'absolute' construction from the above, and in what way that nominative should affect our understanding of the construction. One can easily find instances where, for a word both object of a main verb and subject of an infinitive, the accusative case is maintained despite syntactic complexity:

> 21. I have fownde myn Lord of Oxenforth singuler very good and kynde lord to myn lord and me, and stedefaste in hys promys, wher by he hath wonne myn lordys service as longe as he leevth, and *me* [i.e., he hath wonne me/I] *to be* his trewe beedwoman terme of myn lyve. . . .[36]

And in the following example, the subject of the infinitive — which is also in apposition with the indirect object of the main verb — appears in the object case:

> 22. The residue of all my singuler goodes, catallys, and juellys after my dettys payde, and my bequestes performyd and fulfulled, and burying done, I geue and fully bequeth to my sonnys, Ser Edward Ponyngis and Mathew Browne, and *theym* [i.e., bequeth (to) theym/they] *to dispose* and do theire fre will. . . . (*PnL* III 466)[37]

One can observe that, in the two examples just given, the infinitives have the modality characteristic of the 'absolute' construction, though they are not accompanied by nominative subjects. But several factors could have contributed to the use of the nominative case for the subject of an infinitive. One is simply the relative positions of main verb (plus any intervening objects) and that subject: coming before the main verb or following it at some distance, the infinitive's subject might easily be attracted to the nominative case even if it were also felt as object of the main verb. In discourse where this was typical (e.g., wills, with their long strings of clauses), the nominative could become part of a pattern capable of spreading to other instances where it was less widely separated from the main verb. Another factor is the variety of semantic relationships that can exist between a main verb and a sentence complement. With verbs of 'perception,' for instance, characteristically followed by the

---

[35] Mustanoja points out that 'the use of *to* may be due to the fact that the infinitive is separated from the finite verb by several words' (529).

[36] *The Paston Letters* (hereafter *PnL*), ed. James Gairdner (Westminster 1900–1) III 323.

[37] The last two examples are cited by Carstensen (83), who regards both pronouns as accusatives and as aberrations of the expected Nom. + *to* + Inf. of the 'Testationsformel.'

Acc. + Inf., it is obvious that the subject of the infinitive is strongly sensed as object of the main verb (cf. example 19). But with, for example, verbs of 'decreeing,' it seems more likely that an entire sentence could be sensed as complement (whether as object or as adverbial), and that the subject of the infinitive be marked as nominative.[38] In the following examples, attraction away from the main verb and to the infinitive might explain the nominative case:

23. Let hym fynde a sarasyn
    And *y to fynde* a knyght of myn [i.e., let me/y to fynde]
    The batell vpon them schall goo . . .[39]
24. And thenne hadde she me deuysed to be kyng in this land and soo to regne and *she to be* my quene . . . [i.e., she deuysed herself/she to be].[40]

And there remain those many instances in which one does not honestly know whether to analyse the subject of the infinitive as accusative or nominative:

25. Wȝi schope þou me to wroþer hele,
    To be þus togged and totorn,
    And *oþere to haven* al mi wele ?[41]

Such considerations of the case of an infinitive's subject provide a context in which to view the characteristic 'Nom.' of the absolute construction. Moreover, when one sees in 22 above 'theym to dispose' in a context ('I geue and

---

[38] Such verbs are typically followed by a *that* clause, but can be followed by a *that* clause plus a S + *to* + Inf., by *that* + S + *to* + Inf., or simply by the infinitive construction. Such verbs are more likely than those of 'perception' to act as intransitives followed by an adverbial clause of purpose or result: see esp. ex. 44 and n53 below.

[39] *The Romance of Guy of Warwick: The Second or Fifteenth-Century Version*, ed. Julius Zupitza, EETS 24 (London 1875) 3531–33. The verb 'let' is very susceptible to this in modern English; a speaker who would always say 'let me do it' can frequently be heard to say 'Let John and I do it.' The nominative in the latter is probably due to a number of causes, chief among them its being the second of two subjects (thus separated from object position).

[40] Zeitlin and Dekker cite this passage from *Le Morte Darthur*, ed. H. Oskar Sommer (London 1889) 133.7–8. Vinaver's text (146.2–3) reads: 'And than had she devysed to have me kynge in this londe and so to reigne.' It is possible to see in this construction the modality characteristic of the 'absolute' infinitive. But in other cases a nominative subject may be merely an accident of 'surface' form: cf. ex. 6, of which Mustanoja notes 'it is difficult to see any implication of purpose or even of futurity.' It might best be analyzed as Acc. + *to* + Inf. become Nom. + *to* + Inf. through separation from the verb. The sentence may be paraphrased: 'proud men ought . . . to be ashamed to see their lord . . . ride in this poor array . . . and [at the same time to see] they [themselves] to ride. . . .'

[41] 'The Debate of the Body and the Soul,' cited from O. F. Emerson, *A Middle English Reader* (London 1928) 62.30ff. Einenkel (*Streifzüge* 82 and *Geschichte* 20), Zeitlin (146), and Visser (§993) all call it Nom. + (absolute) Inf. Similarly ambiguous as to case, though they have the modality characteristic of this construction, are examples 5, 27, 29, 30, 32, 37, 39, 40, 42.

bequeth') where one is quite used to seeing 'they'; when one sees in 23 'let . . .
y' where one would more often see 'me'; when one thinks of all the situations
in which a noun subject is not marked for case; then the nominative of the
'absolute' construction begins to appear as a relatively superficial characteristic, one to be noted and acknowledged, but having limited effect on the construction's basic syntax and none on its characteristic modality.

In the light of the foregoing, the most useful and complete way to describe the
'absolute' infinitive under investigation here (Visser §§ 992–96, Mustanoja's
second type) seems to be as follows. It is a subspecies of the general infinitive
transformation whereby a sentence, or nexus, is made into a subordinate clause.
The construction's specific form is (S) + to + Inf. [+ Modal], with the further
specification that an expressed subject pronoun is typically nominative. The
most important characteristics of the construction are the to marker, which it
seems always to have;[42] and its modality, which derives from the modality of
the main clause. Its nominative pronoun is the result of the subject of the
subordinate clause being sensed more strongly as subject of that clause than as
object of the main verb. One can, if one chooses, distinguish it from other
infinitive constructions by means of any of these criteria: absence of to, accusative pronoun as subject of the infinitive, absence of modality.[43] But the
characteristics which seem most crucial to the construction here considered
are to + Inf. [+ Modal].

It remains to attempt some account of the construction's syntactic function.
We have seen that some grammarians note how the construction functions like
some clauses introduced by that.[44] It is, in fact, often coordinate with a that
clause:

---

[42] The only passage cited without to is pointed out by Kenyon (140): ' "Chese now," quod
she, "on of thise thynges tweye: / To han me foul and old til that I deye, / And be to you a
trewe, humble wyf, / And nevere you displese in all my lyf"' (Chaucer CT D1219–22). But
he adds that be and displese may better be regarded as complementary infinitives after chese,
second and third in a series begun by to han. In any event, to is expressed with the first
infinitive — which is doubly marked (to -n).

[43] By the absence of to, one could distinguish it from many complementary infinitives, most
Acc. + Inf., and some other 'absolute' infinitives (the interrogative, exclamatory, and historical infinitives sometimes occur without the to marker). One could distinguish it from
any infinitive construction with an expressed accusative subject, regardless of to or modality.
And on the basis of modality, one could distinguish it from the historical infinitive, from
most Acc. + Inf., and from many complementary infinitives. It can be further distinguished
from the exclamatory, interrogative, and imperative infinitives by means of the semantic
element those terms imply. On the basis of syntactic function it might be distinguished from
those 'absolute' constructions which share its other features: e.g., the parenthetical infinitive is typically a sentence adverb.

[44] See esp. Mätzner 54; Baldwin 74; Einenkel, Geschichte 18–20; Dekker 142–43; Mustanoja
542–43. Cf. Curme III 457.

26. N'yn him desir noon other fownes bredde,
But argumentes to this conclusioun,
That she of him wolde han compassioun,
And he to be hire man, while he may dure. (Chaucer *T&C* 1.465–69)
27. It was accordyd betwen the seyd William and Walter *that* thei schuld
stande and obeye to the ordinaunce . . . of all the seyd matiers of
tweyne of these iiij persones . . ., *and* elles the *decree and jugement* of
a nounpier *to be chosen* by the same arbitores. (*PnL* I 14)
28. ' I seye this, be ye redy with good herte
To al my lust, and *that* I frely may,
As me best thynketh, do you laughe or smerte,
And never *ye to grucche* it, nyght ne day?' (Chaucer *CT* E351–54)[45]

Related to the above are those blended, or contaminated, constructions in
which *that*, after an interruption, is followed by the infinitive construction:

29. And anone the kynge commaunded *that none* of them upon payne of
dethe *to myssaye* them ne doo them ony harme. (Malory 187.3–5)[46]

But the majority of 'absolute' infinitives under consideration here does not
occur coordinate to such a clause or in a *that* blend. Rather the construction is
used without any expressed conjunction or connective word — a characteristic
of infinitive constructions in general and a fact which, along with the non-finite
form, has led to the designation 'absolute.' One can suggest that the (S) +
to + Inf. [+ Modal] was used, in the examples just cited as well as in those to
follow, because it was easy and efficient to do so: the infinitive conveys the
appropriate modality, an awkward or inadequate auxiliary is unnecessary,
and no conjunction need be specified. Nevertheless, these examples can be
seen to perform functions typical of subordinate clauses, and these may be
considered in traditional categories: object clause; subject clause; noun modifier
(relative clause, noun complement); adverbial clause ('result' or 'purpose'
clause, adjective complement). These functions may be illustrated as follows.
(In the brief analysis after each quotation, the clause is referred to as *S*, and
[that], [so that] are used to suggest the function intended.)

The construction as object:
30. He desyryth my Lord Chaunccellor should wryte to hym speciallye yff
he most nedes com upp, and a *bille to be made* yn to Parlement for re-
cuvere of my Lord Bedford godes. (*PnL* I 374)[47]
(desyryth [that] *S*)

---

[45] This coordination is often found: cf. ex. 16, 18. Some other instances are: *T&C* 3.128–
36; Malory 13.6–9; *PnL* I 90.18 and II 197.9 up; *EEW* 88.32ff. and 129.12ff.; *Secreta secre-
torum*, ed. Robert Steele, EETS ES 74 (London 1898) 36.29–32; *Wills and Inventories from
the Registers of the Commissary of Bury St. Edmunds and the Archdeacon of Sudbury*, ed.
Samuel Tymms, Camden Society 49 (London 1850) 17.1–3 and 21.13–15.
[46] See also 17 above; further examples are cited by Visser §996 and by Mustanoja 542–43.
[47] For other examples see 1, 16, 29.

The construction as (extraposed) subject:
31. ... and thy fadir slew oure fadir, and *thou to ly* by oure modir is to
    muche shame for us to suffir. (Malory 612.24–26)
    ([that] *S* is to muche shame)
32. And this figure he added eek therto,
    That if gold ruste, what shal iren do ?
    For if a preest be foul, on whom we truste,
    No wonder is a lewed *man to rust* . . . (Chaucer *CT* A499–502)[48]
    ([that] *S* is no wonder)
The construction as relative clause:
33. ... and indewe withinne the seid mancion a collage of vij. religeous
    monkys or pristes, to preye for the soules above seyd in perpetuite,
    of whiche *one to be* cheif governour of hem, and *he to have* x li., . . .
    (*PnL* I 447)
    (There are two relative clauses: the first is introduced by 'of which'
    [monkys or pristes], the second modifies 'one/governour' [that] *S*.)
34. And thanne agreen that I may be *he*,
    Withouten braunche of vice on any wise,
    In trouthe alwey *to don* yow my service . . . (Chaucer *T&C* 3.131–33)[49]
    (he [that] *S*)
The construction as adverbial clause:
35. Some wyes he yaf wit with wordes to shewe,
    To wynne wiþ truþe þat þe world askeþ,
    As prechours and preestes and Prentices of lawe:
    They lelly *to lyue* by labour of tonge,
    And by wit *to wissen* oþere . . . (*PP* 19.229–33)
    (yaf [so that] *S*)
36. Heere i. ȝelde me to þi as þi boonde-man and þi prisoner, & þi perpetuel
    servaunt, and all the dayes of my lif never *to departe* fro þi servyce.[50]
    (ȝelde [so that] *S*)
The construction as adverbial, modifying adjective:
37. If ȝe hit do i ȝou teche
    Siker may ȝe be of wreche
    And ȝoure shame shal be couþ
    Alle *men to haue* ȝou in mouþ (*CM* 4133–36)[51]
    (couþ [so that] *S*)

What is noteworthy about the construction is that it often resists unambiguous categorization. A reader might question some of those just suggested

---

[48] These two passages were cited earlier as constructions Carstensen excludes from the
'Testationsformel' (8, 10 above). They are repeated here with slightly expanded context.
[49] Cf. 26, where the construction seems to function as a noun complement. One could
analyze 18 either as noun complement (custom [that] *S*) or as an infinitive with a new subject
resuming the auxiliary 'wolde' (cf. ex. 15).
[50] *Yorkshire Writers* II 443. This instance could be analyzed as Acc. + Inf., since the
subject of the infinitive is stated only in the accusative case. But it is equally reasonable to
take it here as *to* + Inf. with subject 'I' understood. For adverbial function, cf. ex. 5.
[51] The ex. is from the Trinity MS; other MSS read 'all men sal you haue in mouþ.' Cf. ex.
28 (redy [so that] *S*).

(e.g., are 35 and 36 object rather than result clauses?). Although its subordinate status *vis à vis* a main clause is clear, in the following instances the construction might be called either a relative or an adverbial clause:

38. And Grace gaf Piers of his goodnesse foure stottes,
    Al þat hise oxen eriede *þei to harewen* after. (*PP* 19.267–68)
    (stottes [that] *S*, or, gaf [so that] *S*)
39. The kyng and þe commune and kynde wit þe þridde
    Shopen lawe and leaute, ech *lif to knowe* his owene. (*PP* Prol. 121–22)
    (lawe and leaute [by that] *S*, or, shopen [so that] *S*)
40.   . . . þe chief halle
    That was maad for meles *men to eten* Inne, (*PP* 10.101–2)
    (halle [in that] *S*, or, maad [so that] *S*)

The following might be analyzed as noun complement or adverbial clause:

41. . . . for hym thought no worship to have a knyght at such an avayle,
    he to be on horsebacke and hys adversary on foote . . . (Malory 50.19–21)
    (avayle [that] *S*, or, have [so that] *S*)

As object or adverbial clause:

42. y will the best prest that may be founde, sey for me the saide trentall,
    with the hole diriges, and all the service thurgh-out the yere, and the
    prest to have x li. (*EEW* 88.10–13)
    (will [that] *S*, or, sey [so that] *S*)[52]

Despite hesitation about how specifically to categorize the construction's function in certain instances, however, its subordinate status is clear and the categories used above can serve to describe its behavior.

The (S) + *to* + Inf. [+ Modal] construction being discussed comes closest to meriting the adjective 'absolute' when it seems to function as an independent main clause. If syntactic units were always delimited by such conventions as capital letters and punctuation, then perhaps the following structures would indeed be independent. But if the context in which these clauses occur supplies their larger syntactic matrix, they should be viewed as subordinate clauses:

43. Item I woll Elysabeth Keston have iiij[xx] [80] mark paid to Norman
    Waschebourne for her mariage. And yef he gruche therwith, the *mater*

---

[52] Had 42 read 'and he to have' rather than 'and the prest to have,' the clause might more likely be adverbial, modifying 'sey.' As it stands it seems rather an object of 'y will' parallel with 'prest . . . sey.' Cf. 4, 17. Other examples seem to hover between object and result: cf. 2, 25. An example such as that quoted in *n*7, 'y will þat John . . . [have] al þe led . . . *he to paie*,' might be analyzed as an adverbial clause whose connection to 'y will' could be paraphrased 'with the understanding that, with the subsequent condition that'; but it is equally possible to regard the infinitive construction as an object clause. One reason for hesitating in cases like 2, 4, 25, 42 and the quotation of *n*7 is the fact that *and* can introduce a 'result' clause in ME: see *MED*, *and* 3 and 5, 6. (This sense of *and* must be borne in mind when evaluating the distinction between Visser §§992 and 993). Another reason for hesitation is discussed in the following *n*. As Acc. + *to* + Inf. [-Modal] where the function of the clause is similar, see 21.

so *to be laboryd and sewyd* that he be constrayned ther to do hit. (*EEW* 118.18–21)

(and yef he gruche [then I wol] *S*)

44. I have condescended the rather that my seide Lord of Norffolk shall be preferryd to the purchasse of the seyde maner of Castre . . .; and thys *covenantys to be engroced* upp wythynne shorth tyme . . . . (*PnL* II 323)

(I have condescended [that/so that] *S*)[53]

45. And if all thre sonnes die withoute heires of their bodies, theire moder than lyvyng, then *she for to haue* all the same maners . . . . (*EEW* 124.23–26)

([he will that] *S*)[54]

46. And [i.e., if] Maister Nevyle, the whych hath wedded my Lady Wullughbye, have power or interest to resseyve the Lord Wyllughby ys debts, then *he to be labured* untoo. (*PnL* I.376)

([I desire that] *S*)[55]

The explicit matrix supplied for the last citation is perhaps not compelling. But for the overwhelming majority of 'absolute' infinitives cited by grammarians, a matrix is explicitly present, although it may be necessary to go back a few sentences in order to see it. Moreover, this 'absolute' structure with a non-finite verb clearly originated, and was regularly employed, as a subordinating transformation. But there is nothing to prevent a clause which originated as a subordinate *S* from appearing without its matrix when the latter would convey no new or necessary information. This is a constant phenomenon with phrases and clauses in speech as well as in colloquial writing. And if a context makes it abundantly clear that, for example, 'he wills that . . .,' or 'the law says . . .,' or 'my legal acumen suggests . . .,' then the subordinated form might well appear without an explicit main clause:

47. Also I bequethe to my wyfe alle þe goddis þat be meuablis, and *sche to be* my prinsepall seccutur . . . (*EEW* 80.4–6)

---

[53] *MED*, *condescenden* 2: 'give one's consent . . . agree (to do something or that something be done)'; examples with *that* clauses, *ibid.*, 2b. This is a good example of a verb which can be transitive (followed by an object clause) or intransitive (followed by an adverbial clause). It is as much to this ambivalence of verbs as to the infinitive construction itself that one can trace the hesitation in assigning syntactic functions to such clauses.

[54] Einenkel (*Geschichte* 20) cites this passage without context. But the will reads: '[121] First, the saide [122] Rauf *will* and ordeyneth and prayeth all his ffeffees . . . to performe and fulfille his will yn the forme ensuyng. First, he *will* that Margaret . . . have . . . All-so he *will* that the saide Margarete have . . . And all-so he *will* that . . . Item he *will* that . . . [123] than he *will* that . . . Than he *will* that . . . Thanne he *will* that . . . All-so he *will* that . . . [124] than he *will* that. . . .' There are previous instances of the infinitive construction in the will: e.g., 123.35ff.; 124.3ff.

[55] Cited by Carstensen, without context (82). The passage is lines 22–25. Line 6: 'Item I *desyre* to know . . . [line 17] And therfor y *desyre* that the executors, and such as most have interest in the Lord Wyllughby goodes, may be comyned wyth; that they may [make] purseute for payment of the seyd iiij. m. marc, for hys part to be had, and y shall make for my part. And [i.e., if] Maister Nevyle . . .'

48. The mater is cler to my thynkyng. Titleshale that solde it to Sir J. Fastolf myght as wele a solde hym your lande or myn; and if the sale be lawfull, I shal leve my hands at the first as I said at London. The *distresse to be kept* for that, I wisse it nede not, and it was unlawfully taken. (*PnL* II 315)[56]

If the long-suffering reader can endure one last passage, then the following lines from *Piers Plowman* might be viewed in connection with the 'independent' use of (S) + *to* + Inf.:

49. Ac kynde loue shal come ȝit and Conscience togideres
And make of lawe a laborer; swich loue shal arise
. . . .
Alle þat beren baselard, brood swerd or launce,
Ax ouþer hachet or any wepene ellis,
Shal be demed to þe deeþ but if he do it smyþye
Into sikel or to siþe, to Shaar or to kultour:
　　Conflabunt gladios suos in vomeres, &c.
Ech man to pleye with a plow, Pykoise or spade,
Spynne, or *sprede* donge or *spille* hymself with sleuþe.
Preestes and persons wiþ *Placebo to hunte*
And *dyngen* vpon Dauid eche day til eue . . . . (*PP* 3.299–300, 305–12)

The series of subjects with infinitives in the last four lines might be thought of as nominal complements, following the new law to be decreed (299), a possibility reinforced by the context of the passage from Isaiah (2.4: 'Et iudicabit gentes, et arguet populos multos: et conflabunt gladios...'). Or the infinitives might be thought of as expressing the 'result' of the Latin line and the making of the new law: 'so that,' *etc.*

This long preamble can be summed up as follows. The 'absolute' infinitive here examined has been seen to have the characteristic form (S) + *to* + Inf. [+ Modal]. *To* and modality are its most consistent features. To this it can be added that its syntactic function, though not usually indicated by a connective, is typically as a subordinate clause: object, subject, noun modifier, adverbial. Finally, the construction occasionally occurs independently of an expressed matrix clause. If it were to be renamed, one might well follow Carstensen's reasoning and call it the 'Testationsformel' or 'testamentary infinitive.' And it might best appear in grammars under the heading 'infinitive for finite verb.'

---

[56] I.e., '[I think that] the legal seizure (*distresse*) should be held back for the eventuality that the sale be lawful, although I do not think it will be necessary.' That the same might be argued for the exclamatory and parenthetical infinitives is apparent. Attempts to specify some precise and constant matter of an ellipsis are doomed because speech situations vary so constantly. In the case of the historical infinitive, it can at least be specified that the 'deleted' auxiliary (whatever it might be) is non-modal.

II

Let us now turn to 'The Speech of Book.' Toward the end of that speech,
Book utters the following lines:

> 255 And I, book, wole be brent but Iesus rise to lyue
> In alle myȝtes of man and his moder gladie,
> And conforte al his kyn and out of care brynge,
> And al þe Iewene Ioye vnioynen and vnlouken;
> And but þei reuerensen his roode and his Resurexion
> 260 And bileue on a newe lawe be lost, lif and soule.

The passage contains a number of forms which are potentially ambiguous. The
difficulty has been so to choose among the alternatives as to arrive at the most
plausible translation; and the nub of it is to account for the two verbs of line
258 ('vnioynen and vnlouken') which are, unambiguously, infinitives.[57] The
potential ambiguities are these:

> 255 *but*   the adversative coordinating conjunction 'but,' or
>   the subordinating conjunction 'unless'
>   *rise*   subjunctive or infinitive
>   *to lyue*   infinitive 'to live,' or prepositional phrase 'to life'
> 256–57 *gladie, conforte, brynge*   subjunctives, or infinitives.

There is the further problem of deciding how the verbs *rise, gladie, conforte,*
and *brynge* (whether subjunctive or infinitive) fit into the syntax.[58]

Two readers of the passage, though their interpretations are generally at odds,
agree that in line 255 *to lyue* must be the prepositional phrase 'to life.' R. E.
Kaske argues this partly because 'rise to live' seems of dubious meaning, but
chiefly because he finds 'rise to life' a stereotyped expression, especially in
lyric references to the Resurrection.[59] E. Talbot Donaldson concurs on both

---

[57] They cannot be plural subjunctives, for their subject is the singular 'Iesus.' In addition
to the obvious sense of the passage, 'Iewene' is plural genitive in form, and 'Ioye' is singular
(having its plural in -*s* or -*n*). The sense of the line, then, is that Jesus take apart and undo
all the joy of the Jews.

[58] MS variants do not bring any conclusive evidence to bear on these ambiguities. That
no B-scribe wrote *but if* at 255 is not particularly significant: where *but* clearly means 'unless,'
but (with variant *but if*), *but* (with no variant *but if*), and *but if* occur about equally (some
forty times each). No B-scribe wrote *risen* or *to rise*; but there is no occurrence of either form
in the text, while the bare infinitive in -*e* occurs four times, three of them without variant
in -*n* (5.389; 15.595; 17.70). On the fact that no B-scribe wrote *to lif*, see below. No pattern
emerges from treatment of the forms in 256–58, although scribal vacillation between -*e* and
-*en* suggests possible hesitation between subjunctive and infinitive. One (C²) wrote *gladen*;
three (CrHmM) *conforten* (but none *bryngen*); one (Cr) wrote *vnioyne*, another (Hm) *vnlowke*,
and a third (O) left the -*n* off both.

[59] R. E. Kaske, 'The Speech of "Book" in *Piers Plowman*' (n1 above) 135–36.

points. He reasons that '*rise* is a verb which does not take the infinitive without a fairly strong sense of purpose, so that one must be prepared to accept the heavy-handed translation, ". . . rise in order to live. . . ."' He adds that he could point to no clear occurrence of 'rise to live' in the lyrics.[60] This decision about 'to life' leads to eventual difficulties with line 258. Were *to lyue* an infinitive, the verbs *gladie, conforte, brynge,* as well as *vnioynen and vnlouken* could all be read as infinitives parallel with it. But if *to lyue* is the prepositional phrase 'to life,' one must seek another explanation.

Donaldson argues that in line 255 *but Iesus rise* is most naturally read as a clause of negative condition, 'unless Jesus rise to life.' The verbs *gladie, conforte,* and *brynge* (256–57) follow as subjunctives parallel with *rise*: 'unless Jesus rise . . . and gladden . . . and comfort . . . and bring.' That leaves *vnioynen and vnlouken* of line 258. To explain them, Donaldson urges that they be read as 'absolute infinitives.'[61]

In the light of the full discussion of the 'absolute' infinitive presented above, that suggestion is unacceptable. One cannot base the identification of this construction, as Donaldson seems to do, on the perception that it conveys 'future action strongly hypothesized by the speaker or a present action strongly visualized by him,' and whose 'effect is one of inevitability' (107–8). Grant the infinitives that modal sense. One must still ask if the line shows any other features of the construction. First, its infinitives do not have an expressed subject. It has been argued above that a subject may indeed be understood from context, and lines 255–57 allow 'Jesus/he' to be understood here without difficulty. There are, however, other aspects of this context: as Donaldson interprets the lines, *but* means 'unless' and introduces a series of conditional clauses, with finite subjunctive verbs coordinated by 'and.' Under these circumstances, it seems most likely that, to signal the start of the infinitive clause, the subject would be re-stated in 258. Secondly, the absence of *to* seems crucial. It is, as we have seen, a constant feature of the construction. For it to be omitted at all is implausible; for it to be omitted in the context just described seems quite impossible.

---

[60] E. Talbot Donaldson, 'The Grammar of Book's Speech in "Piers Plowman"' (*n*3 above) 105.

[61] On the construction, Donaldson cites Mustanoja, Einenkel, and Kenyon. As instances in Langland he quotes examples 2 and 49 above, and further adduces two passages from the description of Haukyn's coat (13.274–310 and 320–25). But the infinitives in this description are all adjuncts, modifying nouns and adjectives: *ymagynen, studie, entremeten* (288, 290) modify *Inwit and outwit* (288); *to cacche, telle* (298–99) modify *loos* (298); *to telle, segge, sweren, demen, bosten, witnesse, siggen* (303–6) modify *bostere* (302); *to chide, tellen, blame, bidden, tellen* (322–25) modify *tonge* (322). Each of these two descriptive passages is headed by one main clause (274, 320) containing long strings of parallel participles, adjectives, and nouns; with these the strings of infinitive adjuncts are in stylistic harmony.

The matter can be further clarified by the following experiment:

255 And I, book, wole be brent but Iesus rise to lyue
    In alle myȝtes of man and his moder gladie,
    *And *he to* conforte al his kyn and out of care brynge . . . .

A reader who has mulled through the quotations given above will hear a
pronounced change of mood at the altered line 257, a change from condition
to statement: 'and he will, is surely going to. . . .' Donaldson suggests precisely
such a change of mood between lines 255 and 258, from 'negative condition'
to 'inevitability.' He judges that such a change is just what Langland wished
to convey, and that one might regard the verbs of 256–57 as 'subjunctives
becoming infinitives' (108). But here one comes, inevitably, back to the
actual form of line 258; for the preceding experiment shows clearly that in such
a case the shift of construction is signaled precisely by the statement of subject
plus *to*. Had line 258 read

            *And *he* al þe Iewene Ioye *to* vnioynen and vnlouken

one would have to agree with Donaldson.[62] But to read the line the way he
suggests in the absence of *he* is at best problematical; to read it that way in the
absence of *to* seems, in all honesty, more implausible than the readings he seeks
to reject.[63]

Neither of those rejected readings, it must be admitted, is without its difficulties. The first was proposed by Kaske. He begins, as has already been

---

[62] For Langland's use of the construction, see examples 35, 38, 39, 40, and 49 above. In 35,
note that the subject is expressed even though its reference is clear and its antecedent present
in each of the three preceding lines; after the construction is initiated, *to* but not the subject
is repeated (last line of the quotation). In 49 the bare infinitive is used only after S + *to*
initiate the series.

[63] In Donaldson's reading, the 'absolute' construction of 258 would best be analyzed as an
'independent testamentary infinitive' (cf. ex. 43–49), an object clause whose understood
matrix is something like 'I, Book, prophesy [that] S.' One difficulty with this is immediate
context. Although Book's speech does indeed begin 'I wol bere witnesse / That . . .' (232–
33), the governing main clause is, rather, 'I, book, wole be brent but . . .' One could al-
ternatively suggest that an 'absolute' construction functioned as a result clause introduced
by *and*, which could give good sense. Ultimately, however, the form of line 258 resists
any such reading; without S + *to* signaling a shift in construction, *and* would
naturally be read as coordinating the line with the verbs of 255–57 — verbs of conditional
clauses. Donaldson recognizes this typical form elsewhere in his discussion. Commenting
on line 260 he says: 'Actually, if we could get Langland's ghost to fill out the line so that it
would be entirely unambiguous for modern readers, I suspect he would use the infinitive:
"And but þei reuerencen his roode and his Resurexion / And beleue on a new lawe *þei to* be
lost, lif and soule"' (208, italics added). This remark implies that he takes the line, as it
stands (without *þei to*), as one with a subjunctive verb; and that he agrees the 'absolute'
construction is indeed signaled by S + *to*.

noted, by taking *to lyue* as 'to life,' and his solution to line 258 arises from his treatment of *but Iesus rise.* He reads line 255: 'I, book, will be burned, but Jesus (will) rise to life' (135–36). Thus he takes *but* as the coordinating conjunction and *rise* as an infinitive governed by *wole,* understood. He then reads all the following verbs as infinitives parallel with *rise.* About his interpretation of line 255, Kaske remarks: 'The awkwardness of this construction lies in its rather unusual omission of the . . . auxiliary in a second co-ordinate clause, here aggravated by the further change from a first-person to a third-person subject and a consequent forcing of the co-ordinating *but* into syntactic ambiguity' (136).

Kaske is able to cite other instances of such a construction where the conjunction is *and,* but none where *but* joins the two clauses.[64] There is one clear example of it, however, in the B-text of *Piers Plowman.* 'Pernele proud-herte' has been moved to promise:

> She sholde vnsowen hir serk and sette þere an heyre
> To affaiten hire flessh þat fiers was to synne.
> 67 'Shal neuere heiȝ herte me hente, but holde me lowe
> And suffre to be mysseyd, and so dide I neuere.' (*PP* 5.65–68)

In prose order, line 67 would read: 'heiȝ herte shal neuere hente me, but [I shall] holde me lowe.' The line really admits of no other interpretation, and one is faced with a situation very like the one described by Kaske: omission of an auxiliary in a second coordinate clause, a change of subject from third to first person, a bare infinitive in *-e,* and two clauses coordinated by *but.* Were it not for the comma which the editors have most properly placed in line 67, one might at first be misled into reading *but holde* as 'unless (proud heart) hold'; but here context would immediately correct such a misreading.[65] At 18.255 the context is less helpful. What would lead a reader to reject 'unless Jesus rise'? As Kaske reads the passage, it could be only the infinitives eventually encountered at line 258. One might well wonder why Langland, had he intended 'but Jesus (will) rise,' would not have marked the infinitive unmis-

---

[64] See 136–37; Kaske notes that *and,* in such cases, has a potential ambiguity very similar to that imposed by his reading on *but* (137*n*4).

[65] Donaldson writes that 'unless' is the 'unmistakable' meaning of *but* 'when it is followed by a recognizable subjunctive' (104). Since in late ME a 'recognizable subjunctive' is very often an equally recognizable infinitive, Donaldson surely means to imply the qualification 'and when the context indicates a clause of negative condition.' Context is decisive for 5.67 (where *holde* is morphologically ambiguous). Cf. 10.61–62: 'Is noon to nyme hym in, ne his noy amende, / But *hunsen* hym as an hound and *hoten* hym go þennes.' Here *hunsen* and *hoten* are morphologically ambiguous, but context tells us to read them as infinitives parallel with *to nyme* and *amende;* the subject has changed from *noon* to an indefinite 'they,' and the governance of the infinitives has shifted from *is noon* to something like *are þo,* yet context disallows reading *but hunsen . . . hoten* as 'unless' plus subjunctive.

takably with *to/-n.* Kaske's reading, while given additional support by 5.67, remains difficult.

If Donaldson's reading has proved implausible and Kaske's is difficult, it might be worthwhile reconsidering a third possibility they both reject: understanding *to lyue* in 255 as an infinitive and all the subsequent verb forms as infinitives parallel with it.[66] The translation, then, would begin: 'And I, book, will be burned unless Jesus rise to live. . . .' This most straightforward reading, we recall, has been set aside because it seemed to make no sense and was thought to violate Middle English idiom. Let us briefly re-examine the problem of *to lyue.*

The charge that 'rise to live' is tautological or heavy-handed can be countered by suggesting a plausible meaning for it. If one takes into consideration the beginning of the next line, good sense results: 'rise to live in all the powers of a man,' that is, 'rise so as to live with all the powers which belong to a viable human being.'[67] The expression, then, would be an emphatic one, stressing the completeness and total efficacy which must characterize the Resurrection.

The argument that *rise to lyue* is a stereotyped phrase for 'rise to life' is potentially more telling. Kaske (135*n*3) cites one nearly exact parallel.[68] But six other instances involve a form of *rise* and the expression 'from death to life,'[69] while one last instance is the phrase 'come to lyve a-ȝen.'[70] Such parallels clearly show that the phrase in question may well mean 'to life,' but they are not so copious, nor with one exception so exact, as to show that *rise to lyue* could have no other meaning.[71] There is one other occurrence of *to lyue* in the B-text which may well mean 'to life':

---

[66] This has been most recently suggested by Richard L. Hoffman, 'The Burning of "Boke" in *Piers Plowman,*' *Modern Language Quarterly* 25 (1964) 59–60. (Hoffman writes in criticism of Kaske; Donaldson, in reaction to both.) Hoffman unfortunately offers little evidence and, as Donaldson points out, goes on to mistranslate line 260.

[67] Donaldson's claim that an infinitive after *rise* must signify purpose (105, quoted above) cannot be tested in *PP,* for the text shows no instance except the possibility in question. Chaucer's practice (which can be examined by means of a concordance) bears the generalization out. But short of an exhaustive concordance of ME, there seems to be no *a priori* prohibition to its being followed by an infinitive expressing result.

[68] *English Lyrics of the XIIIth Century,* ed. Carleton Brown (Oxford 1932) 28.32: 'ros to liue'; that *liue* is the noun is confirmed by its rhyme on the long *i* of *blyþe.*

[69] To these can be added Chaucer, *CT* B2265 (Melibeus) referring to the Resurrection: 'risen fro deeth to lyve.'

[70] Alois Brandl and Otto Zippel, edd., *Mittelenglische Sprach- und Literaturproben* (Berlin 1917) 112.196. For other occurrences of 'to life' see Kaske 135*n*2; also *MED, lif,* esp. 985.2, 986.1, 987.2.

[71] Donaldson regards the fact that no B-scribe wrote *to lyuen* as negative but 'weighty' evidence supporting 'to life' (105). But of fifteen occurrences of the infinitive in the B-text, ten show no variant in *-n* (12.207; 14.42, 130; 15.366, 423, 497; 19.217, 248; 20.63, 311).

> And as Adam and alle þoruʒ a tree deyden,
> Adam and alle þoruʒ a tree shul turne *to lyue* . . . . (18.358–59)

That *turne to lyue* means 'return to life' is certainly possible.[72] *Turne* could also have the sense 'to change so as to be, to become' or even 'to adopt . . . a good life, to be converted,' and the entire phrase could be rendered 'to become alive (again)' or 'to be converted to life (in Christ).'[73] Yet even here there is a plausible alternative which takes *to lyue* as an infinitive and translates: 'change so as to, in order to, live (again)' or 'be converted so as to, in order to, live (in Christ).'[74]

One further bit of evidence can be adduced for taking *to lyue*, in both the cases just discussed, as an infinitive; it is suggestive, but far from conclusive. The scribe of the Kane–Donaldson copy text is very consistent with regard to an inflectional -*e* on the singular noun *lif*.[75] The cases just discussed are, of course, open to debate. But *to* plus *lif* occurs one other time: 'to ech lif' (13.16). After other prepositions (*on*, *wiþ*, *of*, *for*, *in*) the noun is regularly uninflected; the few exceptions to this are equally regular and easily defined: those in which a monosyllabic possessive pronoun intervenes between preposition and noun.[76] Otherwise, whatever its function, the singular noun *lif* occurs without -*e*. And given the potential ambiguity of the lines, it is noteworthy that the editors report no variant *lif* at either 18.255 or 18.359.

Of the proposed translations of lines 255–60, then, the least likely is that which treats line 258 as an 'absolute' infinitive construction. Reading line 255 as 'but Jesus (will) rise to life' is possible, but it is made difficult by the failure of grammatical context to clarify the reading until line 258 — and then the clarification would come only if readers could be counted on to understand 'to lyue' as a prepositional phrase. Reading line 255 as 'unless Jesus rise to live' is grammatically simplest, but runs against what is a reasonably similar

---

[72] On *turne* as 'return' see *OED, turn, v* 20, 21; cf. *PP* 17.122.

[73] *OED, turn, v* 39, 30; cf. *PP* 16.110 and 13.210.

[74] For *turn* used absolutely in the sense of 'convert,' see *PP* 3.327 and 15.503. The infinitive would be an adverbial adjunct, expressing result or purpose.

[75] This copy text (*W*, Trinity College Cambridge B.15.17) is the MS most sensitive and consistent in matters of grammar among all extant *PP* copies (*ed. cit.* 215). What other B-scribes did cannot be known from this ed., since the editors could not record -*e* variants where these had no clear semantic or metrical (syllabic) import (218).

[76] The cases are: *in þi lyue* (5.365, 10.125, 14.24); *by my lyue* (6.101); *by his lyue* (11.135, 13.451); *in my lyue* (14.98). Contrast *of oure lif* (10.92), *in good lif* (8.97). The cases listed above, and the two cases in dispute here, are the only forms of *lif* with -*e* among some 120 occurrences of the word.

Middle English idiom in some comparable contexts, supported by a plausible translation of the very similar 'tourne to lyue' of 18.359.[77]

Professor Donaldson concludes his discussion of the passage by reminding us that 'it was Dame Study who first caused grammar to be written; and since it is the ground of all, she will beat us with birch unless we learn it.' Admonished by this threat of the rod, and having bent over his books, the present writer would choose the last of the three readings set out just above. It is, based solely on such evidence as grammar and textual transmission can offer, the least anomalous interpretation. But Kaske's reading is possible and cannot be made the butt of Dame Study's vexation. Moreover, while no one would urge that the literary critic ignore what Grammar has to teach, this may be one of those cases in which her science yields no conclusive answer and so remains ancillary to loftier disciplines: Philosophy, Theology, and the larger meaning of the poem.

University of North Carolina,
Chapel Hill

---

[77] Kaske's reading could easily accommodate lines 259–60. Abbreviating the entire passage: 'but Jesus (will) rise to life and (will) gladden and (will) comfort and bring out of care and (will) take apart and undo all the joy of the Jews and, unless they reverence his cross and Resurrection and believe in a new Law, (they will) be lost life and soul.' The last reading suggested would take *be* (260) as subjunctive following the negative condition *but* (259). Again abbreviating the entire passage: 'unless Jesus rise to live and (to) gladden and (to) comfort and bring out of care and (to) take apart and undo all the joy of the Jews; and, unless they reverence his cross and Resurrection and believe in a new law, (they) be lost life and soul.' On the form line 260 would have if it were an 'absolute' infinitive, see *n*63.

GENIUS AND INTERPRETATION IN THE 'CONFESSIO AMANTIS'

By WINTHROP WETHERBEE

The *Confessio Amantis* is a highly complex poem, but employs a minimum of overt artistry. The style can seem forbiddingly plain or even dull at a first hearing, but its evenness of tone and movement is finely calculated: what stands out stands out for a reason. Like the *Lais* of Marie de France, a poet whom he resembles in many ways, Gower's narratives are unvaryingly chronological and so sparse in detail as often to seem hardly longer than the Latin summaries which accompany them. He is deeply concerned with moral psychology, but rarely takes us inside his characters' minds, though as C. S. Lewis remarks, he often tells us a great deal simply by telling us *that* they are thinking.[1] His diction is comparably spare: Christopher Ricks has noted the striking effects he achieves with words like 'thing' and 'soft.'[2]

It is perhaps this utter lack of flamboyance that has made critics take for granted the impeccable orthodoxy of Gower's artistic intentions. Whereas in the *Canterbury Tales* dramatic interrelations among the Tales seem more important than any overriding theme, and Chaucer deliberately exploits the diversity of genre and 'entente' among his many tale-tellers, Gower's Genius carefully adapts each tale to its place in the exposition of a moral system, often simplifying characterization, flattening out historical perspective, adjusting chronology, or eliminating episodic material in the interest of clarity.[3] Chaucer's proliferating structure and his use of Harry Baily as master of ceremonies seem to reflect a deliberate refusal to establish a controlling center in his poem, an acceptance of a world of division and opposition, but Gower uses Genius' mediating role to relate all his narratives to a framework of moral, political, and cosmological ideas which express a deep commitment to hierarchy.[4]

Commentators have seen this structure as expressing in itself the essential character of the poem. For J. H. Fisher 'the heart of Gower's matter' is the Prologue and the moralizing digressions; the poem is about love as 'social

---

[1] *The Allegory of Love* (Oxford 1936) 199.

[2] 'Metamorphosis in Other Words,' in *Gower's* CONFESSIO AMANTIS: *Responses and Reassessments*, ed. A. J. Minnis (Woodbridge, Suffolk, and Totowa, N.J. 1983) 28–31.

[3] On the narrative characteristics of Gower's tales see J. A. Burrow, *Medieval Writers and Their Work* (Oxford 1982) 109–14; Charles Runacres, 'Art and Ethics in the "Exempla" of "Confessio Amantis,"' in *Gower's* CONFESSIO AMANTIS 106–34.

[4] See Paul Strohm, 'Form and Social Statement in *Confessio Amantis* and the *Canterbury Tales*,' *Studies in the Age of Chaucer* 1 (1979) 17–40.

cement,' and might equally well be described as a mirror for princes.[5] A. J. Minnis takes pains to incorporate the love-theme into his characterization, but views its treatment of love-folly, like that of Ovid as explained by medieval commentators, as wholly ironic, a way of judging such love by an implicit standard of 'just' or 'honest' love. The poem is in effect an ethical treatise, framed by the wider theme of its Prologue as a medieval commentary is framed by an 'extrinsic' prologue which sets its theme in the context of wisdom in general.[6] Pamela Gradon argues that the true theme of the *Confessio*, as of its Prologue, is not love, but 'rihtwisnesse' or equity, a disciplining of will and appetite by rational discretion which is the basis equally of personal and social order.[7]

All these critics touch on important aspects of the *Confessio*, but none addresses the problem posed by the nature of the material they would subsume under the broad heading of justice or wisdom or political order.[8] The great bulk of the *Confessio Amantis* consists of tales, complex in themselves and made still more so by the complexity of their interrelation. All are ostensibly illustrative of the poem's moral argument, and many touch directly on social and political issues raised in the Prologue, but as it will be the purpose of this paper to illustrate, few make their points in a straightforward way. Further problems are posed by the framing penitential dialogue. The stories address the plight of the troubled lover Amans, yet he seems almost perversely unable to extract a serious message from them. And Gower's confessor-priest is Genius, whose treatment of the lover must be meticulous by the standards of the penitential tradition, but whose role requires that he also teach him love

> After the disposicioun
> Of Venus, whos condicioun
> I moste folwe, as I am holde.   (1.259–61)[9]

Although Genius has an important and complex literary history, his first long speech (1.233–88) provides us with all the definition Gower will give us of his role. We must note both his repeated emphasis on his subservience to Venus and his reluctance to define his function wholly in terms of this relation-

---

[5] *John Gower: Moral Philosopher and Friend of Chaucer* (New York 1964) 187–89.

[6] 'John Gower, *Sapiens* in Ethics and Politics,' *Medium Aevum* 49 (1980) 207–29.

[7] 'John Gower and the Concept of Righteousness,' *Poetica* (Tokyo) 8 (1977) 61–71.

[8] An exception is Russell Peck, whose *Kingship and Common Profit in Gower's* CONFESSIO AMANTIS (Carbondale, Ill. 1978) is the first full-scale interpretation based on a reading of the actual poem. But Peck seeks to read the entire poem in terms of a single idea, 'common profit,' and his readings of particular tales, frequently excellent in detail, are too often reductive in their overall emphasis.

[9] The text for all references to Gower's poetry is that of G. C. Macauley, ed., *The Complete Works of John Gower*, 4 vols. (Oxford 1899–1902).

ship. He is Venus' priest 'touchende of love' (236), but also feels enjoined by
his office as priest to deal with the vices in general, though here too the emphasis
is on their relation to love and the standards of conduct in love set by Venus
(237–61).[10] Although limited in his grasp of virtue and vice, which Venus'
books do not treat, he nonetheless declares,

> Of my Presthode after the forme
> I wol thi shrifte so enforme,
> That ate leste thou schalt hiere
> The vices, and to thi matiere
> Of love I schal hem so remene,
> That thou schalt knowe what thei mene.   (1.275–80)

Throughout this long speech, full of 'buts' and qualifying phrases, we can see
Genius striving to affirm the intrinsic importance of virtue in the face of
Venus' dominating influence, and these lines define a kind of honorable compromise. Love is inescapably the theme of his dealings with Amans, and he
himself is acutely sensitive to its power, but he will contrive to make this
theme a focus for consideration of virtue and vice as such. In what Genius
calls the 'form' of his priestly office, we can see traces of the priest of Nature
in Alain de Lille's *Complaint of Nature*, a link to the human condition before the
Fall, for whom love and sexual conduct are a test of man's psychic integrity,
his responsiveness to the ultimately divine promptings of his higher nature.[11]
Genius' dual perspective, conditioned both by Venus and by his ability to see
his subservience to Venus in relation to a prelapsarian model of human behavior, greatly complicates his treatment of the stories which are his primary
means of appeal.

These stories present themselves to Genius' use already equipped with moral
commentary, and their morals often seem mere foils, serving by their harshness,
obtuseness, or inappropriateness to set off Genius' instinctively more sympathetic response to the story he is telling.[12] But Genius' sympathy is itself no
simple thing. As Venus' priest, he is unfailingly responsive to the plight of
those who try to accommodate their lives to the power of sexual passion, and
strongly critical of those who deny or evade what he sees as their responsibility
to love. But he is also intuitively aware that the failings for which he shows

---

[10] Fisher seems to me to misread this passage when he finds in it, and in lines 254–60 in
particular, evidence that Genius will provide instruction in 'the degrees of love, beginning
with the vices of animal love and ending with the virtues of spiritual love' (*John Gower* 193).
On the constant tension between Genius and Venus, see Burrow, *Medieval Writers* 91–92.

[11] On Genius in Alain and in the *Roman de la Rose*, see my *Platonism and Poetry in the
Twelfth Century* (Princeton 1972) 198–210, 258–65.

[12] See Derek Pearsall, 'Gower's Narrative Art,' *Publications of the Modern Language
Association of America* 81 (1966) 476; Runacres, 'Art and Ethics' 126–34.

such tolerance reflect an underlying failure of reason, will, and vision; and this, though he does not recognize it as such, is a result of the Fall, a measure of man's alienation from a once harmonious relationship with nature and with his fellow humans.

In practice this means that Genius' stories tend to resist their overt moral purpose precisely insofar as they are informed by what we may call the 'genial' perspective of the teller. Again and again he unwittingly subverts or complicates the lesson of a tale by making us aware that the innocence, ignorance, or overmastering passion that gave rise to the sin being illustrated is grounded in a fundamental limitation of perception and understanding basic to the human condition. Gower is not always given credit for a sense of humor, but in fact the *Confessio* is pervaded by what Anthony Farnham calls 'the comedy of high prosaic seriousness,'[13] an inclination to play upon the habits and mechanics of conventional *moralisatio*. The ease and frequency with which the poem discovers complexity of meaning by reducing the workings of its moral argument to the level of quiet parody is one of its most striking and disconcerting features. Like the artfully bungled moralizing of Chaucer's *Legend of Good Women*, the calculated ineptitudes of Gower's Genius are a critical reflection on interpretive methods borrowed from the traditions of moralizing commentary on the poets and the use of brief tales or *exempla* to point a moral in preaching and homiletics.[14]

One of the main purposes of the first few stories of Book I of the *Confessio*, which deal with sins of the eyes and ears, is to advertise the complexity of the poem's argument by showing the limits of moralization. Here, amid such examples as Acteon, Medusa, and the Sirens, there appears a brief bit of scientific lore which may serve as an emblem of Gower's critique. There is, Genius declares, a serpent, 'Aspidis,' who bears within his head a precious stone coveted by enchanters. When these seek to overcome him with spells, he lies with one ear to the ground and thrusts his tail into his other ear so t6at he becomes deaf to their incantations:

> And in this wise himself he skiereth,
> So that he hath the wordes weyved
> And thurgh his Ere is noght deceived.   (1.478–80)

---

[13] Anthony E. Farnham, 'The Art of High Prosaic Seriousness: John Gower as Didactic Raconteur,' in *The Learned and the Lewed: Studies in Chaucer and Medieval Literature*, ed. Larry D. Benson, Harvard English Studies 5 (Cambridge, Mass. 1974) 161–73.

[14] On Gower and the commentary tradition see Minnis, 'John Gower, *Sapiens*' 207–15; '"Moral Gower" and Medieval Literary Theory,' in *Gower's* CONFESSIO AMANTIS 54–58. On Gower's use of the *exemplum*, see especially Runacres, 'Art and Ethics'; also Burrow, *Medieval Writers* 107–18; Judith Shaw, 'John Gower's Illustrative Tales,' *Neuphilologische Mitteilungen* 84 (1983) 437–48.

The source of this figure is Psalm 57.4–5, where the adder who 'stoppeth her ears' to the voice of the charmer stands for the wicked who are deaf to the voice of wisdom. Augustine develops the idea in his *Enarrationes*, and it was a standard sermon exemplum.[15] Isidore, cataloguing serpents in his *Etymologiae* (12.4.12), supplies the particulars of the asp's method of rendering itself deaf, and Brunetto Latini, Gower's immediate source, adds the detail of the stone in the asp's head (*Trésor* 1.138). Gower himself interprets the asp *in bono* in the *Mirour de l'omme*, linking it to Matthew 10.16, where Christ bids the apostles be 'wise as serpents, and harmless as doves.' The serpent embodies prudence: with its ear to the ground it recalls our origin, 'du vile terre et de merdaille'; its use of its tail foretells our 'end,' when we will revert to earth again. The twofold gesture warns us not to covet earthly life (*Mirour* 15253–76).[16]

In the *Confessio*, however, the asp is again explicitly an exemplum (460, 482), but we are not invited to read it figurally, whether *in bono* or *in malo*. As in Brunetto's encyclopedia, it is simply a natural fact. The only hint of its meaning is Genius' broad injunction 'to kepe wel an Ere' (461). As a model for direct emulation, it has no more practical value than an invitation to hide one's head in the sand,[17] yet there is no hint that it is to be treated as moral allegory, or an image of radical *contemptus mundi*. Its status is wholly equivocal, and I think this is Gower's point. The odd little creature, deaf to the world and immune to the wiles of the enchanters, is literally and figuratively a closed circle, impervious to interpretation, an image as enigmatic and daunting in its modest way as any in the *Confessio*.

Perhaps the clearest example of Gower's exploitation of the tradition of *moralisatio* to his own ends in full-scale narrative is his handling of the Narcissus story, borrowed, as Genius acknowledges, from 'the clerk Ovide,' but so altered in his telling as almost literally to outgrow its assigned moral. Amans has just complained that Genius' exempla are insufficiently concerned with 'loves cause' (1.2258–61), and it is perhaps to meet this criticism that Genius offers a version of the story which diverges markedly from Ovid and from earlier medieval versions. Gower's Narcissus takes his image in the fountain for a nymph, rather than a young man, and instead of wasting away like Ovid's hero, he is driven by the nymph's seeming unresponsiveness to destroy himself actively. In a further striking embellishment, found only in a

---

[15] See G. R. Owst, *Literature and Pulpit in Medieval England*, 2nd ed. (Oxford 1966) 198.

[16] Giraldus Cambrensis offers a strikingly pragmatic application of the serpent/dove exemplum to 'prudence' in politics, *De principum instructione* 1.11, ed. G. F. Warner, Rolls Series 21.8 (London 1891) 40.

[17] Richard de Fournival contrasts the vulnerability of the lover's senses to the self-protective powers of the asp, *Li Bestiaires d'Amours*, ed. Cesare Segre (Milan 1957) 31–32.

late recension of the story,[18] a host of nymphs and other woodland beings appear at Narcissus' death to bury his body, and a profusion of flowers springs forth from his grave.

These new details do not deter Genius from asserting that Narcissus was justly punished for his disdain of love (2359–62), but for a reader not wholly predisposed to accept Genius' moral position, the alterations work against the impression of unfeeling aloofness that would seem necessary to Narcissus' exemplary role. And Gower has made many subtler adjustments which work to the same contradictory effect. In Ovid, Narcissus' devotion to the hunt is closely linked to his isolation and indifference to feeling, and the wilderness into which Echo pursues him expresses his condition. He becomes permanently relegated to this wilderness, discovers a solitary passion, and is, like Echo, consumed by it. Gower, on the other hand, takes pains to ground Narcissus' experience as much as possible in the ordinary world, and to stress its universal aspect. Narcissus' pride and his scorning of love are made plain, but there is no mention of his rejecting the appeals of lovers, and the hunt which leads to his discovery of the fatal fountain is a social occasion, described in concrete and realistic detail. The strictly chronological narration provides an explanation of his eventual isolation that seems more circumstantial than symbolic. Ovid had carefully placed his description of the mysterious fountain, never visited by shepherds' flocks or wild animals, and sustaining its surrounding verdure with no help from the larger processes of nature (*Metamorphoses* 3.407–12); it is closely juxtaposed with his conjuring up of Nemesis (406), an ominous prologue to Narcissus' experience. But Gower's fountain is simply a 'lusty welle,' and we discover it only as Narcissus himself does, after he has outstripped the hunt and begun to feel the day's heat. Gower's account of Narcissus' fatal glance is also simpler than Ovid's, but carefully articulated:

> He sih the like of his visage,
> And wende ther were an ymage
> Of such a Nimphe as tho was faie,
> Wherof that love his herte assaie
> Began, as it was after sene,
> Of his sotie and made him wene
> It were a womman that he syh.   (1.2315–21)

The two distinct stages of the experience, in which he seems to behold first the 'image' of a nymph and then simply 'a womman,' express the growth of

---

[18] I am of course assuming that deliberate alterations in the so-called 'third recension' manuscripts of the *Confessio* reflect late revision. See Macaulay, *Complete Works* II cxxvii–cxxxviii; Fisher, *John Gower* 116–27. That the chronology of the different versions is still an open question is shown by Peter Nicholson, 'Gower's Revisions in the *Confessio Amantis*,' *Chaucer Review* 19 (1985) 123–43.

feeling in Narcissus rather than his delusion. The emphasis is sustained as Gower describes the image's mirroring of Narcissus' tears and appeals, in lines which bear no trace of Ovid's calculated fatuity and archness in dramatizing his hero's frustrated confusion (420–36, 450–62). Gower's Narcissus is undergoing nothing more or less than the birth of love, 'the newe wo, / That whilom was to him so strange' (1.2328–29), and the description of his anguish could refer to the *dolor* of any courtly lover:

> And ever among he gan to loute,
> And preith that sche to him come oute;
> And otherwhile he goth a ferr,
> And otherwhile he draweth nerre,
> And ever he fond hire in o place.
> He wepth, he crith, he axeth grace,
> There as he mihte gete non.   (1.2333–39)

Gower quietly but carefully stresses the causality linking the events which follow. Narcissus can obtain no 'grace,' and therefore dashes himself against a rock until he dies, whereupon the Nymphs, 'for pure pite' (2347), perform his burial. Ovid's hero had discovered the truth of his situation, yet remained trapped within it, wasting away with his eyes still fixed adoringly on what he knew to be an illusion (503). But the Narcissus of the *Confessio* experiences only the despair of the rejected lover, and it is this normalizing of the love-dilemma that elicits the pity of the Nymphs, whose coming forth from their 'welles' is a posthumous fulfillment of his prayer, and seems further to confirm the naturalness of his desire. In Ovid the Naiads fail to recover Narcissus' body, finding in its place only a pale flower. That in Gower's version an actual burial is performed further distances his story from Ovid's, reclaiming Narcissus for the world of universal human experience.

Genius wholly ignores these shifts of emphasis, and finds a stern moral in the flowers which flourish in un-Ovidian profusion on Narcissus' grave:

> For in the wynter freyssche and faire
> The floures ben, which is contraire
> To kynde, and so was the folie
> Which fell of his Surquiderie.   (1.2355–58)

The spluttering energy of the mid-line shifts from clause to clause and the oddness of Genius' attack on the innocent flowers would be enough to undercut his moral stance, but in fact his claim that the situation is contrary to 'kynde' has already been denied by the Nymphs. Their burial of Narcissus is an expression of sympathy that pre-empts Genius' authority, concluding the tale more effectively than a moral could have done. Appropriately, the flowers that spring from Narcissus' grave bear no causal relation to the narrative: they appear 'par aventure' (2350), outside the boundaries of the story; and Genius' situation, as he attempts to deal with these unruly products of his own imagination in frustrated isolation, amounts to a burlesque of the plight of Narcissus himself.

Genius' failure to locate the real conclusion of the tale is complemented by the truncated version of the story and its moral presented in the Latin marginal gloss.[19] Here Narcissus is said to have mistaken his reflection for that of 'the nymph whom the poets call Echo,' and fallen instantly in love with it. The confused reminiscence of Ovid undercuts the story's ostensible moral by suggesting Narcissus' ready responsiveness to a beauty not his own, and obscures the point of Gower's careful analysis of the stages of Narcissus' response to the image he sees. The Latin summary of the narrative ends with Narcissus' self-destruction, viewed as the appropriate reward for his pride, but associates it ambiguously with extreme fatigue (*nimio languore*), leaving open the possibility that Narcissus collapsed from exhaustion and in the process brained himself accidentally. In both its narrative and its moral aspect, the gloss gives a misleading account of the English tale, and it omits any mention of the tale's actual, uncanonical conclusion. Like Genius' moral, which overshoots that conclusion, it thus serves, in the end, to set off precisely that element in the story which defies moral categorization.

Ovid's importance for Gower is vast, and we must recognize that, while well versed in medieval Ovidian material,[20] he was also a careful and independent reader of the *Metamorphoses*. It has lately been argued that his use of Ovid is in the tradition of those commentators who deal with Ovid's tales by 'reverently' distorting their overt character to emphasize those elements most conformable to religious and moral orthodoxy.[21] That this is an oversimplification will, I hope, be evident from Gower's handling of the story of Narcissus, and it is clearer still in Genius' first two exempla, the stories of Acteon and Medusa, both of which carefully rework Ovid's narratives to complicate their own ostensible morals.

Ovid had declared that his story of Acteon had no moral, stressing the role of fate (*Met.* 3.141–42, 175–76), and making the gods themselves question the justice of Acteon's punishment (253–55). Genius' ostensible purpose in borrowing the story is to give moral weight to this tale of hapless error, yet he manages to outdo Ovid's stress on innocence, and his version advertises itself from the outset as naïvely straightforward. Ovid had opened his narrative with an impressionistic preview of the culminating metamorphosis, 'the fore-

---

[19] The authorship of the Latin glosses has never been seriously examined, but they are found in the great majority of the manuscripts of the *Confessio*, and there would seem to be no strong reason for questioning Gower's responsibility for them.

[20] See Conrad Mainzer, 'John Gower's Use of the "Medieval Ovid" in the *Confessio Amantis*,' *Medium Aevum* 41 (1972) 215–29.

[21] See Minnis, 'John Gower, *Sapiens*' 207–15; Lewis, *Allegory of Love* 199.

head endowed with alien horns' and 'dogs sated with a master's blood' (*Met.* 3.139–40). At the corresponding moment in Gower, 'Houndes' and 'grete Hornes' appear (1.343), but here they are the still-innocent accouterments of the chase (Ovid's grotesque *cornua* have become hunting-horns). There is no trace of Ovid's Theban landscape, steeped in the blood of slaughtered animals (143); Gower's Acteon moves through a forest filled with flowers and the song of birds.

The one adjustment that would seem to justify Genius' moral application of the story is his treatment of the moment of discovery. In Ovid the single, indirect indication that Acteon has actually seen Diana bathing is the passive participle *visae* (185), used of Diana herself, a word barely visible amid an elaborate description of the goddess' shock and anger. Genius is explicit:

> Bot he his yhe awey ne swerveth
> Fro hire, which was naked al . . . .   (1.366–67)

The Latin gloss nudges us toward a stern view of this moment, declaring that Acteon *would* not avert his gaze, and noting further that he looked at the goddess 'attentively' (*diligencius*). Russell Peck has found these promptings salutary: 'Having mislocated his proper purview by gazing lecherously on the chaste Diana, Acteon commits himself to an impropriety which transforms him into a beast.'[22] But neither lechery nor commitment is evident in the English text, and in all versions Acteon is transformed, not by 'impropriety,' but by Diana. The goddess' wrath is implicitly condemned by Ovid, and Genius himself applies to it the term 'wonder' (368), commonly used in the *Confessio* of things, often monstrous things, which the speaker cannot comprehend. He notes that Acteon's 'unhappy' end was due to vengeance (376–78), and can offer no stronger judgment than that it is often better 'to winke than to loke' (384).

The innocence of Acteon's behavior, reinforced by the idyllic setting in which we view him, clearly defies moralization. A world in which Acteon is punished so harshly for the innocent impulse which keeps his gaze fixed on Diana's beauty is clearly not Edenic, yet the question of what is wrong is still wholly unfocused: it is as though nature, rather than mankind, had fallen into passion and violence, and Acteon may well seem to be destroyed simply for being a man. In a sense this is the case: the real horror of the story is in its illustration of the tension inherent in the confrontation between the sexes in the fallen world, and of the feminine instinct to perceive any masculine intrusion as a potentially appropriative gesture. Although Genius hints at a moral-psychological view of Acteon, noting at the outset an aristocratic tendency to set

---

[22] Peck, *Kingship and Common Profit* 39. Farnham, 'The Art of High Prosaic Seriousness,' gives a very different view of Gower's Acteon.

himself 'above al othre' (341), he obviously embodies the plight of post-lapsarian man in only the most tentative way. But his story is the first of a series in Book I in which the stated theme of pride is complemented by an emphasis on situations in which problems of perception, and men's perceptions of women in particular, test the reader's moral awareness on a practical level at which the standard categories of the penitential manual have little meaning.

At first sight, Gower's version of the story of Medusa, which follows immediately, appears badly confused. The tale occupies fewer than fifty lines, but nearly half of it is taken up with garbled classical lore which has no clear bearing on the story proper. It begins by identifying Medusa and her two sister-Gorgons as daughters of Phorcas (here conceived as a nobleman rather than a sea-monster), born through 'constellacion' in the shape of serpents, and assigns to them the single eye, passed about from one to another, which in ancient versions is the attribute of their sisters, the Graiae (389–410). Having mentioned this eye to no clear purpose, Genius breaks off abruptly in order to remark on a further 'wonder,' the sister's petrifying effect on those who beheld them, and then suddenly introduces a brief account of Perseus' arming by Pallas and Mercury and his slaying of the three sisters (411–35).

The names of Medusa's sisters and their serpentine form, the conflation of Gorgons and Graiae, the mention of the sword of Mercury, and the fact that Perseus slays all three sisters, rather than Medusa alone, are drawn from medieval mythography.[23] But in the conduct of his narrative, Gower is clearly following Ovid's version, narrated by Perseus himself. The randomness of the early portion of Genius' tale, its clumsy transitions, and its confused recollection of the Graiae, are in fact closely imitated from Perseus' report. Perseus tells of the Graiae and his theft of their single eye (*Met.* 4.772–77), but his point is as unclear as in Gower (we learn how the eye was stolen, but not why), and the whole narrative is comparably disjointed. Perseus is plainly more interested in his adventures as such than in their coherence or meaning. In telling of Medusa, he gives more attention to the ominous landscape, strewn with the stony forms of Medusa's victims, and to the thrill of seeing her reflection in his shield than to his brief encounter with the Gorgon herself, whom he had found fast asleep and dispatched quickly (777–85). All of this, down to the final anticlimax, is faithfully reflected in Genius' account, the high point of which is the hero's readying of his arms for a battle which is over almost at once:

> Bot he, which wisdom and prouesse
> Hadde of the god and the godesse,
> The Schield of Pallas gan enbrace,

---

[23] See Mainzer, 'Gower's Use of the "Medieval Ovid"' 216.

With which he covereth sauf his face,
Mercuries Swerd and out he drowh,
And so he bar him that he slowh
These dredful Monstres alle thre.   (1.429–35)

The payoff here is presumably the labeling of Perseus' 'wisdom and prou-
esse,' the divine gifts symbolized by the divine sword and shield which both
enable him to slay the Gorgons and endow the act with a plausible moral
significance.[24] To this extent Gower seems clearly to be thinking in terms of
conventional mythographic analysis. But it remains to be seen why he chooses
to combine this with a studious imitation of Ovid's artfully perfunctory telling
of the story. The answer to this question will, I think, give us a key to the
complex moral focus of Gower's exemplum.

Ovid's Perseus, as his headlong narrative style suggests, is more an ad-
venturer than a true hero. As a son of Jove, fitted out with winged shoes and
god-given weapons, he enjoys a certain official status, but he is less an embodiment of human *virtus* than the product of divine sanction. Even his
divine gifts serve no serious purpose, and there is a generous amount of parody
in Ovid's account of his exploits. Whatever value we read into his slaying of
Medusa is reduced when he appropriates her power for himself, and uses it to
massive and random effect in the grotesquely un-Homeric battle which erupts at
his wedding (*Met.* 5.177–249).

Gower was clearly alert to the incongruities in Ovid's treatment of Perseus,
and I would suggest that in combining a faithful imitation of Ovid's narrative
with the elements of a mythographic interpretation, he is inviting us to see
a parallel between Perseus' heroism and the moralizing function to which
Genius subjects it. The labeling of Perseus' arms with the names of heroic
attributes is an interpretive act as arbitrary and as barren of real moral significance as the bestowal of the arms themselves, no more instructive about the
perils of sight and 'fol delit' (442) than the legend of the Graiae and their single
eye which both poets treat so casually. So used, the tools of moralization are
as efficient, and as meaningless, as the petrifying power of Medusa in the hands
of Perseus, subjecting human events to their effect in a wholly coercive way.
The slaying of Medusa, a legend which exhibits the form of heroic action without the substance, is finally an image of how moralization can perform its
task yet wholly fail to realize the essence of a human situation.

What the appropriately sympathetic response to the Medusa story might be is
not clear from Gower's highly compressed narrative, but a clue is provided
by the conclusion of the episode in Ovid. After relating briefly his killing of the

---

[24] The complementarity of the shield of Pallas and the sword of Mercury, commonly glossed
as the wisdom and eloquence of the virtuous man, is a standard theme of glosses on the
Perseus story, present, as Mainzer notes (216), in the *Ovidius moralizatus* of Pierre Bersuire.

monster, Perseus instantly spins away into tales of other perilous adventures, but is then prevailed upon to tell the history of Medusa herself. She had been a beautiful maiden, her hair her most beautiful attribute, until she was raped by Poseidon in the temple of Minerva and punished by Minerva herself with transformation into the being whom Perseus slays (*Met.* 4.794–801).[25]

This brief, shocking coda gives us for an instant a very different perspective on Medusa's story, one in which, as in the case of Acteon, the plight of the human victim would resist any attempt to see a moral in her destruction. But with or without the further coordinate provided by Ovid's last-minute unveiling of Medusa's own story, it is plain that the 'moral' story of Perseus is distanced from that of Acteon's unwitting encounter with the wrath of Diana by a radical shift of emphasis. Now the vindication of the hero and the casting of the female figure in a destructive role have become part of a deliberate design which bears no clear relation to the sympathetic tenor of the tale: *moralisatio*, effectively powerless in the earlier tale, has here subordinated the authentic story to its own purposes, and thereby precluded a direct response to the human situation enacted.

There is no way to prove that Medusa's violation and transformation was in Gower's mind as he reworked the Perseus story, but the motif of an innocent woman violated at a shrine recurs in the tale of Mundus and Paulina, and I am tempted to see this as an acknowledgment of its omission in the earlier story. Here the noble Mundus is overcome by love of Paulina and, when gold and prayers have failed to move her, bribes two priests to help him. Exploiting her great piety, the priests convince her that the god Anubis loves her, and with her husband's consent she agrees to await his appearance by night in a temple. There Mundus presents himself as the god and has his will. When Paulina meets Mundus the next day, he reveals his knowledge of the event and by a coarse joke makes the truth plain to her. Horrified, she appeals to her husband and he to the king. The priests are put to death and Mundus is banished from the city.

In one sense the tale is about the defeat of hypocrisy by openness, a triumph of community, political and spiritual.[26] First there is a grotesque inversion of values, as the Mary-like purity and faith of Paulina are placed by false priests at the disposal of a pseudo-god who promises to beget upon her a son whom all the world will worship (915–21).[27] But the essential health of the community reasserts itself as Paulina, her husband, the citizenry, and the court respond

---

[25] In Ovid the transformation affects only Medusa's hair (*Met.* 4.801).

[26] See Peck, *Kingship and Common Profit* 41–45.

[27] The implications of this parody are explored at length by Patrick J. Gallacher, *Love, the Word, and Mercury: A Reading of John Gower's* Confessio Amantis (Albuquerque, N.M. 1975) 35–37.

in turn to the wrong that has been done, and the values of marriage, the state, and religion are reaffirmed. There can be no real objection to such a reading, but there is a danger that the role of Paulina will be obscured by it. For the story is really about the failure of the community, and Genius, to do justice to Paulina herself.

Paulina's peculiar status is implicit in Genius' introduction to the story, most of which concerns the irresistible power of love and beauty and aims to explain the behavior of Mundus. We have heard a good deal of such talk from Genius, and it is easy, borne along by the genial sweep of the passage as a whole, to accept the lines with which it ends as more of the same:

> This wif, which in hire lustes grene
> Was fair and freissh and tendre of age,
> Sche may moght lette the corage
> Of him that wole on hire assote.   (1.778–81)

But Genius' compassion can catch us off guard. Whatever sympathy we feel for Mundus becomes empty and patronizing when extended to Paulina: her 'lustes grene' have no place in the story, and her inability to keep the 'corage' of Mundus at bay is due not to any youthful weakness in her but to her remarkable piety. Genius is in fact condoning a basic lack of discretion which, as the tale proceeds, will become a general condition.

Throughout the tale Paulina acts with complete integrity, 'fulfild of alle holinesse' (895).[28] While Mundus lurks behind secrecy and 'blinde tales,' she is unfailingly open and direct. On the morning following her deception, after Mundus has withdrawn 'prively,' she prays kneeling 'upon the bare ground,' bestows generous offerings on the priests, and returns home openly, 'be the Strete' (934–38). Even when her belief that she has taken part in a divine mystery is shattered by Mundus, who accosts her to announce that Anubis has made him his 'lieutenant' and entitled him to enjoy her love in the god's place, she 'bar it stille' (952), and when alone she breaks down only for a moment before coming to herself and vowing to God never to be deceived again (954–64).

But this strength is fully visible only to us, and within the story a certain male officiousness tends to misrepresent it. Genius himself, in general highly respectful of Paulina's piety, treats the apparition of Mundus in the temple, which for her constitutes an epiphany, as virtually a stock love scene, in which 'softe wordes' overcome 'wommanyssche drede':

---

[28] Gower's emphasis is very different from that of his source, the fourth-century Latin version of Josephus known by the name of 'Hegesippus' (2.4), which stresses Paulina's superstition, her credulous ambition to enjoy the god's favor, and the joy of both Paulina and her husband at the news that she will bear a divine child.

> With suche wordes and with mo,
> The whiche he feigneth in his speche,
> This lady wit was al to seche,
> As sche which alle trowthe weneth.   (1.922–25)

Genius has rebuked Amans' witlessness in terms like these (570); here they help to make Paulina's faith in divine 'trowthe' appear like the mere credulity of a young girl. Later, when she confesses to her husband, he sees only her chagrin at the violation of her role as a wife; all he can offer in response is the assurance that he is not angry given the circumstances ('For wel he wot sche may ther noght' 987), a view of the affair at once as sympathetic and as limited as Genius' apology for her 'lustes grene.'

Paulina's own view of her situation comes close to surfacing in her words to her husband after discovering Mundus' deception. Feeling that she has betrayed 'wifhode' itself, she declares

> 'I am non other than a beste,
> Now I defouled am of tuo.'   (1.976–77)

Just who Paulina considers her two defilers to be is uncertain (a case could be made for Mundus and her husband or for the two priests), and I suspect that the ambiguity is intentional, an invitation to us to contrast the complexity of her actual situation with the male view of it that dominates the rest of the story. The lines just quoted are her last gesture, and their ambiguity is left unresolved. Henceforth the issue is her husband's desire to avenge the 'despit.' (Whose wrong he feels it to be is not made clear.) 'A day or two' are given to comforting and 'desporting' Paulina (1001–4), but she has no further role. Once her plight is known she is reduced to a lady in distress, virtually indistinguishable from the Dorigen of Chaucer's *Franklin's Tale* and other such 'noble wyves,' and then disappears altogether. The obliteration of the heroine and her values from the tale is confirmed symbolically when Genius, expanding on an incidental detail in the Latin source, describes the purification of the temple and the casting of its idol into the Tiber. Earlier the idol had been named as Isis, goddess of childbirth, whose pilgrimage is the center of Paulina's religious life (801–6), and its desecration is a symbolic re-enactment of the rape of Paulina herself. To the community, however, it is only an 'ymage' (1039), as Paulina herself has been reduced to a symbolic, almost invisible, occasion for concern. The casting out of the image is part of a great venting of righteous indignation against the two false priests, who, however, are put to death for abetting the folly of Mundus rather than for deceiving Paulina (1018–22, 1025–29). And the tale ends much as it had begun, couching Mundus' milder sentence of exile amid condoning reflections on the power of the love which had led him astray (1048–55).

Genius' failure to do justice to the positive qualities embodied in Paulina provides a valuable reminder of the limitation of his perspective. Although the menace earlier associated with feminine figures has vanished, and the tale advertises itself as sympathetic to love, this new genial emphasis leads to an exaggeration of the power of one kind of love at the expense of another, higher kind. No positive value is assigned to Mundus' folly, but Genius' sympathy with his passion has an effect comparable to that of his moralizing perspective on the earlier tales. In the end, it renders Paulina and her faith utterly invisible, just as the maiden Medusa with her beautiful hair is invisible in Genius' account of Perseus' conquest.

It could be argued that male misperceptions of the feminine, and the moral and psychological problems they dramatize, are the unifying element in Book I of the *Confessio*, Gower's chosen way of focusing his treatment of the sin of pride. The theme appears clearly in Albinus' crude treatment of Rosemund, or in the exemplum of the Sirens, less directly in such a tale as 'The Trump of Death,' where the problem is less a flawed perception of the feminine than a desire to view the whole of life as a courtly idyll.

The story of Florent, a version of the tale told by Chaucer's Wife of Bath, might be seen as an answer to the episode of Perseus and Medusa. Compelled to marry a loathsome old woman, and so repelled by her ugliness that he lies in his marriage bed as if petrified, 'stille as eny stone' (1794), Florent is compelled by honor to turn to his wife, and finds her, too, 'turned,' into a beautiful young 'lady.'[29] It is tempting to see in this second turning not just the reward, but in some sense the result of the first: Florent has accepted his wife, the first of Gower's male protagonists to concede a legitimate role to a female figure, and the consequence of this triumph of chivalry is the emergence of her womanhood in full flower.

But the acceptance is at this point a matter of honor prevailing over physical revulsion, and at no point can the acknowledgment which releases the young lady from her magically 'forshapen' state be clearly seen as a triumph of love or generosity. Indeed, it is possible to see the story's conclusion as replacing one kind of enchantment by another: in the lady's obscurely motivated generosity and in her promise that her beauty will remain undiminished until death (1836–40), there is a strong hint of male fantasy,[30] a recoil from the heavy emphasis earlier in the tale on the ugliness of the old woman (1674–93) and on Florent's anxiety in the face of it — an anxiety which not only renders him immobile on his wedding night, but had earlier led him to think ignobly of marooning his wife on an island where she might live out her few remaining years undiscovered (1568–80).

---

[29] The importance of 'turning' in this passage is noted by Ricks, 'Metamorphosis in Other Words' 39–42.

[30] On this problem see Lee Patterson, ' "For the Wyves Love of Bath": Feminine Rhetoric and Poetic Resolution in the *Roman de la Rose* and the *Canterbury Tales*,' *Speculum* 58 (1983) 684–93.

It is against this background of male encounters with the feminine that we must view the climactic tale of Book I, a story which in itself contains no confrontation with the feminine, but which alludes in a unique and striking way to the concerns of the earlier stories. This is Genius' account of the dream of Nebuchadnezzar, which had its realization when the king was driven from his city to live in the wild and eat grass like an ox, until he was drawn by his humiliation to acknowledge the supremacy of God, and finally restored to his kingdom. Genius' account closely follows Daniel 4, but at the end he diverges to enlarge on the king's experience of the life of a beast. Gower's Nebuchadnezzar actually *becomes* a beast, but when his allotted seven years of animal existence are over, certain very human attitudes revive: he becomes suddenly aware of his diet and environment, and above all of his physical appearance:

> In stede of man a bestes lyke
> He syh; and thanne he gan to syke
> For cloth of gold and for perrie,
> Which him was wont to magnefie.   (1.2995–98)

At first the king thinks instinctively of veiling harsh reality, denying the deeper implications of his bestiality by disguising it from himself. But then he sees through such self-delusion: incapable of human speech, he nonetheless speaks within his heart to affirm the power of God and the essential worth and equality of all humanity: 'In thin aspect ben alle liche, / The povere man and ek the riche' (3009–10).

Here, it would seem, is the victory over pride we have been waiting for. Nebuchadnezzar has witnessed his own helpless degradation and learned, like Lear, to accept the condition of all men. But Gower carries the king's testing further, and goes to remarkable lengths to stress the coexistence of beast and man in the final phase of his ordeal. The point well made in the description of his initial recovery of self-awareness is made again still more vividly in the prayer which follows his vow of humility:

> . . . thogh him lacke vois and speche,
> He gan up with his feet areche,
> And wailende in his bestly stevene
> He made his pleignte unto the hevene.
> He kneleth in his wise and braieth,
> To seche merci and assaieth
> His god, which made him nothing strange,
> Whan that he sih his pride change.   (1.3023–30)

The contrast between outer and inner condition is focused by the punning use of 'braieth,' a bestial sound conveying deep human feeling, which confirms by a spontaneous impulse of the spirit the rational acceptance of God's power already conveyed by the speech of the king's heart. The pun perfectly expresses both Nebuchadnezzar's humble acceptance of his state and the reverence that informs his appeal for readmission to the human community.[31] The very beast in Nebuchadnezzar, once disciplined by humility, reinforces the sincerity of his prayer. An instant later the humanity disguised by the animal form and sound emerges, and he recovers both human form and kingship, the outward manifestations of a dignity already expressed in humility and love for God.

But while Nebuchadnezzar's self-discovery illustrates a kind of vision that has been lacking in earlier tales, Gower's treatment of the final stages of his experience hints at other, unresolved elements in the larger argument of Book I. The king's braying prayer and a number of details of his experience as a beast are imitated from Ovid's story of the nymph Io, whom Jove first raped and then, fearful that Juno would discover his amour, transformed into a heifer. Driven wild by Juno, she wanders through the world and comes at last to the Nile, where, kneeling like Nebuchadnezzar, she directs a 'sorrowful mooing' (*luctisono mugitu*) to Jove for an end to her troubles (*Met.* 1.729–33). Like Nebuchadnezzar, too, Io prays with her face toward the sky, the posture which affirms the special dignity of mankind among earthly creatures,[32] and both are answered with the restoration of human form.

Here the resemblance ends: while Nebuchadnezzar's prayer restores stability to his life, Io is still subject to divine whim, and resumes human form only to be elevated abruptly to the status of a goddess and worshipped as Isis (738–50). Her experience echoes that of Medusa, transformed in punishment for having unwittingly aroused the lust of a god. Like Paulina, who is first degraded and then made the symbol of a cause, it is Io's fate to remain estranged from common human experience even after her transformation is undone. Her personal wrong, like theirs, is forgotten in the course of her story, and her final metamorphosis into the goddess Isis is as arbitrary as the fate of the statue of that same goddess which Paulina's well-meaning fellow citizens cast into the Tiber.

Superimposing the experience of Nebuchadnezzar on that of Io does more than call attention one last time to the contingent status of women in Book I. It reminds us that the monstrous or bestial qualities associated with the female figures of the earlier stories are really reflections of the inability of men, and

---

[31] See Ricks, 'Metamorphosis in Other Words' 31–32. Nicholson, 'Gower's Revisions' 129–30, suggests that the 'braieth' reading is probably due to scribal error, though the allusion to Ovid's Io suggested below would seem to me to provide indirect support for taking it as a deliberate revision.

[32] See *Met.* 1.84–86, 731; cf. *Conf.* 1.3001, 3024–26, and the account of newly created man in *Vox Clamantis* 7.555–56.

of humanity generally, to deal objectively with their unstable desires. It is prideful self-deception that projects our vulnerability to error onto those more vulnerable still, or disguises it by idealizing the objects of our confused impulses. Paulina, deceived by Mundus, had felt herself 'non other than a beste'; in Gower's dramatization of the experience of Nebuchadnezzar, that beast discovers its true home.

In the tale of the Three Questions which concludes Book I, a woman is granted an unambiguously positive role, and the moral of the tale depends on her successfully overcoming male pride. A young king, proud of his wisdom and envious of the ease with which one of his knights answers his hardest questions, challenges the knight on penalty of death to solve three riddles: what thing in the world has least need of help, though men help it the most? What thing is worth most and costs least? What costs most and is worth least? Confounded and anxious, the knight is comforted by his daughter, who gains his permission to answer on his behalf. Her answers not only liberate her father, but so impress the king with her wisdom that he expresses the wish that her social station allowed them to marry. The daughter persuades the king to make her father an earl and then points out to him that she is now an earl's daughter. The king, already in love with her, claims her in marriage. Genius ends by noting that the tale is historical and names the three principals, King Alphonso of Spain, the knight Don Pedro, and his daughter Petronilla.

The tale is introduced by three Latin couplets on humility, the remedy of pride, which raise the argument of Book I to a new level:

> Est virtus humilis, per quam deus altus ad yma
> Se tulit et nostre viscera carnis habet.   (1.12.1–2)
> [It was through the virtue of humility that the high God descended to this low estate, and assumed our fleshly body.]

This description of the Incarnation both recalls the humiliation and regeneration of Nebuchadnezzar, and anticipates the special character of the tale to come, in which the antidote to pride is expounded and illustrated with a straightforwardness virtually unique in the *Confessio*.

The three questions recapitulate fundamental issues of Book I. The answer to the first is the earth (*humus*, the basis of *humilitas*), which flourishes with no help from the great labor men expend on it. What costs least and is worth most is humility itself, embodied in Mary, who became the dwelling place of God in his humble human form. The antithesis of fulfilling humility, the most costly and worthless of things, is pride, which cannot accept its condition and must continually assert itself in wasteful and destructive ways. In reflecting on the earth's self-renewing properties, the knight's daughter reveals the truth that Nebuchadnezzar had learned with difficulty, the common existence of man, bird, and beast, earthly things which earth will reclaim again (3260–65). This insight is the first stage in the assimilation of humility, and the honoring of Mary as the embodiment of this quality acknowledges virtues which the treatment of women in earlier tales had tended to ignore or suppress.[33]

But here as always in the *Confessio*, moralization is a foil to the concrete embodiment of Gower's message. The real confirmation of the daughter's wisdom is her ensuing dialogue with the young king, which abandons all reference to the preceding discourse in favor of practical considerations.[34] The king is made 'inly glad' by the maiden's answers (3324–25), and immediately begins to exhibit a new largesse, but he also finds 'grace' in her appearance. His wish that they could marry is born of the twofold appeal 'of thin ansuere and ek of thee' (3332), and his acts of royal largesse are performed in the 'freisshe hete' of love (3353). She on her part is perpetually kneeling, a very icon of humility, yet there is nothing passive or unworldly in the wit with which she intervenes for her father, induces the young king to exercise 'noble grace,' and then, kneeling all the while, negotiates her father's pardon and ennoblement and finally her own marriage. Nothing could be more open or less morally doctrinaire than the terms on which the story's human relations are resolved, and we may ask what connection exists between the two parts of the tale.

A possible answer is that here for the first time a higher kind of allegory has entered the *Confessio*. The maiden, 'full of grace' (3397), is in a sense humility itself, in the light of which the answers to the king's three questions become efficacious, releasing in him a capacity for charity and enabling him to claim humility as his own. His perception is limited: at first he can accept the maiden's authority only in a rational way (3322), and the humbleness of her social position is an obstacle to his accepting her. But when he is inspired by love of her to exercise royal generosity, and bestow freely what has been bestowed on him by grace of his God-given role,[35] she is his reward.

But if the structure of this episode adumbrates a true, spiritual conquest of pride by humility, it is only an imperfect embodiment of such a triumph: as Genius' concluding historical footnote reminds us, the principals are not ideal types, but human beings. The king's submission is prompted by a very human love, and the maiden's appeal to his 'noble grace' on her father's behalf may

---

[33] See Gallacher, *Love, the Word, and Mercury* 37–40.

[34] That the final episode is a new departure is suggested also by the Latin gloss, which carries the story only as far as the daughter's answers to the three questions.

[35] Gower points to this aspect of the king's role in noting that the earldom he bestows on the knight had lately 'fallen' into his hands through escheat (3354–55), whereby property reverts to a feudal overlord in the absence of a legitimate heir.

flatter his pride rather than humble it. Perhaps the best that can be said about the episode as a resolution to the problems of Book I is that in it we can see male pride and passion being manipulated to 'genial' ends, brought into the service of an instinctive responsiveness to the beauty of virtue. The story and its explicit *moralitas* are still imperfectly united, as in the earlier tales, but here at last they are in sympathy.[36]

Cornell University

----

[36] I would like to thank Tom Stillinger and Sylvia Huot for their generous and helpful comments on an earlier version of this essay.

KONRAD GESNER AND NEOPLATONIC POETICS

By WESLEY TRIMPI*

In 1542, Konrad Gesner published an abbreviated Latin translation of the sixth 'Dissertation' of Proclus' commentary on Plato's *Republic*. Because of its rarity, of the entirely different interests most commonly associated with its author, and of its generally unrecognized importance for literary criticism after the Renaissance, the book is something of a curiosity. After briefly describing Proclus' commentary and Gesner's epitome of it, I shall transcribe three chapters of his translation which offer important distinctions as an example of how he renders Greek literary terms in Latin and tightens, at least in these passages, the rather serpentine presentation of Proclus' exegesis.

In his commentary on the *Republic*, which contains the most detailed defense of poetry in late antiquity, Proclus tries to reconcile Plato's apparent admiration for Homer, as revealed in frequent citations, with his ultimate banishment of the poet from the polis. Proclus resolves this contradiction by attributing to Homer an allegorical intention and practice in accordance with philosophical presuppositions about reality derived from Plotinus and other Neoplatonists. He adds to the logical exposition of ontological realities, already latent in the Plotinian correspondences of force and magnitude, a precision akin to that of geometrical demonstration expressed in his own *Commentary on the First Book of Euclid's* ELEMENTS and *Elements of Theology*. Since he discusses the subjects and methods both of geometry and of poetry in terms analogous to those in Plato's metaphor of the Divided Line, his treatment of the imagination in his commentary on Euclid offers a formal paradigm for his treatment of mimetic and symbolic representation in his *Commentary on the* REPUBLIC. Indeed, the logic of geometry could offer a paradigm against which to measure the coherence of *all* discursive disciplines, even of an art like poetry whose subject matter is human experience rather than mathematical relationship. Once all discursive reasoning, that is to say, has taken to geometrical reasoning as its model, all other forms of cognitive and judicative, to

---

* Like many other students of literature, I have become increasingly indebted to Professor Kaske over the years for many things, and for none perhaps so much as for his dedication and generosity as an editor of *Traditio*. The first and third parts of *Muses of One Mind* (Princeton 1983) are revised versions of articles appearing there in 1971 and 1974 respectively, and had it not been time for me to bring all these materials together in a book, I should in all likelihood have submitted the second part to him as well. It is perhaps appropriate, therefore, that the following observations have grown out of my concern in Part Two with the Neoplatonic transmission of ancient literary theory.

say nothing of poetic, argumentation must either accommodate themselves to that of mathematics or justify their proceeding on other than discursive principles. When seeking a model for coherent structure in mathematical propositions, literary intentions tend to become increasingly 'formalistic,' and one way in which this formalism expresses itself is in the Neoplatonic preference of symbolic over mimetic procedures of representation.[1]

As the Neoplatonists describe their knowledge of both ontological and psychological realities in terms of logical proportions of unity to extension, so Proclus discusses both poetry and geometry in terms of levels of cognition whose objects are related to one another as powers to magnitudes in accordance with the Platonic metaphor of the Divided Line (*Rep.* 509D–511E). Here Plato represents the degree of intelligibility among apprehensible entities by gradations on a perpendicular line. He divides this scale by a horizontal line which separates intelligible entities (νοητόν) above the line from visible entities (ὁρατόν) below it. He then subdivides each of these divisions into two. The resulting four categories correspond to a hierarchy of entities, based upon the degree of clarity and certainty with which they can be known. This scale begins with the lower subdivision of the visible objects and rises to the higher subdivision of intelligible objects. The lowest category is composed of images (εἰκόνες), the objects of conjecture (εἰκασία), such as shadows (σκιάς) and reflections (φαντάσματα) on water and 'on surfaces of dense, smooth, and bright texture.' The second consists of actual objects, animate and inanimate, which have the power to cast such reflections and which form the material of belief (πίστις) or opinion (δόξα). These two categories include all visible entities. The third and fourth categories contain intelligible entities. The third has the same relation to the second as the second to the first; that is, it casts as its images those objects of the second category which, in turn, cast their images to form the objects of the lowest category. The third category, which includes the objects of mathematics and deductive reasoning, is under the control of the understanding (διάνοια). The fourth category consists of first principles, the objects of reason (νοῦς), which, independent of the sensory images still necessary for dianoetic demonstration, work dialectically with

---

[1] For a more detailed discussion of the Neoplatonic contribution to formalism and symbolic representation as summarized briefly in this and the following paragraphs, see my *Muses of One Mind* (Princeton 1983) Chap. 8, esp. 200–19 on Proclus' commentaries. I have used here, as there, *Proclus Diadochus in Platonis* REM PUBLICAM *commentarii*, ed. G. Kroll, 2 vols. (Leipzig 1899), and my English versions of the Greek text are adapted from *Proclus: Commentaire sur la République*, trans. A. J. Festugière, 3 vols. (Paris 1970). For an investigation of Proclus' sources and intentions, see A. D. R. Sheppard, *Studies on the 5th and 6th Essays of Proclus' Commentary on the* REPUBLIC (*Hypomnemata* 61 [Göttingen 1980]) and my comments in *Muses* 202n36.

ideas alone. The four faculties 'participate in clearness (σαφηνείας) and precision in the same degree as their objects partake of truth (ἀληθείας) and reality' (511ε). Plato's metaphor offers a paradigmatic structure for the 'kinds' of poetry distinguished in the passages quoted below from Gesner's epitome as well as for Proclus' commentary itself.[2]

Gesner's small volume contains three translations whose titles are followed on the title page by *Interprete Conrado Gesnero Medico, Tigurino. Omnia nunc primum nata, & excusa Tiguri apud Froschouerum* [1542]. The first title is MORALIS INTERPRETATIO *Errorum Vlyssis Homerici*; the second is COMMENTATIO PORPHYRII *Philosophi de Nympharum antro in XIII. libro Odysseae Homericae, multiplici cognitione rerum uariarum instructissima*; and the third, that of our epitome, is EX COMMENTARIIS PROCLI *Lycij, Philosophi Platonici in libros Platonis de Repub. apologiae quaedam pro Homero, & fabularum aliquot enarrationes*. Where the epitome occurs later in the text itself, it bears the title LVCVBRATIO PROCLI LYCII DIADOCHI *De dictis aduersus Homerum & Poëticen in Republica Platonis*.[3]

The reasons for Gesner's original interest in Proclus' commentary and indeed the subsequent history of his translation remain somewhat obscure. While his famous biological compendia suggest very different interests, his *Bibliotheca vniversalis, siue Catalogus* (Zürich 1545) lists the epitome in his account

---

[2] *Republic*, trans. P. Shorey in *The Collected Dialogues of Plato*, edd. E. Hamilton and H. Cairns (New York 1963). Proclus is explicit about associating his four kinds of poetry with the four categories of the Divided Line: 'It is in this way, then, that Plato has thought good also to divide up the kinds of poetry (γένη τῆς ποιητικῆς): one as being superior to scientific knowledge (ἐπιστήμης), the second as having such knowledge, the third as having responsible opinion (ὀρθοδοξαστικόν), and the fourth as being inferior to responsible opinion' (1.191.26–29). Cf. *Muses* 202n36.

[3] Though there are two copies in the British Library, whose call numbers are 1067.h.4.(2.) and 1067.h.8.(1.), the book is quite rare. For Renaissance accounts of Gesner's life and publications, see his own autobiographical entry (under Conradus) in his *Bibliotheca universalis, siue Catalogus* (Zürich 1545) and his supplement to this volume in his *Appendix bibliothecae Conradi Gesneri* (Zürich 1555). Josias Simler, drawing on both these works, gives an abbreviated account of Gesner's life in his *Epitome bibliothecae Conradi Gesneri* (Zürich 1555). A facsimile reproduction of all three of these works has been published in 2 volumes (Osnabrück 1966). Simler subsequently brought out an enlarged version of the *Catalogus* in 1574 and a third, still larger, edition of it in 1583, entitled *Bibliotheca instituta et collecta primum a Conrado Gesnero: Deinde in Epitomen redacta, & novorum librorum accessione locupletata, tertiò recognita, & in duplum post priores editiones aucta, per Iosiam Simlerum*, which contains the fullest article on Gesner himself (161–68). For modern bibliographical studies, see Hans Fischer, 'Conrad Gessner (1516–1565) as Bibliographer and Encyclopedist,' *The Library*, Dec. 1966, 269–81 [= Bibliog. Soc. (London) Trans. 5th ser., 21.4]; the 'Nachwort' by Hans Widmann which concludes the Osnabrück facsimile of 1966 mentioned above; and a volume of essays commemorating Gesner's 450th anniversary, *Conrad Gessner, 1516–1565: Universalgelehrter, Naturforscher, Arzt* (Zürich 1967).

of his own life,[4] and in Volume II, *Pandectarum siue Partitionum universalium
. . . libri XXI* (Zürich 1548), of the complete *Bibliotheca vniversalis* (1545–55),
he cites Proclus' commentary several times with very specific reference to his
own translation.[5] Other publications listed in the *Catalogus* indicate as well his
interest in Neoplatonic views of poetry: *Heraclidis Pontici de allegorijs Homeri
liber, Porphyrij philosophi quaestiones Homericae,* and *Marini Neapolitani liber
de Procli Vita et felicitate.* The *Vita,* which he says in the *Catalogus* (under
Marinus) *Graecè & Latinè editus est Tiguri apud Gesneros fratres,* was published
with his Greek edition of Marcus Aurelius in 1558. To his own Latin translation of *Procli philosophi Platonici Vita scriptore Marino Neapolitano,* dedicated to Richard Bentley in 1703, J. A. Fabricius appends a useful essay, *De
Procli scriptis editis.* In it, as an extended title of Proclus' commentary on
Plato's *Republic,* Fabricius gives the slightly modified version of Gesner's
description (quoted in *n*4) which appears in Simler's *Bibliotheca instituta* of
1583. Drawing frequently on the information in Fabricius' essay, Thomas
Taylor later translated a number of Proclus' works into English, including the
commentary on Euclid's *Elements* and sections of that on Plato's *Republic* —
for which he explicitly says he consulted Gesner's epitome.[6]

The distinctions between 'kinds,' as opposed to 'genres,' of poetry contained in Chapters 22–24 transcribed below might best be introduced by il-

---

[4] He describes the contents of the volume as follows: 'Moralis interpretatio errorum Vlyssis
Homerici, authoris incerti. Commentatio Porphyrij philosophi de nympharum antro in
decimotertio libro Odysseae Homericae, multiplici cognitione rerum uariarum instructissima.
Apologiae quaedam pro Homero & arte poëtica fabularumque aliquot enarrationes ex com-
mentarijs Procli Lycij Diadochi Philosophi Platonici in libros Platonis de republica: in
quibus plurimae de dijs fabulae, non iuxta grammaticorum uulgus historice, physice, aut
ethice tractantur: sed theologicis aut metaphysicis rationibus explanantur. Omnia nunc
primum à Graeco sermone conversa & impressa Tiguri 1542. in 8. chartis 12. In Procli
Apologijs libere uertimus aliâs epitomen aliâs paraphrasin usurpantes, uitio Graeci exemplaris
admodum corrupti, sensum tamen ubique saluum reddidimus.'

[5] The *Catalogus* of 1545, whose individual history is described in *n*3, became the first of
three [four counting the *Appendix*] volumes making up the complete *Bibliotheca universalis.*
In the second (1548) and third (1549) volumes, called *Pandectae,* Gesner broke down the
works and their authors (listed in Volume I) under topics which could then serve as an extended index of subject matters.

[6] *Thomas Taylor the Platonist,* edd. K. Raine and G. M. Harper (Princeton 1969) 449
(in the index to this volume references to Konrad Gesner are absorbed under the name of
Johann Matthias Gesner). A single instance may suffice here to suggest the importance of
Proclus' commentaries for literary criticism in the eighteenth and nineteenth centuries.
On the basis of the marginalia in his copy of Taylor's translation of Proclus' commentary on
Euclid (1792), it is arguable, I think, that Coleridge drew much of the terminology for his
famous distinction between the primary and secondary imagination from Taylor's version of
Proclus.

lustrating their function in the Neoplatonic 'program' for poetry. In a characteristic passage Proclus describes how poets are to 'explicate' (literally 'unfold') divine truths into mythological narratives:

> Indeed, as the fathers of mythology have seen that nature, which produces images of immaterial and intelligible forms and which decorates this visible world with varied imitations of these forms, represents the indivisible by what is divided, the eternal by what is in temporal process, the intelligible by the sensible, the immaterial in a material way, the unextended with spatial extension, and existence firm in repose by constant change — these fathers, following nature and the procession of being in their appearance under visible and figurative guise, imitate the surpassing quality of the models by rendering the creations of the divine by means of expressions as antithetical as possible to the divine. Those who go the furthest in this direction reveal by those things which [in us] are contrary to nature the very things which, in the gods, are superior to nature, by failures of rational calculation what is more divine than reason itself, and by objects which appear ugly to us what transcends in its simple wholeness the beauty of any individual part. In this way, these fathers are likely to put us in mind again of the surpassing eminence of the gods.[7]

The unfolding of divine truths in a sensible form which is most remote from, and antithetical to, their significance requires symbolic, as opposed to mimetic, forms of representation. Each god remains one and the same in his simplicity without attempting to deceive anyone, but he appears in various forms to his human worshipers who must ascertain the divine properties according to their own limited capacities. While he remains uniform, human beings 'participate' in his nature according either to their intellect ($\nu o \tilde{\nu} \varsigma$), which grasps things directly in their totality, or to their rational soul ($\psi v \chi \grave{\eta}$ $\nu o \varepsilon \varrho \acute{a}$), which arrives at things discursively, or to their imagination ($\varphi a \nu \tau a \sigma \acute{\iota} a$), which knows things figuratively, or to their sensation ($a \mathring{\iota} \sigma \theta \eta \sigma \iota \varsigma$), which knows things only as

---

[7] My translation, also used in *Muses* 217, is adapted from Festugière's French translation of 1.77.13–30 in Kroll's edition. The following is Gesner's corresponding summary with some Greek words introduced from Kroll: 'Certe ipsa natura fabricans imagines intelligibilium, & sine omni materia idearum, multis uarijsque modis hoc propositum assequitur. Per partes enim imitatur impertia, aeterna temporaneis, intelligibilia sensilibus, simplicia mixtis, quantitatis expertia dimensionibus, stabilia mutationibus, quantum eius fieri potest, & apparentium rerum aptitudo permittit, exprimere conatur. Hoc animaduerso fabularum authores ipsi quoque simulachra & imagines diuinorum carminibus fingentes, eximiam uim exemplarium contrarijs ($\mathring{\varepsilon} \nu a \nu \tau \iota \acute{\omega} \tau a \tau o \iota \varsigma$) & remotissimis ($\mathring{a} \varphi \varepsilon \sigma \tau \eta \varkappa \acute{o} \sigma \iota \nu$) adumbrationibus imitantur, nempe rebus praeter naturam ($\pi a \varrho \grave{a}$ $\varphi \acute{v} \sigma \iota \nu$), deorum naturae praestantiam ($\tau \grave{o}$ $\mathring{v} \pi \grave{\varepsilon} \varrho$ $\varphi \acute{v} \sigma \iota \nu$): irrationalibus ($\pi a \varrho a \lambda \acute{o} \gamma o \iota \varsigma$), uim omni ratione diuiniorem; turpibus, ut apparent, pulchritudinem omnia corporea superantem utcunque referunt, ac ita diuinitatis excellentiam omnia quae dici fingique possunt longissimum excedentem ob oculos ponunt' (36^{r-v}).

impressions. Thus the divine nature is uniform in itself but multiform with respect to our varying methods of cognition.[8]

To accommodate such a broad range of human perspectives and faculties, identifiable with the four levels of intelligibility on Plato's Divided Line, Proclus develops a hierarchy of four different 'kinds' (γένη) of poetry. This hierarchy is based on the types of experience the poet wishes to represent and, therefore, reflects indirectly poetic genres and styles. Mimetic representation, most congenial to reporting and shaping the world of the senses, and a style most sensitive to recording and manipulating sensory impressions are confined to experiences associated with the two epistemological categories below the line. As one ascends above the line, the experience to be treated becomes less and less amenable to mimetic representation and an impressionistic style and more and more appropriate to symbolism and stylistic simplicity. Proclus argues that Plato rejected only those subjects, and the genres conventionally associated with them, most committed to mimetic kinds of representation and that most of Homer's subjects, when properly interpreted, were the materials appropriate for the noetic and dianoetic faculties.

I have chosen Chapters 22–24 of Gesner's epitome to transcribe as exemplary of his method for several reasons. First, in defining the kinds of poetry mentioned above and identifying the poets associated with each, they make distinctions which are important for the history of literary criticism. Second, they contain Latin renderings of important Greek critical terms (given in parenthesis) and show some inevitable flattening of connotation which accompanies translation. Third, these chapters may be taken as a unit, to some degree, and show one of Gesner's happier consolidations of Proclus' exegesis.[9] I

---

[8] This paraphrases Festugière's rendering of Kroll 1.111.16–27. Gesner's corresponding summary is as follows: 'Simplex (τὸ ἁπλοῦν) enim deorum essentia uidentibus apparet uaria (ποικίλον), cum dij tamen neque mutentur, neque fallere uelint: sed ipsa natura pro modo diuersitateque participantium proprietates deorum determinat. Nam etsi unum sit quod participatur, aliter tamen atque aliter diuersa suscipientia participant. Mens enim indiuisibiliter (ἀμερίστως), intelligibilis anima colligendo & ratiocinando (ἀνειλιγμένως), phantasia imaginando (μορφωτικῶς), sensus patiendo (παθητικῶς) participant. Itaque participatum substantia quidem est uniformi, & immutabile per se constansque: multiforme autem participatione uidetur, & diuersas imaginationes mouet propter imbecillitatem iudicij participantium' (54ᵛ).

[9] In Book IV, entitled *De poetica*, of Volume II of his completed *Bibliotheca universalis*, Gesner specifically refers to his translation of Proclus' account of these 'kinds' of poetry: 'Quod tria sint genera poeticae, & primum de diuino, Proclus in rempub. Platonis ex nostra translatione, cap. 22. De secundo, quod rationale nominamus, cap. 23. De tertio quod imitatorium uocatur, ac in coniecturale et phantasticum subdiuidit, cap. 24.' Among the various categorizations of poetry by 'kinds' in the Renaissance, Sir Philip Sidney's division, long associated by editors with that of J. C. Scaliger (*Poetics* 1.2), is noteworthy in that it clearly reveals his Aristotelian, as opposed to Neoplatonic, presuppositions in setting both noetic and dianoetic categories of subject matter aside in favor of those appropriate for mimetic representation (*An Apology for Poetry*, ed. G. Sheppard [London 1967] 101–3).

have indicated in additional parentheses (*a*) certain transliterated Greek words and (*b*) the page and the approximate line numbers, in Volume I of Kroll's edition, of the Greek passages which Gesner is translating at each point — pages and line numbers which Festugière also records in the margins of his French translation. I have given both Gesner's pagination and passages in Plato to which Proclus specifically refers in brackets, while double parentheses indicate transitional passages which Gesner has added to Proclus.

Stanford University

[88ʳ]   CAPVT XXII

Quod tria sint genera poëticae, & primum de diuino.

Posthac dispiciamus, quae & quot genera poëtices iuxta Platonem sint, & quodnam ex illis respiciens in lib. 10. Reipub. Socrates poëticen accusauerit (177.4–12). Primum igitur secundum tres animae diuersas facultates mentem, rationem & opinionem, tres quoque poëticae formas esse dicimus (178.7–11). ((Itaque singulas seorsim explanabimus, Platonis quoque sententiam afferentes, & apud Homerum exempla uniuscuiusque ostendentes.

Prima poëticae differentia menti similis est.)) Est autem mens animae uis optima, perfectissima, diuinissima, diuinae uitae simillima, eius contemplationi dedita, deorum iuris est, non sui, ex illorum lumine suum accendit, supernaturali unitati simplicissimam suam essentiam coniungit (177.17–23). Sic & praestantissimum poëticae genus, animam diuinitate beat, inter deos collocat, ineffabili unione (ἕνωσιν ἄρρητον) participato participans, & replenti repletum coniungit, ab omni materia abstrahit, coelesti lumine illustrat, diuino igne inflammat, ac totam inferiorem animae constitutionem soli menti unice parere cogit. Hic sanè furor (μανία) quauis temperantia melior est, symmetria & proportione diuinitatis animum instruit, adeo ut erumpentia quoque uerba, qui effectus eius ultimi sunt, mensuris et numeris ornata uideantur. Vt enim uatum furor ex ueritate, amatorum ex pulchritudine, sic poëtarum [88ᵛ] ex diuina symmetria (συμμετρίαν θείαν) nascitur, qua dijs penitissime coniunguntur (178.12–179.1). De hac Plato in Phaedro scribit [245A], 'quod Musarum occupatio sit & furor teneris intactisque animis superne immissus. Opus eius esse dicit suscitare & afflare secundum odas & reliquam poësim: finem uero, ut infinita antiquorum gesta celebrans, posteros instruat.' Ex his uerbis dilucidum fit, primum quidem Platonem huic generi poëtices diuinitatem ascribere, ut quod à Musis deducat, quae cuncta mundi tum intelligibilia tum sensibilia opera harmonia paterna complent, & concinno motu: Et occupationem appellare, quia totus animus illustratus, illustrantis diuinitatis praesenti effectui se permittit: furorem uero, quia proprium ingenium relinquit, & pro numinis impulsu fertur. Deinde uero animae occupandae habitum describere (180.11–

181.2). Teneram enim inquit esse oportere, & intactam, non rigidam, duram, nec alijs multis uarijsque (ποικίλων) & alienis à numine (ἀλλοτρίων τοῦ θείου) opinionibus plenam. Nam mollis & tenera debet esse, ut diuinam inspirationem facile admittat: intacta autem, ut ab alijs omnibus uacua synceraque sit. Tertio addit commune opus, quod perficitur Musis quidem afflantibus, anima uero ad recipiendum disposita. Porrò suscitatio animae est erectio, & minime deprauata operatio, & à lapsu in generationem conuersa ad deum excitatio. Afflatus, motus est diuinus, & chorea indefessa ad deum (181.3–30). Postremo res humanas [89ʳ] diuino ore prolatas, perfectiores, illustriores, & ad ueram doctrinam auditoribus commodiores fieri testatur. Non quod adolescentibus docendis conueniat haec poësis: sed iam perfectis in politica disciplina, & mysticam de diuinis rebus traditionem desiderantibus omnium est commodissima ad docendum, si modo recondita ueritas enucleetur. Quare merito ipsam Plato omnibus humanis artibus praefert. 'Qui autem' (ut ibidem scribit) 'absque furore Musarum poëticas ad fores accedit, confidens arte quadam poëtam se bonum euasurum, inanis erit & ipse & eius poësis, prae illa quae ex furore procedit, qua quidem haec quae ex prudentia fit euanescit' [245ᴀ]. Hactenus ex Phaedro (182.1–20).

His non dissimilia in Ione Socrates edisserit [533ᴅ]. Cum enim Rhapsodus dixisset abundare se dicendi copia de Homero, de reliquis autem poëtis non item: Socrates causam rei subijcit dicens ita fieri, quoniam non ex arte id faciat, sed ui diuina moueatur: alioquin enim in omnibus similibus idem, quod in Homero praestiturum, nisi diuino instinctu peculiariter ad Homerum inclinaret. Deum autem siue Musam, id est diuinam causam primum inquit esse mouens, inde poëtam concitari, ab eo rursus rhapsodos: Sic ut poëtarum furor medius sit inter diuinum principium, & rhapsodos, movens simul & motus, & superne accepta inferioribus distribuens latente quodam consensu, per quem isti gradus [89ᵛ] non secus inter se cohaerent, quàm multi annuli ferrei à magnete pendentes, qui proximum annulum attrahens suam ei uim illicem ferri communicat, ille sequenti quoque, ac ita deinceps. Sic in poëtica diuinum esse quiddam oportet quod ultima primae monadi per media connectat. Hoc ut Homerus, sic & Plato nunc in plurali numero Musas uocant, nunc in singulari Musam, aliâs ad multitudinem catenae Musarum habito respectu, aliâs uero ad cohaerentem omnium unionem, quae à prima causa inferioribus inseritur. Est enim poëtica arcano quodam & uniformi modo (μονειδῶς) in primo mouente, deinde in poëtis ab illa unitate concitis reuolutim,¹⁰ ut ita loquar: in rhap-

---

¹⁰ To *reuolutim* Gesner appends a marginal gloss: '*ἀνειλιγμένως*, id est, sicut ex glomere fila reuoluuntur.' The Greek adverb, meaning 'explicitly' (= in an 'explicated' or 'unfolded' manner), is formed from the perfect passive participle of *ἀνελίσσειν*: to unroll (a book); to interpret, unravel, or explicate; to roll back, counteract, or reverse direction. In the Latin passage quoted in *n*8, Gesner renders the adverb *colligendo & ratiocinando* which describes the

sodis uero secundum infimum & subministrantem gradum (182.25–184.7). ((Haec ex Ione allegasse satis sit in praesentia, qui desiderat alia multa ibidem inueniet primum hoc & diuinum poëtarum genus comprobantia.))

Adijciamus Atheniensis hospitis & Timaei testimonia [40D]. 'Hic enim sequi hortatur Apollineo furore captos poëtas, utpote deorum filios, & res progenitorum suorum optime scientes, etsi sine argumentis & demonstrationibus pronuncient.' Ille uero lib. tertio Legum sic scribit [682A]: 'Poëtarum genus diuinum est, dijs agitur, hymnosque sacros concinit, & cum Gratijs Musisque ueritatem passim contingit' (185.8–15). Ad haec in Alcibiade primo: 'Natura,' inquit, 'aenigmatica poësis est, & non cuiusuis [90ʳ] intellectui patet' [Second Alcib. 147B]. Sed iam satis superque clarum esse uidetur quid de Homero senserit Plato, & quod praestantissimam hanc & diuinam poëticae formam planè calculo suo comprobauerit, qua potitos etiam uenerari cum silentio iubet [Rep. 378A]. Quod autem adolescentibus non conueniat [Rep. 378D] (186.12–19), ((non amplius repetendum est, ne quis brassicam bis coctam nobis obijciat.))

Porrò apud Homerum omnia quidem poëticae genera inuenias, sed imaginationis ac imitationis minus habet, excellit autem in primo (192.7–9), ((quo de nunc agimus:)) ut cum Musis & furore plenus, mysticos diuinitatis sensus proponit, quales sunt de unitate opifice, triplici uniuersitatis diuisione, Vulcani uinculis, & Iouis cum Iunone concubitu. Quin & ipse de Demodoco (sub cuius persona seipsum innuere uoluit, quare caecum etiam fuisse tradit) dicit, cantorem fuisse diuinum, Musis amatum, & Apollini Musarum duci [Od. 8.64, 488–90] (193.11–24).

CAPVT XXIII

De secundo genere poëtices, quod rationale nominamus.

((Hactenus de diuina & furibunda poësi actum. Nunc transeamus ad alterum genus, quod illam animae facultatem imitatur, quam Graeci διάνοιαν uocant, nos si libet rationem uertamus.)) Est igitur ratio dignitate & potentia mente inferior, mentem tamen actionum suarum ducem sequitur, ac inter ipsam opinionemque [90ᵛ] media est: & ut anima per mentem dijs coniungitur, sic ratione in seipsam conuertitur: haec multitudinem argumentorum reuoluit, uarias formarum differentias considerat, intelligens & intellectum in unum

---

activity of διάνοια, the faculty appropriate to the second kind of poetry and to mathematical reasoning (cf. Proclus' commentary on Euclid). The metaphor of thread unwound from a ball or spool suggests not only the Neoplatonic dissipation of the unified idea in discursively extended syntax but the ancient comparison of all artistic discourse with weaving and hence with becoming a *textum* or 'text.'

colligit, ac intelligibilem essentiam imitatur. Cum autem opus rationis prudentia sit, secundum poëticae genus ei attribuimus, quod medium est inter supra
dictum, & tertium proxime dicendum. Cognoscit autem haec rationalis poësis
essentias rerum, circa honesta & bona tum uerba tum facta libenter uersatur,
ea contemplatur, singula concinnis numeris & rythmis effert, sententias mora-
les, optima consilia, intelligibilem moderationem, omnem denique uirtutem
proponit, animae circuitus, immortalitatem, & uarias facultates explicat (179.3–
15): haec multa nomina incorporeae naturae mortalibus patefecit, multa quoque corporeae substantiae probabilia dogmata produxit. Huiusmodi poësis
est Theognidis, ut Atheniensis hospes testatur [*Laws* 629ε], quae cum omnem
uirtutem doceat & commendet, iure praefertur poësi Tyrtaei, quae ad solam
fortitudinem hortatur (186.25–187.7). Item in Alcibiade secundo de recta &
tutissima ad deum oratione loquens, testimonium eius ab hoc genere poëtices
nempe scientia prudentiaque claro deducit, his uerbis [142ε]: 'Quare prudens
mihi uidetur poëta ille, qui amicis insipientibus usus, cum eos uideret & agentes
& orantes, quae ipsis minime conducebant, [91ʳ] cum tamen eis utilia uideren-
tur, communem pro omnibus orationem instituit in his uersibus:

> Summe deus largire bonum poscentibus, & non,
> Sed mala quamuis te quis roget ipsa, neges.'

Hic Socrates poëtam prudentem (ποιητὴν φρόνιμον) appellans apparet hoc
genus poësis constituere, non enim furibunde (ἐνθουσιασμόν) haec prolata
sunt, nec ad imitationem expressa, quare diuersum genus esse relinquitur,
quod iudicio & ratione pollet (187.24–188.14). Hanc autem repraesentat Homerus, cum animae uitam, diuersas animae partium substantias, simulachri
differentiam ab usurpante anima, differentias in natura, elementorum uniuersi
ordinem, ciuilia officia, & huiusmodi describit (193.5–9). Quinetiam ipsemet
Homerus Phemium Musicum in hoc genere peritum fecisse uidetur [*Od.* 1.137–
38], ubi Penelope ipsum dicit

> Oblectamina plurima nosse,
> Facta hominumque deûmque   (194.13–18).

CAPVT XXIIII

De tertio genere poëtices, quod imitatorium uocatur,
ac in coniecturale (εἰκαστικόν) & phantasticum (φανταστικόν) subdiuiditur.

((Post duo superiora genera poëtices, primum, inquam, furibundum, alterum rationale, superest ut de imitatorio loquamur. Hoc igitur postremum
genus longe discedit ab aliorum praestantia:)) imaginationibus (φαντασίαις)
[91ᵛ] enim, opinionibus (δόξαις) & sensibus irrationalibus utitur, unde multum
uitij contrahit, praecipue altera eius pars, quae phantastica dicitur. Modicas
enim affectiones ualde extollit, audientes perturbat, unà cum uocabulis uarijs-

que harmonijs & numeris animorum affectus immutat: rerum naturas, non quales sunt, sed ut uulgo uidentur, adumbrat (σκιαγραφία),[11] non secundum exactam cognitionem (ἀκριβὴς γνῶσις) exponit: finem sibi proponit delectationem audientium: animae partem passionibus obnoxiam, ut gaudio & tristitiae obnoxiam, maxime respicit. Subdiuiditur autem in alia duo genera, quorum unum εἰκαστικόν & ὀρθοδοξαστικόν Graece nominatur, Latine coniecturale aut assimilatorium dici licebit: alterum phantasticum (φανταστικόν). Hoc nihil aliud quàm apparentem imitationem & similitudinem, non ueram, repraesentat, & satis efficere sibi uidetur, si uoluptatem ac oblectationem secundum phantasiam auditoribus pepererit. Illud uero non tam captat auram popularem, quàm rectae & congruae imitationi studet, ut ipsas res exprimat, & ob oculos ponat exquisita imagine, de quibus uerba facit, ac exemplaria quae imitatur quàm proxime referat (179.16–32). Sed utriusque differentias ex ipso Platone sub Eleatae hospitis persona proferemus, qui ita loquitur [*Soph.* 235D–236A]: 'Duas nunc imitationis species cernere mihi uideor, unam quidem coniecturalem uel assimilandi artem, cuius opus est secundum exemplar, quod ad longitudinem, latitudinem, [92r] profunditatem, conuenientesque colores attinet, aemule imaginem fabricare. THEAET. Nónne quicunque aliquid imitantur, hoc idem pro uiribus agunt? HOSPES. Non illi, qui magnum aliquod opus fingunt aut pingunt. Si enim ueram pulchrorum commensurationem simulachris praeberent, minora quàm decet superiora membra, maiora uero quae infra sunt apparerent: propterea quod illa eminus, haec comminus à nobis conspiciantur. THEAET. Omnino. HOS. Ergo artifices ueritate dimissa, non eas quae reuera sunt, sed quae uidentur pulchrae commensurationes, simulachris ipsis accommodant.' Ex his uerbis clarum fit utrunque genus imitandi Platonem distinxisse, ut in pictura & statuaria, sic & in poësi, quae illis comparatur. Caeterum de coniecturali seorsim Atheniensis hospes loquitur, ubi de Musica agit, quae sibi non uoluptatem, sed ueram & simillimam exemplaris imitationem proponit (189.3–190.6), ((quem locum, qui uoluerit libro secundo de Legibus requirat [667C–668C], nos hic breuitatis causa omittimus.)) Porrò de phantastico genere Socrates lib. 10. reipub. sermonem instituit [597E–598B], comparans ipsam picturae, quae non naturae, sed opificum opera repraesentat:

---

[11] Proclus uses the metaphor of a picture roughed out in shadow or shading (σκιαγραφία) for the mimetic representation of experiences associated with the categories below the Divided Line. In his *Lexicon graecolatinum* (Basle 1552), Gesner defines σκιαγραφία as 'adumbratio, prima picturae lineamenta' and σκιαγράφω as 'adumbro, hoc est rem non solidam exprimo, sed per umbram, edo, ac fallaci simulacro repraesento, quales sunt imagines picturae umbratilis.' For early metaphorical uses of these terms from Plato on, see *Traditio* 34 (1978) 403–13. This whole section distinguishing eicastic from phantastic imitation is a rare instance of Gesner's expanding a passage in Proclus (1.179.24–32) for emphasis or clarity, which perhaps suggests a strong Renaissance interest in the distinction.

non qualia sunt, sed qualia uidentur: nec ueritatem eorum, sed phantasma imitatur. Huiusmodi phantasticam quoque poësin esse, & tertio gradu à ueritate discessisse demonstrat (190.27–191.26). Inuenitur autem hoc imitatorium genus utrunque etiam apud [92ᵛ] Homerum. Phantasticus enim tum dicendus est, cum secundum uulgi opinionem aliquid effert, ut cum ortum & occasum solis describit à locis, non ueris, sed apparentibus secundum sensus, qui ob loci distantiam falluntur. Vbi uero imitationis typos rebus & personis conuenientes seruat, ut cum heroës pugnantes, consultantes, & loquentes imitatur, singulis pro uitae & studiorum decoro aptas orationes, & facta convenientia affingens, coniecturalis (εἰκαστικῆς) poëta nominari debet (192.22–193.4). Huiusmodi fortassis etiam ille Clytaemnestrae cantor fuerit, qui recta opinione temperantiae exempla tam docte imitabatur, ut Clytaemnestra nihil planè deliquerit, quandiu illum apud se habuit [Od. 3.267–68]. Phantasticum autem Thamyrin Musicum appellare licebit, qui pro antiqua & simplici Musica, multis modis uariantem (πολυτροπωτέραν) & uulgo placentem sensibusque iucundiorem (αἰσθητικωτέραν) inducere conabatur: propterea cum ipsis Musis certasse fingitur, & ab ipsis ira commotis excaecatus esse [Il. 2.599], non quod iracundia Musae tangantur, sed quia ipse ad ueram, simplicem, ueteremque Musicam ineptus erat, non rectam opinionem aut scientiam imitandi sequutus, sed affectus tantum & imaginationem quomodocunque; commouere satagens. Hactenus omnia poëticae genera distinximus, & in Homero ostendimus: quorum postremum, nempe phantasticum in eius poësi minimum inest, ueruntamen ut etiam uulgo placeret, eius quoque nonnihil [93ʳ] admiscuit. Caeterum Tragoedi, etiam illa quae Homerus absolute cum ratione prudentiaque protulit, in imitationem uerterunt, ut auribus uulgi accommodarent, & quae secundum rectam coniecturam descripsit, aemulati sunt phantastice, quod ipsorum non Homeri uitium est. Non secus quàm si quispiam ciuitatem ingressus bene institutam, in qua etiam ebrietas utilitatis alicuius causa exerceatur: hanc solam imitetur, non autem prudentiam, & totam ciuitatis ordinationem: ipsius id culpa, non reipub. factum dicemus. Sed concedamus age Homerum authorem esse Tragoediae, quatenus quod in ipso ultimum & uilissimum est, Tragoedi aemulantur. At non Tragoediae solum, sed omnium Platonis operum secundum imitationem conscriptorum, & totius apud ipsum philosophicae contemplationis eundem faciemus ducem & praeceptorem (194.19–196.13).

POETRY AND PAINTING IN LOPE'S
'EL CASTIGO SIN VENGANZA'

By ROBERTO GONZÁLEZ ECHEVARRÍA

No play of Lope's has puzzled critics more than *El castigo sin venganza* (1631). *Peribáñez*, *Fuenteovejuna*, and to some degree *El caballero de Olmedo* have elicited the kind of criticism that can be considered cumulative; generations of scholars have added their knowledge and insights to our understanding of these plays. But our assumptions about Lope's work remain largely untouched. This is not the case with *El castigo*, a play that has provoked polemics as has no other work by Lope and that, in spite of the amount of criticism it has received, always makes us feel that we are at ground zero in our effort to understand it.[1] Those of us who have been inspired by R. E. Kaske's work and to the best of our abilities emulate his vast learning and exegetical perseverance are inevitably led to such problematic texts. I have rarely been more impressed by an act of reading than by Kaske's prodigious feats of interpretation of obscure passages in Dante. I remember one in particular that he performed at a symposium on 'difficult literature,' a gathering where *El castigo* would surely have been at home.[2]

The position of *El castigo* in Lope's *œuvre* seems to have destined it for such a polemical reception. One of the last plays of Lope's voluminous production, it was performed at a court feast at a delicate political moment, had a theme that could be interpreted as an allusion to an embarrassing event in the history of the Spanish monarchy, and appeared at a time when Lope's successors, most notably Tirso and Calderón, had already produced masterpieces of their own.[3] Around that banner year of 1631, Calderón would produce *La vida es sueño*, and Tirso his *El burlador de Sevilla*. In poetry, the great Góngora, who had died a few years earlier, in 1627, had provoked bitter controversies,

---

[1] *El castigo* has been studied by some of the greatest Hispanists of the century, from Amado Alonso to Edward M. Wilson and Alexander A. Parker. For a commentary on the debates the play has provoked, see Gerald E. Wade, 'The "comedia's" Plurality of Worlds: Some Observations,' *Hispania* 65 (1982) 334–45. There are good bibliographies in the two modern editions of the play by C. A. Jones (Oxford 1966) and A. David Kossoff (Madrid 1970).

[2] 'Dante's *Purgatorio* XXXII and XXXIII: A Survey of Christian History,' *University of Toronto Quarterly* 43 (1974) 194–214.

[3] 'Many saw in the events of the play a reminiscence of the love of Prince Carlos, son of Philip II, for Isabel, who became Philip's Queen and thereby Carlos' stepmother' (C. A. Jones 4). The Duke's womanizing could also have been taken as an allusion to Philip IV. Kossoff, in the introduction to his edition, is skeptical about the allusiveness of the play.

but his manner prevailed over that of Lope, his enemy and detractor. In *El castigo*, Lope had the unparalleled and disturbing privilege of revising his own revisionists. These circumstances, it seems to me, weighed heavily upon Lope as he wrote this beautiful and enigmatic product of his old age, one in which *el fénix de los ingenios* attempted to be born anew from the ashes of the literary wars that had beset Madrid in the first decades of the seventeenth century.

It seems to me that Lope, at the end of his life, sensed that his successful formula for the theater was being radically revamped by his followers, and he wanted to regain his pre-eminent position. He wanted, in a manner of speaking, to be his own successor, his own literary son. What the upstarts had done, chiefly Calderón, but also Tirso, was to dramatize the incompatibility of the two forces that shape Lope's theatrical universe: love, in the guise of the post-Petrarchan poetic mode, and honor, as the system of social conventions that hold love in check, and thus shape Spanish society. In Lope's theater they are, of course, also in conflict, but love and honor provide solutions as well as clashes, and their validity as mainsprings for action is rarely questioned. In Tirso, the inherent evils of love are displayed to their fullest by Don Juan, a character who eschews all amatory courtesy and makes a mockery of honor and valor. In Calderón, honor appears as a destructive force that is at odds with the most elementary Christian tenets.[4] Together, these two annihilating passions would produce some of Calderón's most chilling tragedies: *El médico de su honra*, *El pintor de su deshonra*, and *A secreto agravio, secreta venganza*. In *Peribáñez*, love and honor triumph. In *El caballero de Olmedo*, they produce a tragic hero. In *El médico de su honra* and *El pintor de su deshonra*, love and honor yield psychotic killers.[5] In *El castigo sin venganza*, Lope sets out to go further than Tirso and Calderón, to delve into the deepest source of the tragic contradiction that his successors found in his dramatic formula. The theme of incest, I will argue, pitting a son and his father against each other as rivals for the same woman, is a result of this quest to revise himself, both as a way of recasting the love–honor dyad and as a reflection of the problematic transition from Lope to Calderón. This turning-point in literary history, which conventional criticism has up to now explained in terms of continuity and stylization, was more polemical than has been suspected.[6]

---

[4] Peter N. Dunn, 'Honour and the Christian Background in Calderón,' in *Critical Essays on the Theatre of Calderón*, ed. Bruce W. Wardropper (New York 1965), 24–60.

[5] On *El médico* and *El pintor*, see the following articles by Bruce W. Wardropper: 'Poetry and Drama in Calderón's *El médico de su honra*,' *Romanic Review* 49 (1958) 3–11; 'The Unconscious Mind in Calderón's *El pintor de su deshonra*,' *Hispanic Review* 18 (1950) 285–301.

[6] Albert E. Sloman has studied how Calderón rewrote plays by Lope and other playwrights in *The Dramatic Craftsmanship of Calderón* (Oxford 1958).

Critical efforts to translate *El castigo sin venganza* into logical formulations, that is to say, attempts to interpret the play, have failed because the play is about an impossibility, such as Currie K. Thompson has seen in one of the most perceptive pieces on it.[7] The 'meaning' of *El castigo* cannot be rendered discursively because the play's 'meaning' is essentially about a breakdown in language, a breakdown that is brought about by contradictions that language cannot simultaneously hold. These warring contraries affect the possibility of representation; they are distorted reflections of each other that do not produce meaning as something that can be exchanged, but error and violence. Their thematic projection in the play is the sexual relationships between the protagonists. So conceived, as it were, language always distorts its object, in the same way that the Duque kills the Conde by loving him too much. The Phaedra myth lurking underneath the surface of the play is also concerned with a breakdown in re-production, as are the various Biblical stories to which the play alludes.[8] Incest is a contradictory redoubling in which the original is distorted by repetition. The son returns to the mother's womb in the most literal sense. The father inflicts wounds on himself by inadvertently killing his son, whose desire for the same woman he has unwittingly provoked.

The breakdown in language is signaled by an appeal to images, image-making, and imagery — in short, to painting. It is not a question here of so-called comparative aesthetics, or simply of the influence that the great painters of the period had on Lope, but one where speculation (*valga la palabra*) about perception and expression leads away from the verbal to the visual. Incest, narcissism, and the tragedy they bring about are intimately related in *El castigo*. The only way to 'interpret' the play is to show how these themes are deployed and relate to one another. In doing so, I will argue, Lope suggests an aesthetic

---

[7] Thompson writes, even anticipating my image of the gallery of mirrors in *El castigo*: 'Lope has destroyed a basic "platform" (as Booth would say) of human speech and thought; in its place he has given us a gestalt puzzle which clicks back and forth between two contradictory images. The gestalt puzzle has been discussed by Booth as distinguishing stable from unstable irony, for in it there is no hierarchical placement in which one image is shown to be correct and another incorrect. Perception depends ultimately upon the "eyes of the beholder"; man exists in the midst of a gallery of mirrors' (Currie K. Thompson, 'Unstable Irony in Lope de Vega's *El castigo sin venganza*,' *Hispanófila* 36 [1981] 232). Perception depends more on the desire of the beholder, which breaks down the ironic relation. In addition, Lope goes further than the kind of Boothian irony invoked by Thompson by making contraries reflect each other. Infinite repetition is not just situational or perspectival, but a way of dissembling even individual perspective, as will be seen later in this paper. Thompson does not connect the mirror to her excellent study of the various ironies. David M. Gitlitz does devote a page to it in his 'Ironía e imágenes en *El castigo sin venganza*,' *Revista de Estudios Hispánicos* 14 (1980) 22–23.

[8] Kossoff denies the importance of the Phaedra myth and insists on the Biblical background, particularly that of David and Absalom.

theory that is already modern, as daring as that of the great painters of the age, and as much an anticipation of modern theories of cognition as their canvases. Most criticism of *El castigo* has been led astray by focusing on the relationship between Federico and Casandra, while overlooking that between the Duque and his son. The central issue of the play hovers on that relationship, and if one were to look for a tragic hero, the Duque would have to be the most likely candidate, for his actions set in motion the action of the play.[9] It is clear throughout *El castigo* that the Duque feels great love for his bastard son. The Duque's motives for action — or, as we shall see, inaction — are determined by that love, not by his penchant for easy women. When the play begins we soon discover that the Duque has postponed marrying so as not to produce a legitimate child who will rob Federico of his chance to inherit him. What appear to be the philanderings of the Duque really turn out to be delaying tactics to preserve the rights of Federico. Once he does marry, impelled by *razón de estado*, the Duque's lack of ardor for his wife can be attributed to the same motive:

> porque es Federico, Aurora,
> lo que más mi alma adora,
> y fue casarme traición
> que hago a mi propio gusto.   (665–68)

[Federico is that which my soul adores the most, and by marrying I was a traitor to my own desire.][10]

Later in the play, Batín tells Federico that he is the light in his father's eyes ('eres el sol de sus ojos' 2153), a very significant image, as we shall see later. The more the Duque loves Federico the less he can love Casandra, for loving her threatens Federico. Critics bent on a moralistic reading of the play see the Duque's gallivanting as his worst fault, and attribute his downfall to it. But at issue is not what the Duque does to other women as much as what he does not do to his wife. Casandra is quite clear on this point. She is not inspired by the Victorian morals of most critics of the play. Casandra does not care about the Duque's 'mujercillas'; she resents the little attention her husband devotes to her:

---

[9] Kossoff and Thompson are the only two critics who focus their attention on the relationship between father and son. Alexander A. Parker studies the concatenation of events in the play according to his theory of poetic justice in Golden Age drama, *The Approach to the Spanish Drama of the Golden Age* (London 1957). Edward M. Wilson offers a different perspective in 'Cuando Lope quiere, quiere,' *Cuadernos Hispanoamericanos* 161–62 (1963) 265–98.

[10] I am quoting from Kossoff's edition. The translations, which I have often revised, come from Jill Booty in *Lope de Vega: Five Plays*, ed. R. D. F. Pring-Mill (New York 1961). The editor's introduction is excellent on the play and its critics.

> Que venga un hombre a su casa,
> cuando viene al mundo el día,
> que viva a su fantasía,
> por libertad de hombre pasa.
> ¿ quién puede ponerle tasa?
> Pero que con tal desprecio
> trate una mujer de precio,
> de que es casado olvidado,
> o quiere ser desdichado
> o tiene mucho de necio.   (1047–52)

[It seems it passes for freedom in a man that he should live as he chooses and not come home till dawn. Who can prevent him? But he who forgets he is married, and treats a noblewoman with such scorn, must either be a fool or one who seeks his own disgrace.]

It is by this non-action that the Duque brings about the tragedy. His reluctance to make love to his wife and therefore reproduce in the manner prescribed by society thrusts Casandra into the arms of Federico. It is true, as we shall soon see, that there are other strong forces leading both lovers in that direction, but what favors their actual reunion is the absence of love on the part of the Duque. The Duque constantly refuses to act as a husband, and it is tragically ironic that at the end, when he has to punish Federico, he does so as a father, not as a husband, for as a husband he would have had to take revenge: 'Seré padre y no marido / dando la justicia santa' ('I will act as a father, not as a husband, in administering saintly justice' 2846–47). The Duque is always a father, seldom a husband. He is a master of negativity and non-action. Thus we can say that because of his excessive love for his son, the Duque sets in motion a series of actions that lead to the destruction of that very son, his own wife, and ultimately of his public and private life. At this level one can readily see the tragic element in *El castigo sin venganza*: the Duque brings onto himself and the object of his love precisely that which he wishes to avoid.

But one cannot be entirely satisfied with this interpretation. The question remains: why the excessive love for his son on the part of the Duque, and why must this kind of filial love bring about the tragedy? If we left our interpretation here, we would have to accept that the meaning of the play is moralistic. The Duque has made an imprudent error in putting his son's love above his duty as a husband and as a man of state. But can we really be satisfied with such vapid moralism in reading a play as full of disturbing overtones as *El castigo*, a play in which Casandra is willing to risk her life for her passion, a loving son is capable of committing adultery with his own stepmother, and a loving father has his son slaughtered? Tragedy in *El castigo sin venganza* is not the result of moral defects on the part of the characters that could conceivably be amended. Tragedy is the result of overpowering dark forces in human nature that are irrevocably at odds with the social contract. These dark forces are a kind of negative vision.

The Duque loves the Conde so much because he is in the grips of a narcissistic passion. Being the light or — more literally — the sun in his eyes, Federico both guides him and blinds him. It is evident throughout the play that for the Duque, Federico is a reflection of himself, his very picture, as he and Casandra ironically refer to him toward the end. 'Un retrato vuestro ha sido' ('he has been your living portrait'), she says, to which he replies, now with the full knowledge of their misdeeds:

> Ya sé que me ha retratado
> tan igual en todo estado,
> que por mí le habéis tenido   (2656–59)

[I have heard so much. I hear that he has been in everything so much my image that you have treated him as if he were myself.]

The Duque's love of self in Federico, and thus his self-annihilation through the destruction of that image of self, is central in what turns out to be a whole series of specular reflections whose motive is love. Love in *El castigo* will always be love of a reflection. A good deal of the imagery of the play revolves around the issue of image-making, of the imagination, and of *pensamiento*, as well as of the ability of both to be bound by moral restrictions. Tragedy in *El castigo* stems from the penchant in humankind to love images of self, a penchant that leads to destruction and self-destruction. Tragedy in this play of Lope's, then, is — beyond the themes of love and honor — the eternal struggle created by the contradictory presence of death within love. To love the tangible, colorful representation of self, to produce images, is the central mimetic activity, the activity that produces art, art like *El castigo* itself.[11] One of the enduring values of this statement of Lope's is the suggestion that his art is born of desire, like much else in his life. In the play, Lope bridges the gap between the role of the imagination as a creative force in the Golden Age dramatists and as a destructive one in the characters they create; if the imagination leads to error and deceit in the fiction, it does so also outside of it.[12]

---

[11] I am not unaware that the description of the imagination that I offer here is contaminated by Lacan's version of the *imaginaire*. For a more conscious and conscientious application of Lacan to Hispanic texts (as well as to various Shakespeare plays that have much in common with *El castigo*), see Eduardo González, *La persona y el relato: Proyecto de lectura psicoanalítica* (Madrid 1985).

[12] 'Quedamos, pues, en que la imaginación es al mismo tiempo la facultad *creadora* en los poetas y la facultad *traidora* de los personajes imaginados por él.' Bruce W. Wardropper, 'La imaginación en el metateatro calderoniano,' in *Studia Hispanica in Honorem R. Lapesa* (Madrid 1972) 619. This article offers a precise and useful survey of the theories of the imagination prevalent in Spain during the Golden Age to which I am indebted. Following Wardropper, Susan L. Fischer has written a perceptive article on 'Lope's *El castigo sin*

The boldest image-maker in *El castigo sin venganza* is Casandra, who longs for Federico and ponders if to want him is in and of itself a sin. But she figures incorrectly that the mistake she has committed is merely an 'error pintado' ('an image of error' or 'a painted error' 1585). Soon this image will come to life when she puts into practice what her imagination proposes. Imagination, rendered both as 'imaginación' and 'pensamiento' in the play, makes the impossible look possible, oblivious to reason and ethics; hence it is removed from discursive activity and always cast in the language of the visible: 'que no hay tan grande imposible / que no le juzguen visible / los ojos del pensamiento' ('there is nothing so impossible that the eyes of the imagination cannot consider it possible' 1559–61).[13] Federico had closed the first act with a similar meditation on the freedom of the imagination to conjure up impossible images. But the imagination is not free. This is so not only because of Batín's theological injunction that in the freedom of the soul man should see an image of his immortality, and hence should always choose the good (Calderón's argument in *La vida es sueño*), but because the imagination inevitably conjures up the impossible. Through the imagination, desire creates a vivid representation of the forbidden. Imagination is always allied both to creation and to self-destruction in the play.

The characters' fatal inclination to love reflections of themselves is brought forth very early in *El castigo sin venganza*, when Casandra and Federico meet for the first time. This meeting occurs by chance. Federico, who has gone to meet Casandra, wanders off to a forest to consider his predicament, and there he meets his stepmother, whose carriage has foundered on a river bank. She has also wandered off the road, as if drawn by a magic force to be a specular image of Federico. The overtones of the encounter are clear. The lovers are impelled by fate to meet in this *locus amoenus*, this Petrarchan site where the 'dolce, chiare e fresche acque' run through a beautiful forest. The results of the encounter are predictable. The Petrarchan echoes of the scene are fairly distinct in the *silvas* Federico recites upon entering the wood. He has stopped to consider his present state, a reflective gesture that has even clearer Petrar-

---

venganza and the Imagination,' *Kentucky Romance Quarterly* 28 (1981) 23–36. Fischer relates the imagination to instances of 'metatheater' within the play. To her and Wardropper, the characters create — in these instances — that which their concupiscent imaginations dictate, only to be thwarted by reality. I link the imagination more to image-making and suggest that in *El castigo* it prevails over the constraints of the real world by absorbing it.

[13] *Pensamiento* meant something akin to the imagination in the Golden Age, whereas in modern Spanish the word is closer to the English 'thought.' Here 'ojos del pensamiento' can mean 'the mind's eye,' if we think of mind as the ability to conjure up images. It is, of course, relevant here to recall that Federico is 'el sol' in the Duque's eyes.

chan and Garcilasian resonances ('Cuando me paro a contemplar mi estado').[14]
There, 'fatigado / de varios pensamientos' ('wearied by various imaginings'
240–41), he sits at the foot of trees that 'atentos'

> a las dormidas ondas de este río,
> en su puro cristal, sonoro y frío,
> mirando están sus copas,
> después que los vistió de verdes ropas,
> de mí mismo quisiera retirarme,   (242–47)

[listening to the sleepy waves of this river, and looking at their own tops in
its cold, pure, sonorous crystal, on which they appeared dressed in green;
here I would like to take leave of myself.]

The fatal coincidence of the encounter between Federico and Casandra height-
ens the tragic nature of the play. But one must take notice of where they meet.
The literary allusions already mentioned make it abundantly clear that Federico
and Casandra meet in a place saturated with the aura of the courtly love tradition. This poetic grove is full of dangers. The waters of the river create an
inverted reflection of the trees; the lovers meet at the juncture between reality
and its mirror-image. They meet on the sheen of the mirror. This game of
mirrors is itself a reflection of the mirror-like actions of the two lovers, who
have wandered off the road at the same time to meet and reflect each other
in what is very much like a house of mirrors. Federico and Casandra are
caught from the beginning in this world of images, of the imagination, a world
that is far from free, and whose machine-like precision is rendered visible by a
'fearful symmetry,' as Margaret Van Antwerp has called it, echoing Blake
in one of the most powerful readings of the play to date.[15] The word-play
'yerro–erro' that appears so frequently in this scene to convey the ambiguity
between 'to err' and 'to wander off' is the linguistic version of this gallery of
reflections into which the lovers have entered: each word is a slightly distorted
mirror-image of the other. The bearely audible y is the transparent wall that
separates them. In the grove-become-gallery-of-mirrors, there is no longer a

---

[14] The ambience of this grove is very much out of Garcilaso's *Egloga Primera*. I quote
Garcilaso's Sonnet 1 from the *Obras* (Madrid 1963).

[15] 'Fearful Symmetry: The Poetic World of Lope's *El castigo sin venganza*,' *Bulletin of
Hispanic Studies* 58 (1981) 205–16. Van Antwerp brilliantly outdistances previous criticism
of the play by showing that Lope presents a systematic balancing of contraries that denies
any possibility of a moralistic conclusion. She has seen that even the characters hold within
themselves warring contraries simultaneously, thus making it impossible to pass final judgment on them. In my view, Van Antwerp's only error is not to follow the lead of her title,
by showing how the fear of symmetry leads to violence and aggression, which in turn makes
the game of reflections not a stable balancing of contraries, but a frightful destruction of
images, mostly self-images. Van Antwerp's piece is by far the most advanced on *El castigo*
and I recognize a great debt to it.

distinction between reality and reflection, for every appearance is the product
of desire. Hence, as we have seen, in the world of the imagination contraries
can coexist side by side.

The world of the lovers, once they surrender to their passion, is a house of
mirrors. This is conveyed in a masterful scene in which Aurora, who loves
Federico and is spurned by him (and is, in a sense, a counter-image of Casandra,
who is shunned by the Duque), reveals to the Marqués the activities of the stepmother and her son.

Everything is significant in this second-hand description of the lovers'
embrace, not the least of which is its source. Aurora admits that she is led to
spy on Casandra and Federico by her jealousy, that is to say, by her desire for
him. This desire turns walls into translucent glass:

> Pues viéndome despreciada
> y a Federico tan libre,
> di en inquirir la ocasión,
> y como son los celos linces
> que las paredes penetran,
> a saber la causa vine.   (2061–67)

[So seeing myself scorned, and Federico acting so unconcerned, I wished to
know the reason, and since jealousy is lynx-eyed and sees through walls, I
soon discovered why.]

Aurora does not really see the lovers through glass, but reflected in a mirror.
The arrangement of Casandra's boudoir and how Aurora manages to lay eyes on
the lovers are of the utmost significance:

> En correspondencia tiene,
> sirviéndole de tapices
> retratos, vidrios y espejos,
> dos iguales camarines
> el tocador de Casandra;
> y como sospechas pisen
> tan quedo, dos cuadras antes
> miré y vi ¡ caso terrible !
> en el cristal de un espejo
> que el conde las rosas mide
> de Casandra con los labios.   (2067–77)

[In Casandra's bedroom there are two corresponding closets which have
their walls covered not in tapestries, but in mirrors and portraits. Suspicion
counseled me to tread stealthily, and, to my horror, from two anterooms
away I saw reflected in a mirror Count Federico measuring the roses of
Casandra's lips with his own.][16]

---

[16] Kossoff comments: 'Lope tiene una imaginación espacial, y la idea de estos versos
probablemente es ésta: el tocador de Casandra tenía dos camarines llenos de retratos, vidrios
y espejos a tal punto que ornamentaban el tocador como si los camarines fuesen tapices;
Aurora, llena de sospechas, se acercó silenciosa y aun antes de llegar al primer camarín vio en

What Aurora reports seeing is a Genet-like play of reflections (I am thinking, of course, of *Le Balcon*). Not only does she turn the walls of Casandras's boudoir to glass, but these walls are covered with mirrors and portraits. More importantly, these two 'camarines' or closets are in 'correspondencia,' that is to say, they face and reflect each other, creating an infinitely receding sequence. Like the inverted tree-tops in the scene when the lovers first meet, their kiss takes place in a gallery of mirror-images that projects them into infinity, multiplying endlessly their act as in a nightmare. Aurora, appropriately, does not see the lovers, but their reflection, or perhaps a reflection of their reflection. The lines are beautifully precise in this respect: the lovers are seen on 'the glass of a mirror,' not in its depths. Their image is all surface, visibility. In a sense, the lovers *are* their reflection, the image each has of the other as a projection of desire. It is this image that acts upon the other characters.

But let us return to the boudoir. Aurora has seen the lovers through a correspondence of mirrors, but she does not see them from a perspective that keeps her safely outside the play of reflections. In order to see, Aurora has to be seen. To look into the mirror, she has to surrender her own image to it. Somewhere in that gallery of mirrors Aurora's own image is reflected. If the lovers were to turn to the mirror, they would be able to see her reflection in the act of looking, like the character at the back of Velázquez' *Las meninas*. Perhaps another observer would be able to see the three characters at once, framed in one mirror, a monstrous assemblage that would nevertheless be allowed by the play of reflections and would indicate to what degree Aurora is implicated in the image that she reports having seen. Like the Duque, she sees herself in the image of her desire, and by revealing what she has seen she seeks to destroy it. The mirror's ability to contain warring contraries, that is to say, the impossible, makes it a symbol of the imagination, which in the play is capable of forming images that are monstrous in their heterogeneity. There is an inexorable multiplication of images, owing to very precise physical and geometrical laws. These laws determine what is seen and how more than each character's individual vision determines what is reality. Reality is the sum total of the errors of perception of the characters, a composite of the images they create, and the

---

un espejo el beso de los amantes, que se suponían escondidos a la vista de otros. La descripción del beso sugiere que Federico saboreaba las mejillas, moviendo su boca por la cara de ella como midiendo las distancias entre los lugares besados, o quiza Federico tenía los labios apartados como si fueran dedos separados para tomar la medida de un objeto, en este caso las *rosas* que deben ser, como en Góngora las mejillas o pómulos de la dama . . .' (327). I do not believe that we have to be so specific with regard to *rosas*, which are full of suggestions and possible visual meanings. I am more inclined to think of them as lips. A kiss on the lips also sets the lovers in a specular relation to each other. 'Tomar la medida de algo,' to take the measure of something, is also an act of possession.

reflections of those images. Each character's body is snatched by these reflections and placed in this game of correspondences that make up reality. No character can see without at the same time being seen. To see is to be caught in a ruthless mechanism whose end-result is an anticipation of death, a giving up of the body; one lives in the image projected by the desire of the other, a projection that kills, as with the three protagonists, who kill themselves through their passion for each other.

It is, of course, quite revealing that the walls of Casandra's boudoir are covered not only by mirrors but also by portraits. She lives in a world of reflections, of representations of representations. We have already seen the perverse meaning of 'retrato' in the play, as applied to Federico's supplanting of his father. Paintings and mirrors are equivalent in their function as walls here. They are walls that do not divide and thus arrest one's gaze, but return one's image and reflect vast non-existing spaces, abolishing in fact the distinction between real and fictional space. The space where love and reflection take place, where painting exists, is the imagination in the sense already noted: a pictorial image that is the projection of desire. For this reason, it seems to me that Aurora's description of the kiss has the configuration of a painting. The lovers are seen as if caught in the web of lines that a painter would draw to put them in the proper perspective. They occupy a center, around which reflections of their action appear. Even the metaphor used to describe the kiss is of a spatial and chromatic nature: Federico *measures* Casandra's *roses* with his lips. The action is framed not only by the real stage, but by the *camarines* that center the lovers. It is not difficult, in short, to imagine a painting depicting this scene, one that would include the prying Aurora, who would, in turn, be reflecting our own role in the scene as spectators.[17]

By looking and being caught in the act by the mirror, Aurora shows that the audience in *El castigo sin venganza* is also caught in the play's game of reflections. She indicates that we too are voyeurs whose own libidinal forces are spent in observing the reflection of this repetitive lover's triangle, the images of it that the theater offers. In this respect Lope's aesthetics turn modern in a manner not too dissimilar from that of Velázquez and other great painters of the period. This is where Lope's appeal to painting is most profound: as a reflection on the act of re-presenting reality. Painting as a hypostasis of desire is a commonplace in Golden Age literature, and Lope often uses it as such. In *Peribáñez*, the Comendador has a painter do a portrait of Casilda. Casilda's

---

[17] I have learned much in this respect from Julián Gállego, *Visión y símbolos en la pintura española del Siglo de Oro* (Madrid 1972), and from the papers in 'Painting in Spain 1650–1700,' a special issue of *Record of the Art Museum of Princeton University*, 41.2 (1982), particularly Bruce W. Wardropper's 'Calderón de la Barca and Late Seventeenth-Century Theater,' 35–41.

image is a reflection of the Comendador's desire for her, and the portrait a way of possessing that reflection of hers.[18] In Cervantes' *Persiles*, the characters carry on their voyages painted images of the beloved and of that which they desire. Lope goes further in *El castigo* by demonstrating that depiction issues from the inside as much as from a perception of reality, and that such depiction not only affects that which is depicted, but thrusts him who depicts into the fictional realm he has created, much like Velázquez' own self-portrait in *Las meninas*.

The most searing meditation on this is offered by the ending of the play. Here, like the protagonist of *El pintor de su deshonra*, the Duque creates a picture in which he destroys the objects of his desire.[19] In the unforgettable last scenes of *El castigo*, the Duque creates a fiction. He tells Federico that the person bound, gagged, and covered has conspired against his rule and orders him to kill the traitor. The person is, of course, Casandra, who by her actions has indeed threatened the stability of the realm. Then the Duque has his minions slay Federico, claiming that this bastard son has killed his stepmother because she was pregnant with him who would be a rightful heir. The Duque's fiction is as complex as the game of mirrors in Casandra's boudoir and the reflections of the waters in the *locus amoenus* where the lovers met. Like the gallery of mirrors, the Duque's fiction contains truth and lies enmeshed in a play of corresponding images.

Casandra is at once a traitor and the *duquesa*, Federico's mother and his lover. That is, she has produced him (even if only metaphorically) and is capable of re-producing him. In fact, according to the Duque's fiction, Federico kills her because she is pregnant with an heir. But if she were pregnant, it would have to be by Federico, not the Duque. Therefore, like his father, Federico kills his own son in the realm of reflections and images in which they dwell. Federico has unwittingly become — again — his father's *retrato*. Like him he kills his own son and, in murdering Casandra, destroys the person he loves most. Casandra too has brought about Federico's death, so that she gives him both life and death as a mother and a lover. The Duque, in killing his wife through Federico, makes his son also reflect his actions. Casandra's body, like her boudoir, is a locus of refractions and reflections; she is loved and killed

---

[18] On *Peribáñez* see Mary Gaylord Randel, 'The Portrait and the Creation of *Peribáñez*,' *Romanische Forschungen* 85 (1973) 145–58. On painting in Lope and Golden Age theater, see Frederick de Armas' work, particularly 'Lope de Vega and Titian,' *Comparative Literature* 30 (1978) 338–53, and 'Lope de Vega and Michelangelo,' *Hispania* 65 (1982) 172–79; also Jean Babelon, 'Pintura y poesía en el Siglo de Oro,' *Clavileño* 1.2 (1950) 16–21; E. George Erdman, Jr., 'An Additional Note on the Retrato Motif in Lope,' *Romance Notes* 5 (1964) 183–86; Myron A. Peyton, 'The *retrato* as Motif and Device in Lope de Vega,' *Romance Notes* 4 (1962) 51–57.

[19] On this point, see Fischer (*n*12).

by Federico, making loving and killing activities that are mirror-images of each other. Life and death face each in *El castigo sin venganza*, creating an infinite series of images of each other.

The *descubrimiento* scene at the very end of the play is the Duque's last creation. It is clear from all the evidence we have concerning the scenography of Golden Age drama that this kind of scene had a picture-like arrangement: it was like a *tableau vivant*.[20] This is reinforced by the fact that the characters themselves become spectators and talk of looking one last time at the dead lovers, whose bodies are uncovered for that purpose. The Duque exclaims that 'En tanta / desdicha aun quieren los ojos / verle muerto con Casandra' ('Amid so much misfortune, still my eyes long to see him dead beside Casandra' 3009–11). And after the bodies are displayed, the Marqués reports, as the Conde looks at the lovers: 'Vuelve a mirar el castigo / sin venganza' ('He has wrought justice without revenge. See, how he looks upon them yet again' 3012–13). The Marqués reports not the bodies, but the Duque looking at the bodies. Like Aurora before him, he depicts an image, a reflection, and rightly so, one that is a repetition ('yet again'). In both scenes, Casandra and Federico are frozen in a gesture. They are motionless, yet their image is repeated in love as well as in death. The Duque's last deed is to cast Federico and Casandra onto a picture, the *escena de descubrimiento*, where he and the spectators become one as onlookers. Our playing a role like the Duke's is of the utmost significance here. We are spectators/killers too, viewing with relish a monstrous image that is a projection of our own desire. Like the scene of the kiss, this one contains the impossible made possible in the realm of the visible: a mother and son joined by love and death, killed by the husband-father.

Like the Duque's creation, Lope's play moves from the verbal to the visual, from the language of poetry to that of painting. In the last scene, taking advantage of the tradition of the discovery scene, the stage becomes a picture, and the players themselves, except those who play the roles of the dead lovers, become spectators. The development of Golden Age theater toward more ornate scenery and better-equipped houses did not stem solely from technical and social reasons. There was an inner development toward the painterly in the poetry of the *comedia*. *El castigo sin venganza* marks the transition and lays out the reasons for it. *El castigo*, like the gallery of mirrors where Casandra meets Federico, is made up of reflections and repetitions. These are as sig-

---

[20] For the 'discovery scene' see N. D. Shergold, *A History of the Spanish Stage from Medieval Times until the End of the Seventeenth Century* (Oxford 1967). If we visualize the scene of the kiss, as does Kossoff, the discovery of the bodies would take place on the same spot on the stage as Casandra's boudoir.

nificant as Federico's being an image of his father and as trivial as Batín's mimicking Federico's actions at the scene of the first meeting, where the *gracioso* proposes to Lucrecia. Scenes are repeated with slight variations, situations are reversed, characters meet their doubles. Even Casandra's unborn son appears as a reflection of Federico and of the Duque's worst fears. Like painting, the *comedia* has an inner construction made up of images of images, of divisions as troublesome as the walls of Casandra's room, of appearances (*apariencia* was, of course, the name for stage props).

Beyond morality, and perhaps even beyond Christianity, Lope's tragedy offers a picture of humankind as prey to an insoluble dilemma, in which love, even filial love, is at once the creator and the destroyer of life. The blindness provoked by desire is what allows us to create images, and we live in the images of others. Parker and Durán have insisted, and rightly so, on the fact that the Spanish Golden Age theater is one of action, not of characters.[21] I would add to this that action means here the *inter*action between the various images that the characters have of each other. In short: a character is not only his or her actions, but his or her reflections on others, be they doubles, counter-images, or creations of others. For this reason characters often bewail being 'fuera de sí' or, more memorably, in the beautiful gloss included in the play, 'sin mí, sin vos y sin Dios.' Being without oneself or God is endemic in *El castigo sin venganza*, as we have seen. This living in one's image, in one's reflection, and the persistent errors of perception in which the characters fall, compelled by the brightness of those images (like the son in the Duque's eyes), constitute one of the enduring messages of Baroque theater in Spain, as Wardropper has persuasively argued in discussing a late play of Calderón's.[22] But Lope had already seen, as it were, where things were going, and gave a fairly full anticipation of it in *El castigo*.

Would it be too much to read into the struggle between the Duque and the Conde a reflection of the competition between Lope and Calderón? There is no question, as others have noted, that *El castigo sin venganza* is a very Calderonian play, from the themes to the imagery, but, in my view, above all

---

[21] Parker (*n9 supra*) and Manuel Durán, 'Lope y el teatro de acción,' *Hispanófila* 18 (1963) 3–14.

[22] 'Calderón de la Barca and Late Seventeenth-Century Theater' (*n17*). Here Wardropper analyzes the use of the mirror device in *Hado y divisa de Leónido y Marfisa* (1680), Calderón's last secular play. Calderón has added a last twist to the mirror-portrait game by having a portrait represent a mirror. A real mirror facing the king, as Wardropper perceptively argues, would have reflected irrelevant images from various perspectives, not the image of the king. Thus the creator of images — the mirror — is itself rendered as an artificial image in Calderón.

in the geometry.[23] The world-view of the cosmos as a mechanistic play of geometrical reflections is Calderón's, not Lope's.[24] Lope's adoption of this, plus the other elements mentioned, clearly indicates that he has consciously or unconsciously imitated what Calderón had added to this theatrical formula. Calderón has become the precursor, to use Harold Bloom's terminology, and Lope the ephebe.[25] Only here we have an inversion of Bloom's formula. In playing the ephebe, Lope turns the tables on his disciple, making himself into a *puer senex* who will claim the new again as his own. Lope usurps both roles in the Oedipal confrontation. He is both precursor and successor, original and copy. Driven, like the Duque, by his narcissistic passion, Lope claims both sides of the mirror. His disproportionate claim, his anxiety to be original, has the Romantic ring that his modern aesthetics already anticipate.

Yale University

---

[23] '*El castigo sin venganza* may, I believe, be profitably examined in the light of some of the principal characteristics of Calderonian tragedy, for between the older and the younger dramatist there is often in this particular respect a striking confluence of dramatic vision' (Gwynne Edwards, 'Lope and Calderón: The Tragic Pattern of *El castigo sin venganza*,' *Bulletin of the Comediantes* 33 [1981] 107–20).

[24] On this topic, see my 'El "monstruo de una especie y otra": *La vida es sueño* III.2725,' Co-Textes (Montpellier) 3: *Calderón: Códigos, monstruo, icones*, ed. Javier Herrero (1982) 27–58.

[25] Harold Bloom, *A Map of Misreading* (New York 1975).

PUBLICATIONS OF R. E. KASKE

1. 'The Use of Simple Figures of Speech in *Piers Plowman* B: A Study in the Figurative Expression of Ideas and Opinions,' *Studies in Philology* 48 (1951) 571–600 (= *Studies in Mediaeval Culture Presented to George Raleigh Coffman*).
2. 'A Note on *bras* in *Piers Plowman* A, III, 189; B, III, 195,' *Philological Quarterly* 31 (1952) 427–30.
3. 'Gigas the Giant in *Piers Plowman*,' *Journal of English and Germanic Philology* 56 (1957) 177–85.
4. 'Langland and the *Paradisus Claustralis*,' *Modern Language Notes* 72 (1957) 481–83.
5. 'The Knight's Interruption of the *Monk's Tale*,' *ELH: A Journal of English Literary History* 24 (1957) 249–68.
6. '*Sapientia et Fortitudo* as the Controlling Theme of *Beowulf*,' *Studies in Philology* 55 (1958) 423–56; reprinted in *An Anthology of* BEOWULF *Criticism*, ed. Lewis E. Nicholson (Notre Dame 1963) 269–310.
7. review of: Robert W. Frank, Jr., PIERS PLOWMAN *and the Scheme of Salvation* (New Haven 1957), in *Modern Language Notes* 74 (1959) 730–33.
8. 'The Summoner's "Garleek, Oynons, and eek Lekes,"' *Modern Language Notes* 74 (1959) 481–84.
9. 'The Speech of "Book" in *Piers Plowman*,' *Anglia* 77 (1959) 117–44.
10. 'An Aube in the *Reeve's Tale*,' *ELH: A Journal of English Literary History* 26 (1959) 295–310.
11. 'Langland's Walnut-Simile,' *Journal of English and Germanic Philology* 58 (1959) 650–54.
12. 'The Sigemund–Heremod and Hama–Hygelac Passages in *Beowulf*,' *Publications of the Modern Language Association of America* 74 (1959) 489–94.
13. 'Two Cruxes in *Pearl*: 596 and 609–10,' *Traditio* 15 (1959) 418–28.
14. 'Eve's "Leaps" in the *Ancrene Riwle*,' *Medium Aevum* 29 (1960) 22–24.
15. 'January's "Aube,"' *Modern Language Notes* 75 (1960) 1–4.
16. 'Patristic Exegesis in the Criticism of Medieval Literature: The Defense,' in *Critical Approaches to Medieval Literature: Selected Papers from the English Institute, 1958–1959*, ed. Dorothy Bethurum (New York 1960) 27–60 and 158–59; abridged in *Interpretations of* PIERS PLOWMAN, ed. Edward Vasta (Notre Dame 1968) 319–38; and in *Geoffrey Chaucer: A Critical Anthology*, ed. J. A. Burrow (Baltimore 1969) 233–39.

17. 'Weohstan's Sword,' *Modern Language Notes* 75 (1960) 465–68.
18. 'The Aube in Chaucer's *Troilus*,' in *Chaucer Criticism*, II: TROILUS AND CRISEYDE *and the Minor Poems*, edd. Richard J. Schoeck and Jerome Taylor (Notre Dame 1961) 167–79.
19. 'Dante's "DXV" and "Veltro,"' *Traditio* 17 (1961) 185–254; abridged, with some important additions, as 'Dante's *DXV*,' in *Dante: A Collection of Critical Essays*, ed. John Freccero, Twentieth Century Views (Englewood Cliffs, N.J. 1965) 122–40.
20. 'The *Canticum Canticorum* in the *Miller's Tale*,' *Studies in Philology* 59 (1962) 479–500.
21. review of: Morton W. Bloomfield, PIERS PLOWMAN *as a Fourteenth-Century Apocalypse* (New Brunswick, N.J. 1962), in *Journal of English and Germanic Philology* 62 (1963) 202–8.
22. review of: David C. Fowler, PIERS THE PLOWMAN: *Literary Relations of the A and B Texts* (Seattle 1961), in *Journal of English and Germanic Philology* 62 (1963) 208–13.
23. '*Ex vi transicionis* and Its Passage in *Piers Plowman*,' *Journal of English and Germanic Philology* 62 (1963) 32–60; reprinted in *Style and Symbolism in* PIERS PLOWMAN: *A Modern Critical Anthology*, ed. Robert J. Blanch (Knoxville, Tenn. 1969) 228–63.
24. 'Chaucer and Medieval Allegory,' *ELH: A Journal of English Literary History* 30 (1963) 175–92 (article reviewing D. W. Robertson, Jr., *A Preface to Chaucer* [Princeton 1962]).
25. '"Hygelac" and "Hygd,"' in *Studies in Old English Literature in Honor of Arthur G. Brodeur*, ed. Stanley B. Greenfield (Eugene, Ore. 1963) 200–6 (reissued New York 1973 with an addendum on 206).
26. 'Weland and the *wurmas* in *Deor*,' *English Studies* 44 (1963) 190–91.
27. 'The Reading *genyre* in *The Husband's Message*, Line 49,' *Medium Aevum* 33 (1964) 204–6.
28. 'The Character *"Figura"* in *Le Mystère d'Adam*,' in *Mediaeval Studies in Honor of Urban Tigner Holmes, Jr.*, edd. John F. Mahoney and John Esten Keller (Chapel Hill, N.C. 1966) 103–10.
29. review of: George Kane, PIERS PLOWMAN: *The Evidence for Authorship* (London 1965), in *Journal of English and Germanic Philology* 65 (1966) 583–86.
30. review of: Hans Schabram, *Superbia: Studien zum altenglischen Wortschatz*, I (Munich 1965), in *Speculum* 41 (1966) 762–64.
31. 'A Poem of the Cross in the Exeter Book: "Riddle 60" and "The Husband's Message,"' *Traditio* 23 (1967) 41–71.
32. 'The *Eotenas* in *Beowulf*,' in *Old English Poetry: Fifteen Essays*, ed. Robert P. Creed (Providence, R.I. 1967) 285–310.

33. review of: Rosemond Tuve, *Allegorical Imagery: Some Medieval Books and Their Posterity* (Princeton 1966), in *Speculum* 42 (1967) 196–99.
34. 'The Silver Spoons of Sutton Hoo,' *Speculum* 42 (1967) 670–72.
35. '*Piers Plowman* and Local Iconography,' *Journal of the Warburg and Courtauld Institutes* 31 (1968) 159–69.
36. 'Some Newly-Discovered Wall-Paintings at Madley, Herefordshire,' *Traditio* 24 (1968) 464–71.
37. review of: P. M. Kean, THE PEARL: *An Interpretation* (New York 1967), in *English Language Notes* 6 (1968) 48–52.
38. '*Beowulf*,' in *Critical Approaches to Six Major English Works:* BEOWULF *through* PARADISE LOST, edd. Robert M. Lumiansky and Herschel Baker (Philadelphia 1968) 3–40; abridged in *Beowulf*, ed. Joseph F. Tuso, Norton Critical Editions (New York 1975) 118–31.
39. 'Gawain's Green Chapel and the Cave at Wetton Mill,' in *Medieval Literature and Folklore Studies: Essays in Honor of Francis Lee Utley*, edd. Jerome Mandel and Bruce A. Rosenberg (New Brunswick, N.J. 1970) 111–12 and 357–58.
40. review of: Edward B. Irving, Jr., *A Reading of* BEOWULF (New Haven 1968), in *Journal of English and Germanic Philology* 69 (1970) 159–61.
41. '*Beowulf* and the Book of Enoch,' *Speculum* 46 (1971) 421–31.
42. '"Sì si conserva il seme d'ogne giusto" (*Purg.*, XXXII, 48),' *Dante Studies* 89 (1971) 49–54.
43. review of: Ian Bishop, PEARL *in Its Setting: A Critical Study in the Structure and Meaning of the Middle English Poem* (Oxford 1968), in *Anglia* 89 (1971) 135–37.
44. review of: Sarah Appleton Weber, *Theology and Poetry in the Middle English Lyric: A Study of Sacred History and Aesthetic Form* (Columbus, Oh. 1969), in *Speculum* 46 (1971) 188–90.
45. 'Horn and Ivory in the *Summoner's Tale*,' *Neuphilologische Mitteilungen* 73 (1972) 122–26 (= *Studies Presented to Tauno F. Mustanoja on the Occasion of His Sixtieth Birthday*).
46. 'Chaucer's Marriage Group,' in *Chaucer the Love Poet*, edd. Jerome Mitchell and William Provost (Athens, Ga. 1973) 45–65.
47. 'Holy Church's Speech and the Structure of *Piers Plowman*,' in *Chaucer and Middle English Studies in Honour of Rossell Hope Robbins*, ed. Beryl Rowland (London 1974) 320–27.
48. 'Dante's *Purgatorio* XXXII and XXXIII: A Survey of Christian History,' *University of Toronto Quarterly* 43 (1974) 193–214.
49. review of: Stanley B. Greenfield, *The Interpretation of Old English Poems* (London 1972), in *Modern Philology* 72 (1974) 190–94.
50. 'A Dagger in Relief on Stonehenge?' *Traditio* 31 (1975) 315–16.

51. 'The Conclusion of the Old English "Descent into Hell,"' in Παράδοσις: *Studies in Memory of Edwin A. Quain* (New York 1976) 47–59.

52. '*Clericus Adam* and Chaucer's *Adam Scriveyn*,' in *Chaucerian Problems and Perspectives: Essays Presented to Paul E. Beichner, C.S.C.*, edd. Edward Vasta and Zacharias P. Thundy (Notre Dame 1979) 114–18.

53. '*Sapientia et Fortitudo* in the Old English *Judith*,' in *The Wisdom of Poetry: Essays in Early English Literature in Honor of Morton W. Bloomfield*, edd. Larry D. Benson and Siegfried Wenzel (Kalamazoo, Mich. 1982) 13–19 and 264–68.

54. 'The Seven *Status Ecclesiae* in *Purgatorio* XXXII and XXXIII,' in *Dante, Petrarch, Boccaccio: Studies in the Italian Trecento in Honor of Charles S. Singleton*, edd. Aldo S. Bernardo and Anthony L. Pellegrini, Medieval and Renaissance Texts and Studies 22 (Binghamton, N.Y. 1983) 89–113.

55. 'The Coastwarden's Maxim in *Beowulf*: A Clarification,' *Notes and Queries* NS 31 (1984) 16–18.

56. '*Sir Gawain and the Green Knight*,' in *Medieval and Renaissance Studies: Proceedings of the Southeastern Institute of Medieval and Renaissance Studies. Summer 1979* [No. 10], ed. George Mallary Masters (Chapel Hill, N.C. 1984) 24–44.

57. 'The *gifstol* Crux in *Beowulf*,' in *Sources and Relations: Studies in Honour of J. E. Cross*, Leeds Studies in English NS 16 (1985) 142–51.

58. 'Causality and Miracle: Philosophical Perspectives in the *Knight's Tale* and the *Man of Law's Tale*,' to appear in *New Views on Old Masterpieces: Essays on British Literature of the Middle Ages and the Renaissance*, edd. David G. Allen and Robert A. White; papers from the Fifth Citadel Conference on Literature, March 14–16, 1985.

59. *Medieval Christian Literary Imagery: A Guide to Interpretation* (Toronto, to appear 1987).

60. 'Pandarus' "Corounes Tweyne" in *Troilus*,' to appear in a volume in memory of Judson B. Allen.

61. 'The Character "Hunger" in *Piers Plowman*,' to appear in a forthcoming Festschrift.